THE ILLUSTRATED CHILDREN'S
ENCYCLOPEDIA OF THE

THE ILLUSTRATED CHILDREN'S ENCYCLOPEDIA OF THE

ANCIENT
WORLD

STEP BACK IN TIME TO DISCOVER THE WONDERS OF THE STONE AGE,
ANCIENT EGYPT, ANCIENT GREECE, ANCIENT ROME, THE AZTECS
AND MAYA, THE INCAS, ANCIENT CHINA AND ANCIENT JAPAN

Consultant editors: John Haywood, Charlotte Hurdman, Richard Tames,
Philip Steele & Fiona Macdonald

southwater

CONTENTS

CIVILIZATIONS IN TIME

THE TIMECHART gives a perspective of world history, showing how the civilizations featured in this book fit into time, and how they relate to each other. At the base of the chart, in the distant past, are the ancient civilizations that form the foundations of human history. The perspective narrows to the point of the present day, taking in key civilizations across the world.

Each of the four vertical sections represents a continent, so that you can see immediately that while successive civilizations became increasingly complex and sophisticated in Europe, Africa and Asia, little was happening in North America. Here, the simple hunter-gatherer lifestyle of the Native American peoples persisted until relatively recent times. Then, in Central and South America, the Maya, Aztec and Inca civilizations rose and fell within a few centuries. The timechart enables you to compare the brief lives of these civilizatons to those of ancient Egypt, which spanned the European Stone Age and the civilizations of ancient Greece and Rome, or of China, where an unbroken pattern of empires and cultural development endured until the early 1900s.

ARCHITECTURE: Like the ancient peoples of Egypt, the Maya built tall pyramids to be closer to their gods. Temples were often the most complex buildings of early societies.

KEY

EUROPE

Mycenaean Greek	1
Classical Greek	2
Roman	3

AFRICA

Ancient Egyptian	4

ASIA

Shang China	5
Zhou China	6
Chinese Empires	7
Yamato Japan	8
Heian Japan	9
Japanese Shogunate	10

AMERICAS

Maya	11
Aztec	12
Inca	13

RELIGION: The Buddha lived around 500BC. He introduced a religion that spread from India to Sri Lanka and Southeast Asia, and that is still practised today.

TECHNOLOGY: The wheel was developed in Mesopotamia, possibly as early as 3500BC.

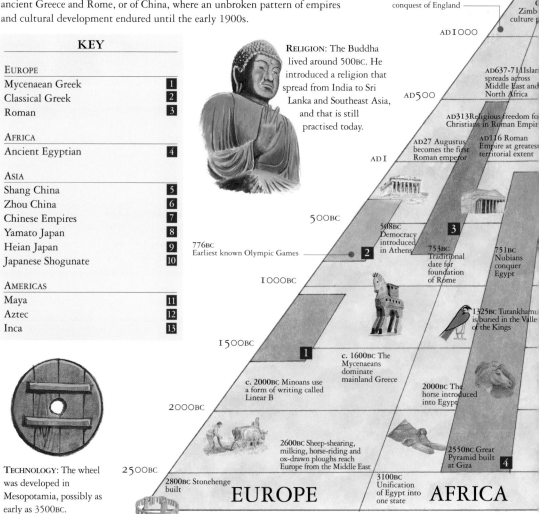

c. AD1460 Portuguese begin African slave trade

AD1500

D1066 Norman conquest of England

AD
Zimb
culture

AD1000

AD637-711 Islam spreads across Middle East and North Africa

AD500

AD313 Religious freedom for Christians in Roman Empire

AD27 Augustus becomes the first Roman emperor

AD116 Roman Empire at greatest territorial extent

AD1

508BC Democracy introduced in Athens

500BC

776BC Earliest known Olympic Games

753BC Traditional date for foundation of Rome

751BC Nubians conquer Egypt

1000BC

1325BC Tutankhamu is buried in the Valle of the Kings

1500BC

c. 1600BC The Mycenaeans dominate mainland Greece

c. 2000BC Minoans use a form of writing called Linear B

2000BC The horse introduced into Egypt

2000BC

2600BC Sheep-shearing, milking, horse-riding and ox-drawn ploughs reach Europe from the Middle East

2550BC Great Pyramid built at Giza

2500BC

2800BC Stonehenge built

EUROPE

3100BC Unification of Egypt into one state

AFRICA

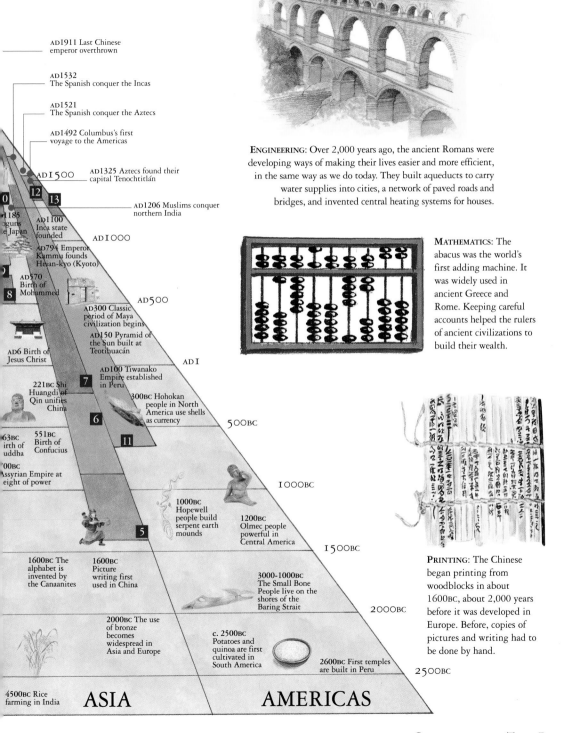

AD1911 Last Chinese emperor overthrown

AD1532 The Spanish conquer the Incas

AD1521 The Spanish conquer the Aztecs

AD1492 Columbus's first voyage to the Americas

AD1500

AD1325 Aztecs found their capital Tenochtitlán

12

13

AD1206 Muslims conquer northern India

1185 oguns e Japan

AD1100 Inca state founded

AD1000

AD794 Emperor Kammu founds Heian-kyo (Kyoto)

AD570 Birth of Mohammed

8

AD300 Classic period of Maya civilization begins

AD500

AD150 Pyramid of the Sun built at Teotihuacán

AD1

AD6 Birth of Jesus Christ

AD100 Tiwanako Empire established in Peru

221BC Shi Huangdi of Qin unifies China

7

300BC Hohokan people in North America use shells as currency

6

500BC

63BC irth of uddha

551BC Birth of Confucius

11

00BC ssyrian Empire at eight of power

1000BC

1000BC Hopewell people build serpent earth mounds

1200BC Olmec people powerful in Central America

1500BC

5

1600BC The alphabet is invented by the Canaanites

1600BC Picture writing first used in China

3000-1000BC The Small Bone People live on the shores of the Baring Strait

2000BC

2000BC The use of bronze becomes widespread in Asia and Europe

c. 2500BC Potatoes and quinoa are first cultivated in South America

2600BC First temples are built in Peru

2500BC

4500BC Rice farming in India

ASIA

AMERICAS

ENGINEERING: Over 2,000 years ago, the ancient Romans were developing ways of making their lives easier and more efficient, in the same way as we do today. They built aqueducts to carry water supplies into cities, a network of paved roads and bridges, and invented central heating systems for houses.

MATHEMATICS: The abacus was the world's first adding machine. It was widely used in ancient Greece and Rome. Keeping careful accounts helped the rulers of ancient civilizations to build their wealth.

PRINTING: The Chinese began printing from woodblocks in about 1600BC, about 2,000 years before it was developed in Europe. Before, copies of pictures and writing had to be done by hand.

THE RISE OF CIVILIZATION

THIS BOOK describes some of the most important and influential ancient civilizations in world history. If asked, some people might say that the word civilization had something to do with decent behaviour or living comfortably. When governments treat their people cruelly, or a person is rude, we may describe them as uncivilized. For archaeologists and ancient historians, however, the word has a different meaning. They use it to refer to a large community of people with a government. Almost everybody in the world today lives in a community like this.

The Beginnings

For most of human history people did not live in civilizations. For over two million years, our ancestors lived in small family groups, hunting wild animals, gathering wild plant foods and sheltering in caves and simple huts. Beginning around 11,000 years ago in the Middle East, people began to settle into a farming way of life. Instead of living a wandering life in the quest for food to hunt and gather, they began to stay in one place, to keep animals in enclosures, and to grow crops. By about 2,000 years ago most people in the world had given up the hunting and gathering existence, and relied on farming for their food. It was this change to agriculture that led to more permanent homes, the growth of settlements, and eventually, the development of the first civilizations.

FOOD FOR THE POT
Hunting was an important way of obtaining meat in the past. This ancient Greek plate shows a hunter returning from a successful day's sport.

The Population Explodes

Farming caused important social changes. Some farmers were more successful than others, perhaps because they had better land or because they worked harder, and grew more food than they needed to support their own families. They could exchange their surplus food for luxuries such as fine jewellery and weapons, or use their extra supplies to win power and influence over other people. As a result, inequalities of wealth and power began to develop in farming communities. Powerful individuals were able to become chiefs, ruling over people

RICE FARMING
Rice was a major crop for many early farming communities in China, Japan and India where there was enough rain and flat land.

Egyptian pyramids were a symbol of the wealth and power of ruling pharaohs. They were feats of architectural engineering. The Great Pyramid at Giza is larger than Nelson's Column, London, the Sydney Opera House, and New York's Statue of Liberty.

and controlling their land. Because farming increased the food supply, the human population began to rise quickly.

The Growth of Cities

The population rose fastest in the places where there were the fertile soils, low-lying land, reliable water supply and climate suitable for growing crops, such as on the flood plains of great rivers. Towns and cities with thousands of inhabitants gradually evolved from settlements that had become established on the banks of the Nile in Egypt, the Tigris and Euphrates in Iraq, the Indus in Pakistan and the Yellow River in China. The first civilizations develope in these regions between 5,500 and 3,500 years ago. The old system of local chiefs was no longer sufficient to control such large communities as cities. More complicated systems of government took their place, and rulers with greater power, wealth and influence emerged in the form of monarchs and emperors.

The Need for Organization

Farmers brought their surplus food to the cities to pay it to the ruler as taxes. The ruler, in turn, used what he or she did not need to support people who provided essential services. Ruling the large communities involved a lot of organization. People with full-time, specialist jobs were needed, such as administrators to run the government, soldiers to guard territory, builders and craftworkers

ANIMAL CARVINGS
With increased civilization, skills and artistic creativity developed. This figure of a bison licking its back was carved from a reindeer's antler in about 12,000BC.

WRITE IT DOWN
Pen-cases were often used by scribes, who were the official writers in early civilizations. Rulers and their helpers needed to keep careful records.

to make increasingly elaborate homes, palaces and temples. Systems of writing and counting were invented to help rulers and administrators record

A LONG HOUSE
As people settled into farming life, they built more permanent homes, using local materials such as stone, mud-brick, or timber and thatch. This is a reconstruction of an early European house.

LIFE BY THE NILE
Tomb paintings in ancient
Egypt give valuable
information on how people
lived at the time.

everything they needed to do their jobs properly. To strengthen their power, rulers issued laws which everyone was expected to obey – and they needed to pay people to make sure that the laws were kept.

Pioneering Peoples

The very first civilization was founded by the Sumerian people on the flood plain of the Tigris and Euphrates rivers in Mesopotamia (modern Iraq) about 5,500 years ago. The people lived in cities, each of which was an independent state with its own king. The civilization flourished for over 1,000 years, and then gradually went into decline. A second civilization was already established by this time, on the banks of the River Nile in Egypt. It became one of the most successful in history, lasting for over 3,000 years. The towns and cities of Egypt were united in a single kingdom, forming the world's first nation. The Egyptians were also great builders. Many of their buildings, like the pyramids, still survive today, over 4,000 years after they were completed.

SHIPS AND SAILORS
A widespread empire needed feeding. This Roman merchant ship is stacked with grain.

The Birth of Europe

The power and wealth of Egypt and Mesopotamia had a knock-on effect on neighbouring regions, which in time, led to other civilizations arising. The most important was Greece, which became one of the most creative civilizations in history. Its achievements are still seen and felt in today's world. Ancient Greek states were the first to allow citizens to have a say in how they were governed. The new system was called democracy – which is how most countries in Europe and the Americas are

ACTORS' MASKS
The ancient Greeks were the first people to have theatres and dramas. Actors wore masks and wigs to show the type of character they were playing.

CLASSICAL TASTE
The ancient Greeks worked out how to make elegant buildings. Many of their styles and methods are still used today.

governed today. The Greeks founded cities throughout the Mediterranean and the Middle East. They had some of the first scientists, philosophers and historians, and their art and building styles are still copied.

As the golden age of Greece came to an end, the Roman people of Italy had already laid the foundations of their own civilization, around 800BC. They were tough soldiers and conquered so much territory that their empire became one of the largest in history – both Greece and Egypt came under Roman rule. The Empire ended over 1,500 years ago, but its calendar and alphabet are still in use throughout the world.

Worlds Apart

Far away from Europe and the Middle East, other civilizations developed independently. The greatest began in China over 3,500 years ago and lasted until modern times. The Chinese were amazingly inventive. They could make silk, paper and gunpowder, for example, hundreds of years before these skills were mastered in Europe.

SPINNING SILK THREAD
Making silk was one of the crafts of ancient China – long before the method was discovered in the West.

In the Americas, the Maya people produced brilliant mathematicians and astronomers, while the Aztecs believed the world would end if they did not sacrifice thousands of people to their gods every year. The Incas built temples, fortresses and even roads, but had not invented the wheel. No one in Europe or Asia even suspected that these civilizations existed before the explorer Christopher Columbus sailed to what Europeans called the New World in 1492.

STARS AND PLANETS
Like this Inca astrologer, many ancient peoples watched the Sun, Moon and stars to work out a calendar of days and years.

TEMPLE TOMB
The Maya, Inca and Aztecs built temples as centres of worship.

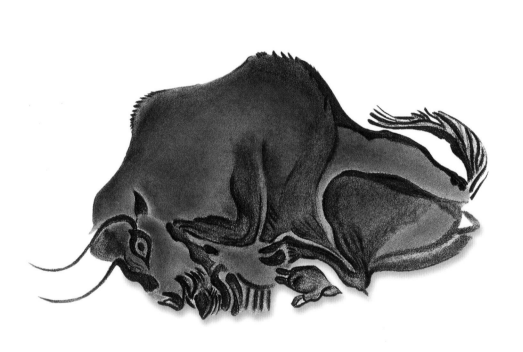

THE
STONE AGE

*The Stone Age spans over two million years –
which is most of the history of humankind. It is
called the Stone Age because many of the tools and
weapons used in everyday life were made from
stones and flints. Over a very long period of time,
people began to build homes and villages, and
make pottery and ploughs.*

CHARLOTTE HURDMAN
Consultant: Dr Robin Holgate, Luton Museum

The Dawn of Humankind

THE FIRST PERIOD in human history is called the Stone Age. Stone was used to make tools and other objects. Some of these objects survive today. Wood, bone and plant fibres were also used, but they rotted, leaving little trace.

Our earliest human ancestors were making tools from stone at least two million years ago, but our story really starts with the arrival of modern humans, called *Homo sapiens sapiens*, about 100,000 years ago. The Stone Age is part of human prehistory, which means that it took place before there were any written records. Archaeologists have to be detectives, piecing together what might have happened. Special techniques, such as radiocarbon dating, help experts to work out what life was like thousands of years ago. We can also look at modern-day hunter-gatherer cultures for clues as to how people lived.

SKELETONS AND BURIALS
This is the skeleton of a Neanderthal man who was buried about 60,000 years ago. Human remains and the objects buried with them can tell experts a lot about early people.

CAVE PAINTINGS
This beautiful painting of a bison is from the caves at Altamira in Spain. It was painted in about 13,000BC by prehistoric hunters. Cave paintings often show animals that were hunted at the time.

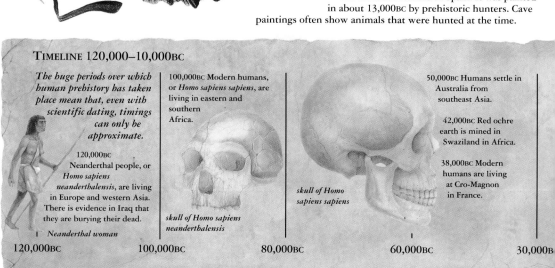

TIMELINE 120,000–10,000BC

The huge periods over which human prehistory has taken place mean that, even with scientific dating, timings can only be approximate.

120,000BC Neanderthal people, or *Homo sapiens neanderthalensis*, are living in Europe and western Asia. There is evidence in Iraq that they are burying their dead.

Neanderthal woman

100,000BC Modern humans, or *Homo sapiens sapiens*, are living in eastern and southern Africa.

skull of *Homo sapiens neanderthalensis*

skull of *Homo sapiens sapiens*

50,000BC Humans settle in Australia from southeast Asia.

42,000BC Red ochre earth is mined in Swaziland in Africa.

38,000BC Modern humans are living at Cro-Magnon in France.

120,000BC   100,000BC   80,000BC   60,000BC   30,000B

SCENES FROM LIFE

This rock engraving, or carving, from Namibia shows two giraffes. It was carved by hunters in southern Africa, around 6000BC. The North American continent is the only one where early prehistoric art like this has not yet been found.

SCULPTURES

Small carvings of prehistoric women are called Venus figurines. This one was made in about 23,000BC. The many sculptures that have been found can give clues to Stone Age people's ideas and beliefs.

TOOLS

Looking at stone tools can tell us how they may have been made and used. Tools, such as this hand-axe and these scrapers, were used for preparing meat and hides.

CLUES IN CAVES

Many rock shelters and natural caves, like this one in Malta, have been lived in for thousands of years. Much of our knowledge about prehistoric people has been found by carefully digging through layers of rock and soil in sites like this. Many rock homes seem to have been lived in for thousands of years before being abandoned.

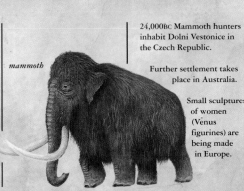

mammoth

24,000BC Mammoth hunters inhabit Dolni Vestonice in the Czech Republic.

Further settlement takes place in Australia.

Small sculptures of women (Venus figurines) are being made in Europe.

cave painting

16,000BC The last glacial period, sometimes called the last Ice Age, is at its coldest.

15,000BC The finest Stone Age cave paintings and carvings of bone and antler so far discovered are being made in Europe.

10,500BC Pottery is made in Japan.

Asian people who travelled across the American continent have now reached South America. Some live at Monte Verde in Chile.

| 30,000BC | 25,000BC | 20,000BC | 15,000BC | 10,000BC |

The Stone Age World

THE STONE AGE is the longest period of human history. It covers such a vast time period that it is often divided into stages, according to the type of tools people were using. The first and by far the longest division was the Palaeolithic period, or Old Stone Age, which began more than two million years ago. During this time, people made the first stone tools. It was followed by the Mesolithic period, or Middle Stone Age, around 10,000BC. During this period people began to use new tools, such as bows and arrows, to hunt deer and wild pigs. From about 8000BC, the Neolithic period, or New Stone Age, began with the start of farming. However, the Stone Age has lasted for different periods of time in different parts of the world, so these divisions are not always helpful. The Stone Age came to an end when people began to work metals on a large scale.

Modern human beings now live all over the Earth, but views vary about how this happened. Some experts think we evolved, or developed, in Africa, before spreading out into Asia and Europe. Others think we evolved separately in different parts of the world. The first people to reach America probably crossed from Siberia in Russia when the Bering Strait was dry land. This may have been around 13,000BC or even earlier. By about 10,000BC, however, people had reached right to the tip of South America.

mastodon, Canada
20,000BC

bisons,
North America
9000BC

NORTH AMERICA

CENTRAL AMER

agriculture, South America
7000BC

Origins of agriculture

cave art, Argentin
8500BC

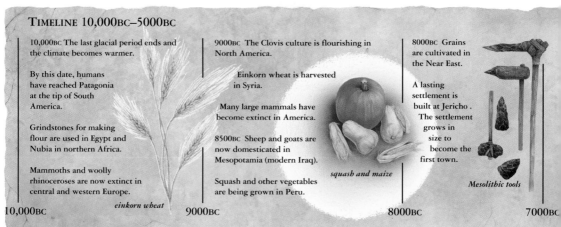

TIMELINE 10,000BC–5000BC

10,000BC The last glacial period ends and the climate becomes warmer.

By this date, humans have reached Patagonia at the tip of South America.

Grindstones for making flour are used in Egypt and Nubia in northern Africa.

Mammoths and woolly rhinoceroses are now extinct in central and western Europe.

einkorn wheat

9000BC The Clovis culture is flourishing in North America.

Einkorn wheat is harvested in Syria.

Many large mammals have become extinct in America.

8500BC Sheep and goats are now domesticated in Mesopotamia (modern Iraq).

Squash and other vegetables are being grown in Peru.

squash and maize

8000BC Grains are cultivated in the Near East.

A lasting settlement is built at Jericho . The settlement grows in size to become the first town.

Mesolithic tools

10,000BC   9000BC   8000BC   7000BC

EUROPE

migrating reindeer, Russia
15,000BC

clay figurine,
Czech Republic
24,000BC

ASIA

cave art, France
15,000BC

pottery, Japan
10,500BC

settlement,
Turkey
6,500BC

rock art,
Sahara
6000BC

Peking Man, China
460,0000BC

Homo erectus *skull*,
Java, 120,000BC

AFRICA

Homo habilis *skull*, Kenya
2.5 million years ago

SOUTH AMERICA

N

AUSTRALIA

cave art, Namibia
8000BC

THE STONE AGE WORLD
This map shows places of
importance during the Stone Age.

indigenous peoples,
Australia
50,000BC

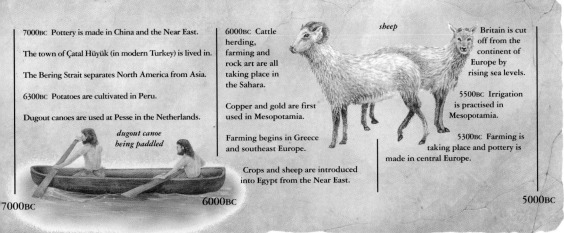

7000BC Pottery is made in China and the Near East.

The town of Çatal Hüyük (in modern Turkey) is lived in.

The Bering Strait separates North America from Asia.

6300BC Potatoes are cultivated in Peru.

Dugout canoes are used at Pesse in the Netherlands.

*dugout canoe
being paddled*

6000BC Cattle
herding,
farming and
rock art are all
taking place in
the Sahara.

Copper and gold are first
used in Mesopotamia.

Farming begins in Greece
and southeast Europe.

Crops and sheep are introduced
into Egypt from the Near East.

sheep

Britain is cut
off from the
continent of
Europe by
rising sea levels.

5500BC Irrigation
is practised in
Mesopotamia.

5300BC Farming is
taking place and pottery is
made in central Europe.

7000BC   6000BC   5000BC

People from the Past

MODERN HUMANS and their most recent ancestors are called hominids. The first hominids formed two main groups – *Australopithecus* and *Homo*. *Australopithecus* first appeared about four million years ago and died out about one million years ago. The first *Homo*, named *Homo habilis*, appeared about two and a half million years ago and, like *Australopithecus*, lived in southern and eastern Africa.

About two million years ago, a new kind of hominid, *Homo erectus*, appeared. This was the first hominid to leave Africa, moving into Asia and later Europe. Eventually, *Homo erectus* evolved, or developed, into *Homo sapiens*, which evolved into *Homo sapiens sapiens*, or modern humans. By 10,000BC *Homo sapiens sapiens* had settled on every continent except Antarctica.

PEKING MAN
This reconstruction is of a type of *Homo erectus* whose remains were found in China. Peking Man lived here from about 460,000 to 230,000 years ago. Experts believe *Homo erectus* were the first people to make regular use of fire.

CRO-MAGNON PEOPLE
The Cro-Magnons were the first modern people to live in Europe, about 40,000 years ago. The burial of a young Cro-Magnon man, whose remains were found in a Welsh cave, is shown in this picture. The body was sprinkled with red ochre and had bracelets and a necklace of animal teeth.

TIMELINE 5000BC–2000BC

5000BC Rice farming is being carried out in waterlogged fields in eastern China.

Large areas of southeast Asia are isolated by rising sea levels.

New Guinea and Tasmania have become separated from Australia.

wild rice

4500BC Rice farming begins in India.

Farming begins in northwest Europe.

4400BC Wild horses are domesticated on the steppes, or plains, of Russia.

4200BC Megalithic tombs, made of huge stones, are built in western Europe.

4100BC Sorghum and rice are cultivated in the Sudan in Africa.

4000BC Bronze casting begins in the Near East.

Flint-mining in northern and western Europe increases.

early domesticated horse

3500BC The llama is domesticated in Peru.

The first cities are built in Sumer, Mesopotamia.

The plough and wheel are invented in the Near East and spread to Europe.

3400BC Walled towns are built in Egypt.

3200BC Egyptians use sailing ships on the river Nile.

| 5000BC | 4500BC | 4000BC | 3500BC | 3200BC |

Australopithecus
.5 to 2 million years ago

Archaeologists believe that our earliest ancestors came from Africa. One group, Australopithecus Africanus, walked upright.

Homo Habilis
2 to 1.6 million years ago

Homo habilis *walked upright but had long arms. Habilis was probably the first hominid to make stone tools and to hunt.*

Homo Erectus
1.6 million to 400,000 years ago

This hominid had a bigger brain than habilis *and may have been as tall and heavy as modern people. Erectus was a skilful hunter.*

Broken Hill Man

This hominid was another Homo erectus. Erectus *invented new kinds of tools, used fire, lived in rock shelters and built huts.*

Neanderthal Man
120,000 to 33,000 years ago

Homo sapiens neanderthalensis *(Neanderthals) made flint tools. Neanderthals are thought to have been the first people to bury their dead.*

Modern Man
100,000 years ago

Our own subspecies, Homo sapiens sapiens *(modern man), developed over 100,000 years ago.*

Neanderthal People

The Neanderthals were a subspecies of *Homo sapiens* who flourished in Europe and western Asia. They lived from about 120,000 to 33,000 years ago, during the last glacial, or cold, period. Neanderthals had larger brains than modern humans, with sloping foreheads and heavy brows.

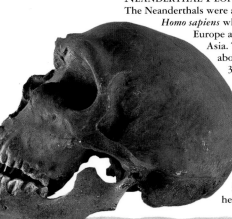

Homo Sapiens

This skull belonged to an early human being. The species *Homo sapiens* may have evolved about 400,000 years ago.

3200BC The Newgrange passage grave is built in Ireland.

3100BC The first script, called *cuneiform*, develops in Mesopotamia.

3000BC Maize is domesticated in central America.

Skara Brae in the Orkney Islands is inhabited.

2800BC The first earthworks are begun at Stonehenge in England.

Flint is mined at Grimes Graves in England.

development of maize

Stonehenge, a prehistoric circle of standing stones in England

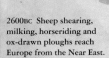

2600BC Sheep shearing, milking, horseriding and ox-drawn ploughs reach Europe from the Near East.

2000BC The use of bronze is widespread in Asia and Europe.

3200BC	2800BC	2600BC	2400BC	2000BC

Climate and Survival

COVERED BY ICE
Ancient ice still forms this Alaskan glacier. The height of the last glacial was reached about 18,000 years ago. At this time almost 30 per cent of the Earth was covered by ice, including large parts of North America, Europe and Asia, as well as New Zealand and southern Argentina. Temperatures dropped, and sea levels fell by over 100m.

ONE CHANGING ASPECT of our Earth affected Stone Age people more than anything else – the climate. Over many thousands of years, the climate gradually grew cooler and then just as slowly warmed up again. This cycle happened many times, changing the landscape and the plants and animals that lived in it.

During cool periods, called glacials, sea levels dropped, exposing more land. Herds of animals grazed vast grasslands and the cold, bare tundra farther north. When temperatures rose, so did sea levels, isolating people on newly formed islands. Woodlands gradually covered the plains.

DEER HUNTER
In warmer periods, forest animals, like this red deer, replaced bison, mammoths and reindeer, which moved north. Humans followed the grazing herds or began to hunt forest game.

ANIMALS OF THE COLD
Mammoths were the largest mammals adapted to a colder climate, grazing the northern plains. The related mastodon was found in North America. Reindeer, horses, musk oxen, woolly rhinoceroses and bison were common too.

ANIMAL EXTINCTIONS

This painting of a mammoth is from a cave in southwest France. By 10,000BC, mammoths and woolly rhinoceroses were extinct in central and western Europe, as were bison and reindeer. In North America, mammoths, mastodons, camelids and many other large animal species vanished abruptly by 9000BC. Even in tropical Africa, the rich variety of animals of the savanna was reduced at the end of the last glacial period.

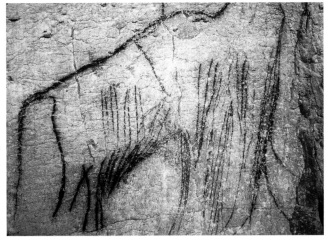

WILD BOAR

Pigs, such as wild boar, are adapted to living in a forest habitat. They use their snouts and feet to root for food on the forest floor. Pigs were one of the first animals to be domesticated because they will eat almost anything.

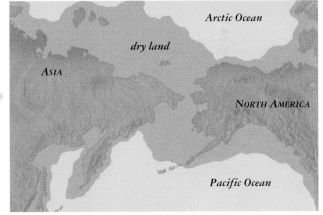

Arctic Ocean

dry land

ASIA

NORTH AMERICA

Pacific Ocean

ISOLATED ISLANDS

The White Cliffs of Dover are a famous landmark on England's southeast coast, but this was not always so. During the last glacial, Ireland, Great Britain and France were linked. When the ice began to melt, areas of low-lying land were gradually flooded, causing Britain to become an island by 6000BC.

LAND BRIDGES

This illustration shows how two continents were joined by tundra during the last glacial period. Early man could migrate across the dry land that had been created over the Bering Straits and cross from Asia to North America. When the ice melted, the crossing was no longer possible and the continents were once again separated by sea. There were many land bridges during the glacial periods, including one that connected Great Britain to continental Europe.

Migration and Nomads

MIGRATING HERDS
A huge herd of reindeer begins its spring migration across northern Norway. The Sami, or Lapp people, have lived in the Arctic regions of Sweden and Norway since ancient times. They herd reindeer for their meat and milk, following the herds north in the spring and camping in tents called *lavos*.

THE FIRST HUMANS did not lead a settled life, living in the same place all the time. Instead they were nomads, moving around throughout the year. They did this in order to find food. Early people did not grow crops or keep animals. They hunted wild animals and collected berries, nuts and other plants. This is called a hunter-gatherer way of life. Moving from one place to another is called migration. Some Stone Age migrations were seasonal, following the herds of game. Others were caused by natural disasters, such as forest fires or volcanic eruptions. Changes in the climate and rising populations also forced people to move in search of new territory. After humans learned how to farm, many settled down in permanent homes to raise their crops.

ANTLER HARPOON
This antler harpoon was found at Star Carr, in North Yorkshire, England. Antler is easily carved into barbed points to make harpoons. The points were tied to spears and used for fishing and hunting.

SEASONAL CAMPS
In mesolithic times, the hunter-gatherers moved camp at different times of year. In late spring and summer, inland and coastal camps were used. Red and roe deer were hunted in the woods. Fish, shellfish, seals and wild birds were caught or gathered. Meat, hides and antlers were cut up and prepared, then taken to a more sheltered winter settlement.

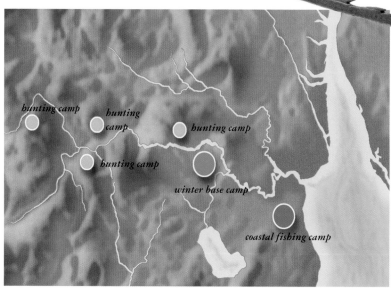

hunting camp

hunting camp

hunting camp

hunting camp

winter base camp

coastal fishing camp

TREES
The changing climate caused changes in vegetation. Heather, mosses and lichens grew on the cold tundra that covered much of the land during glacials. On the edge of the tundra were forests of pine, larch and spruce. As the climate warmed, the first trees to colonize open areas were silver birches. Gradually, the birches were replaced by oaks, hazels and elms. As forests grew up, people found there was enough food to hunt and gather in one area without the need to migrate.

moss   *pine*

NATIVE AMERICANS
The Plains Indians of North America were nomads, living in cone-shaped buffalo-hide tents called tepees. Native Americans of the eastern plains, such as the Dakota shown above, lived mainly in permanent settlements, using their tepees for summer and autumn hunts. In the 1800s, the Plains Indians were forced by the United States government to live on reservations. They took their tepees with them and tried to preserve part of their traditional way of life.

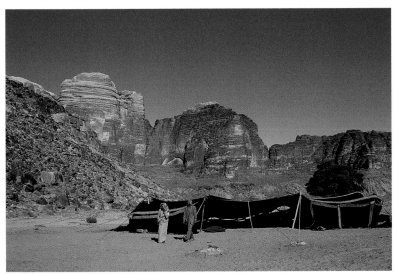

NOMADS IN THE DESERT
Although their numbers are dwindling, the Bedouin still live as nomadic herders in the dry regions of the Near East and Africa. They keep camels, sheep and goats to provide them with milk and meat. Their animals are also sold for other foods such as flour, dates and coffee. Bedouins live in tents made from woven goat hair. They move from place to place in search of grazing for their animals, just as people have done for thousands of years.

Social Structure

IN STONE AGE TIMES, there were very few people in the world. Experts estimate that the world's population in 13,000BC was only about 8 million. Today it is nearer 6 billion. We can make guesses about how Stone Age people lived together by looking at hunter-gatherer societies of today.

Although people lived in families as we do, these families themselves lived together in groups called clans. All the members of a clan were related to each other, usually through their mother's family or by marriage. Clans were large enough to protect and feed everyone, but not so large that they were unmanageable. All the members of a clan, including children, were involved in finding and gathering food for everyone. Clans were probably also part of larger tribes, which may have met up at certain times of year, such as for the summer hunt. The members of a tribe shared a language and a way of life. When people learned how to farm, populations increased and societies began to be organized in more complicated ways.

MOTHER GODDESSES

This baked-clay sculpture from Turkey was made in about 6000BC. She may have been worshipped as a goddess of motherhood. Families were often traced through the female line because mothers give birth, while fathers may remain unknown.

SHAMAN LEADERS

This painting from the 1800s shows Native American shamans performing a ritual dance. Shamans were the spiritual leaders of their tribes. They knew the dances, chants, prayers and ceremonies that would bring good luck and please the spirits. Shamanism is found in hunter-gatherer societies around the world today and was practised in prehistoric times.

TRIBAL CHIEF

This man is a
Zulu chief
from South
Africa. His
higher rank
is shown
by what
he wears.
In prehistoric
times, tribes
might have
been ruled by
chiefs or councils
of elders. An old
man buried at
Sungir in Russia
around 23,000BC
was probably a
chief. His body
was found richly
decorated with
fox teeth and
beads made of
mammoth ivory.

SCENES FROM LONG AGO

Paintings on cliff walls in
the Sahara Desert show
hippopotamuses being
hunted and herders tending
cattle. Other images show a
woman pounding flour, as
well as wedding ceremonies
and a family with a dog. They
show that, in 6000BC, it was
a fertile area with highly
organized communities.

A CYCLADIC FIGURINE

Between 3000
and 2000BC,
some of the
finest prehistoric
sculpture was made
on the Cycladic
Islands of Greece.
This figurine is made
of ground marble and
shows a slender woman
with her arms folded
above her waist. Figurines
showing musicians with harps
and flutes have also been
found. Such sculptures come
from complex societies.

A TRADITIONAL WAY OF LIFE

The man on the left is helping a boy
prepare for his coming-of-age
ceremony in Papua New Guinea.
Traditional ways of life are still
strong in that country, where there
are many remote tribes. In some
villages, all the men live together,
rather than with their wives and
children. This allows them to
organize their work, such as
hunting, more easily.

Communication and Counting

Our early human ancestors were communicating with each other using words and gestures as long ago as 300,000BC. Eventually, complex languages began to develop to pass on skills and knowledge. Hunters may have used a special sign language when tracking game, leaving markers to signal the route and imitating animal and bird sounds.

From about 37,000BC, people began to carve marks on bones and to use pebbles as simple counting devices. Days may have been counted on calendar sticks. In some cave paintings, experts have noticed dots and symbols that may be counting tallies or the beginnings of a writing system.

TALLY STICK
Notches carved on wooden sticks, or in this case on the leg bone of a baboon, may have been used as counting devices or as simple calendars. This one dates from about 35,000BC. Similar sticks are used by some groups of people living in southern Africa today.

By about 7000BC, tokens with symbols to represent numbers and objects were being used by traders in the Near East. Such tokens may have led to the first written script. This developed in about 3100BC and was a kind of picture writing called *cuneiform*.

PICTURES AND SYMBOLS
This cave painting of a wild horse comes from Lascaux in southwest France. It was painted in about 15,000BC. The horse is surrounded by symbols which, along with dots and notches, may have been a way of keeping track of migrating animals.

HAND ART
You will need: self-drying clay, rolling pin and board, modelling tool, sandpaper, yellow and red acrylic paints, water, two spray bottles.

1 Roll out the clay, giving it a lumpy surface like a cave wall. Trim the edges with a modelling tool to make a stone tablet.

2 Leave the clay to dry. When it is hard, rub the tablet with sandpaper to get rid of sharp edges and make a smooth surface.

3 Mix the paint with water and fill the spray bottles. Put one hand on the tablet and spray plenty of yellow paint around it.

DEVELOPING WRITING

This Sumerian clay tablet was made in about 3100BC. It uses characters based on picture symbols to give an account of a year's harvest. As cuneiform writing developed, people wanted to express abstract ideas, such as good or bad, so they changed symbols already in use, often by adding marks.

SMOKE SIGNALS

This engraving from the late 1800s shows Native Americans using smoke signals to communicate with each other. Human beings have spent most of their history without written language, but this does not mean they were always unable to communicate or record important information.

HANDS ON

These hand stencils are from a cave in Argentina. They are similar to those found on rock walls in Europe, Africa and Australia. They may have been a way for prehistoric artists to sign their work.

4 Keeping your hand in exactly the same place, spray on the red paint, so that you are left with a clear, sharp outline.

5 When you have finished spraying, remove your hand. Be careful not to smudge the paint, and leave the tablet to dry.

The artist of the original Argentinian hand painting sprayed paint around his or her hand. This was done either by blowing through a reed, or by spitting paint on to the cave wall!

Shelter

PEOPLE HAVE always needed protection from the weather. During most of the last 100,000 years, the Earth's climate was much colder than it is today. People lived in huts in the open during summer, but when harsh weather came, families moved into caves. They built stone windbreaks across the entrances and put up huts inside to give further protection from the storms and cold. In summer, as they followed the herds of game, hunters built shelters of branches and leaves. Families lived in camps of huts made of branches and animal skins. Farther north, where there were no caves and few trees, people built huts from mammoths' leg bones and tusks. Wherever they settled, however, it was very important to be near a supply of fresh water.

CAVES AND ROCK SHELTERS
This is the entrance to a rock shelter in southwest France. Neanderthal people were the first to occupy this site, in about 100,000BC. People usually lived close to the entrance of a cave, where the light was best and the sun's warmth could reach them.

MAMMOTH-BONE HOME
This is a reconstruction of a mammoth-hunter's house. It was built in about 13,000BC in Ukraine. The gaps between the bones were filled with moss and shrubs. The entire structure was then covered with mammoth hide or turf.

A HUNTER'S HOME
You will need: self-drying clay, board, modelling tool, cardboard, brown-green acrylic paint, water pot, paintbrush, twigs, ruler, scissors, PVA glue, fake grass or green fabric.

1 Roll out lengths of clay to form long and short mammoth bones and tusks. Then make some stones in different sizes.

2 Use the modelling tool to shape the ends of the bones and make the stones uneven. Leave the pieces, carefully separated, to dry.

3 Spread some modelling clay roughly over a piece of cardboard. Paint the clay a brown-green colour and leave to dry.

MOBILE HOME

This model tepee was made in 1904 by the Cheyenne people of the Great Plains in the USA. Prehistoric people may have lived in tents or huts like this, made from branches covered with animal hides. They were quick to put up and take down, and could be folded for carrying. Portable homes were essential for people following migrating herds of animals.

SHELTERS OF TURF AND STONE

This is the outside of a Neolithic house in the village of Skara Brae in the Orkney Islands. It was built around 3000BC. The buildings were sunk into the ground and surrounded with turf to protect them from bad storms. Covered passages linked the houses.

A BURIED SITE

The village of Skara Brae in the Orkney Islands was built of stone because there were no local trees for building. Even the furniture inside was made of stone. In about 2000BC, the whole village was buried by a sand storm, preserving the site until it was exposed by a great storm in 1850.

Where wood was scarce, heavy mammoth bones were used to weight down grass and animal hides covering a hunter's house.

4 Use a pair of scissors to cut the twigs so that they are about 15cm long. You will need about eight evenly sized twigs in all.

5 Push the twigs into the modelling clay to form a cone-shaped frame. Glue a few stones on to the clay at the base of the twigs.

6 Cover the twigs with pieces of fake grass or fabric glued in place. Be sure not to cover up the stones around the base.

7 Neatly glue the long mammoth bones and tusks all over the outside. Fill in gaps with smaller bones. Leave it all to dry.

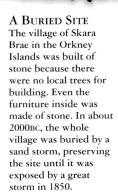

Fire and Light

OUR ANCESTOR *Homo erectus* learned to use fire at least 700,000 years ago. This early human ate cooked food and had warmth and light at night. Fire was useful to keep wild animals away and to harden the tips of wooden spears. Hunters waving flaming branches could scare large animals into ambushes. *Homo erectus* probably did not know how to make fire, but found smouldering logs after natural forest fires. Campfires were carefully kept alight, and hot ashes may have been carried to each new camp. Eventually, people learned to make fire by rubbing two dry sticks together. Then they found that striking a stone against a kind of rock called pyrite made a spark. By 4000BC, the bow drill had been invented. This made lighting a fire much easier.

STONE LAMP
Prehistoric artists used simple stone lamps like this as they decorated the walls of caves 17,000 years ago. A lighted wick of moss, twine or fur was put in a stone bowl filled with animal fat. Wooden splinters or rushes dipped in beeswax or resin were also used.

AROUND THE HEARTH
This is the inside of a Neolithic house at Skara Brae in the Orkney Islands. In the centre is a stone hearth, surrounded by beds, chairs and a dresser all made from stone. The smoke from the fire escaped through a hole in the turf roof. The large stones surrounding the hearth helped to protect the fire from being put out by draughts.

A MODEL BOW DRILL

You will need: thick piece of dowelling, craft knife, sandpaper, wood stain, water pot, brush, balsa wood, modelling tool, clay, rolling pin, scissors, chamois leather, raffia or straw.

1 Ask an adult to shape one end of the dowelling into a point with a craft knife. The blade should always work away from the body.

2 Lightly sand down the stick and paint it with wood stain. Ask an adult to cut out a balsa-wood base. Paint the base too.

3 Use the modelling tool to gouge a small hole in the centre of the balsa-wood base. The dowelling stick should fit in this hole.

BUSH FIRES

Before people learned to make fire, they made use of accidental fires like this one in Africa, perhaps set off by lightning or the sun's heat. Early people learned to use fire for cooking. Many vegetable plants are poisonous when raw but harmless when cooked. Fire was also used for hunting. A line of fire was lit and then the hunters would catch the animals as they fled.

FIRE STARTER

A Kalahari bushman uses a modern bow drill to start a fire. The string of a bow is used to twist a wooden drill round and round as the bow is moved backwards and forwards. The drill's point rests on a wooden base. The rubbing of the drill on the base creates heat, which is used to set fire to a small heap of tinder, such as moss. The tinder is then added to a pile of dry grass and small sticks.

To hold the drill upright, prehistoric people used a stone or piece of wood at the top. Some had a wooden mouthpiece to hold the drill upright and free the other hand to hold the base.

4 Roll out the clay and cut out a bone shape. Make a hole in each end and smooth the sides with your fingers. Let it harden.

5 Use a pair of scissors to cut a thin strip of leather about twice as long as the bone. This is the thong used to twist the drill.

6 Tie the strip of leather to the bone. Thread the strip through both holes, tying a knot at each end to secure the leather.

7 Scatter straw or raffia around the base. Wrap the leather thong around the drill and place the point in the central hole.

Food for Gathering

MATTOCK
This mattock, or digging tool, was made from an antler. It dates from between 8000 and 4000BC. It has a hole drilled through it, in which a wooden handle would have been fitted.

Stone Age hunter-gatherers had a very varied diet. They gradually discovered which plants they could eat and where they grew. From spring to autumn, women and children foraged for seeds, berries, nuts and roots. They found birds' eggs and the shoots and leaves of vegetable plants. In summer, plants such as peas, beans, squashes and cucumbers were picked, and the seeds of wild grasses were collected. The summer sun also ripened wild dates, grapes, figs, blueberries and cranberries. In autumn, there were nuts, such as almonds, pine nuts, walnuts, hazelnuts and acorns. These were stored underground, while fruits and berries were dried to preserve them. Insects, caterpillars and snails were food too! Wild honeycomb and herbs added flavour. The foragers used digging sticks to unearth roots, while leather bags and woven baskets held food safely.

INSECT GRUB
This is a witchetty grub, the large white larva of a goat moth. These grubs are eaten as a delicacy by Australian Aboriginals. Insects such as ants, grasshoppers, beetles and termites were healthy, high-protein food for Stone Age people.

BIRDS' EGGS
Prehistoric people ate many kinds of birds' eggs, from tiny quails' eggs to huge ostrich eggs. These eggs were laid by a pheasant, a bird native to Asia. Eggs are rich in protein, vitamins and minerals, which makes them a valuable food. Eggshells were also used to make beads for jewellery.

STEWED FRUIT
You will need: a large saucepan, 500g blueberries, 500g blackberries, 200g hazelnuts, wooden spoon, honeycomb, tablespoon, ladle, serving bowl.

1 Always choose firm, fresh fruit and wash it and your hands before you begin. First pour the blueberries into the pan.

2 Next pour in the blackberries. Use a wooden spoon to stir them gently into the blueberries, without crushing the fruit.

3 Shake in the whole hazelnuts and carefully stir the fruit and nuts once again until they are all thoroughly mixed.

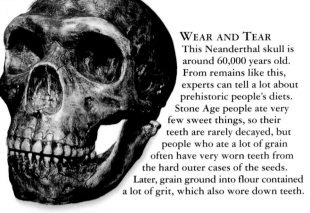

WEAR AND TEAR

This Neanderthal skull is around 60,000 years old. From remains like this, experts can tell a lot about prehistoric people's diets. Stone Age people ate very few sweet things, so their teeth are rarely decayed, but people who ate a lot of grain often have very worn teeth from the hard outer cases of the seeds. Later, grain ground into flour contained a lot of grit, which also wore down teeth.

nettle leaves

dandelion leaves *woodland fungus*

LOOKING FOR HONEY

This Mbuti man in the Republic of Congo is smoking out bees from their nest in order to collect the honey more easily. Prehistoric people may also have used fire to rob bees of their store. Collecting honey was worth the danger as it is rich in energy-giving carbohydrates, and its sweetness made other foods tasty.

Prehistoric people would have cooked fruit in a similar way to preserve it as jam. Clay pots, rather than metal saucepans, were used for cooking and storing.

4 Add six tablespoons of honey from the comb. Now ask an adult to put the pan on the stove and bring it slowly to the boil.

5 Simmer the fruit and nuts very gently for 20 minutes. Leave to cool. Use a ladle to transfer your dessert to a serving bowl.

Fish and Shells

OWARDS THE END of the last glacial period, about 12,000 years ago, the world's climate began to warm up. Melting ice flooded low-lying plains and fed many lakes, marshes and rivers. Trees grew across the grasslands and tundra, and bands of hunters started to settle down in campsites, some of which were permanent, beside seashores, lakes and rivers. Fishing and gathering shellfish became increasingly important sources of food for many people. Along the seashore, they foraged for seaweed and shellfish, such as mussels, whelks, clams and crabs. They also hunted many kinds of fish, seals and seabirds. Rivers and lakes were full of fish such as salmon and pike, as well as crayfish, turtles, ducks and other water birds. Fishing was done from boats or the shore, using hooks, harpoons and nets. Traps made of woven willow were put at one end of a dam built across a stream. As fish swam through, they were caught in the trap.

SEAL HUNTER
The traditional way of life of the Inuit is probably very similar to that of prehistoric hunter-fishers. They have lived along Arctic coasts for thousands of years.

BONE HARPOONS
These bone harpoon heads from southwest France date from around 12,000BC. They would have had wooden shafts and been attached to lines of leather or sinew.

A MODEL HARPOON
You will need: dowelling, craft knife, wood stain, self-drying clay, wooden board, ruler, pencil, white card, scissors, modelling tool, PVA glue, paintbrush, paint, water pot, leather laces or strong string.

1 Ask an adult to cut down one end of a length of thick dowelling using a craft knife. Cuts should be made away from the body.

2 Paint the dowelling with wood stain and leave it to dry. The stain will darken the wood to make it look older and stronger.

3 Roll out a piece of white clay to make a shaft about 15 cm long. Shape one end of the clay to a rounded point.

FOOD FROM THE SEASHORE

The seashore provided a plentiful source of food all year round. Mussels, cockles, whelks, oysters, scallops, winkles, razors, crabs and lobsters could be found along sandy beaches and in rock pools. Seaweed and the fleshy leaves of rock samphire were also collected from rocks and cliffs.

edible crab

mussel   *rock samphire*

FEARSOME FIGHTER

The pike lives in lakes and rivers. It is a powerful fish and a terrifying predator. Prehistoric people fished for pike from dugout canoes in late spring and early summer.

FISHING TACKLE

Fish hooks, made from carved bone, wood, antler, flint or shell, were attached to a strong line. A caught fish was stunned with a club before being hauled into the canoe.

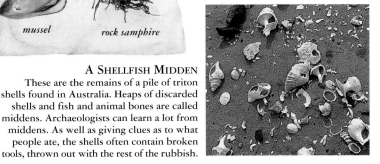

A SHELLFISH MIDDEN

These are the remains of a pile of triton shells found in Australia. Heaps of discarded shells and fish and animal bones are called middens. Archaeologists can learn a lot from middens. As well as giving clues as to what people ate, the shells often contain broken tools, thrown out with the rest of the rubbish.

Prehistoric hunters used harpoons for catching fish and hunting reindeer and bison.

4 Draw out a serrated edge for a row of barbs on a strip of card about 3 cm x 10 cm, as shown. Carefully cut out the barbs.

5 Use a modelling tool to make a slot down one side of the clay harpoon. Leave the clay to dry, then glue the barbs into the slot.

6 When the glue has dried, paint the head of your harpoon a suitable stone colour, such as a greyish brown.

7 Using a leather lace or strong string, tightly bind the harpoon head to the cut-down end of the wooden shaft.

Hunting Animals

URING THE LAST GLACIAL PERIOD, clans hunted great herds of bison, horses, reindeer and mammoths that roamed the tundra and grasslands. At first they used stone axes and wooden spears. Later, spears with bone or flint barbs were developed, and spear-throwers were used to throw the spears farther and harder. Animals were attacked directly or caught in pitfall traps and snares. Alternatively, a whole herd might be chased over a cliff or into an ambush. This was a good way to build up a large supply of meat. As forests spread over the land, forest animals were hunted with bows and arrows. By about 12,000BC, hunters were using tame dogs to help in the chase. Every part of a kill was used. The meat was cooked for food or dried to preserve it. Hides were made into clothes and animal fat was used in lamps. Bones and antlers were made into tools and weapons.

ANIMAL CARVINGS
This figure of a bison licking its back was carved from a reindeer's antler in about 12,000BC. It may have been part of a spear-thrower. Hunters often decorated their weapons with carvings of the animals they hunted.

BISON CAVE PAINTING
These two bison were painted on a cave wall in France in about 16,000BC. The walls of caves in southwest France and northern Spain are covered with almost life-sized paintings of animals that were hunted at the time. Early hunters knew the regular migration routes of large animals such as bison and reindeer. They looked for sick or weak animals, or attacked at vulnerable moments, such as when the animals were crossing a river.

THE GAME CYCLE

This illustration shows the animals people hunted in southwest France between about 33,000BC and 10,000BC. There was plenty of game to choose from. The hunters intercepted the animals at different times of the year as they followed their regular migration routes.

MAMMOTH HUNTERS
This woolly mammoth was carved from an animal's shoulder blade. Hunters worked in groups to kill these large mammals, one of which could feed a family for several months.

LEAP OF DEATH
In the engraving below, hunters are stampeding a herd of horses over a cliff in France. The hunters probably crept up to the animals, then, at a signal, jumped to their feet, yelling to startle the herd. Skeletons of 10,000 wild horses have been found at this site.

MUSK OXEN
Today, one of the few large mammals that can survive the harsh winters of the tundra is the musk ox. Their thickset bodies have a dense covering of fur with a shaggy outer coat. During the last glacial, musk oxen were widely hunted in Europe, Asia and North America.

The First Crops

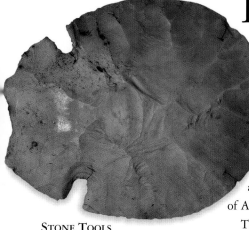

I N ABOUT 8000BC, people in the Near East began growing their own food for the first time. Instead of simply gathering the seeds of wild grasses, such as wheat and barley, they saved some of it. Then, the following year, they planted it to produce a crop. As they began to control their food sources, the first farmers found that a small area of land could now feed a much larger population. People began living in permanent settlements in order to tend their crops and guard their harvest. Over the next 5000 years, farming spread from the Near East to western Asia, Europe and Africa. Farming also developed separately in other parts of Asia around 6500BC and in America by about 7000BC.

The first farms were in hill country where wheat and barley grew naturally and there was enough rain for crops to grow. As populations increased, villages began to appear along river valleys, where farmers could water their crops at dry times of the year.

STONE TOOLS
This chipped flint is the blade of a hoe. It was used in North America between about AD900 and AD1200, but it is very similar to the hoes used by the first farmers to break up the soil. Rakes made of deer antlers were used to cover over the seeds. Ripe corn was harvested with sharp flint sickle blades.

SICKLE BLADE
This flint sickle blade has been hafted, or inserted, into a modern wooden handle. Ears of ripe corn would either have been plucked by hand or harvested with sickles such as this.

WILD RICE
Rice is a type of grass that grows in hot, damp areas, such as swamps. It was a good food source for early hunter-gatherers along rivers and coasts in southern Asia. The seeds were collected when ripe and stored for use when little other food was available. The grain could be kept for many months.

WORLD CROPS

The first plants to be domesticated, or farmed, were those that grew naturally in an area. Wheat and barley grew wild in the Near East. In India, China and southeast Asia, rice was domesticated by 5000BC and soon became the main food crop. Around 3000BC in Mexico, farmers grew maize, beans and squash. Farther south in the Andes mountains, the chief crops were potatoes, sweet potatoes and maize.

maize   *butternut squash*

GRINDING GRAIN

This stone quern, or hand-mill, is 6000 years old. It was used to grind grain into a coarse flour for making porridge or bread. The grain was placed on the flat stone and ground into flour with the smooth, heavy rubbing stone. Flour made in this way often contained quite a lot of grit. To make bread, water was added to the flour. The mixture was then shaped into flat loaves, which were baked in a clay oven.

STRAIGHT TRACK

Several tracks were built across marshes between 4000 and 2000BC in southern England. In some cases these were to link settlements to nearby fields of crops. The long, thin rods used to build the track above tell us a lot about the surrounding woodlands. The trees were coppiced, which means that thin shoots growing from cut hazel trees were harvested every few years.

A STEP UP

These terraced hillsides are in the Andes mountains of Peru. In mountainous areas where rainfall was high, some early farmers began cutting terraces, or steps, into the steep hillsides. The terraces meant that every scrap of soil could be used for planting. They prevented soil from eroding, or washing away. Farmers also used terracing to control the irrigation, or watering, of their crops. One of the first crops to be cultivated in Peru was the potato, which can be successfully grown high above sea level.

Taming Animals

ABOUT THE SAME time that people began to grow crops, they also started to domesticate (tame) wild animals. Wild sheep, goats, pigs and cattle had been hunted for thousands of years before people started to round them up into pens. Hunters may have done this to make the animals easier to catch. These animals gradually got used to people and became tamer. The first animals to be kept like this were probably sheep and goats around 8500BC in the Near East.

Herders soon noticed that larger animals often had larger young. They began to allow only the finest animals to breed, so that domestic animals gradually became much stronger and larger than wild ones. As well as four-legged livestock, chickens were domesticated for their eggs and meat. In South America, the llama was kept for its meat and wool, along with ducks and guinea pigs. In southeast Asia, pigs were the most important domestic animals.

WILD CATTLE
This bull is an aurochs, or wild ox. The aurochs was the ancestor of today's domestic cattle. Taming these huge, fierce animals was much harder than keeping sheep and goats. Wild cattle were probably not tamed until about 7000BC. The aurochs became extinct in AD1627. In the 1930s, a German biologist re-created the animal by crossing domesticated breeds such as Friesians and Highland cattle.

WILD HORSES
Horses were a favourite food for prehistoric hunter-gatherers. This sculpture of a wild horse was found in Germany. It was made around 4000BC. Horses also often appear in cave art. They were probably first domesticated in Russia around 4400BC. In America, horses had become extinct through over-hunting by 9000BC. They were reintroduced by European explorers in the AD1500s.

DINGOES AND DOGS

The dingo is the wild dog of Australia. It is the descendant of tame dogs that were brought to the country more than 10,000 years ago by Aboriginal Australians. Dogs were probably the first animals to be domesticated. Their wolf ancestors were tamed to help with hunting and, later, with herding and guarding. In North America, dogs were used as pack animals and dragged a *travois* (sled) behind them.

DESERT HERDERS

Small herds of wild cattle were probably first domesticated in the Sahara and the Near East. This rock painting comes from the Tassili n'Ajjer area of the Sahara Desert. It was painted in about 6000BC at a time when much of the Sahara was covered by grassland and shallow lakes. The painting shows a group of herders with their cattle outside a plan of their house.

GOATS AND SHEEP

Rock paintings in the Sahara show goats and sheep, among the first animals to be domesticated. They were kept for their meat, milk, hides and wool, and are still some of the most common farmed animals.

LLAMAS

The llama was domesticated in central Peru by at least 3500BC. It was kept first for its meat and wool, but later it was also used for carrying food and goods long distances. A relative of the llama, the alpaca, was also domesticated for its wool.

Stone Technology

EARLY TOOLS
These chipped pebbles from Tanzania in Africa are some of the oldest tools ever found. They were made by *Homo habilis*, an early human ancestor, almost two million years ago.

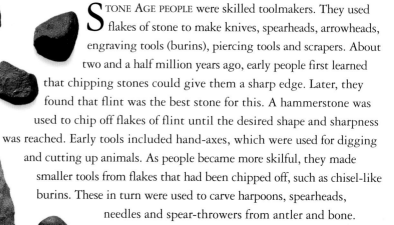

STONE AGE PEOPLE were skilled toolmakers. They used flakes of stone to make knives, spearheads, arrowheads, engraving tools (burins), piercing tools and scrapers. About two and a half million years ago, early people first learned that chipping stones could give them a sharp edge. Later, they found that flint was the best stone for this. A hammerstone was used to chip off flakes of flint until the desired shape and sharpness was reached. Early tools included hand-axes, which were used for digging and cutting up animals. As people became more skilful, they made smaller tools from flakes that had been chipped off, such as chisel-like burins. These in turn were used to carve harpoons, spearheads, needles and spear-throwers from antler and bone.

FLAKING
Neanderthals and *Homo sapiens* were far better toolmakers than earlier people. They chipped flakes off pieces of flint to produce hand-axes (*left and middle*) and chopping tools (*right*). Pointed or oval-shaped hand-axes were used for many different tasks.

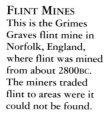

FLINT MINES
This is the Grimes Graves flint mine in Norfolk, England, where flint was mined from about 2800BC. The miners traded flint to areas were it could not be found.

MAKE A MODEL AXE
You will need: self-drying clay, board, modelling tool, sandpaper, grey acrylic paint, wood stain, water pot, paintbrush, thick dowelling, craft knife, ruler, chamois leather, scissors.

1 Pull out the clay into a thick block. With a modelling tool, shape the block into an axe head with a point at one end.

2 When the clay is completely dry, lightly rub down the axe head with sandpaper to remove any rough surfaces.

3 Paint the axe head a stone colour, such as grey. You could use more than one shade if you like. Leave it to dry.

SPEAR POINT

The Cro-Magnons used long, thin flakes of flint to make their tools. This leaf-shaped spear point was made by highly skilled toolmakers about 20,000 years ago. Its finely flaked shape was made by delicately chipping over the entire surface.

STONES FOR TOOLS

Nodules of flint are often found in limestone rock, especially chalk, so it was reasonably easy to obtain. But other kinds of rock were used for toolmaking too. Obsidian, a rock formed from cooled lava, was widely used in the Near East and Mexico. It fractured easily, leaving sharp edges. In parts of Africa, quartz was made into beautiful, hardwearing hand-axes and choppers. A rock called diorite was used for making polished axe heads in Neolithic times.

quartz   *chert (a type of flint)*

STONE AXES

These polished stone battle axes became the most important weapon in Scandinavia by the late Neolithic period. They date from about 1800BC.

TOOLMAKING LESSON

Stone Age people came to depend more and more on the quality of their tools. In this reconstruction, a father is passing on his skill in toolmaking to his son.

Prehistoric people used axes for chopping wood and cutting meat. They shaped a stone blade, then fitted it on to a wooden shaft.

4 Ask an adult to trim one end of a piece of thick dowelling using a craft knife. Paint the piece with wood stain and leave to dry.

5 To bind the axe head to the wooden shaft, first carefully cut a long strip of leather about 2.5cm wide from a chamois cloth.

6 Place the axe head on the trimmed end of the shaft. Wrap the strip of leather around the head and shaft in a criss-cross pattern.

7 Pull the leather strip tight and wrap the ends twice round the shaft below the head. Tie the ends together and trim them.

Carving Wood and Bone

Aʟᴛʜᴏᴜɢʜ ᴛʜɪꜱ ᴩᴇʀɪᴏᴅ is called the Stone Age, wood, bone, antler and ivory were just as important for making tools and other implements. Not only could these materials be carved and shaped by stone tools, but bone and antler hammers and punches were used to shape the stone tools themselves. By using these implements, better cutting edges and finer flakes of stone could be achieved.

Antler, bone, wood and ivory had many different uses. Antler picks were used to dig up roots and chip out lumps of stone. Antlers and bones were carved into spear-throwers and, along with ivory, were used to make needles, fish hooks, harpoon heads and knives. Wood was used to make the handles and mounts for spears, harpoons, axes, sickles and adzes, which were tools used for shaping wood, as well as to make bows and arrows. The shoulder blades of cattle were made into shovels, while smaller bones were used to make awls to punch small holes. Smaller bones were also used to make fine whistles and little paint holders. All these materials were often beautifully carved with pictures of the animals that were hunted and fine decorative patterns.

SPEAR-THROWER
This carving of a reindeer's head is probably part of a spear-thrower. Wood, bone or antler all have natural cracks and flaws in them. Prehistoric carvers often incorporated these into the design to suggest the animal's outline, as well as particular features, such as eyes, mouth and nostrils. Engraved, or carved, pictures in caves also often make use of the natural form of the rock.

ADZE
An adze was a bit like an axe, except that its blade was at right angles to the handle. The flint blade on this adze dates from about 4000ʙᴄ to 2000ʙᴄ. Its wooden handle and binding are modern replacements for the originals, which have rotted away. Adzes were swung in an up-and-down movement and were used for jobs such as hollowing out tree trunks and shaping them to make dugout canoes.

AXE
Early farmers needed axes to clear land for their crops. An experiment in Denmark using a 5,000-year-old axe showed that a man could clear one hectare of woodland in about five weeks. This axe head dating from between 4000ʙᴄ and 2000ʙᴄ has been given a modern wooden handle.

ANTLER PICK

Antlers were as useful to prehistoric humans as to their original owners! This tool comes from a Neolithic site near Avebury in England. Antler picks were used for digging and quarrying. Antler was a very versatile material. It could be made into spear and harpoon points, needles and spear-throwers.

CRAFTSPEOPLE

This engraving shows Stone Age life as imagined by an artist from the 1800s. It shows tools being used and great care being taken over the work. Even everyday items were often finely carved and decorated by the craftspeople who made them.

CARVED BATON

This ivory object is known as a *bâton de commandement*. Several of these batons have been found, especially in France. But no one is sure what they were used for. Some experts think they were status symbols, showing the importance of the person carrying them. Others think that the holes were used to straighten arrows. Whatever their use, the batons are often decorated with fine animal carvings and geometric designs.

ANTLERS AT WORK

Two stags (male deer) fight. Male deer have large antlers, which they use to battle with each other to win territory and females. The stags shed and grow a new set of antlers each year, so prehistoric hunters and artists had a ready supply of material.

Crafts

THE VERY FIRST HANDICRAFT was probably basketmaking, using river reeds and twigs woven together. Baskets were quick to make and easy to carry, but not very durable. Pottery was harder-wearing. The discovery that baking clay made it stronger may have happened by accident, perhaps when a clay-lined basket fell into the fire. Baked clay figures were made from about 24,000BC, but it took thousands of years for people to realize that pottery could be useful for cooking and storing food and drink. The first pots were made in Japan around 10,500BC. Pots were shaped from coils or lumps of clay. Their sides were smoothed and decorated before being fired in an open hearth or kiln.

Another neolithic invention was the loom, around 6000BC. The first cloth was probably made of wool, cotton or flax (which could be made into linen).

BAKED CLAY FIGURINE

This is one of the oldest fired-clay objects in the world. It is one of many similar figurines made around 24,000BC at Dolni Vestonice in the Czech Republic. Here, people hunted mammoths, woolly rhinoceroses and horses. They built homes with small, oval-shaped ovens, in which they fired their figurines.

CHINESE JAR

It is amazing to think that this elegant pot was for everyday use in 4500BC. It was made in Banpo, near Shanghai. The people of Banpo were some of China's earliest farmers. They grew millet and kept pigs and dogs for meat. The potters made a high quality black pottery for important occasions and this cheaper grey pottery for everyday use.

MAKE A CLAY POT

You will need: terracotta modelling clay, wooden board, modelling tool, plastic flower pot, decorating tool, varnish, brush, sandpaper.

1 Roll out a long, thick sausage of clay on a wooden board. It should be at least 1cm in diameter.

2 Form the roll of clay into a coil to make the base of your pot. A fairly small base can be made into a pot, a larger one into a bowl.

3 Now make a fatter roll of clay. Carefully coil this around the base to make the sides of your pot.

HOUSEHOLD POTS

Many early pots were decorated with basket-like patterns. This one has a simple geometric design and was made in Thailand in about 3500BC. Clay pots like this were used for storing food, carrying water or cooking.

STEATITE IDOL

Steatite, or soapstone, has been used to make this carving from the Cycladic Islands of Greece. Soapstone is very soft and easy to carve. Figurines like this one were often used in funeral ceremonies. They could also be used either as the object of worship itself or as a ritual offering to a god. This figure has a cross around its neck. Although the symbol certainly has no Christian significance, no one really knows what it means.

WOVEN THREADS

The earliest woven objects may have looked like this rope and cane mat from Nazca in Peru. It was made around AD1000. Prehistoric people used plant-fibre rope to weave baskets and bags. The oldest known fabric dates from about 6500BC and was found at Çatal Hüyük in Turkey. Few woven objects have survived, as they rot quickly.

Fired-clay pots could only be made where there were natural deposits of clay, so some areas seem to have specialized in baked-clay pottery and sculpture. The patterns used to decorate the pots vary from area to area.

4 With a modelling tool, smooth down the edges of the coil to make it flat and smooth. Make sure there are no air spaces.

5 Place your pot over a flower pot to support it. Keep adding more rolls of clay to build up the sides of your pot.

6 Smooth down the sides as you add more rolls. Then use a decorating tool with a serrated end to make different patterns.

7 Leave your pot to dry out. When the clay is dry, varnish the outside. Use sandpaper to smooth the inside of your pot.

Clothing

THE HUNTERS of the last glacial period were probably the first people to wear clothes. They needed them for protection from the cold. Clothes were made of animal hides sewn together with strips of leather. The first clothes included simple trousers, tunics and cloaks, decorated with beads of coloured rock, teeth and shells. Fur boots were also worn, tied on with leather laces.

Furs were prepared by stretching out the hides and scraping them clean. The clothes were cut out and holes were made around the edges of the pieces with a sharp, pointed stone called an awl. The holes made it much easier to pass a bone needle through the hide. Cleaned hides were also used to make tents, bags and bedding.

Some time after sheep farming began in the Near East, wool was used to weave cloth. In other parts of the world, plant fibres, such as flax, cotton, bark and cactus, were used. The cloth was coloured and decorated with plant dyes.

PREPARING HIDES
An Inuit woman uses her teeth to soften a seal skin. Prehistoric hunter-gatherers probably also softened hides like this. Animal hides were first pegged out and scraped clean. Then they were washed and stretched taut on a wooden frame to stop them shrinking as they dried. The stiff, dry hide was then softened and cut to shape for clothing.

PINS AND NEEDLES
These are 5000-year-old bone pins from Skara Brae in the Orkney Islands. Prehistoric people made pins and needles from slithers of bone or antler, their sides were then smoothed by rubbing them on a stone.

DYEING CLOTH
You will need: natural dyes such as walnuts, elderberries and safflower, saucepan, water, tablespoon, sieve, bowl, chamois leather, white card, white t-shirt, wooden spoon. (Dyes can be found in health food shops.)

1 Choose your first dye and put approximately 8-12 tablespoons of it into an old pan. You may need to crush or shred it first.

2 Ask an adult to boil the dye and then simmer it for one hour. Leave to cool. Pour the dye through a sieve to remove lumps.

3 Test a patch of chamois leather by dipping it in the dye for a few minutes. You could wear rubber gloves for protection.

NATURE'S COLOURS

Stone Age people used the flowers, stems, bark and leaves of many plants to make dyes. The flowers of dyer's broom and dyer's chamomile gave a range of colours from bright yellow to khaki. Plants such as woad and indigo gave a rich blue dye, while the bark, leaves and husks of the walnut made a deep brown. Plants were also used to prepare hides. Skins were softened by being soaked with oak bark in water.

dyer's broom

birch bark

oak bark

RAW MATERIALS

This engraving shows an Inuit man hunting a seal in the Arctic. Animals provided skin for cloth, sinews for thread and bones for needles. Clothes made of animal skin kept out the cold and rain, and allowed early people to live farther north.

KEEPING WARM

This Nenet woman from Siberia in Russia is wearing a reindeer-skin coat called a *yagushka*. Prehistoric people probably dressed in a similar way to keep out the cold. Waterproof trousers, hooded parkas, boots and mittens would have been worn.

GRASS SOCKS

Until recently the Inuit of North America gathered grasses in summer and braided them into socks like these. The socks were shaped to fit the foot snugly and were worn under seal-skin boots.

4 Lay the patch on a piece of white card and leave it to dry. Be careful not to drip the dye over clothes or upholstery as you work.

5 Make up the other two dyes and test them out in the same way. Compare the patches and choose your favourite colour.

6 Dye a white t-shirt by preparing it in your chosen dye. Try to make sure that the t-shirt is dyed evenly all over.

Safflower flowers for dyeing were picked when first open, then dried.

Ornament and Decoration

CEREMONIAL DRESS
The amazing headdress, face painting and jewellery still seen at ceremonies in Papua New Guinea may echo the richness of decoration in Stone Age times.

Both men and women wore jewellery in the Stone Age. Necklaces and pendants were made from all sorts of natural objects. Brightly coloured pebbles, snail shells, fishbones, animal teeth, seashells, eggshells, nuts and seeds were all used. Later, semi-precious amber and jade, fossilized jet and hand-made clay beads were also made. The beads were threaded on to thin strips of leather or twine made from plant fibres.

Other jewellery included bracelets made of slices of elephant or mammoth tusk. Strings of shells and teeth were made into beautiful headbands. Women plaited their hair and put it up with combs and pins. People probably decorated their bodies and outlined their eyes with pigments such as red ochre. They may have tattooed and pierced their bodies too.

BODY PAINT
These Australian Aboriginal children have painted their bodies with clay. They have used patterns that are thousands of years old.

BONES AND TEETH
This necklace is made from the bones and teeth of a walrus. It comes from Skara Brae in the Orkney Islands. A hole was made in each bead with a stone tool, or with a wooden stick spun by a bow drill. The beads were then strung on to a strip of leather or twine.

MAKE A NECKLACE
You will need: self-drying clay, rolling pin and board, modelling tool, sandpaper, ivory and black acrylic paint, paintbrush, water pot, ruler, scissors, chamois leather, card, double-sided sticky tape, PVA glue, leather laces.

1 Roll out the clay on a board and cut out four crescent shapes with the modelling tool. Leave them on the board to dry.

2 Rub the crescents lightly with sandpaper and paint them an ivory colour. You could varnish them later to make them shiny.

3 Cut four strips of leather about 9cm x 3cm. Use the edge of a piece of card to make a black criss-cross pattern on the strips.

NATURAL DECORATION

We know about the wide variety of materials used in Stone Age jewellery from cave paintings and ornaments discovered in graves. Shells were highly prized and some were traded over long distances. Other materials included deers' teeth, mammoth and walrus ivory, fish bones and birds' feathers.

a selection of sea shells

A WARRIOR'S HEADDRESS

This Yali warrior from Indonesia has a headdress of wild boars' teeth and a necklace made of shells and bone. Headdresses and necklaces made of animals' teeth may have had a spiritual meaning for Stone Age people. The wearer may have believed that the teeth brought the strength or courage of the animal from which they came.

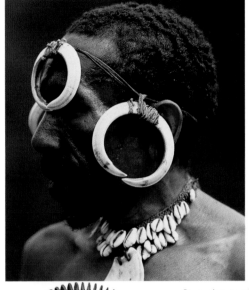

BANGLES AND EAR STUDS

This jewellery comes from Harappa in Pakistan. It dates from between 2300BC and 1750BC and is made from shells and coloured pottery. Archaeologists in Harappa have found the remains of dozens of shops that sold jewellery.

Stone Age people believed that wearing a leopard claw necklace brought them magical powers.

4 When they are dry, fold back the edges of each strip and hold in place with double-sided sticky tape.

5 Brush the middle of each crescent with glue and wrap the leather around, forming a loop at the top, as shown.

6 Plait together three leather laces to make a thong. Make the thong long enough to go around your neck and be tied.

7 Thread the leopard's claws on to the middle of the thong, arranging them so that there are small spaces between them.

The Arts

STONE AGE ARTISTS were wonderfully skilled, working in stone, antler, bone, ivory and clay. They painted rock walls, engraved stone and ivory and carved musical instruments. They created images of the animals they hunted, as well as human figures and abstract designs. No one knows for sure why they were so creative.

The earliest works of art date from around 40,000BC and were etched on to rocks in Australia. In Europe, the oldest works of art are cave paintings from about 28,000BC. Most cave paintings, however, date from around 16,000BC. The walls of caves in northern Spain and southwest France are covered with paintings and engravings of animals. Stone Age artists also carved female figures, called Venus figurines, and decorated their tools and weapons. This explosion in art ended in about 10,000BC.

VENUS FIGURINES
This small figure, called the Venus of Lespugue, was found in France. It dates from about 20,000BC. Her full figure probably represents the fertility of a goddess. She may have been carried as a good luck charm.

MUSIC AND DANCE
Stone Age rock paintings in Europe and Africa show people moving in dance-like patterns. This engraving from a cave on the island of Sicily dates from about 9000BC. Ceremonies in the Stone Age almost certainly included music and dancing, perhaps with drums and whistles too.

MAKE A CAVE PAINTING
You will need: self-drying craft clay, rolling pin and board, modelling tool, sandpaper, acrylic paints, paintbrush, water pot.

1 First roll out the craft clay, giving it a slightly bumpy surface like a cave wall. Cut it into a neat shape with a modelling tool.

2 When the clay has dried, lightly rub down the surface with sandpaper to make it smooth and give a good surface to paint on.

3 Paint the outline of your chosen animal in black. This painting shows a reindeer similar to those in Stone Age cave paintings.

EARLY POTTERY

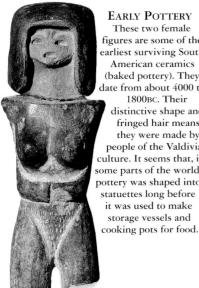

These two female figures are some of the earliest surviving South American ceramics (baked pottery). They date from about 4000 to 1800BC. Their distinctive shape and fringed hair means they were made by people of the Valdivia culture. It seems that, in some parts of the world, pottery was shaped into statuettes long before it was used to make storage vessels and cooking pots for food.

AN ARTIST'S MATERIALS

Prehistoric artists made their paints from soft rocks and minerals such as charcoal and clay. They ground these to a powder and mixed them with water or animal fat. Charcoal from the fire was used for black outlines and shading. Coloured earth, called ochre, gave browns, reds and yellows. A clay called kaolin was used for white paint. The paint was stored in hollow bones. Brushes were made from animal hair, moss or frayed twigs.

ochre   *charcoal*

SPIRAL DESIGNS

These carved stones are from the temple at Tarxien on the island of Malta and date from around 2500BC. Many large stone monuments that were built in Europe from about 4200BC are decorated with geometric patterns.

4 Draw the most obvious features of your animal by exaggerating their size. The sweeping horns of this deer make it very striking.

5 When the outline is dry, mix yellow, red and black to make a warm colour with which to fill in the outline of your animal.

6 Finish off your picture by highlighting some parts of the body with reddish brown paint mixed to resemble red ochre.

Stone Age artists painted in black, white and earthy colours.

Trade and Distribution

S TONE AGE PEOPLE did not use banknotes and coins for money, as we do. Instead they bartered, or exchanged, things. When one person wanted a bowl, for example, he or she had to offer something in exchange to the owner of the bowl – perhaps a tool or ornament. Towards the end of the Stone Age, however, people began to use shells or stone rings as a kind of currency.

Even isolated hunter-gatherer groups came into contact with each other and exchanged things, such as seashells, for tools or hides. With the beginning of farming around 8000BC in the Near East, however, long-distance exchange and a more organized trading system began. New activities, such as farming, pottery and weaving, needed specialized tools, so a high value was put on suitable rocks. In western Europe, flint mines and stone quarries produced axe blades that were prized and traded over great distances. Sometimes goods were traded thousands of kilometres from where they were made.

COWRIE SHELLS
Small, highly polished cowrie shells were popular as decoration for clothes and jewellery in prehistoric times. The shells have been found scattered around skeletons in burial sites, many of which are hundreds of kilometres from the coast. Later, cowrie shells were used as money in Africa and parts of Asia.

AXES
A good strong axe was a valuable commodity. It was particularly important for early farmers, who used it to chop down trees and clear land for crops. Axe heads made of special stone were traded over wide distances.

BURIED WITH WEALTH
This communal burial on the Solomon Islands in the Pacific Ocean shows the deceased accompanied by shells and ornaments. Shells have been used for money for thousands of years – in fact, for longer and over a wider area than any currency including coins. One hoard of shells, found in Iraq, was dated before 18,000BC.

STONE TRADE

During the neolithic period there was a widespread trade in stone for axes. At Graig in Clwyd, Wales (*left*), stone was quarried from the scree slopes and taken all over Britain. The blades were roughed out on site, then transported to other parts of the country, where they were ground and polished into axe heads. Rough, unfinished axes have been found lying on the ground at Graig.

FUR TRAPPER

A modern Cree trapper from the Canadian Arctic is surrounded by his catch of pine marten pelts. Furs were almost certainly a valuable commodity for prehistoric people, especially for hunter-gatherers trading with more settled farmers. They could be traded for food or precious items such as amber or tools.

SKINS AND PELTS

White Arctic fox skins are left to dry in the cold air. In winter, Arctic foxes grow a thick white coat so that they are well camouflaged against the snow. Furs like this have traditionally been particularly valuable to Arctic people, both for the clothing that makes Arctic life possible and for trading.

Transport on Land and Sea

THE EARLIEST MEANS of transport, apart from travelling on foot, was by boat. The first people to reach Australia, perhaps as early as 50,000BC, must have used log or bamboo rafts to cross open water. Later, skin-covered coracles and kayaks (canoes hollowed from tree trunks) and boats made from reeds were used. On land, people dragged goods on wooden sledges or *travois* (triangular platforms of poles lashed together). Logs were used as rollers to move heavy loads. The taming of horses, donkeys and camels in about 4000BC revolutionized land transport. The first roads and causeways in Europe were built around the same time. In about 3500BC, the wheel was invented by metal-using people in Mesopotamia. It quickly spread to Stone Age people in Europe.

HORSE'S HEAD
This rock engraving of a horse's head comes from a cave in France. Some experts think that horses may have been tamed as early as 12,000BC. There are carvings that appear to show bridles around the heads of horses, but the marks may indicate manes.

CORACLE
A man fishes from a coracle, one of the oldest boat designs. Made of animal hide stretched over a wooden frame, the coracle may have been used since about 7600BC.

MAKE A MODEL CANOE
You will need: card, pencil, ruler, scissors, PVA glue, glue brush, masking tape, self-drying clay, double-sided sticky tape, chamois leather, pair of compasses, thread, needle.

canoe top

——— 20cm ———

canoe top

— 10CM —

canoe base

——— 20cm ———

canoe base

—10cm—

1 Cut card to the size of the templates shown on the left. Remember to cut semicircles from the long edge of both top pieces.

2 Glue the bases together and the tops together. Use masking tape to secure them as they dry. Join the top to the base in the same way.

SAILING BOATS

This is a model of a skin-covered boat called an *umiak*, which was used by the Inuit of North America. The figure at the back is the helmsman, whose job is to steer the boat. The other figures are rowing the oars. The ancient Egyptians seem to have been the first people to use sailing ships around 3200BC.

STONE BRIDGE

Walla Brook bridge on Dartmoor is one of the oldest stone bridges in Britain. Bridges make travelling easier, safer and more direct. The first bridges were made by placing tree trunks across rivers, or by laying flat stones in shallow streams.

KAYAK FRAME

This wooden frame for a kayak was made by an Inuit fisherman. It has been built without any nails, the joints being lashed together with strips of leather. Canoes such as this have been in use for thousands of years.

Inuit kayaks give clues about how Stone Age boats may have looked. The outsides were covered with skin.

3 Draw three circles the size of the holes in the top, with smaller circles inside. Cut them out. Make clay rings the same size.

4 Cover the clay and the card rings with double-sided tape. These rings form the seats where the paddlers will sit.

5 Cover your canoe with chamois leather, leaving holes for seats. Glue it tightly in place so that all the cardboard is covered.

6 Use a needle and thread to sew up the edges of the leather on the top of the canoe. Position and fix the seats and oars.

Warfare and Weapons

Warfare and fighting were certainly a part of Stone Age life. Prehistoric skeletons often reveal wounds received during a fight. For example, in a cemetery in Egypt dating from about 12,000BC, the skeletons of 58 men, women and children have been found, many with the flint flakes that killed them still stuck in their bones. In South Africa, a rare rock engraving, dating from between 8000 and 3000BC, shows two groups of people fighting each other with bows and arrows. No one knows exactly why people fought each other. After 8000BC, as the population of farmers grew, conflict between farming groups competing for land increased. Early farming villages were often encircled by earthworks, mud-brick walls or high wooden fences for protection.

DEADLY ARROWHEADS
The first arrowheads may have been made of wood, hardened over a fire. Yet flint could be given a much sharper edge. This hoard was found in Brittany, France. Sharp weapons could mean the difference between life and death, so they were very valuable.

AMERICAN POINT
This type of stone weapon was used by hunter-gatherers in North America to hunt bison. It is called a Folsom point and dates from around 8000BC.

A BOW AND ARROW
You will need: self-drying clay, rolling pin and board, modelling tool, sandpaper, acrylic paint, paintbrush, two lengths of thin dowelling (about 40cm and 60cm), craft knife, double-sided sticky tape, scissors, string.

1 Roll out the craft clay and use a modelling tool to cut out an arrowhead shape. When dry, smooth with sandpaper and paint grey.

2 Ask an adult to trim down one end of the shorter length of dowelling with a craft knife. This is the arrow shaft.

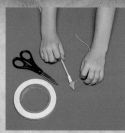

3 Fix the arrow head to the shaft with double-sided sticky tape. Wrap string around the tape to imitate leather binding.

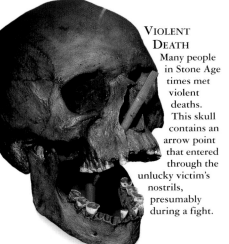

VIOLENT DEATH

Many people in Stone Age times met violent deaths. This skull contains an arrow point that entered through the unlucky victim's nostrils, presumably during a fight.

HUNTERS OR WARRIORS?

This rock painting, dating from around 6000BC, shows hunters or warriors with bows and arrows out on a raid. By about 13,000BC, prehistoric hunters had learned that bows and arrows were more powerful and accurate than spears.

BLADES AND POINTS

A selection of flint arrow heads and knife blades from Egypt shows fine workmanship. Flakes of flint about 20cm long were used as lanceheads. Shorter ones were made into javelins, knives and arrows. The heads were mounted on to wooden shafts with tree resin glue and strips of leather.

Prehistoric hunter-gatherers carried small, lightweight bows from which they could fire many arrows quickly.

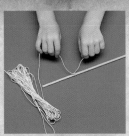

4 Use the longer length of dowelling to make the bow. Tie a long length of string securely to one end of the bow.

5 Ask an adult to help you carefully bend back the bow and tie the string to the other end. Sticky tape will help to secure the string.

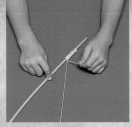

6 To tighten and secure the bowstring further, wind the string round each end several times. Then tie it and cut off the end.

7 Using double-sided sticky tape, wrap another piece of string around the middle of the bow as a rest for the arrow.

Religion and Magic

W E CAN ONLY GUESS at the beliefs of Stone Age people. The first people we know of who buried their dead were the Neanderthals. This suggests that they believed in a spirit world. Early people probably worshipped the spirits of the animals they hunted and other natural things. Some paintings and engravings on rocks and in caves may have a magical or religious purpose. Small statues, called Venus figurines, were probably worshipped as goddesses of fertility or plenty. Prehistoric people probably thought illnesses and accidents were caused by evil spirits. It may have been the job of one person, called a shaman, to speak to the spirits and interpret what should be done.

As farming spread and settlements grew into towns, more organized religions began. Shrines decorated with religious pictures have been found at Çatal Hüyük in Turkey, the site of a well-preserved town dating from around 7000BC.

ANCIENT BURIAL
The skull of the skeleton from this burial found in France has been scattered with red ochre earth. Red may have represented blood or life for Stone Age people. Bodies were often buried on their sides, with their knees pulled up to their chins. Tools, ornaments, food and weapons were put in the graves. Later Stone Age people built elaborate tombs for their dead.

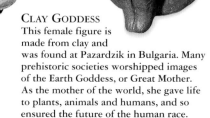

RITUAL ANTLERS
These antlers are from a red stag and were found at Star Carr in England. Some experts think that antlers were worn by a kind of priest called a shaman, perhaps in a coming-of-age ceremony or to bring good luck in that season's hunt.

CLAY GODDESS
This female figure is made from clay and was found at Pazardzik in Bulgaria. Many prehistoric societies worshipped images of the Earth Goddess, or Great Mother. As the mother of the world, she gave life to plants, animals and humans, and so ensured the future of the human race.

TREPANNING

Cutting a hole in a person's head is called trepanning. It was practised in prehistoric times from about 5000BC. A sharp flint tool was used to cut a hole in the skull in order to let illness escape from the body. Several skulls have been found that show the hole starting to close – evidence that some patients even survived the blood-curdling procedure!

SPELLS AND POTIONS

In many hunter-gatherer societies today, a shaman (witch doctor) can speak with the spirits from the world of the dead. In cultures such as the Amazonian Indians, shamen also administer potions from plants to cure illness. They use plants such as quinine, coca and curare.

Stone Age people probably behaved in a similar way. There is evidence that neolithic farmers in northwestern Europe grew poppies and hemp, possibly for use in magic potions and rituals.

poppy

ANCESTOR WORSHIP

This skull comes from Jericho in the Near East and dates from about 6500BC. Before the people of Jericho buried their dead, they removed the skulls. These were covered with plaster and painted to look like the features of the dead person. Cowrie shells were used for eyes. Some experts believe that this was done as a form of ancestor worship.

RITUAL DANCE

A modern painting shows a traditional Australian Aboriginal dance. Traditional ceremonies are an important part of Aboriginal life. Evidence of them has been found on prehistoric sites in Australia. Aboriginal beliefs are designed to maintain the delicate balance between people and their environment.

Monuments of Wood and Stone

THE FIRST GREAT STONE MONUMENTS were built in Europe and date from around 4200BC. They are called megaliths, which means large stones in Greek, and were built by early farming communities from Scandinavia to the Mediterranean. Some of the first megaliths were dolmens, made up of a large flat stone supported by several upright stones. They are the remains of ancient burial places, called chambered tombs. They may also have been used to mark a community's territory. Others are called passage graves. These were communal graves where many people were buried. Later, larger monuments were constructed. Wood or stone circles called henges, such as Stonehenge in England, were built. No one knows why these circles were made. They may have been temples, meeting places or giant calendars, since they are aligned with the Sun, Moon and stars.

DOLMEN
The bare stones shown here are all that is left of a chambered tomb once covered by a large mound of earth. Called a dolmen, the huge slabs once surrounded a burial chamber.

WOOD HENGE
This is a modern reconstruction of a wooden henge (circle) excavated at Sarn-y-Brn-Caled in Wales. People started building wooden henges around 3000BC. Henges were centres of religious and social life.

A WOODEN HENGE
You will need: card, ruler, compasses, pencil, scissors, terracotta craft clay, rolling pin and board, modelling tool, 1-cm- and 5-mm-thick dowelling, sandpaper, acrylic paint, paintbrush, fake grass, PVA glue, wood stain, brush.

1 Cut out a circle of card about 35cm in diameter. Roll out the clay, place the circle on top and cut around the clay.

2 Press a 1cm-thick stick around the edge to make a ring of evenly spaced post holes. Mark a circle, about 10cm across, inside the first.

3 Press the stick around the second circle to make 5 evenly spaced holes. Leave the base to dry. Sand it and paint it brown.

STANDING STONES

Stonehenge was built over many centuries from about 2800BC to 1400BC. The first Stonehenge was a circular earthwork made up of a bank and ditch. Later, large blocks of dressed (shaped) sarsen stones were put up. The stones are aligned with the midsummer sunrise and midwinter sunset, as well as the positions of the Moon.

PASSAGE GRAVE

This stone lies at the entrance to a passage grave at Newgrange in Ireland. The grave is a circular mound with a single burial chamber at the centre, reached by a long passage. Many of the stone slabs that line the passage are decorated with spirals and circles.

STONE TEMPLE

This is Hgar Quim temple on the island of Malta. Many stone temples were built on Malta between 3600BC and 2500BC. The oldest have walls at least 6m long and 3.5m tall. The most impressive temple is the Hypogeum, carved on three levels deep underground.

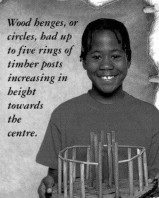

Wood henges, or circles, had up to five rings of timber posts increasing in height towards the centre.

4 Cover the base with uneven pieces of fake grass, glued into place. Be careful not to completely cover up the post holes.

5 Cut short sticks for the posts and lintels. Cut 7 more longer sticks. Paint the sticks with wood stain and leave to dry.

6 Glue the sticks in place using the post holes as guides. When dry, glue the lintels on top to complete your wood circle.

Journey through Life

STONE AGE PEOPLE held ceremonies to mark the significant stages in their lives, such as birth, coming of age, marriage and death. Coming-of-age ceremonies marked the point when boys and girls were thought of as adults, playing a full part in the life of the clan. Lifespans in Stone Age times were much shorter than they are today. Old people were valued members of the clan, as they were able to pass on their skills and knowledge. Most people lived into their thirties, but few survived to their sixties. There was little people could do against illness and infection and many infants died at birth. When game and food were plentiful, however, it seems that hunter-gatherers probably had an easier way of life than later farmers, whose work was hard and unending.

BURIAL SCENE
This burial from northeast France was made in about 4500BC at the time when farming was starting in that area. These early farmers were buried in small cemeteries, often with shell ornaments, adzes and stones for grinding grain.

DOGGU FIGURE
This Jomon human figurine from Japan was made of clay between 2500 and 1000BC. These figurines were often used during funerary rituals and, in some cases, were also buried in graves.

A PASSAGE GRAVE

You will need: card, pair of compasses and pencil, ruler, scissors, rolling pin and board, terracotta self-drying clay, modelling tool, white self-drying clay, PVA glue and gluebrush, compost, spoon, green fabric.

1 Cut out two card circles, with diameters of 20cm and 25cm. Roll out the clay and cut around the larger circle with a modelling tool.

2 Put the smaller circle on top of the larger circle and cover it with clay. With a modelling tool, mark out the passage and chamber.

3 Roll out the white clay and cut it into squares. Form rocks from some squares and model the rest into stone slabs.

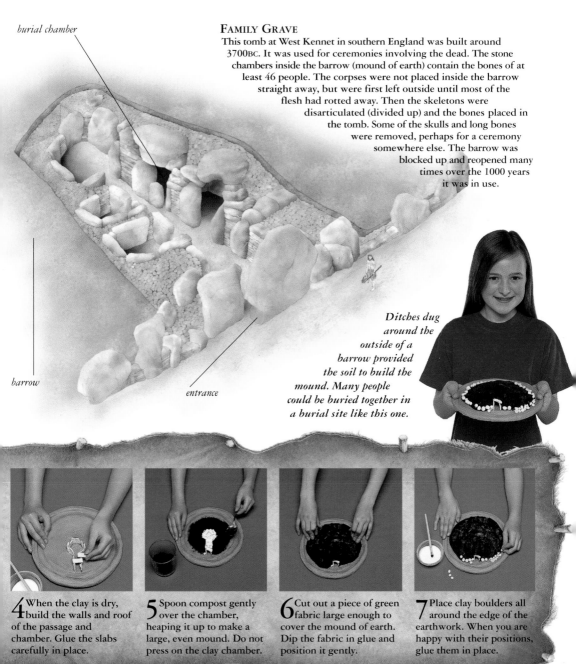

burial chamber

FAMILY GRAVE

This tomb at West Kennet in southern England was built around 3700BC. It was used for ceremonies involving the dead. The stone chambers inside the barrow (mound of earth) contain the bones of at least 46 people. The corpses were not placed inside the barrow straight away, but were first left outside until most of the flesh had rotted away. Then the skeletons were disarticulated (divided up) and the bones placed in the tomb. Some of the skulls and long bones were removed, perhaps for a ceremony somewhere else. The barrow was blocked up and reopened many times over the 1000 years it was in use.

barrow

entrance

Ditches dug around the outside of a barrow provided the soil to build the mound. Many people could be buried together in a burial site like this one.

4 When the clay is dry, build the walls and roof of the passage and chamber. Glue the slabs carefully in place.

5 Spoon compost gently over the chamber, heaping it up to make a large, even mound. Do not press on the clay chamber.

6 Cut out a piece of green fabric large enough to cover the mound of earth. Dip the fabric in glue and position it gently.

7 Place clay boulders all around the edge of the earthwork. When you are happy with their positions, glue them in place.

Neolithic Villages

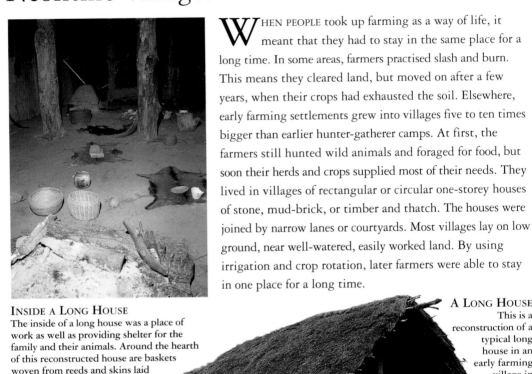

WHEN PEOPLE took up farming as a way of life, it meant that they had to stay in the same place for a long time. In some areas, farmers practised slash and burn. This means they cleared land, but moved on after a few years, when their crops had exhausted the soil. Elsewhere, early farming settlements grew into villages five to ten times bigger than earlier hunter-gatherer camps. At first, the farmers still hunted wild animals and foraged for food, but soon their herds and crops supplied most of their needs. They lived in villages of rectangular or circular one-storey houses of stone, mud-brick, or timber and thatch. The houses were joined by narrow lanes or courtyards. Most villages lay on low ground, near well-watered, easily worked land. By using irrigation and crop rotation, later farmers were able to stay in one place for a long time.

INSIDE A LONG HOUSE
The inside of a long house was a place of work as well as providing shelter for the family and their animals. Around the hearth of this reconstructed house are baskets woven from reeds and skins laid out on the floor. Around the walls, tools are stored.

A LONG HOUSE
This is a reconstruction of a typical long house in an early farming village in Europe. The village dates from around 4500BC.

A Town House

This picture shows how a house at Çatal Hüyük in Turkey may have looked. The walls were made of mud-brick, with poles covered with reeds and mud as the roof. All the houses were joined together, with no streets in between. People went about by climbing over the rooftops, entering their homes by a ladder through the roof.

The main room of each house had raised areas for sitting and sleeping on. More than a thousand houses were packed together like this at Çatal Hüyük.

Stone Walls

These are the remains of the walls of a house in an early farming village in Jordan. It was built around 7000BC. The walls are made of stone collected from the local area.

The first farming towns and villages appeared in the Near East. Most were built of mud-brick and, over hundreds of years, such settlements were often rebuilt many times on the same site.

The Oven

Many houses contained ovens or kilns, used for baking bread and firing pottery. A kiln allowed higher temperatures to be reached than an open hearth, and therefore produced better pottery. Each village probably made its own pottery.

The End of an Era

THE END OF the Stone Age was marked by the growth of towns and cities. The very first town was probably Jericho in the Near East. In about 8000BC, a farming village was built there on the site of an earlier settlement. By about 7800BC, nearly 2700 people lived in Jericho. Çatal Hüyük in Turkey was the site of another, much larger town, dating from about 6500BC and with a population of about 5000. The people who lived in these towns were not just farmers. There were also craftspeople, priests and traders. When metal-working became widespread, better tools allowed people to produce more food. Improved farming led to the first civilizations, with well-organized workforces, armies and governments ruled by kings and priests. These civilizations grew up in the fertile areas of Iraq, Egypt, India and China, heralding the end of the Stone Age.

JERICHO
In about 8000BC, farmers built a settlement at Jericho in the Near East. It was surrounded by a ditch and massive stone walls. The walls were broken by a great round tower, the remains of which are shown here. The people of Jericho traded with bands of nomadic hunter-gatherers.

A SLIM FIGURINE
This female figurine was made around 2000BC on the Cycladic Islands of Greece. Her slender shape contrasts greatly with the fuller figures of earlier female statuettes. She may have been created as a continuation of the tradition of fertility figurines, or mother goddesses, in new, town-based societies.

MAKE A FIGURINE
You will need: board, terracotta self-drying clay, modelling tool, glass tumbler, PVA glue (mixed with water for varnish) and brush.

1 First, mould a flattish, triangular shape from craft clay to form the body. Then roll out a fat sausage for the arms and legs.

2 Trim two lengths from the sausage to form the arms. Then cut the rest of the sausage to form two leg pieces.

3 Join the arms to the body, smoothing down the join and marking the shoulder area lightly with a modelling tool.

SARGON OF AKKAD

This Sumerian carving dates from about 2300BC and depicts Sargon, King of Akkad. Sumer was the first civilization in the world. It arose in southern Mesopotamia (modern Iraq) in about 3200BC. The Sumerians were great traders.

REFINED POTTERY

This beautiful pottery jar is from the Jomon period in Japan and was made around 3000BC. The Japanese were making pottery as early as 10,500BC, and their Jomon culture thrived until as late as around 300BC. Clay continued to be, and still is, an important material for the manufacture of ceramics.

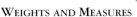

WEIGHTS AND MEASURES

As trade grew, people needed a fair system of weights and measures. These weights and scales come from the city of Mohenjo-Daro, a centre of the Harappan civilization in Pakistan.

A prehistoric clay figure similar to this one has been nicknamed The Thinker. It was made in Romania around 5200BC.

4 Roll out a piece of clay for the neck and a ball for the head. Sculpt features on to the face. Join the head and neck to the body.

5 Lean the figure against a glass to support it. Attach the legs, moulding the feet by pinching the ends of the rolls, as shown.

6 Bend each arm in turn and position them so that the hands support the figurine's head and the elbows rest on its knees.

7 Leave the clay to dry, then gently remove the glass. Varnish the figurine lightly and leave it to dry again before moving it.

The Stone Age Today

THE SPREAD OF METAL-WORKING and farming changed the way people lived, but only very slowly. Huge areas of the world continued to live in the Stone Age. In many areas, people carried on living a hunter-gatherer way of life even when they knew about farming methods. In addition, large parts of the world remained isolated from each other until quite recently. Without the use of metal, Stone Age people evolved complicated and advanced societies of their own. Incredibly, by 1000BC, people from southeast Asia had colonized many of the Pacific islands, crossing up to 600km of open ocean. This was a great deal farther than people elsewhere dared to travel without being in sight of land.

Stone Age societies have survived right up to the twentieth century. The Inuit of the Arctic, the Aborigines of Australia and the San hunter-gatherers of southern Africa continue to preserve a way of life that is many thousands of years old.

ARCTIC PEOPLES

This is a Nenet man from Siberia in Russia. The Nenet share a traditional way of life with the Inuit of North America. Today, most live in small settlements or towns, but they are very proud of their culture. They preserve their own language, art and songs, and regard hunting as an essential part of their way of life.

PAPUA NEW GUINEA

These men are taking part in one of the spectacular traditional dances of Papua New Guinea. The highland areas of Papua New Guinea have formed a natural barrier between different groups of people. This has helped to preserve a rich variety of cultures and languages. Many people in small villages continue to grow their own food and hunt for animals in the dense forests.

THE KINGDOM OF EGYPT
This map of Egypt today shows where there were important cities and sites in ancient times. The ancient Egyptians lived mostly along the banks of the river Nile and in the green, fertile lands of the delta. Through the ages, the Egyptians built many imposing temples in honour of their gods and mysterious tombs to house their dead. Most of these temples and tombs were built close to the major cities of Memphis and Thebes.

SURVIVORS OF THE DESERT
The face of the great pharaoh Ramesses II stares out at us. Huge statues of Ramesses were part of a temple cut from the rock face at Abu Simbel in 1269BC. During the 1960s the statues had to be raised because a new dam at Aswan turned this part of the Nile into a lake. Temples, tombs and statues such as those at Abu Simbel have survived for thousands of years in the dry desert heat. More recently, many monuments have started to disintegrate because of the polluted air around modern cities such as Luxor.

c4000–3500BC Reed shrines are built.

The first buildings are made from mud brick.

Craftsmen paint the first wall paintings and make stone statues.

one of over 750 hieroglyphic symbols in the Egyptian writing system

c3400BC Walled towns are built in Egypt.

3100BC The first of the great royal families govern Egypt. The Early Dynastic period begins.

King Narmer unites Egypt. He creates a capital at Memphis.

Egyptians use hieroglyphs.

2686BC Old Kingdom period.

2667BC Zoser becomes pharaoh.

2650BC Stepped pyramid built at Saqqara.

Stepped Pyramid
2600BC Pyramid built at Maidum.

2589BC Khufu becomes pharaoh. He later builds the Great Pyramid at Giza.

Great Sphinx

c2500BC Khafra, son of Khufu, dies. During his reign the Great Sphinx was built at Giza.

2181BC The Old Kingdom comes to an end.

The Intermediate Period begins. Minor kings in power.

4000BC   3500BC   3000BC   2500BC   2000BC

A Great Civilization

The story of ancient Egypt began about 8,000 years ago when farmers started to plant crops and raise animals in the Nile Valley. By about 3400BC the Egyptians were building walled towns. Soon after that the northern part of the country (Lower Egypt) was united with the lands upstream (Upper Egypt) to form one country under a single king. The capital of this new kingdom was established at Memphis.

The first great period of Egyptian civilization is called the Old Kingdom. It lasted from 2686BC to 2181BC. This was when the pharaohs built great pyramids, the massive pointed tombs that still stand in the desert today.

During the Middle Kingdom (2050–1786BC), the capital was moved to the southern city of Thebes. The Egyptians gained control of Nubia and extended the area of land being farmed. Despite this period of success, the rule of the royal families of ancient Egypt was sometimes interrupted by disorder. In 1663BC, control of the country fell into foreign hands. The Hyksos, a group of Asian settlers, ruled Egypt for almost 100 years.

In 1567BC the Hyksos were overthrown by the princes of Thebes. The Thebans established the New Kingdom. This was the highest point of Egyptian civilization. Traders and soldiers travelled into Africa, Asia and the lands of the Mediterranean. However, by 525BC, the might of the Egyptians was coming to an end and Egypt became part of the Persian Empire. In 332BC rule passed to the Greeks. Finally, in 30BC, conquest was complete as Egypt fell under the control of the Roman Empire.

AFRICA

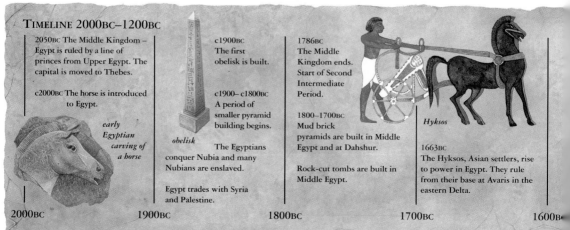

Timeline 2000BC–1200BC

2050BC The Middle Kingdom – Egypt is ruled by a line of princes from Upper Egypt. The capital is moved to Thebes.

c2000BC The horse is introduced to Egypt.

early Egyptian carving of a horse

obelisk

c1900BC The first obelisk is built.

c1900– c1800BC A period of smaller pyramid building begins.

The Egyptians conquer Nubia and many Nubians are enslaved.

Egypt trades with Syria and Palestine.

1786BC The Middle Kingdom ends. Start of Second Intermediate Period.

1800–1700BC Mud brick pyramids are built in Middle Egypt and at Dahshur.

Rock-cut tombs are built in Middle Egypt.

Hyksos

1663BC The Hyksos, Asian settlers, rise to power in Egypt. They rule from their base at Avaris in the eastern Delta.

2000BC   1900BC   1800BC   1700BC   1600BC

EUROPE

Kadesh battle site

...aean Empire

Hittite Empire

MINOAN CRETE

Byblos

LEVANT

SYRIA

Mediterranean Sea

Megiddo

Jerusalem

Avaris

PALESTINE

MESOPOTAMIA

ASIA

LOWER EGYPT

Sinai

Memphis

EGYPT

River Nile

Western Desert

Thebes

UPPER
EGYPT

NUBIA

Red Sea

ARABIA

NORTH

MAP OF THE NEAR EAST
In 1279BC, at the height of
the New Kingdom,
Egypt was a leading
power in the Near East.
The country was prosperous
and rich, trading with Minoan Crete,
Syria, the Levant and Nubia.
Nevertheless, it faced threats from
enemies such as the Hittites.

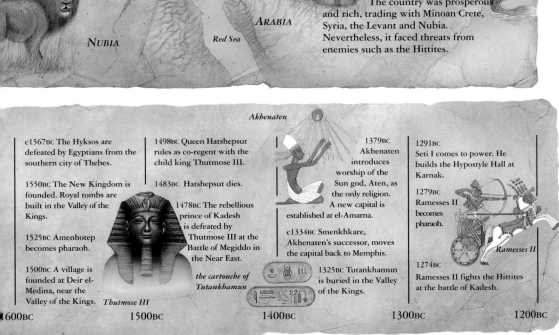

c1567BC The Hyksos are
defeated by Egyptians from the
southern city of Thebes.

1550BC The New Kingdom is
founded. Royal tombs are
built in the Valley of the
Kings.

1525BC Amenhotep
becomes pharaoh.

1500BC A village is
founded at Deir el-
Medina, near the
Valley of the Kings.

Thutmose III

1498BC Queen Hatshepsut
rules as co-regent with the
child king Thutmose III.

1483BC Hatshepsut dies.

1478BC The rebellious
prince of Kadesh
is defeated by
Thutmose III at the
Battle of Megiddo in
the Near East.

*the cartouche of
Tutankhamun*

Akhenaten

1379BC
Akhenaten
introduces
worship of the
Sun god, Aten, as
the only religion.
A new capital is
established at el-Amarna.

c1334BC Smenkhkare,
Akhenaten's successor, moves
the capital back to Memphis.

1325BC Tutankhamun
is buried in the Valley
of the Kings.

1291BC
Seti I comes to power. He
builds the Hypostyle Hall at
Karnak.

1279BC
Ramesses II
becomes
pharaoh.

Ramesses II

1274BC
Ramesses II fights the Hittites
at the battle of Kadesh.

1600BC   1500BC   1400BC   1300BC   1200BC

Famous Pharaohs

F OR THOUSANDS OF YEARS ancient Egypt was ruled by royal families. We know much about the pharaohs and queens from these great dynasties because of their magnificent tombs and the public monuments raised in their honour.

Egypt's first ruler was King Narmer, who united the country in about 3100BC. Later pharaohs such as Zoser and Khufu are remembered for the great pyramids they had built as their tombs.

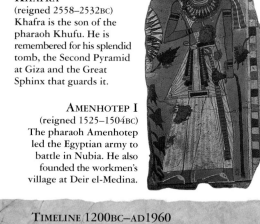

Pharaohs usually succeeded to the throne through royal birth. However, in some cases military commanders such as Horemheb came to power. Although Egypt's rulers were traditionally men, a few powerful women were made pharaoh. The most famous of these is the Greek queen Cleopatra, who ruled Egypt in 51BC.

KHAFRA
(reigned 2558–2532BC)
Khafra is the son of the pharaoh Khufu. He is remembered for his splendid tomb, the Second Pyramid at Giza and the Great Sphinx that guards it.

AMENHOTEP I
(reigned 1525–1504BC)
The pharaoh Amenhotep led the Egyptian army to battle in Nubia. He also founded the workmen's village at Deir el-Medina.

HATSHEPSUT
(reigned 1498–1483BC)
Hatshepsut was the half-sister and wife of Thutmose II. When her husband died, she was appointed to rule Egypt until her young stepson Thutmose III was old enough. However Queen Hatshepsut was ambitious and had herself crowned pharaoh. Hatshepsut is famous for her trading expeditions to the land of Punt. The walls of her temple at Deir el-Bahri show these exotic trips.

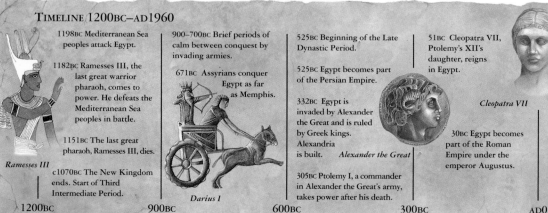

TIMELINE 1200BC–AD1960

1198BC Mediterranean Sea peoples attack Egypt.

1182BC Ramesses III, the last great warrior pharaoh, comes to power. He defeats the Mediterranean Sea peoples in battle.

1151BC The last great pharaoh, Ramesses III, dies.

Ramesses III

c1070BC The New Kingdom ends. Start of Third Intermediate Period.

900–700BC Brief periods of calm between conquest by invading armies.

671BC Assyrians conquer Egypt as far as Memphis.

Darius I

525BC Beginning of the Late Dynastic Period.

525BC Egypt becomes part of the Persian Empire.

332BC Egypt is invaded by Alexander the Great and is ruled by Greek kings. Alexandria is built. *Alexander the Great*

305BC Ptolemy I, a commander in Alexander the Great's army, takes power after his death.

51BC Cleopatra VII, Ptolemy's XII's daughter, reigns in Egypt.

Cleopatra VII

30BC Egypt becomes part of the Roman Empire under the emperor Augustus.

1200BC · 900BC · 600BC · 300BC · AD0

TUTANKHAMUN
(reigned 1334–1325BC)
This pharaoh came to the throne when he was only nine years old. He died at the age of 18. Tutankhamun is remembered for his tomb in the Valley of the Kings, which was packed with amazing treasure.

THUTMOSE III
(reigned 1479–1425BC)
Thutmose III is remembered as a brave warrior king. He launched many military campaigns against the Syrians in the Near East. Records from the time tell of Thutmose marching fearlessly into battle at the head of his army, unconcerned about his own safety. He won a famous victory at Megiddo and then later at Kadesh. Thutmose III was buried in the Valley of the Kings.

AKHENATEN
(reigned 1379–1334BC)
The Egyptians believed in many gods. However, when Akhenaten came to power, he introduced worship of one god, the Sun disc Aten. He moved the capital from Memphis to Akhetaten (now known as el-Amarna). His chief wife was the beautiful Queen Nefertiti.

RAMESSES II
(reigned 1279–1212BC)
One of the most famous pharaohs of all, Ramesses II, was the son of Seti I. He built many fine temples and defeated the Hittites at the Battle of Kadesh in 1274BC. The chief queen of Ramesses was Nefertari. Carvings of this graceful queen can be seen on Ramesses II's temple at Abu Simbel. Ramesses lived a long life and died at the age of 92. He was buried in the Valley of the Kings.

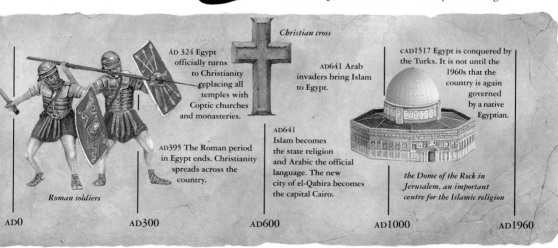

Christian cross

AD 324 Egypt officially turns to Christianity replacing all temples with Coptic churches and monasteries.

AD641 Arab invaders bring Islam to Egypt.

cAD1517 Egypt is conquered by the Turks. It is not until the 1960s that the country is again governed by a native Egyptian.

AD395 The Roman period in Egypt ends. Christianity spreads across the country.

AD641 Islam becomes the state religion and Arabic the official language. The new city of el-Qahira becomes the capital Cairo.

the Dome of the Rock in Jerusalem, an important centre for the Islamic religion

Roman soldiers

AD0   AD300   AD600   AD1000   AD1960

The Land of the Gods

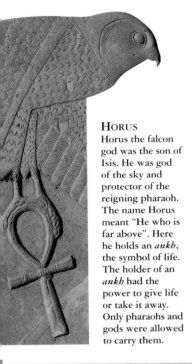

T HE ANCIENT EGYPTIANS believed that the ordered world in which they lived had been created out of nothingness. Chaos and darkness could return at any time if the proper religious rituals were not followed. The spirit of the gods lived inside the pharaohs, who were honoured as god-kings. They looked after the everyday world for the gods. Over 2,000 gods were worshipped in ancient Egypt. Many gods were linked to a particular region. The mighty Amun was the god of Thebes. Some gods appeared as animals – Sebek the water god was a crocodile. Gods were also connected with jobs and interests. The hippopotamus goddess, Tawaret, looked after babies and childbirth.

Many ordinary Egyptians understood little about the religion of the court and nobles. They believed in magic, local spirits and superstitions.

HORUS
Horus the falcon god was the son of Isis. He was god of the sky and protector of the reigning pharaoh. The name Horus meant "He who is far above". Here he holds an *ankh*, the symbol of life. The holder of an *ankh* had the power to give life or take it away. Only pharaohs and gods were allowed to carry them.

LOTUS FLOWER
The lotus was a very important flower to the Egyptians. This sacred symbol was used to represent Upper Egypt.

THE GODDESS NUT
Nut, covered in stars, was goddess of the heavens. She is often shown with her body stretched across the sky. The Egyptians believed that Nut swallowed the Sun each evening and gave birth to it the next morning. She was married to the Earth god, Geb, and gave birth to the gods Isis and Osiris.

AMUN OF THEBES
Amun was originally the god of the city of Thebes. He later became popular throughout Egypt as the god of creation. By the time of the New Kingdom, Amun was combined with other powerful gods such as Ra, god of the Sun, and became known as Amun-Ra. He was believed to be the most powerful god of all. Amun is sometimes shown as a ram.

HOLY BEETLES
Scarabs are beetles that were sacred to the ancient Egyptians. Pottery or stone scarabs were used as lucky charms, seals, or as ring decorations. The base of these scarabs was often inscribed with stories telling of some great event.

OSIRIS, KING OF THE UNDERWORLD
The great god Osiris stands dressed as a king. He was one of the most important gods in ancient Egypt, the master of life and the spirit world. He was also the god of farming. Egyptian tales told how Osiris was murdered and cut into pieces by his brother Seth, the god of chaos. Anubis, the jackal-headed god of embalming, gathered the pieces together and his sister, Isis, brought Osiris back to life.

CAT MUMMIES
The Egyptians worshipped gods in the forms of animals from the Old Kingdom onwards. The cat goddess Bastet was said to be the daughter of the great Sun god, Ra. Cats were so holy to the Egyptians that at one time many of them were embalmed, wrapped in linen bandages and preserved as mummies. It is thought that bronze cat figures and these mummified cats were left as offerings to Bastet at her temple.

MIW THE CAT
Cats were holy animals in ancient Egypt. They even had their own god! The Egyptians' love of cats dated back to the early farmers who tamed cats to protect stores of grain from mice. Cats soon became popular pets. The Egyptian word for cat was *miw*, which was rather like a mew or miaow!

Priest, Politician and God

THE CROOK AND FLAIL
These emblems of the god Osiris became badges of royal authority. The crook stood for kingship and the flail for the fertility of the land.

flail

crook

THE WORD PHARAOH comes from the Egyptian *per-aa*, which meant great house or palace. It later came to mean the man who lived in the palace, the ruler. Pictures and statues show pharaohs with special badges of royalty, such as crowns, headcloths, false beards, sceptres and a crook and flail held in each hand.

The pharaoh was the most important person in Egypt. As a god-ruler, he was the link between the people and their gods. He therefore had to be protected and cared for. The pharaoh led a busy life. He was the high priest, the chief law-maker, the commander of the army and in charge of the country's wealth. He had to be a clever politician, too. The ancient Egyptians believed that on his death, the pharaoh became a god in his own right.

Pharaohs were generally men, but queens sometimes ruled Egypt if the pharaoh was too young. A pharaoh could take several wives. Within royal families it was common for fathers to marry daughters and for brothers to marry sisters. Sometimes pharaohs married foreign princesses in order to make an alliance with another country.

MOTHER GODDESS OF THE PHARAOHS
Hathor was worshipped as the mother goddess of each pharaoh. Here she is shown welcoming the pharaoh Horemheb to the afterlife. Horemheb was a nobleman who became a brilliant military commander. He was made pharaoh in 1323BC.

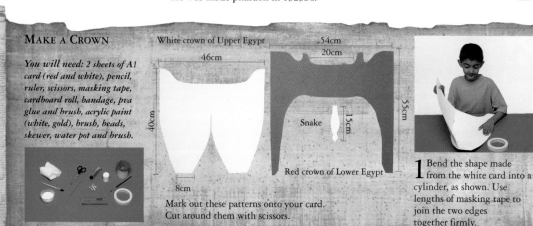

MAKE A CROWN

You will need: 2 sheets of A1 card (red and white), pencil, ruler, scissors, masking tape, cardboard roll, bandage, pva glue and brush, acrylic paint (white, gold), brush, beads, skewer, water pot and brush.

White crown of Upper Egypt

54cm

46cm

20cm

40cm

55cm

15cm

Snake

8cm

Red crown of Lower Egypt

Mark out these patterns onto your card. Cut around them with scissors.

1 Bend the shape made from the white card into a cylinder, as shown. Use lengths of masking tape to join the two edges together firmly.

RAMESSES MEETS THE GODS

This painting shows the dead pharaoh Ramesses I meeting the gods Horus (left) and Anubis (right). Pharaohs had to pass safely through the after-life or the link between the gods and the world would be broken forever.

THE QUEEN'S TEMPLE

This great temple (*below*) was built in honour of Queen Hatshepsut. It lies at the foot of towering cliffs at Deir el-Bahri, on the west bank of the Nile near the Valley of the Kings. The queen had the temple built as a place for her body to be prepared for burial. Pyramids, tombs and temples were important symbols of power in Egypt. By building this temple, Hatshepsut wanted people to remember her as a pharaoh in her own right.

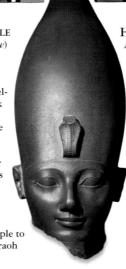

HATSHEPSUT

A female pharaoh was so unusual that pictures of Queen Hatshepsut show her with all the badges of a male king, including a false beard! Here she wears the pharaoh's crown. The cobra on the front of the crown is the badge of Lower Egypt.

The double crown worn by the pharaohs was called the pschent. *It symbolized the unification of the two kingdoms. The white section at the top (*hedjet*) stood for Upper Egypt, and the red section at the bottom (*deshret*) for Lower Egypt.*

2 Tape a cardboard roll into the hole at the top. Plug its end with a ball of bandage. Then tape the bandage in position and glue down the edges.

3 Wrap the white section with lengths of bandage. Paint over these with an equal mixture of white paint and glue. Leave the crown in a warm place to dry.

4 Now take the shape made from the red card. Wrap it tightly around the white section, as shown, joining the edges with masking tape.

5 Now paint the snake gold, sticking on beads as eyes. When dry, score lines across its body. Bend the snake's body and glue it to the crown, as shown.

Court and Nobles

EGYPTIAN PALACES were vast complexes. They included splendid public buildings where the pharaoh would meet foreign rulers and carry out important ceremonies. Members of the royal family lived in luxury in beautiful townhouses with painted walls and tiled floors near the palace.

The governors of Egypt's regions also lived like princes, and pharaohs had to be careful that they did not become too rich and powerful. The royal court included large numbers of officials and royal advisors. There were lawyers, architects, tax officials, priests and army officers. The most important court official of all was the vizier, who carried out many of the pharaoh's duties for him.

The officials and nobles were at the top of Egyptian society. But most of the hard work that kept the country running smoothly was carried out by merchants and craft workers, by farmers, labourers and slaves.

GREAT LADIES
Ahmose-Nefertari was the wife of Ahmose I. She carries a lotus flower and a flail. Kings could take many wives and it was also common for them to have a harem of beautiful women.

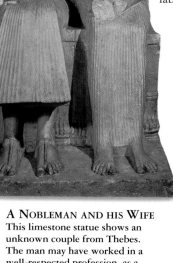

A NOBLEMAN AND HIS WIFE
This limestone statue shows an unknown couple from Thebes. The man may have worked in a well-respected profession, as a doctor, government official, or engineer. Noblewomen did not work but were quite independent. Any property that a wife brought into her marriage remained hers.

THE SPLENDOURS OF THE COURT
This is the throne room of Ramesses III's palace at Medinet Habu, on the west bank of the Nile near Thebes. Pharaohs often had many palaces and Medinet Habu was one of Ramesses III's lesser ones. Surviving fragments of tiles and furniture give us an idea of just how splendid the royal court must have been. A chamber to one side of the throne room is even believed to be an early version of a shower cubicle!

RELAXATION

Ankherhau (*above*), a wealthy overseer of workmen, relaxes at home with his wife. They are listening to a harpist. Life was pleasant for those who could afford it. Kings and nobles had dancers, musicians and acrobats to entertain them. Cooks worked in their kitchens preparing sumptuous meals. By comparison, ordinary people ate simple food, rarely eating meat except for the small animals they caught themselves.

HAIR CARE

The royal family was waited on by domestic servants who attended to their every need. Here (*left*), the young Queen Kawit, wife of the pharaoh Mentuhotep II, has her hair dressed by her personal maid. Although many of the female servants employed in wealthy households were slaves, a large number of servants were free. This meant that they had the right to leave their employer at any time.

Towns, Homes and Gardens

THE GREAT CITIES of ancient Egypt, such as Memphis and Thebes, were built along the banks of the river Nile. Small towns grew up haphazardly around them. Special workmen's towns such as Deir el-Medina were also set up around major burial sites and temples to help with building work.

Egyptian towns were defended by thick walls and the streets were planned on a grid pattern. The straight dirt roads had a stone drainage channel, or gutter, running down the middle. Parts of the town housed important officials, while other parts were home to craft workers and poor labourers.

Only temples were built to last. They were made of stone. Mud brick was used to construct all other buildings from royal palaces to workers' dwellings. Most Egyptian homes had roofs supported with palm logs and floors made of packed earth. In the homes of wealthier Egyptians, walls were sometimes plastered and painted. The rooms of their houses included bedrooms, living rooms, kitchens in thatched courtyards and workshops. Homes were furnished with beds, chairs, stools and benches. In the cool of the evenings people would sit on the flat roofs or walk and talk in cool, shady gardens.

THE GARDEN OF NAKHT
The royal scribe Nakht and his wife Tjiui take an evening stroll through their garden. Trees and shrubs surround a peaceful pool. Egyptian gardens included date palms, pomegranates, grape vines, scarlet poppies and blue and pink lotus flowers. Artists in ancient Egypt showed objects in the same picture from different angles, so the trees around Nakht's pool are flattened out.

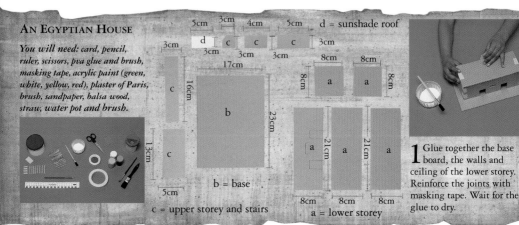

AN EGYPTIAN HOUSE

You will need: card, pencil, ruler, scissors, pva glue and brush, masking tape, acrylic paint (green, white, yellow, red), plaster of Paris, brush, sandpaper, balsa wood, straw, water pot and brush.

d = sunshade roof

5cm 3cm 4cm 5cm

3cm   d   c   c   c   3cm
       3cm   3cm   3cm
       17cm   8cm   8cm

16cm   a   a

b   23cm

          a   a   a   a
                 21cm   21cm

13cm

5cm

b = base

c = upper storey and stairs

8cm 8cm 8cm

a = lower storey

1 Glue together the base board, the walls and ceiling of the lower storey. Reinforce the joints with masking tape. Wait for the glue to dry.

ABOVE THE FLOODS

The homes of wealthy people were often built on platforms to stop damp passing through the mud brick walls. This also raised it above the level of any possible flood damage.

SOUL HOUSES

Pottery models give us a good idea of how the homes of poorer Egyptians looked. During the Middle Kingdom, these soul houses were left as tomb offerings. The Egyptians placed food in the courtyard of the house to feed the person's soul after death.

MUD BRICK

The Egyptians made mud bricks from the thick clay soil left behind by the Nile floods. The clay was taken to the brickyard and mixed with water, pebbles and chopped straw. Mud brick is still used as a building material for houses in Egypt today and is made in the same way.

straw

mud

BRICK MAKING

A group of labourers make bricks. First mud was collected in leather buckets and taken to the building site. There, it was mixed with straw and pebbles. Finally the mixture was put into a mould. At this stage, bricks were sometimes stamped with the name of the pharaoh or the building for which they were made. They were then left to dry in the hot sunshine for several days, before being carried away in a sling.

Egyptian houses had a large main room that opened directly onto the street. In many homes, stairs led up to the roof. People would often sleep there during very hot weather.

2 Now glue together the top storey and stairs. Again, use masking tape to reinforce the joints. When the top storey is dry, glue it to the lower storey.

3 Glue the balsa pillars into the front of the top storey. When the house is dry, cover it in wet paste of plaster of Paris. Paint the pillars red or a colour of your choice.

4 Paint the whole building a dried mud colour. Next paint a green strip along the side. Use masking tape to ensure straight edges. Sand any rough edges.

5 Now make a shelter for the rooftop. Use four balsa struts as supports. The roof can be made of card glued with straw. Glue the shelter into place.

Skilled Workers

I N ANCIENT EGYPT, skilled workers formed a middle class between the poor labourers and the rich officials and nobles. Wall paintings and models show us craft workers carving stone or wood, making pottery, or working precious metals. There were boat builders and chariot makers, too.

Artists and craft workers could be well rewarded for their skills, and some became famous for their work. The house and workshops of a sculptor called Thutmose was excavated in el-Amarna in 1912. He was very successful in his career and was a favourite of the royal family.

Craft workers often lived in their own part of town. A special village was built at Deir el-Medina, near Thebes, for the builders of the magnificent, but secret, royal tombs. Among the 100 or so houses there, archaeologists found delivery notes for goods, sketches and plans drawn on broken pottery. Working conditions cannot always have been very good, for records show that the workers once went on strike. They may well have helped to rob the tombs that they themselves had built.

GLASS IN GOLD
This pendant shows the skill of Egyptian craft workers. It is in the form of Nekhbet the vulture, goddess of Upper Egypt. Glass of many colours has been set in solid gold using a technique called cloisonné. Like many other such beautiful objects, it was found in the tomb of Tutankhamun.

JEWELLERS AT WORK
Jewellers are shown at their work benches in this wall painting from 1395BC. One is making an ornamental collar while the others are working with precious stones or beads. The bow strings are being used to power metal drill bits.

A HIVE OF INDUSTRY

Skilled craftsmen are hard at work in this bustling workshop. Carpenters are sawing and drilling wood, potters are painting pottery jars, and masons are chiselling stone. A foreman would inspect the quality of each finished item.

DEIR EL-MEDINA

The stone foundations of the village of Deir el-Medina may still be seen on the west bank of the Nile. They are about 3,500 years old. In its day, Deir el-Medina housed the skilled workers who built and decorated the royal tombs in the Valley of the Kings. The men worked for eight days out of ten. The village existed for four centuries and was large and prosperous. Nevertheless, the workmen's village did not have its own water supply, so water had to be carried to the site and stored in a guarded tank.

SURVEYING THE LAND

Officials stretch a cord across a field to calculate its area. These men have been employed to survey an estate for government records.

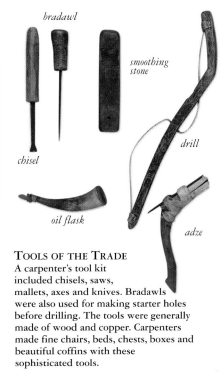

bradawl

smoothing stone

bow drill

drill

chisel

oil flask

adze

axe

saw

pull saw

TOOLS OF THE TRADE

A carpenter's tool kit included chisels, saws, mallets, axes and knives. Bradawls were also used for making starter holes before drilling. The tools were generally made of wood and copper. Carpenters made fine chairs, beds, chests, boxes and beautiful coffins with these sophisticated tools.

Arts and Crafts

THE ANCIENT EGYPTIANS loved beautiful objects, and the craft items that have survived still amaze us today. There are shining gold rings and pendants, necklaces inlaid with glass and a dazzling blue pottery called faience. Jars made of a smooth white stone called alabaster have been preserved in almost perfect condition, along with chairs and chests made of cedar wood imported from the Near East.

Egyptians made beautiful baskets and storage pots. Some pottery was made from river clay, but the finest pots were made from a chalky clay found at Quena. Pots were shaped by hand or, later, on a potter's wheel. Some were polished with a smooth pebble until their surface shone. We know so much about Egyptian craft work because many beautiful items were placed in tombs, so that the dead person could use them in the next world.

ALABASTER ART
This elaborate jar was among the treasures in the tomb of Tutankhamun. Jars such as this would have held precious oils and perfumes.

GLASS FISH
This beautiful stripy fish looks as if it should be swimming in the reefs of the Red Sea. In fact it is a glass jar used to store oils. Glass-making became popular in Egypt after 1500BC. The glass was made from sand and salty crystals. It would then have been coloured with metals and shaped while still hot.

MAKE A LOTUS TILE

You will need: card (2 sheets), pencil, ruler, scissors, self-drying clay, modelling tool, sandpaper acrylic paint (blue, gold, green, yellow ochre), water pot and brush. Optional: rolling pin & board.

1 Using the final picture as reference, draw both tile shapes onto card. Cut them out. Draw the whole pattern of tiles onto the sheet of card and cut around the border.

2 Roll out the clay on a board with a rolling pin or bottle. Place the overall outline over the clay and carefully trim off the edges. Discard the extra clay.

3 Mark the individual tile patterns into the clay, following the outlines carefully. Cut through the lines, but do not separate them out yet.

DESERT RICHES

The dwellers of the green Nile valley feared and disliked the desert. They called it the Red Land. However, the deserts did provide them with great mineral wealth, including blue-green turquoise, purple amethyst and blue agate.

blue agate   *turquoise*   *amethyst*

ROYAL TILES

Many beautiful tiles have been discovered by archaeologists. It is thought that they were used to decorate furniture and floors in the palaces of the Egyptian pharaohs.

TUTANKHAMUN'S WAR CHEST

This painted chest shows Tutankhamun in battle against the Syrians and the Nubians. On the lid, the young king is also seen hunting in the desert. The incredible detail of the painting shows that this was the work of a very skilled artist. When Tutankhamun's tomb was opened, the chest was found to contain children's clothes. The desert air was so dry that neither the wood, leather nor fabric had rotted.

NEKHBET COLLAR

This splendid collar was one of 17 found in Tutankhamun's tomb. The spectacular wings of the vulture goddess Nekhbet include 250 feather sections made of coloured glass set in gold. The vulture's beak and eye are made from a black, volcanic glass called obsidian. This and other amazing objects found in the young king's tomb show us the incredible skill of Egyptian craftsmen.

4 Now use the tool to score patterns of leaves and flowers into the surface of the soft clay, as shown. Separate the pieces and allow them to dry.

5 When one side of each tile has dried, turn it over. Leave the other side to dry. Then sand down the edges of the tiles until they are smooth.

6 The tiles are now ready for painting. Carefully paint the patterns in green, yellow ochre, gold and blue. Leave them in a warm place to dry.

These tiles are similar to those found at a royal palace in Thebes. The design looks rather like a lotus, the sacred waterlily of ancient Egypt.

The Pyramid Builders

THE PYRAMIDS were massive four-sided tombs, built for the pharaohs of the Old Kingdom. Each side, shaped like a triangle, met together in a point at the top. The first Egyptian pyramid was built at Saqqara in about 2650BC. It had stepped sides. The most impressive pyramids, built at Giza over 100 years later, had flat sides. The summit of each pyramid was probably capped in gold. Inside the pyramids were burial chambers and secret passages. No one really knows why the Egyptians built these tombs in pyramid shapes, but it may have been seen as a stairway to heaven to help the pharaoh achieve eternal life.

The pyramids were built with fantastic skill and mathematical accuracy by a team of architects, engineers and stonemasons. They still stand today. The manual labour was provided not by slaves, but by about 100,000 ordinary people. These unskilled workers had to offer their services each year when the flooding Nile made work in the fields impossible.

WORN DOWN BY THE WIND
This pyramid at Dahshur was built for pharaoh Amenemhat III. Once the limestone casing had been stolen, its mud-brick core was easily worn down by the harsh desert winds. Pyramids had become popular burial monuments after the building of the first step pyramid at Saqqara. Examples can be seen at Maidum, Dahshur and Giza. However, Amenemhat's pyramid is typical of those built during the Middle Kingdom when inferior materials were used.

THE STEP PYRAMID
The earliest step pyramid was built at Saqqara for the pharaoh Zoser. The tomb probably started out as a mastaba, an older type of burial site made up of a brick structure over an underground tomb. The upper levels of Zoser's mastaba were redesigned as a pyramid with six huge steps. It was 60m high and towered above the desert sands. It covered the underground tomb of the pharaoh and included 11 burial chambers for the other members of the royal family.

ROYAL ARCHITECT
Imhotep was vizier, or treasurer, in the court of the great pharaoh Zoser. He designed the huge step pyramid at Saqqara. This pyramid was the first large monument made entirely of stone. Imhotep was also a wise man who was an accomplished scribe, astronomer, doctor, priest and architect. In the late period of the Egyptian empire, he was worshipped as a god of medicine.

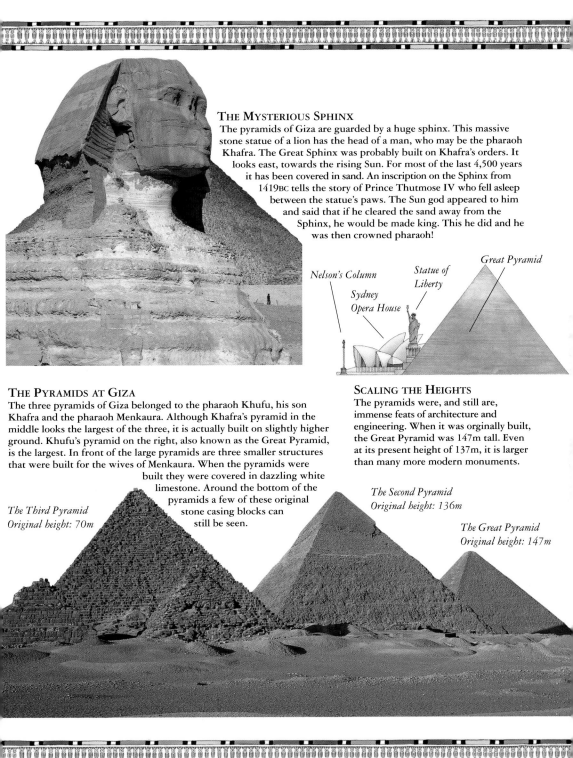

THE MYSTERIOUS SPHINX

The pyramids of Giza are guarded by a huge sphinx. This massive stone statue of a lion has the head of a man, who may be the pharaoh Khafra. The Great Sphinx was probably built on Khafra's orders. It looks east, towards the rising Sun. For most of the last 4,500 years it has been covered in sand. An inscription on the Sphinx from 1419BC tells the story of Prince Thutmose IV who fell asleep between the statue's paws. The Sun god appeared to him and said that if he cleared the sand away from the Sphinx, he would be made king. This he did and he was then crowned pharaoh!

Nelson's Column

Sydney Opera House

Statue of Liberty

Great Pyramid

THE PYRAMIDS AT GIZA

The three pyramids of Giza belonged to the pharaoh Khufu, his son Khafra and the pharaoh Menkaura. Although Khafra's pyramid in the middle looks the largest of the three, it is actually built on slightly higher ground. Khufu's pyramid on the right, also known as the Great Pyramid, is the largest. In front of the large pyramids are three smaller structures that were built for the wives of Menkaura. When the pyramids were built they were covered in dazzling white limestone. Around the bottom of the pyramids a few of these original stone casing blocks can still be seen.

The Third Pyramid
Original height: 70m

SCALING THE HEIGHTS

The pyramids were, and still are, immense feats of architecture and engineering. When it was orginally built, the Great Pyramid was 147m tall. Even at its present height of 137m, it is larger than many more modern monuments.

The Second Pyramid
Original height: 136m

The Great Pyramid
Original height: 147m

Wonder of the World

EARLY TOURISM
In the 1800s, many tourists climbed to the top of the Great Pyramid. From here, the best view of the Giza complex could be had. However, it was a dangerous climb and some visitors fell to their death.

For MANY YEARS the Great Pyramid at Giza was the largest building in the world. Its base is about 230m square, and its original point was 147m high. It is made up of about 2,300,000 massive blocks of stone, each one weighing about 2.5 tonnes. It was the oldest of the seven ancient wonders of the world and is the only one left standing today. Even in ancient times, tourists came to marvel at the size of the Great Pyramid, and vast numbers of people still come to Giza today.

The Great Pyramid is incredible in terms of both scale and age. It was built for the pharaoh Khufu, who died in 2566BC. Nearby was a great temple built in his honour. The purpose of the pyramid was to protect Khufu's body while he journeyed to meet the gods after his death. A 47m long passage leads to one of the three burial chambers inside the pyramid, but the pharaoh's body was never found in the tomb. It had been robbed long ago.

GRAND GALLERY
This steep passage is known as the Grand Gallery. It leads up to the burial chamber in the Great Pyramid. After King Khufu's funeral, granite blocks were slid down the gallery to seal off the chamber. However, ancient Egyptian tomb robbers still managed to break into the chamber and steal its contents.

MAKE A PYRAMID

You will need: card, pencil, ruler, scissors, pva glue and brush, masking tape, acrylic paint (yellow, white, gold), plaster paste, sandpaper, water pot and brush.

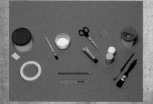

a

b

16 cm

a

32cm

15.5 cm

b

31.5cm

c

c

19.5 cm

c

c

21.5 cm

Make the pyramid in two halves. Cut out one triangle (a) for the base, one triangle (b) for the inside and two of triangle (c) for the sides of each half section.

1 Glue the half section of the pyramid together, binding the joints with pieces of masking tape, as shown. Now make the second half section in the same way.

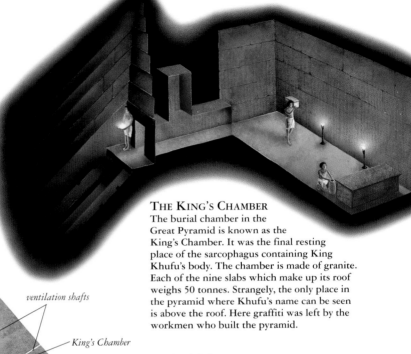

INSIDE A PYRAMID

This cross-section shows the inside of the Great Pyramid. The design of the interior changed several times during its construction. An underground chamber may originally have been intended as Khufu's burial place. This chamber was never finished. A second chamber, known as the Queen's Chamber, was also found empty. The pharaoh was actually buried in the King's Chamber. Once the funeral was over, the tomb had to be sealed from the inside. Blocks of stone were slid down the Grand Gallery. The workmen left through a shaft and along a corridor before the stones thudded into place.

THE KING'S CHAMBER

The burial chamber in the Great Pyramid is known as the King's Chamber. It was the final resting place of the sarcophagus containing King Khufu's body. The chamber is made of granite. Each of the nine slabs which make up its roof weighs 50 tonnes. Strangely, the only place in the pyramid where Khufu's name can be seen is above the roof. Here graffiti was left by the workmen who built the pyramid.

ventilation shafts

King's Chamber

Grand Gallery

Queen's Chamber

escape shaft for workers

corridor

unfinished chamber

2 Mix up yellow and white paint with a little plaster paste to achieve a sandy texture. Then add a little glue so that it sticks to the card. Paint the pyramid sections.

3 Leave the painted pyramid sections to dry in a warm place. When they are completely dry, sand down the tips until they are smooth and mask them off with tape.

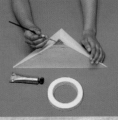

4 Now paint the tips of each half of the pyramid gold and leave to dry. Finally, glue the two halves together and place your pyramid on a bed of sand to display.

The building of the Great Pyramid probably took about 23 years. Originally the pyramids were cased in pale limestone, so they would have looked a brilliant white. The capstone at the very top of the pyramid was probably covered in gold.

The Valley of the Kings

In 1550BC, the capital of Egypt moved south to Thebes. This marked the beginning of the New Kingdom. The ancient Egyptians no longer built pyramids as they were obvious targets for tomb robbers. The people still raised great temples to honour their dead rulers, but now the pharaohs were buried in secret underground tombs. These were hidden away in the cliffs bordering the desert on the west bank of the Nile, where the Sun set each night. It was from here that the pharaoh would journey to meet the Sun god on his death.

The burial sites near Thebes included the Valley of the Kings, the Valley of the Queens and the Valley of the Nobles. The tombs were packed with glittering treasure. Practical

items that the pharaoh would need in the next life were buried there too, such as food, royal clothing, gilded furniture, jewellery, weapons and chariots.

The tombs were guarded by a secret police force and were designed with traps to foil any intruders. Even so, many sites were robbed in ancient times. Luckily, some remained unspoiled and have given archaeologists an amazing look into the world of ancient Egypt.

THE KINGDOM OF THE DEAD
The Valley of the Kings lies across the Nile from the modern town of Luxor, on the edge of the Western desert. Sixty-two New Kingdom tombs have been discovered here so far.

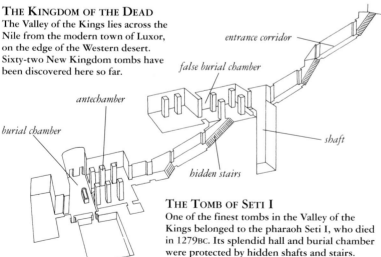

entrance corridor

false burial chamber

antechamber

burial chamber

shaft

hidden stairs

THE TOMB OF SETI I
One of the finest tombs in the Valley of the Kings belonged to the pharaoh Seti I, who died in 1279BC. Its splendid hall and burial chamber were protected by hidden shafts and stairs.

THE MASK
This beautiful mask was placed over the face of Tutankhamun's mummy. It presents the pharaoh in the image of the Sun god, Ra. This mask is made of solid gold and a blue stone called lapis lazuli. Tutankhamun's tomb was the most spectacular find in the Valley of the Kings. The inner chambers had not been disturbed for over 3,260 years.

GRAVE ROBBERS

When Howard Carter entered the tomb of Tutankhamun, he discovered that robbers had reached its outer chambers in ancient times. The Valley guards had resealed the tomb, but many items were left in heaps and piles. This picture shows two chariots, two beds, a chest, stools and food boxes.

UNTOLD TREASURES

This gold perfume box was found in Tutankhamun's burial chamber. The

oval-shaped designs are called cartouches. They contain pictures of the pharaoh as a boy.

WORKERS ON SITE

The excavations of the 1800s and 1900s brought teams of Egyptian workers back into the Valley of the Kings for the first time in thousands of years. They dug down into tombs, carried out soil in baskets and shifted rocks. This photograph was taken in 1922 during Howard Carter's excavations that uncovered the tomb of Tutankhamun.

Mummies and Coffins

THE EARLY EGYPTIANS found out that people buried in the desert were often preserved in the dry sand. Their bodies dried out and became mummified. Over the ages, the Egyptians became experts at preserving bodies by embalming them. They believed that the dead would need to use their bodies in the next life.

The methods of mummification varied over the years. The process usually took about 70 days. The brains were hooked out through the nose and the other organs were removed and placed in special jars. Only the heart was left so that it could be weighed in the next life. Embalming involved drying the body out with salty crystals of natron. Afterwards it was stuffed and covered with oils and ointments and then wrapped in bandages. The mummy was then placed inside a series of coffins in the shape of the body.

MUMMY CASE
This beautiful gold case contains the mummy of a priestess. Once the embalmed body had been wrapped in bandages it was placed in a richly decorated coffin. Both the inside and outside would be covered in spells to help the dead person in the underworld. Sometimes more than one coffin was used. The inner coffins would be of brightly painted or gilded wood (*as left*) and the outer coffin would be a stone sarcophagus.

CANOPIC JARS
Special jars were used to store the body's organs. The human-headed jar held the liver. The baboon jar contained the lungs. The stomach was put in the jackal-headed jar and finally the guts were placed in the falcon-headed jar.

CANOPIC JARS

You will need: self-drying clay, rolling pin and board, ruler, modelling tool, sandpaper, masking tape, acrylic paint (white, blue, green, yellow, black), water pot and brush.

1 Roll out ³/₄ of the clay and cut out a circle about 7cm in diameter. This is the base of the jar. Now roll out thin strips of clay. Coil these from the base to make the sides.

2 Carefully press out the bumps between the coils until the sides of the jar are smooth and round. Finally trim the top of the jar with a modelling tool.

3 Now make a lid for the jar. Measure the size needed and cut out a circle of the remaining clay. Mould it into a dome. Model the head of a baboon on to the lid.

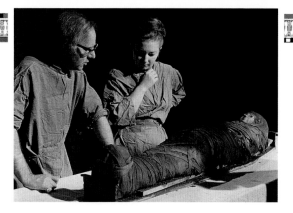

BENEATH THE BANDAGES

Unwrapping a mummy is a delicate operation. Today, archaeologists can use scanning or X-ray equipment to examine the mummies' bodies. It is possible to tell what food they once ate, the work they did and the illnesses they suffered from. X-rays also show the stuffing used to replace the internal organs.

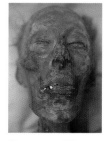

RAMESSES II

This is the unwrapped head of the mummy of Ramesses II. Wadding was placed in his eye sockets to stop the natron (preserving salts) from destroying his features.

It was believed that any part of a person's body could be used against them. For this reason the organs were removed and stored in canopic jars. Spells written on the jars protected them.

THE OPENING OF THE MOUTH CEREMONY

The last ritual before burial was led by a priest wearing the mask of the god Anubis. The human-shaped coffin was held upright and its face was touched with magical instruments. This ceremony enabled the mummy to speak, see and hear in the next world.

4 Hapy the baboon guarded the mummy's lungs, Use the modelling tool to make the baboon's eyes and long nose. Leave the lid in a warm place to dry.

5 When both the jar and the lid are completely dry, rub them down with sandpaper until they are smooth. The lid should fit snugly on to the jar.

6 It is now time to paint your jar. Use the masking tape to protect the baboon's face and to help you get the stripes straight. Follow the colours in the picture above.

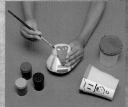

7 Paint hieroglyphs down the front of the jar as shown. Use the letters on page 46 to help you. The canopic jar is now ready for the funeral.

Egyptian Funerals

W HEN A PHARAOH died, everything possible was done to make sure he completed his journey to the gods in safety. During the New Kingdom, the ruler's coffin, containing his mummy, would be placed on a boat and ferried from Thebes to the west bank of the Nile. There it was placed in a shrine and hauled on a sled drawn by oxen to the Valley of the Kings. The funeral procession was spectacular. Priests scattered offerings of milk and burned incense. Women played the part of official mourners, screaming and weeping. In front of the tomb there was dancing and a priest read out spells. After a ceremony and a banquet, the coffin was placed in the tomb with food, drink and treasure. The tomb was then sealed.

LIFE AFTER DEATH
The *ba*, or personality, of a dead person hovers over the mummy. It appears as a bird. Its job is to help the dead body rejoin its spirit, or *ka*, so it can live in the next world. This picture is taken from a papyrus called the Book of the Dead. This book acted as a guide to the after-life for the dead. It contained spells to guarantee safe passage through the underworld. Priests read from it at the funeral and then it was buried with the mummy.

SHABTI FIGURES
Shabti were model figures placed in a tomb. Their purpose was to work for the dead person in the next life, acting as servants or labourers. They would be brought to life by a spell.

MAKE AN UDJAT EYE
You will need: self-drying clay, modelling tool, sandpaper, acrylic paint (red, blue, black, white), water pot and brush.
Optional: rolling pin and board.

1 Begin by rolling out the clay on the board. Use the modelling tool to cut in the pattern of the eye pieces. Refer to step 2 for the shape of each piece.

2 Remove all extra clay and arrange the eye pieces on the board. The eye is meant to represent the eye of the falcon-headed god Horus.

3 Next, press the pieces together until you have the full shape of the eye. Use the modelling tool if necessary. Now leave the eye to dry.

THE FUNERAL PROCESSION

The coffin lies inside a boat-shaped shrine on a sled. The priests chant and pray as they begin to haul the sled up towards the burial place. A burial site such as the Valley of the Kings is called a necropolis, which means 'the city of the dead'. The coffin would be taken into the tomb through a deep corridor to its final resting place. In the burial chamber, it would be surrounded by fine objects and riches.

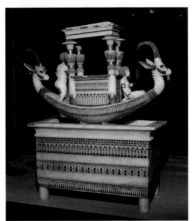

FUNERARY BOAT

This beautiful model boat was placed in the tomb of Tutankhamun. It is made of alabaster and shows two female mourners who represent the goddess Isis and her sister Nephthys. They are mourning the death of the murdered god Osiris. Between them is an empty sarcophagus (stone coffin casing), which may once have been used to hold oils. Many other boats were found in the tomb. They were meant to carry the pharaoh after he had died, just as a boat had carried Ra, the Sun god, through *Dwat*, the underworld.

4 Smooth the surface with fine sandpaper. The eye of Horus is now ready for painting. Horus was said to have lost his eye in a battle with Seth, the god of Chaos.

5 Paint in the white of the eye and add the black eyebrow and pupil. Next, paint in the red liner. Finally, paint the rest of the eye charm blue and leave to dry.

When Horus lost his eye, it was made better by the goddess Hathor. Udjat meant making better. Charms like this were wrapped up with mummies to protect them in the next life.

Priests, Temples and Festivals

MASSIVE TEMPLES were built in honour of the Egyptian gods. Many can still be seen today. They have great pillars and massive gates, courtyards and avenues of statues. Once, these would have led to a shrine that was believed to be the home of a god.

Ordinary people did not gather to worship in an Egyptian temple as they might today in a church. Only priests were allowed in the temples. They carried out rituals on behalf of the pharaoh, making offerings of food, burning incense, playing music and singing. They had complicated rules about washing and shaving their heads, and some had to wear special clothes such as leopard skins. Noblewomen served as priestesses during some ceremonies. Many priests had little knowledge of religion and just served in the temple for three months before returning to their normal work. Other priests studied the stars and spells.

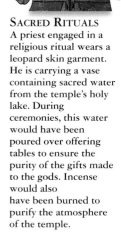

There were many religious festivals during which the god's shrine would be carried to other temples in a great procession. This was when ordinary Egyptians joined in worship. Offerings of food made to the gods were given back to the people for public feasting.

SACRED RITUALS
A priest engaged in a religious ritual wears a leopard skin garment. He is carrying a vase containing sacred water from the temple's holy lake. During ceremonies, this water would have been poured over offering tables to ensure the purity of the gifts made to the gods. Incense would also have been burned to purify the atmosphere of the temple.

KARNAK
This painting by David Roberts shows the massive temple of Karnak as it appeared in 1850. It still stands just outside the modern town of Luxor. The temple's most important god was Amun-Ra. The site also includes courts and buildings sacred to other gods and goddesses, including Mut (a vulture goddess, wife of Amun) and Khons (the Moon god, son of Amun). The Great Temple was enlarged and rebuilt over about 2,000 years.

ANUBIS THE EMBALMER

A priest wears the mask of Anubis to embalm a body. This jackal-headed god was said to have prepared the body of the god Osiris for burial. He and his priests had strong links with mummies and the practice of embalming.

TEMPLE OF HORUS

A statue of Horus, the falcon god, guards the temple at Edfu. There was a temple on this site during the New Kingdom. However, the building that still stands today dates back to the period of Greek rule. This temple was dedicated to Horus and his wife, the cow goddess Hathor. Inside the temple there are stone carvings showing Horus fighting the enemies of Osiris, his father.

KALABSHA TEMPLE

The Kalabsha temple was one of the largest temples in Lower Nubia. In the 1960s, the Aswan Dam was built and Lower Nubia was flooded. Many monuments such as the temples at Abu Simbel and Philae had to be moved. The temple at Kalabsha was dismantled, and its 13,000 blocks of stone were moved to New Kalabsha, where it was rebuilt.

GATEWAY TO ISIS

The temple of Philae (*above*) was built in honour of Isis, the mother goddess. Isis was worshipped all over Egypt and in many other lands, too. Massive gateways called pylons guard the temple of Philae. Pylons guard the way to many Egyptian temples and were used for special ceremonies.

Workers and Slaves

T HE PHARAOHS may have believed that it was their links with the gods that kept Egypt going, but really it was the hard work of the ordinary people. It was they who dug the soil, worked in the mines and quarries, sailed the boats on the river Nile, marched with the army into Syria or Nubia, cooked food and raised children.

Slavery was not very important in ancient Egypt, but it did exist. Most of the slaves were prisoners who had been captured during the many wars that Egypt fought with their neighbours in the Near East. Slaves were usually treated well and were allowed to own property.

Many Egyptian workers were serfs. This meant that their freedom was limited. They could be bought and sold along with the estates where they worked. Farmers had to be registered with the government. They had to sell crops at a fixed price and pay taxes in the form of produce. During the season of the Nile floods, when the fields lay under water, many workers were recruited into public building projects. Punishment for those who ran away was harsh.

PLOUGHING WITH OXEN
This model figure from a tomb is ploughing the soil with oxen. The Egyptian farm workers' daily toil was hard. Unskilled peasant labourers did not own land and were paid little.

TRANSPORTING A STATUE
These workers are moving a huge stone statue on a wooden sled hauled by ropes. Many farm workers had to labour on large public building works, building dams or pyramids, each summer and autumn. Their food and lodging were provided, but they were not paid wages. Only the official classes were exempt from this service, but anyone rich enough could pay someone else to do the work for them. Slaves were used for really hard labour, such as mining and quarrying.

104 ANCIENT EGYPT

COUNTING GEESE

A farmer's flock of geese is counted out in this wall painting. Every other year, government officials visited each farm. They would count the animals to see how much tax had to be paid to the pharaoh. Taxes were paid in produce rather than money. The scribe on the left is recording this information. Scribes were members of the official classes and therefore had a higher position than other workers.

GIVE THAT MAN A BEATING

This tomb painting shows an official overseeing work in the fields. Unskilled peasant farmers were attached to an estate belonging to the pharaoh, a temple, or a rich landowner. Farmers who could not or would not give a large percentage of their harvest in rent and taxes to the pharaoh were punished harshly. They might be beaten, and their tools or their house could be seized as payment. There were law courts, judges and local magistrates in place to punish tax collectors who took bribes.

CARRYING BREAD

A woman carries a tray of loaves on her head. Most of the cooking in large houses and palaces was done by male servants, but baking bread was the job of the women. Baking was one of the few public jobs open to women.

GRINDING CORN

This model from 2325BC shows a female servant grinding wheat or barley grains into flour. She is using a stone hand-mill called a quern.

Farmers and Crops

HARVEST FESTIVAL
A priestess makes an offering of harvest produce in the tomb of Nakht. The picture shows some of the delicious fruits grown in Egypt. These included figs, grapes and pomegranates.

FARMING TOOLS
Hoes were used to break up soil that had been too heavy for the ploughs. They were also used for digging soil. The sharp sickle was used to cut grain.

sickle   *hoes*

THE ANCIENT EGYPTIANS called the banks of the Nile the Black Land because of the mud that was washed downstream each year from Central Africa. The Nile flooded in June, depositing this rich, fertile mud in Egypt. The land remained underwater until autumn.

By November the ground was ready for ploughing and then sowing. Seeds were scattered over the soil and trampled in by the hooves of sheep or goats. During the drier periods of the year, farmers dug channels and canals to bring water to irrigate their land. In the New Kingdom, a lifting system called the *shaduf* was introduced to raise water from the river. The success of this farming cycle was vital. Years of low flood or drought could spell disaster. If the crops failed, people went hungry.

Farm animals included ducks, geese, pigs, sheep and goats. Cows grazed the fringes of the desert or the greener lands of the delta region. Oxen were used for hauling ploughs and donkeys were widely used to carry goods.

TOILING IN THE FIELDS
Grain crops were usually harvested in March or April, before the great heat began. The ears of wheat or barley were cut off with a sickle made of wood and sharpened flint. In some well-irrigated areas there was a second harvest later in the summer.

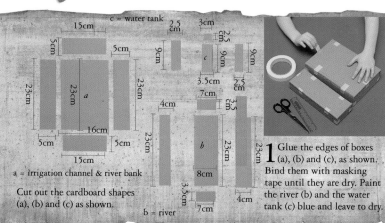

MAKE A SHADUF
You will need: card, pencil, ruler, scissors, pva glue, masking tape, acrylic paint (blue, green, brown), water pot and brush, balsa wood strips, small stones, twig, clay, hessian, string .
Note: mix green paint with dried herbs for the grass mixture.

c = water tank

15cm · 2.5 cm · 3cm

5cm · 5cm · 9cm · c · 9cm

23cm · 23cm · a · 23cm · 3.5cm · 2.5 cm · 7cm

16cm · 4cm

5cm · 5cm

15cm

a = irrigation channel & river bank

Cut out the cardboard shapes (a), (b) and (c) as shown.

b · 23cm · 8cm

b = river · 7cm

1 Glue the edges of boxes (a), (b) and (c), as shown. Bind them with masking tape until they are dry. Paint the river (b) and the water tank (c) blue and leave to dry.

HERDING THE OXEN

This New Kingdom wall painting shows oxen being herded in front of a government inspector. Cattle were already being bred along the banks of the Nile in the days before the pharaohs. They provided milk, meat and leather. They hauled wooden ploughs and were killed as sacrifices to the gods in the temples.

NILE CROPS

The chief crops were barley and wheat, used for making beer and bread. Beans and lentils were grown alongside leeks, onions, cabbages, radishes, lettuces and cucumbers. Juicy melons, dates and figs could be grown in desert oases. Grapes were grown in vineyards.

leeks   *onions*

WATERING MACHINE

The *shaduf* has a bucket on one end of a pole and a heavy weight at the other. First the weight is pushed up, lowering the bucket into the river. As the weight is lowered, it raises up the full bucket.

The mechanical lifting system called the shaduf *was invented in the Middle East. It was brought into Egypt about 3,500 years ago.*

2 Paint the river bank with the green grass mixture on top, brown on the sides and the irrigation channel blue. Next, get the balsa strips for the frame of the shaduf.

3 Glue the strips together, supporting them with masking tape and a piece of card. When dry, paint the frame brown. Glue the stones onto the water tank.

4 Use a twig for the shaduf pole. Make a weight from clay wrapped in hessian. Tie it to one end of the pole. Make a bucket from clay, leaving two holes for the string.

5 Thread the string through the bucket and tie to the pole. Tie the pole, with its weight and bucket, to the shaduf frame. Finally, glue the frame to the bank.

Food and Banquets

WORKING PEOPLE in Egypt were often paid in food. They ate bread, onions and salted fish, washed down with a sweet, grainy beer. Flour was often gritty and the teeth of many mummies show signs of severe wear and tear. Dough was kneaded with the feet or by hand, and pastry cooks produced all kinds of cakes and loaves.

BEAUTIFUL BOWLS
Dishes and bowls were often made of faience, a glassy pottery. The usual colour for this attractive tableware was blue-green or turquoise.

A big banquet for a pharaoh was a grand affair, with guests dressed in their finest clothes. A royal menu might include roast goose or stewed beef, kidneys, wild duck or tender gazelle. Lamb was not eaten for religious reasons, and in some regions certain types of fish were also forbidden. Vegetables such as leeks were stewed with milk and cheese. Egyptian cooks were experts at stewing, roasting and baking.

Red and white wines were served at banquets. They were stored in pottery jars marked with their year and their vineyard, just like the labels on modern wine bottles.

A FEAST FIT FOR A KING
New Kingdom noblewomen exchange gossip at a dinner party. They show off their jewellery and best clothes. The Egyptians loved wining and dining. They would be entertained by musicians, dancers and acrobats during the feast.

MAKE A CAKE

You will need: 200g stoneground flour, $\frac{1}{2}$ tsp salt, 1tsp baking powder, 75g butter, 60g honey, 3tbsp milk, caraway seeds, bowl, wooden spoon, floured surface, baking tray.

1 Begin by mixing together the flour, salt and baking powder in the bowl. Next, chop up the butter and add it to the mixture.

2 Using your fingers, rub the butter into the mixture, as shown. Your mixture should look like fine breadcrumbs when you have finished.

3 Now add 40g of your honey. Combine it with your mixture. This will sweeten your cakes. The ancient Egyptians did not have sugar.

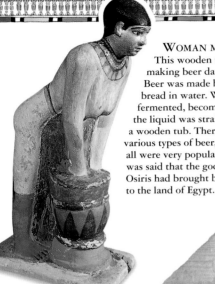

WOMAN MAKING BEER
This wooden tomb model of a woman making beer dates back to 2400BC. Beer was made by mashing barley bread in water. When the mixture fermented, becoming alcoholic, the liquid was strained off into a wooden tub. There were various types of beer, but all were very popular. It was said that the god Osiris had brought beer to the land of Egypt.

DRINKING VESSEL
This beautiful faience cup could have been used to drink wine, water or beer. It is decorated with a pattern of lotus flowers.

DESERT DESSERTS
An Egyptian meal could be finished off with nuts such as almonds or sweet fruits – juicy figs, dates, grapes, pomegranates or melons. Sugar was still unknown so honey was used to sweeten cakes and pastries.

pomegranates

dates

PALACE BAKERY
Whole teams of model cooks and bakers were left in some tombs. This was so that a pharaoh could order them to put on a good banquet to entertain his guests in the other world. Models are shown sifting, mixing and kneading flour, and making pastries. Most of our knowledge about Egyptian food and cooking comes from the food boxes and offerings left in tombs.

Egyptian pastries were often shaped in spirals like these. Other popular shapes were rings like doughnuts, and pyramids. Some were shaped like crocodiles!

4 Add the milk and stir the mixture until it forms a dough. Make your dough into a ball and place it on a floured board or surface. Divide the dough into three.

5 Roll the dough into long strips, as shown. Take the strips and coil them into a spiral to make one cake. Make the other cakes in the same way.

6 Now sprinkle each cake with caraway seeds and place them on a greased baking tray. Finish off by glazing the cakes carefully with a little extra honey.

7 Ask an adult to bake them in an oven at 180°C/Gas Mark 4 for 20 minutes. When they are ready, take them out and leave on a baking rack to cool.

Egyptian Dress

THE MOST COMMON TEXTILE in Egypt was linen. It was mostly a spotless white. Dyes such as iron (red), indigo (blue) and saffron (yellow) were sometimes used, but coloured and patterned clothes were usually the mark of a foreigner. However, the Egyptians did decorate their clothes with beads and beautiful feathers. Wool was not used for weaving in ancient Egypt. Silk and cotton did not appear until foreign rulers came to power in Egypt, after about 1000BC.

The basic items of dress for men were a simple kilt, loin-cloth or tunic. Women wore a long, closely fitting dress of fine fabric. Fashions for both men and women varied over the ages, with changes in the straps, pleating and folds.

Although more elaborate styles of clothing did appear in the New Kingdom, clothing was relatively simple, with elaborate wigs, jewellery and eye make-up creating a more dramatic effect.

LUCKY BRACELET
The bracelet above features an *udjat* eye – this eye charm was thought to protect those who carried it. Many items of jewellery featured such charms for decoration as well as for superstitious reasons. Some necklaces and earrings featured magic charms to prevent snake bites or other disasters.

GOLDEN SANDALS
These gold sandals were found in the tomb of Sheshonq II. Sandals for the rich were usually made of fine leather, while the poor used sandals made of papyrus or woven grass.

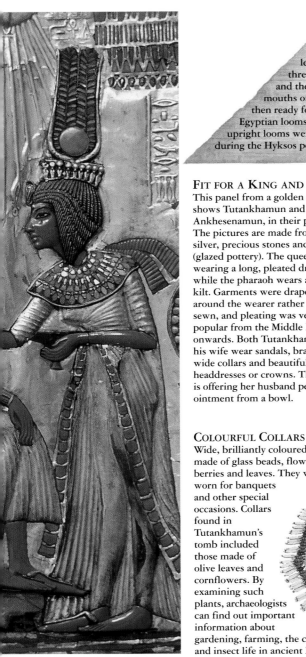

FABRICS

Linen was made from the plant flax. Its stalks were soaked, pounded and then rolled into lengths. The fibre was spun into thread by hand on a whirling spindle, and the thread kept moist in the mouths of the spinners. It was then ready for weaving. The first Egyptian looms were flat, but upright looms were brought in during the Hyksos period.

linen

FIT FOR A KING AND QUEEN

This panel from a golden throne shows Tutankhamun and his wife, Ankhesenamun, in their palace. The pictures are made from glass, silver, precious stones and faience (glazed pottery). The queen is wearing a long, pleated dress, while the pharaoh wears a pleated kilt. Garments were draped around the wearer rather than sewn, and pleating was very popular from the Middle Kingdom onwards. Both Tutankhamun and his wife wear sandals, bracelets, wide collars and beautiful headdresses or crowns. The queen is offering her husband perfume or ointment from a bowl.

FIRST FASHIONS

This shirt was found in the tomb of Tarkhan. It was made nearly 5,000 years ago during the reign of the pharaoh Djet. The fabric is linen and there are pleats across the shoulders.

COLOURFUL COLLARS

Wide, brilliantly coloured collars were made of glass beads, flowers, berries and leaves. They were worn for banquets and other special occasions. Collars found in Tutankhamun's tomb included those made of olive leaves and cornflowers. By examining such plants, archaeologists can find out important information about gardening, farming, the climate and insect life in ancient Egypt.

Looking Beautiful

BOTH EGYPTIAN MEN and women wore cosmetics. Their make-up included green eyeshadow made from a mineral called malachite and black eyeliner made from galena, a type of lead. Lipsticks and blusher were made from red ochre, and the early Egyptians also liked tattoos. Most Egyptian men were clean shaven. Priests also shaved their heads and the short haircut of the pharaoh was always kept covered in public. Wigs were worn by men and women, even by those who had plenty of hair of their own. Grey hair was dyed and there were various remedies for baldness. One was a lotion made from donkey's hoof, dog's paw, date stones and oil!

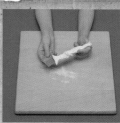

MIRROR, MIRROR
Mirrors were made of polished copper or bronze, with handles of wood or ivory. This bronze mirror is from 1900BC. Mirrors were used by the wealthy for checking hairstyles, applying make-up, or simply for admiring one's own good looks! The poor had to make do with seeing their reflection in water.

A TIMELESS BEAUTY
This limestone head is of Queen Nefertiti, the wife of the Sun-worshipping pharaoh Akhenaten. She seems to be the ideal of Egyptian beauty. She wears a headdress and a necklace. The stone is painted and so we can see that she is also wearing make-up and lipstick.

MAKE A MIRROR

You will need: mirror card, pencil, scissors, self-drying clay, modelling tool, rolling pin and board, small piece of card or sandpaper, gold paint, pva glue and brush, waterpot and brush.

1 Begin by drawing a mirror shape on the white side of a piece of mirror card, as shown. Carefully cut the mirror shape out. Put the card to one side.

2 Take your clay and roll it into a tube. Then mould it into a handle shape, as shown. Decorate the handle with a lotus or papyrus flower, or other design.

3 Now make a slot in the handle with a square piece of card or sandpaper, as shown. This is where the mirror card will slot into the handle.

BIG WIGS AND WAXY CONES

Many pictures show nobles at banquets wearing cones of perfumed grease on their heads. The scent may have been released as the cones melted in the heat. However, some experts believe that the cones were drawn in by artists to show that the person was wearing a scented wig. False hairpieces and wigs were very popular in Egypt. It was common for people to cut their hair short, but some did have long hair that they dressed in elaborate styles.

COSMETICS

During the early years of the Egyptian Empire, black eye kohl was made from galena, a type of poisonous lead! Later soot was used. Henna was painted on the nails and the soles of the feet to make them red. Popular beauty treatments included pumice stone to smooth rough skin and ash face packs.

 face pack   pumice stone   kohl   henna

COSMETICS BOWL

Cosmetics, oils and lotions were prepared and stored in jars and bowls, as well as in hollow reeds or tubes. These containers were made of stone, pottery and glass. Minerals were ground into a powder and then mixed with water in cosmetics bowls to make a paste. Make-up was applied with the fingers or with a special wooden applicator. Two colours of eye make-up were commonly used – green and black. Green was used in the early period, but later the distinctive black eye paint became more popular.

The shape of mirrors and their shining surface reminded Egyptians of the Sun disc, so they became religious symbols. By the New Kingdom, many were decorated with the goddess Hathor or lotus flowers.

4 Place the handle on a wire baking tray and leave it in a warm place to dry. Turn it over after two hours. When it is completely dry, try your mirror for size.

5 It is now time to paint the handle. Paint one side carefully with gold paint and leave it to dry. When it has dried, turn the handle over and paint the other side.

6 Finally, you can assemble your mirror. Cover the base of the mirror card in glue and insert it into the handle slot. Leave it in a warm place to dry.

Papyrus and Scribes

T HE WORD PAPER comes from papyrus, the reed that grows on the banks of the river Nile. To make paper, the Egyptians peeled the outer layer off the reeds. The pith inside the stems was cut into strips, soaked in water and then placed in criss-cross layers. These were hammered until they were squashed together. The surface of the papyrus was then smoothed out with a wooden tool. Other writing materials included fragments of pottery, leather and plastered boards.

It is thought that only about four out of every 1,000 Egyptians could read or write. Scribes were professional writers who would copy out official records and documents, letters, poems and stories. The training of young scribes was thorough, strict and harsh. One teacher, Amenemope, wrote to his students, "pass no day in idleness or you will be beaten". However, most workers envied the scribes for their easy way of life. They were well rewarded for their work.

SCRIBE'S BURNISHER
This beautiful tool was found in the tomb of Tutankhamun. It is made of ivory topped with gold foil. Burnishers were used for smoothing down the surface of freshly-made papyrus.

EXERCISE BOOKS
School exercises were often written on broken pieces of stone or pottery that had been thrown away. These pieces are known as *ostraka*. Young scribes would copy exercises out onto the ostrakon and then have them corrected by a teacher. Many examples of corrected exercises have been discovered in Egypt.

SCRIBES RECORDING THE HARVEST
Kneeling scribes record the size of the grain harvest. The farmer would then have to give a proportion of the grain to the pharaoh as a tax. Many scribes worked in the government, copying out accounts, taxes, orders and laws. They were like civil servants.

WRITING CASE

This scribe's pen-case dates back to around 3000BC. It contains reed pens and an inkwell. The ink was made of charcoal or soot, mixed with water. Scribes carried a grinder for crushing the pigments first. Often the scribe's name and the name of his employer or the pharaoh would be carved into the case.

PENS

In ancient Egypt brushes and pens were made of reed. Blocks of ink were mixed with water on a special palette. Black ink was made from charcoal and red ink was made from ochre (an iron compound). Both were mixed with gum.

charcoal

reed pen

PORTABLE PALETTE

The work of a scribe often meant he had to travel on business, to record official documents. Most had a portable palette like this for when they went away. Scribes often carried a briefcase or document carrier too, to protect the information they had recorded.

FAMOUS SCRIBES

Accroupi sits cross-legged, holding a scroll of papyrus and a pen-case. Accroupi was a famous scribe who lived in Egypt at the time of the Old Kingdom. Scribes were often powerful people in ancient Egypt, and many statues of them have survived. The high standing of scribes is confirmed in the text *Satire of the Trades,* which says: "Behold! no scribe is short of food and of riches from the palace".

SYMBOL FOR A SCRIBE

The hieroglyph for a scribe is made up of a water pot, a brush holder and a palette with cakes of ink. The Egyptian word for scribe or official was *sesh*.

Ways of Writing

WE KNOW so much about the ancient Egyptians because of the written language they left behind. Inscriptions providing detailed information about their lives can be found on everything from obelisks to tombs. From about 3100BC they used pictures called hieroglyphs. Each of these could stand for an object, an idea or a sound. There were originally around 1,000 hieroglyphic symbols. Hieroglyphs were used for thousands of years, but from 1780BC a script called hieratic was also popular. Yet another script, demotic, was used as well as hieroglyphs in the latter days of ancient Egypt.

However, by AD600, long after the last of the pharaohs, no one understood hieroglyphs. The secrets of ancient Egypt were lost for 1,200 years, until the discovery of the Rosetta Stone.

THE ROSETTA STONE

The discovery of the Rosetta Stone was a lucky accident. In 1799, a French soldier discovered a piece of stone at an Egyptian village called el-Rashid or Rosetta. On the stone, the same words were written in three scripts representing two languages. Hieroglyphic text is at the top, demotic text is in the centre, and Greek is at the bottom.

EGYPTIAN CODE CRACKED

French scholar Jean-François Champollion cracked the Rosetta Stone code in 1822. The stone contains a royal decree written in 196BC when the Greek king Ptolemy V was in power in Egypt. The Greek on the stone enabled Champollion to translate the hieroglyphs. This one discovery is central to our understanding of the way the ancient Egyptians used to live.

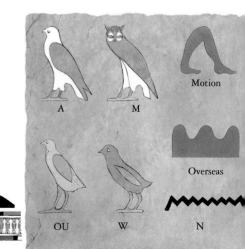

A

M

Motion

OU

W

N

Overseas

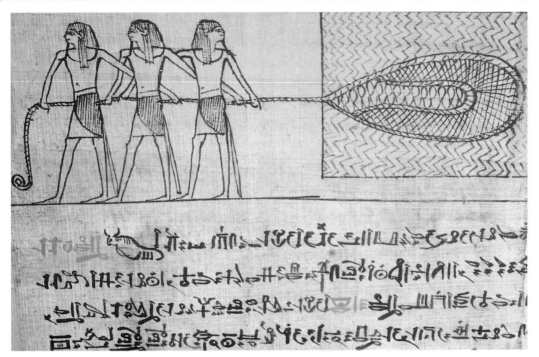

HIERATIC SCRIPT

Hieratic script (*above*) took the picture symbols of hieroglyphs and turned them into shapes that were more like letters. This script was more flowing and could be written quickly. It was used for stories, letters and business contracts. It was always read from right to left.

DEMOTIC SCRIPT

Demotic script (*left*) was introduced towards the end of the Late Kingdom. This could be written even more quickly than hieratic script. Initially it was used for business, but soon it was also being used for religious and scientific writings. It disappeared when Egypt came under Roman rule.

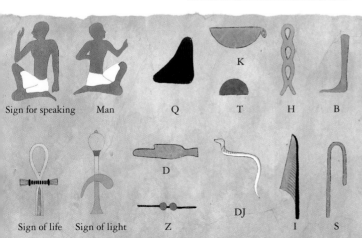

Sign for speaking
Man
K
Q
T
H
B

Sign of life
Sign of light
D
Z
DJ
I
S

HIEROGLYPHS

Hieroglyphs were made up of small pictures. These pictures were based on simplified sketches of birds and snakes, plants, parts of the body, boats and houses. Some hieroglyphs represented complete ideas such as light, travel or life. Others stood for letters or sounds that could be combined to make words.

Science and Technology

THE ANCIENT EGYPTIANS had advanced systems of numbering and measuring. They put their knowledge to good use in building, engineering and in surveying land. However, their knowledge of science was often mixed up with superstitions and belief in magic. For example, doctors understood a lot about broken bones and surgery, but at the same time they used all kinds of spells, amulets and magic potions to ward off disease. Much of their knowledge about the human body came from their experience of preparing the dead for burial.

The priests studied the stars carefully. They thought that the planets must be gods. The Egyptians also worked out a calendar, and this was very important for deciding when the Nile floods would arrive and when to plant crops.

MATHEMATICAL PAPYRUS
This papyrus shows methods for working out the areas of squares, circles and triangles. It dates from around 850BC. These methods would have been used in calculations for land areas and pyramid heights on Egyptian building projects. Other surviving Egyptian writings show mathematical calculations to work out how much grain would fit into a store. The Egyptians used a decimal system of numbering with separate symbols for one, ten, 100 and 1,000. Eight was shown by eight one symbols – 11111111.

CUBIT MEASURE
Units of measurement included the royal cubit of about 52cm and the short cubit of 45cm. A cubit was the length of a man's forearm and was subdivided into palms and fingers.

MAKE A WATER CLOCK
You will need: self-drying clay, plastic flowerpot, modelling tool, skewer, pencil, ruler, masking tape, scissors, yellow acrylic paint, varnish, water pot and brush. Optional: rolling pin and board.

1 Begin by rolling out the clay. Take the plastic flowerpot and press its base firmly into the clay. This will be the bottom of your water clock.

2 Cut out an oblong of clay large enough to mould around the flowerpot. Add the base and use your modelling tool to make the joints smooth.

3 Make a small hole near the bottom of the pot with a skewer, as shown. Leave the pot in a warm place to dry. When the clay has dried, remove the flowerpot.

NILOMETER

A series of steps called a Nilometer was used to measure the depth of the water in the river Nile. The annual floods were desperately important for the farmers living alongside the Nile.
A good flood measured about 7m. More than this and farm buildings and channels might be destroyed. Less than this and the fields might go dry.

STAR OF THE NILE

This astronomical painting is from the ceiling of the tomb of Seti I. The study of the stars was part religion, part science. The brightest star in the sky was Sirius, which we call the dog star. The Egyptians called it Sopdet, after a goddess. This star rose into view at the time when the Nile floods were due and was greeted with a special festival.

MEDICINE

Most Egyptian medicines were based on plants. One cure for headaches included juniper berries, coriander, wormwood and honey. The mixture was rubbed into the scalp. Other remedies included natron (a kind of salt), myrrh and even crocodile droppings. Some Egyptian medicines probably did heal the patients, but others did more harm than good.

coriander

garlic

Time was calculated on water clocks by calculating how long it took for water to drop from level to level. The water level lowered as it dripped through the hole in the bottom of the pot.

4 Mark out lines at 3mm intervals inside the pot. Mask the ends with tape and paint the lines yellow. When dry, remove the tape. Ask an adult to varnish the pot inside.

5 Find or make another two pots and position them as shown. Ask a partner to put their finger over the hole in the clock while you pour water into it.

6 Now ask your partner to take their finger away. The length of time it takes for the level of the water to drop from mark to mark is the measure of time.

Music and Dance

ALTHOUGH MUCH OF OUR KNOWLEDGE about the Egyptians comes from their interest in death, they also loved life. Paintings show how much they enjoyed dancing and music. Also, many musical instruments have been found inside tombs. Music was played for pleasure and entertainment, as well as for religious worship and for marching into battle.

The first Egyptian instruments were probably flutes and harps. Instruments similar to pipes, oboes and trumpets later became popular. During the New Kingdom, lutes and lyres were brought in from Asia. Bells, cymbals, tambourines and drums kept the beat, along with a sacred rattle called the sistrum.

Dancers performed at banquets, sometimes doing acrobatic feats in time to the music. Other dances were more solemn, being performed in temples and at funerals.

THE SISTRUM
A priestess is rattling a sistrum. The ancient Egyptians called this instrument a *seshesht*. It is made of a loop of bronze containing loose rods that rattled when shaken.

STRING SOUNDS
Musicians play a harp, a lyre and a lute at a banquet. These were among the most common string instruments in ancient Egypt. During the New Kingdom female musicians became very popular.

MAKE A RATTLE

You will need: self-drying clay, balsa wood (1.5 x 15cm), card, modelling tool, skewer, wire and 10 washers, pliers, pva glue and brush, acrylic paint (brown or red and black mixed, gold), water pot and brush.

1 For the handle, you will need the block of clay and the balsa wood. Push the balsa wood into the square block of clay to make a hole for the handle.

2 Next, make two slots in the top of the clay block for the card part of the rattle to fit into. The card will form the shaker part of the sistrum.

3 Sculpt the face of the goddess Hathor into the top of the handle. Look at the picture of her on page 82. Now leave the clay in a warm place to dry.

MUSICIANS OF THEBES

This famous wall painting from Thebes is about 3,400 years old. It shows women dancers and musicians performing at a banquet. The Egyptians tended to listen to professional musicians rather than play for their own pleasure. No Egyptian music was written down, but we do still know the words of some of their songs. The hieroglyphs above this picture tell us that the musicians are playing a song in praise of nature. The dancing girls in the painting shake their bodies gracefully to the rhythm of the music.

HARPIST

A male harpist plays a hymn to the god Horus. The first Egyptian harps were plain and simple, but later they were beautifully made, carved and painted gold.

4 Pierce two holes into the card. Thread the wire through the washers and then through the holes in the card. Bend the wire back with pliers to secure it.

5 Push the head of the rattle into the slots in the handle and then glue into position. Paint the rattle brown and rub in gold paint to create a bronze look.

The sistrum was a sacred rattle used by noblewomen and priestesses at religious ceremonies and musical festivities. It was used in the worship of Hathor, the goddess of love.

Entertainment and Leisure

ONE OF THE FAVOURITE PASTIMES of the Egyptians was hunting. They hunted for pleasure as well as for food, using bows and arrows, throwing sticks, spears and nets. Thousands of years ago, many wild animals lived in Egypt. Today most of these are found only in lands far to the south. They included hippopotamuses and lions. Hunting these animals was extremely dangerous, and pictures show the pharaoh setting out bravely for the hunt. In practice the animals were often trapped and released into an enclosure before the pharaoh arrived. There he could easily catch them from the safety of his chariot.

ANIMAL CHAMPIONS
Here the lion and the antelope, two old enemies, are sitting down peacefully for a game of *senet*. This painting dates from about 1150BC. *Senet* could be played on fine boards or on simple grids scratched on stones or drawn in sand.

YOUR MOVE
This noble is playing *senet*, eagerly watched by his wife. The players threw dice to decide how many squares to move over at one time. Some of the squares had forfeits and some had gains. *Senet* was said to be a game of struggle against evil.

Chariots first appeared in Egypt during the Hyksos period, and racing them soon became a fashionable sport with the nobles. One sport that was popular with all Egyptians was wrestling. There was no theatre in Egypt, but storytellers at the royal court and on village streets told fables and stories about battles, gods and magic.

Board games were popular from the early days of Egypt. In the tomb of Tutankhamun there was a beautiful gaming board made of ebony and ivory, designed for two games called *senet* and *tjau*.

MAKE A MEHEN BOARD
You will need: self-drying clay, rolling pin and board, ruler, modelling tool, green paint, cloth, varnish, water pot and brush. For the game: 12 round counters 6 blue on one side/grey on the other, 6 gold on one side/orange on the other, 2 larger counters, dice.

1 Roll out the clay onto the board and cut it to the shape shown. Use the ruler and modelling tool to score on the lines of the snake at regular intervals. Leave to dry.

2 Next, rub the board with diluted green paint to stain the lines. Wipe the excess paint away with a rag. Leave to dry. Finally, ask an adult to varnish it.

3 Each player has 6 counters of the same colours plus a larger piece (the lion). Turn all your counters so they show the same colour. You need to throw a one to start each counter off.

THE LAST GAME

This gaming board comes from Tutankhamun's tomb. Board games were so popular that they were placed in tombs to offer the dead person some fun in the next life.

HOLDS AND THROWS

Wrestling was one sport that any Egyptian could do. It did not need expensive chariots or any other special equipment. It was popular with rich and poor alike.

WILDFOWLING IN THE MARSHES

Nebamun, a nobleman, is enjoying a day's wildfowling in the marshes of the Nile Delta. He stands in his reed boat and hurls a throwing stick, a kind of boomerang, at the birds flying out of the reeds. His cat already seems to have caught several birds.

Mehen, the snake game, was popular in Egypt before 3000BC.

4 You must start each of your counters on the board before advancing any of the others. A throw of one ends a go and allows your opponent to take their turn.

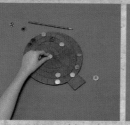

5 Exact numbers are needed to reach the centre. Once at the centre, turn your counter over to start its return journey. When it has got back to the start, your lion piece can begin.

6 The lion moves to the centre in the same way as the other counters. However, on its return journey, it can eat any of your opponent's counters in its way.

7 The winner is the person whose lion has eaten the largest number of counters. Work out the number of counters you got home safely and see who has the most left.

A Child's World

ALTHOUGH EGYPTIAN CHILDREN had only a brief period of childhood before education and work, they did enjoy playing with rattles, balls, spinning tops, toy horses and toy crocodiles. They wrestled in the dust, ran races and swam in the river.

Girls from ordinary Egyptian families received little schooling. They were taught how to look after the household, how to spin, weave and cook. When girls grew up there were few jobs open to them, although they did have legal rights and some noblewomen became very powerful. Boys were mostly trained to do the same jobs as their fathers. Some went to scribe school, where they learned how to read and write. Slow learners were beaten without mercy. Boys and some girls from noble families received a broader education, learning how to read, write and do sums.

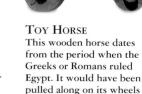

TOY HORSE
This wooden horse dates from the period when the Greeks or Romans ruled Egypt. It would have been pulled along on its wheels by a piece of string.

FUN FOR ALL
Spinning tops were popular toys with children in Egypt. They were made of glazed stone and would have been cheap enough for poorer families to buy.

ISIS AND HORUS
Many statues show the goddess Isis with Horus as a child sitting on his mother's lap. The young Horus was believed to protect families from danger and accidents. The Egyptians had large families and family life was important to them.

A LION THAT ROARS
You will need: self-drying clay, rolling pin and board, modelling tool, a piece of card, skewer, balsa wood, sandpaper, acrylic paint (white, green, red, blue, black, yellow), masking tape, string, water pot & brush.

1 Begin by rolling out the clay. Cut the pieces to the shapes shown. Mould the legs onto the body and the base. Put the bottom jaw piece to one side.

2 Use your modelling tool to make a hole between the lion's upper body and the base, as shown. This hole is for the lower jaw to fit into.

3 Insert the lower jaw into the hole you have just made and prop it up with a piece of card. Make a hole through the upper and lower jaws with the skewer.

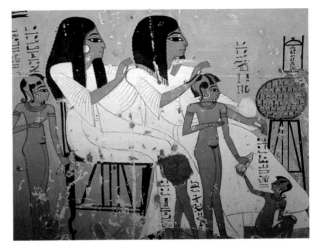

THE LOCK OF YOUTH

When they were young, boys and girls wore a special haircut, a shaved head with a lock of plaited hair. This plait, or lock of youth, was allowed to grow over one side of children's faces. When they reached adulthood, many Egyptians would have their heads shaved and wear an elaborate wig.

Originally this toy would have been made of wood, with a bronze tooth.

BOUNCING BACK

Egyptian children enjoyed playing games with balls made from rags, linen and reeds. However, archaeologists are not certain whether the balls above were used for the playing of games or as a type of rattle for younger children.

A TOY LION

Pull the string, and the lion roars! Or is it a cat miaowing? Children once played with this animal on the banks of the Nile. At the time, this toy would have been brightly painted.

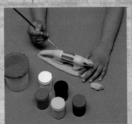

4 Now use the skewer to make a hole from left to right through the lion's upper body. The string will go through these holes later to be connected to the jaw.

5 Push a small piece of balsa wood into the mouth. This will form the lion's tooth. Leave the clay lion to dry and then sand down the surface.

6 Paint the lion in white, yellow, blue, black and red, as shown. Use masking tape to ensure that your lines are straight. Leave the lion in a warm place to dry.

7 Thread the string through the holes in the upper body and tie it to secure. A second string then goes through the lower and upper jaws of your lion.

Weapons and Warriors

EGYPT was surrounded by harsh deserts on three sides. In the north were the marshes of the delta and to the south the Nile ran over a series of rapids and waterfalls, the cataracts. All these formed barriers to invading armies. Even so, Egyptian towns were defended with forts and walls, and many pharaohs went into battle against their neighbours. Wars were fought against the Libyans, the Nubians, the Hittites and the Syrians.

There were professional soldiers in Egypt, but most were forced to join the army. For slaves, fighting in the army was a chance to gain their freedom. At times, foreign troops were also hired to fight. Young men in the villages learned to drill in preparation for war. Soldiers carried shields of leather and wood. They were armed with spears, axes, bows and arrows, daggers and swords. Later, war chariots drawn by horses were used. Special awards, such as the golden fly, were handed out for bravery in battle.

KING DEN

This ivory label from 3000BC shows King Den striding into battle against an eastern enemy. He stands beneath the flag, or standard, of the jackal-headed god Anubis. He is armed with a club, or mace.

RIDING TO VICTORY

Egyptian art often shows scenes of a pharaoh riding into battle or returning home in triumph. The king is shown in a fine chariot, driving prisoners before him. Artists often showed the enemy as very small, to show the importance and power of the pharaoh. This plaque of red gold shows Tutankhamun as the all-conquering hero.

MAKE A GOLDEN FLY

You will need: card, pencil, ruler, scissors, self-drying clay, pva glue and brush, acrylic paint (gold), gold or white ribbon (40cm long x 1cm wide), water pot and brush.

1 Begin by making the body and wings of the fly. Use a ruler and pencil to draw the fly shape onto the card, as shown. Then cut it out carefully with scissors.

2 Next, mould the face of the fly in clay. Roll two small balls for the eyes and outline them with coils of clay. This will make the eyes look larger.

3 Take the card, bend over the tab and glue it down, as shown. This will make a loop. When the fly is finished, ribbon will be threaded through this loop.

BATTLE AXE

This axe has a silver handle and a long blade designed to give a slicing movement. The battle axe was the Egyptian foot soldiers' favourite weapon. Its head of copper or bronze was fitted into a socket or lashed to the wooden handle with leather thongs. Soldiers did not wear armour in battle. Their only protection against weapons such as the heavy axes and spears was large shields made of wood or leather. The mummy of the pharaoh Seqenenre Tao shows terrible wounds to the skull caused by an axe, a dagger and a spear on the battlefield.

The Order of the Golden Fly was a reward for brave soldiers. This is a model of an award given to Queen Aahotep for her part in the war against the Hyksos.

DAGGERS

These ceremonial daggers were found in Tutankhamun's tomb. They are similar to those that would have been used in battle. Egyptian daggers were short and fairly broad. The blades were made of copper or bronze. An iron dagger was also found in Tutankhamun's tomb, but this was very rare. It may have been a gift from the Hittite people, who were mastering the new skill of ironworking.

4 Glue four small strips of white card onto the face, as shown. Push them into the modelling clay. Leave the fly's face in a warm place to dry.

5 Now glue the completed clay fly in place on the card wings. Leave the finished fly to dry for 20 minutes or so before painting it.

6 Carefully paint the fly gold. If your ribbon is white, paint that gold too. Leave the fly and, if necessary, the ribbon to dry. Make two other flies in the same way.

7 Thread the ribbon through the loops in your golden flies, as shown. Originally the golden flies would have been worn on a chain.

Boats and Ships

THE EGYPTIANS were not great seafarers. Their ocean-going ships did sail the Red Sea and the Mediterranean, and may even have reached India, but they mostly kept to coastal waters. However, the Egyptians were experts at river travel, as they are today. They built simple boats from papyrus reed, and these were used for fishing and hunting.

Egypt had little timber, so wooden ships were often built from cedar imported from Lebanon. Boats and model ships were often placed in tombs, and archaeologists have found many well-preserved examples.

The Nile was Egypt's main road, and all kinds of boats travelled up and down. There were barges transporting stones to building sites, ferries taking people across the river, and royal pleasure boats.

THE FINAL VOYAGE
Ships often appear in Egyptian pictures. They were important symbols of the voyage to the next world after death.

ALL ALONG THE NILE
Wooden sailing ships with graceful, triangular sails can still be seen on the river Nile today. They carry goods and people up and down the river. The design of these boats, or *feluccas*, has changed since the time of the ancient Egyptians. The sails on their early boats were tall, upright and narrow. Later designs were broader, like the ones shown above. In Egypt, big towns and cities have always been built along the river, so the Nile has served as an important highway.

MAKE A BOAT

You will need: a large bundle of straw 30cm long, scissors, string, balsa wood, red and yellow card, pva glue and brush.

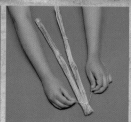

1 Divide the straw into five equal bundles and then cut three of them down to 15cm in length. Tie all five bundles securely at both ends and in the middle, as shown.

2 Take the two long bundles and tie them together at one end as shown. These bundles will form the outer frame of the boat. Put them to one side.

3 Next take the three short bundles of straw and bind them together at both ends. These will form the inner surface of the straw boat.

STEERING ROUND SAND BANKS

This wooden tomb model shows a boat from 1800BC with high curved ends. Long steering oars kept the boat on course through the powerful currents of the flooding river. Although timber was the main material for building larger boats, their designs were similar to those of the simple reed vessels.

SAILING TO ABYDOS

These boats are making a pilgrimage to Abydos. This was the city of Osiris, the god of death and rebirth. Mummies were taken here by boat. Ships and boats played a major part in the religious beliefs of the Egyptians. Ra the Sun god travelled on a boat across the sky. In October 1991, a fleet of 12 boats dating from about 3000BC was found at Abydos near Memphis. The boats were up to 30m in length and had been buried beneath the desert sands. The vessels found in these pits are the oldest surviving large ships in the world.

SIGN OF THE NORTH

The hieroglyph below means boat. It looks a bit like the papyrus reed vessels with their curved ends. This sign later came to mean north. A ship without a sail would always travel north with the current of the Nile.

Early boats were made from papyrus reeds. These were bound with string made from reed fibres.

4 Next push the short bundles into the centre of the long pair firmly. Tie the bundles together with string at one end, as shown.

5 Bring the rear of the long pair of bundles together and tie them securely, as shown. Bind the whole boat together with string.

6 Thread a string lengthwise from one end to the other. The tension on this string should give the high curved prow and stern of your boat.

7 Finally, cut the card and glue it to the balsa sticks to make the boat's paddle and harpoon. Boats like these were used for fishing and hunting hippos.

Trade and Conquest

AT ITS HEIGHT, the Egyptian empire stretched all the way from Nubia to Syria. The peoples of the Near East who were defeated by the pharaohs had to pay tribute in the form of valuable goods such as gold or ostrich feathers. However, the Egyptians were more interested in protecting their own land from invasion than in establishing a huge empire. They preferred to conquer by influence rather than by war.

Egyptian trading influence spread far and wide as official missions set out to find luxury goods for the pharaoh and his court – timber, precious stones or spices. Beautiful pottery was imported from the Minoan kingdom of Crete. Traders employed by the government were called *shwty*. The ancient Egyptians did not have coins, and so goods were exchanged in a system of bartering.

Expeditions also set out to the land of Punt, probably a part of east Africa. The traders brought back pet apes, greyhounds, gold, ivory, ebony and myrrh. Queen Hatshepsut particularly encouraged these trading expeditions. The walls of her mortuary temple record details of them and also show a picture of Eti, the Queen of Punt.

WOODS FROM FARAWAY FORESTS
Few trees grew in Egypt, so timber for making fine furniture had to be imported. Cedarwood came from Lebanon and hardwoods such as ebony from Africa.

ALL THE RICHES OF PUNT
Sailors load a wooden sailing boat with storage jars, plants, spices and apes from the land of Punt. Goods would have been exchanged in Punt for these items. Egyptian trading expeditions travelled to many distant lands and brought back precious goods to the pharaoh. This drawing is copied from the walls of Hatshepsut's temple at Deir el-Bahri.

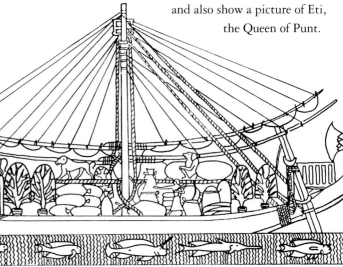

SYRIAN ENVOYS

Foreign rulers from Asia and the Mediterranean lands would send splendid gifts to the pharaoh, and he would send them gifts in return. These Syrians have been sent as representatives of their ruler, or envoys. They have brought perfume containers made of gold, ivory and a beautiful stone called lapis lazuli. The vases are decorated with gold and lotus flower designs. The pharaoh would pass on some of the luxurious foreign gifts to his favourite courtiers.

NUBIANS BRINGING TRIBUTE

Nubians bring goods to the pharaoh Thutmose IV – gold rings, apes and leopard skins. Nubia was the land above the Nile cataracts (rapids), now known as northern Sudan. The Egyptians acquired much of their wealth from Nubia through military campaigns. During times of peace, however, they also traded with the princes of Nubia for minerals and exotic animals.

EXOTIC GOODS

Egyptian craftsmen had to import many of their most valuable materials from abroad. These included gold, elephant tusks (for ivory), hardwoods such as ebony and softwoods such as cedar of Lebanon. Copper was mined in Nubia and bronze (a mixture of copper and tin) was imported from Syria.

ivory

ebony

A WORLD OF TRADE

The Egyptians travelled over the Red Sea to the mysterious land of Punt. This modern map shows the voyage the traders would have made. No one is sure of the exact location of Punt, but it was probably present-day Somalia, Eritrea, Yemen or southern Sudan.

ANCIENT
GREECE

*Over a period of 2,000 years, the ancient Greeks
laid the foundations of the modern world. Many of
their ideas about medicine, mathematics, buildings
and art, and how towns and countries are
governed are still in use. Their heroes, poets,
politicians, and colourful, imperfect gods made
ordinary human existence more exciting and fun.*

RICHARD TAMES
Consultant: Louise Schofield, British Museum

The World of the Ancient Greeks

STEP BACK IN TIME 3,000 YEARS to the shores of the eastern Mediterranean where one of the most enduring and influential civilizations of the Western world is emerging. Ancient Greece was made up of a number of self-supporting city states, each of which developed a strong, individual identity. They developed from an agricultural society that wrote in simple pictograms into a sophisticated culture. Centuries on, the Greek legacy survives in parts of modern society. The origins of democracy, mathematics, medicine and philosophy can be traced back to this time in history. Even some of our words are made up from ancient Greek. "Telephone" comes from the ancient Greek words "tele" meaning far and "phonos" meaning "sound".

A FEAT OF PERFECTION
The Parthenon is regarded as the supreme achievement of Greek architecture. It was the most important building in Athens, where it still sits on top of the Acropolis. The temple took 15 years to build and was dedicated to Athena, guardian goddess of Athens. Around 22,000 tonnes of marble, transported from over 15 km away, were used in its construction.

TIMELINE 6000BC–c.1100BC

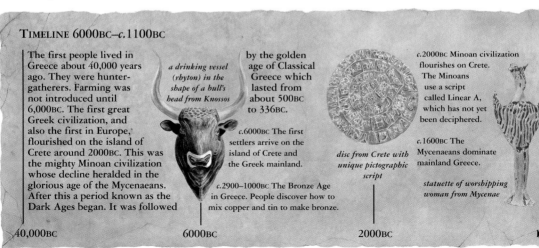

The first people lived in Greece about 40,000 years ago. They were hunter-gatherers. Farming was not introduced until 6,000BC. The first great Greek civilization, and also the first in Europe, flourished on the island of Crete around 2000BC. This was the mighty Minoan civilization whose decline heralded in the glorious age of the Mycenaeans. After this a period known as the Dark Ages began. It was followed by the golden age of Classical Greece which lasted from about 500BC to 336BC.

a drinking vessel (rhyton) in the shape of a bull's head from Knossos

c.6000BC The first settlers arrive on the island of Crete and the Greek mainland.

c.2900–1000BC The Bronze Age in Greece. People discover how to mix copper and tin to make bronze.

disc from Crete with unique pictographic script

c.2000BC Minoan civilization flourishes on Crete. The Minoans use a script called Linear A, which has not yet been deciphered.

c.1600BC The Mycenaeans dominate mainland Greece.

statuette of worshipping woman from Mycenae

40,000BC   6000BC   2000BC

THE ANCIENT GREEK WORLD

The map above shows the main ports and cities through which the Greeks traded. The ancient Greek world centred on the Aegean Sea. The Greeks were adventurous seafarers. Trade took them from the Aegean Sea to the Atlantic Ocean and the shores of the Black Sea, where they formed many settlements. These colonies helped Greece to spread its influence beyond the mainland and its offshore islands.

CENTRE STONE

The omphalos (navel) was a carved stone kept at the shrine at Delphi. The ancient Greeks thought that this holy sanctuary was the centre of the world. The omphalos stone was placed there to mark the centre. It was said to have been put there by Zeus, ruler of the gods. It may have also served as an altar on which sacrifices were made.

THE PAST REVEALED

Archaeological evidence in the shape of pottery such as this vase help us to piece together the history of Greece. This vase is typical of the superior craftsmanship for which the Greeks were admired. It was common for vases to be decorated with pictures showing historical events. In this one, we see a scene from the siege of Troy in which the king is being murdered. The siege was an important event in Greek folklore. These decorative vases were used as containers for liquids such as oil, water and wine. The export of such pottery contributed an enormous amount of wealth to the Greek empire.

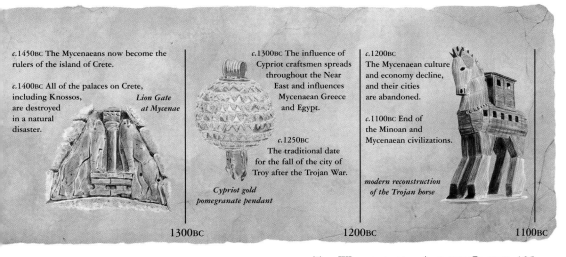

c.1450BC The Mycenaeans now become the rulers of the island of Crete.

c.1400BC All of the palaces on Crete, including Knossos, are destroyed in a natural disaster.

Lion Gate at Mycenae

c.1300BC The influence of Cypriot craftsmen spreads throughout the Near East and influences Mycenaean Greece and Egypt.

c.1250BC The traditional date for the fall of the city of Troy after the Trojan War.

Cypriot gold pomegranate pendant

c.1200BC The Mycenaean culture and economy decline, and their cities are abandoned.

c.1100BC End of the Minoan and Mycenaean civilizations.

modern reconstruction of the Trojan horse

1300BC   1200BC   1100BC

Power and Prosperity

The history of ancient Greece spans 20 centuries. It starts with the Minoan civilization on the island of Crete which reached its height between 1900 and 1450BC. This culture was also the first to develop in Europe. The Minoans were a lively and artistic people who built palaces and towns and were also great seafarers. Their achievements greatly influenced the Mycenaeans, who built their own civilization on the Greek mainland from around 1600BC. Both cultures collapsed, probably under the impact of natural disasters and warfare, to be followed by centuries of poverty.

Revival was under way by 750BC and the Greek world reached its economic peak during the 5th century BC. This period is known as the Classical Age, when Athens was at the height of its power and prosperity. During this century, Athens led the Greeks into a series of victorious battles against Persia. However Athens later suffered an economic decline because of the Peloponnesian Wars fought against Sparta. Then, in the 4th century BC, Greece was conquered by Macedonia. The Macedonian ruler Alexander the Great spread Greek culture throughout his empire. Finally between 168 and 146BC Macedonia and Greece were absorbed into the Roman empire, and Greek civilization became part of the heritage that Rome passed on to the rest of Europe.

TRADE AND EXPANSION
The Classical Age in Greek history dates from around 500 to 336BC. This period was marked by an increase in the wealth of most Greek city states. Greek trade ships were sailing throughout the Mediterranean and Black Sea. Colonies were also being set up on the shorelines of these two seas.

ITALY

• *Locri*

SICILY

• *Naxos*

N

• *Syracuse*

W

S

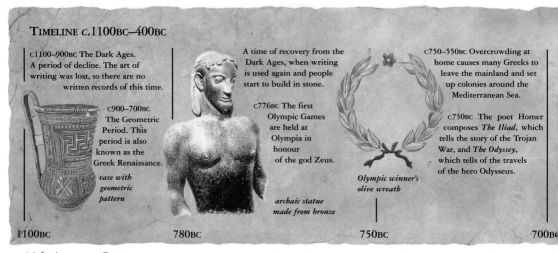

TIMELINE c.1100BC–400BC

c1100–900BC The Dark Ages. A period of decline. The art of writing was lost, so there are no written records of this time.

c900–700BC The Geometric Period. This period is also known as the Greek Renaissance.

vase with geometric pattern

A time of recovery from the Dark Ages, when writing is used again and people start to build in stone.

c776BC The first Olympic Games are held at Olympia in honour of the god Zeus.

archaic statue made from bronze

c750–550BC Overcrowding at home causes many Greeks to leave the mainland and set up colonies around the Mediterranean Sea.

c750BC The poet Homer composes *The Iliad*, which tells the story of the Trojan War, and *The Odyssey*, which tells of the travels of the hero Odysseus.

Olympic winner's olive wreath

1100BC | 780BC | 750BC | 700BC

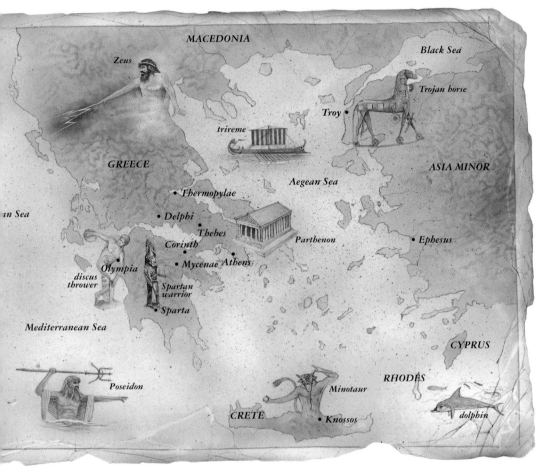

MACEDONIA

Zeus

Black Sea

Trojan horse

Troy

trireme

GREECE

ASIA MINOR

Aegean Sea

an Sea

• *Thermopylae*

• *Delphi*

Thebes

Corinth

Parthenon

• *Ephesus*

discus thrower

Olympia

• *Mycenae* *Athens*

Spartan warrior

• *Sparta*

Mediterranean Sea

CYPRUS

Poseidon

RHODES

Minotaur

CRETE

• *Knossos*

dolphin

---

c700–500BC **The Archaic Period.** During this period Greece expands. Athens becomes the largest and most influential of the city-states that make up Greece.

c508BC **Democracy is introduced in Athens.** Every citizen has the right to speak and vote.

Odysseus gouges out the eye of a Cyclops

c500–336BC **The Classical Age.** Greek culture and learning reaches its height.

c480–479BC **The Persian Wars.** The Greeks are victorious, defeating the Persians at the battles of Marathon and Salamis.

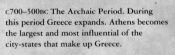

Persian archer

c479–431BC **The golden age of Athens.** Trade flourishes and the city grows very prosperous.

c447–432BC **The Parthenon is built in Athens.**

the Parthenon

500BC   480BC   440BC

Famous Greeks

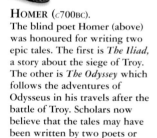

THE GREEKS TREASURED THEIR rich store of myths and legends about gods and heroes, but they also took a keen interest in human history. They valued fame and glory far more than riches. Their ultimate aim in life was to make a name for themselves that would live on long after death. Statues were put up in prominent places to honour Greeks who had won fame in different ways – as generals on the battlefield, as poets, teachers, philosophers, mathematicians, orators or sportsmen. These heroes represented the human qualities the Greeks most admired – physical courage, endurance and strength, and the intelligence to create, invent, explain and persuade.

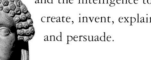

HOMER (*c*700BC).
The blind poet Homer (above) was honoured for writing two epic tales. The first is *The Iliad,* a story about the siege of Troy. The other is *The Odyssey* which follows the adventures of Odysseus in his travels after the battle of Troy. Scholars now believe that the tales may have been written by two poets or even groups of several poets.

SAPPHO (*c*600BC)
The poet Sappho was born on the island of Lesbos. She wrote nine books of poetry, but only one complete poem survives. Beauty and love were the subjects of her poetry. Her work inspired other artists of the time and influenced many writers and poets in later centuries.

SOPHOCLES (496–406BC)
Only seven of Sophocles' plays have survived. He is thought to have written 123 altogether. Besides being a playwright, Sophocles was also a respected general and politician. His name means "famed for wisdom".

TIMELINE 440BC–140BC

443–429BC The great statesman, Pericles, dominates politics in Athens.

431–404BC The Peloponnesian Wars take place between Athens and its great rival, Sparta. The Spartans defeat the Athenians.

399BC The Athenian philosopher, Socrates is condemned to death because his views prove unpopular.

marble bust of the philosopher, Socrates

371BC Sparta is defeated by Thebes. Thebes becomes the leading power in Greece.

362BC Sparta and Athens combine forces to defeat the Thebans at the battle of Mantinea.

338BC The Greeks are defeated by the Macedonians at the battle of Chaeronea. Philip II of Macedonia becomes ruler of Greece.

iron corselet which is thought to have belonged to Philip II of Macedonia

336BC Philip II of Macedonia dies and is succeeded by his son, Alexander the Great. Alexander builds a huge empire, stretching from Greece as far east as India.

bronze statuette of Alexander the Great

440BC   371BC   336BC   334BC

PERICLES (495–429BC)

A popular figure and brilliant public speaker, Pericles was elected as a general 20 times. While in office, he built up a powerful navy and organized the building of strong defences, beautiful temples and fine monuments. He also gave ordinary citizens more say in government. Pericles' career ended after he led Athens into a disastrous war against Sparta. He was ostracized (expelled) as punishment for his misjudgement.

ALEXANDER THE GREAT (356–323BC)

Alexander was the son of Philip II of Macedonia. His life was spent in conquest of new territory, and his empire stretched across the Middle East, Persia and Afghanistan as far as the river Indus. His empire was swiftly divided when he died after suspected poisoning.

SOCRATES (469–399BC)

A renowned teacher and philosopher, Socrates encouraged people to think about how to live a good life. The Athenians sentenced him to die by drinking hemlock (a poison). Plato, Socrates' most brilliant pupil and himself a great philosopher, recorded his teacher's last days.

ARCHIMEDES (287–211BC)

The mathematician, scientist, astronomer and inventor, Archimedes came from Syracuse. When his city was besieged by the Romans, he designed a huge lens that focused sunlight on the Roman ships and set them on fire. He also devised a screw for raising water out of the ground and studied the concepts of floating and balance.

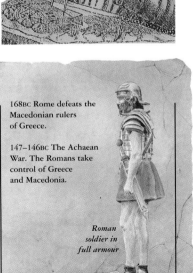

334BC Alexander the Great invades Persia to include it in his empire.

333BC The Persian army, led by King Darius, is defeated by Alexander the Great at the battle of Issus.

331BC Alexander the Great becomes king of Persia after defeating the Persians at the battle of Gaugamela.

King Darius of Persia

Romulus and Remus, legendary founders of Rome

323BC Alexander the Great dies, and his successors fight over the throne.

275BC Greek colonies are taken over by the Romans.

168BC Rome defeats the Macedonian rulers of Greece.

147–146BC The Achaean War. The Romans take control of Greece and Macedonia.

Roman soldier in full armour

323BC   196BC   146BC

The Minoans

AT THE HEART OF THE MINOAN CIVILIZATION was a huge palace at Knossos. The palace was a great political and cultural centre, and it controlled much of central Crete. At the height of its prosperity around 2000BC, over 10,000 people lived in the palace. Despite its obvious wealth, the palace was left unfortified because its rulers believed that their fleet could overcome any invaders. However, around 1450BC, the warlike Mycenaean Greeks captured Knossos and destroyed all the other Minoan palaces and towns.

In the early 1900s, British archaeologist Sir Arthur Evans unearthed the splendid remains of an ancient civilization on the island of Crete. He named it "Minoan" after the legendary Cretan king Minos, son of Zeus. It was discovered that the Minoans did not speak Greek and their writing, known as Linear A, has still not been decoded.

PURPOSEFUL POT
This brightly decorated pot from Knossos was probably used to hold water or wine. Sir Arthur Evans used the changes in pottery style to work out a chronology of the Minoan civilization. This pot was made around 1700–1550BC, on a potter's wheel.

A SPECIAL OCCASION
Frescoes were a popular art form used to decorate the walls of Cretan palaces. In order to make them last, frescoes were painted straight on to the wet plaster walls. This fresco shows a group of women gathered to watch a show or ceremony. Brightly coloured outfits with tight bodices and flounced skirts, as worn by the women here, were typical of the period.

MINOAN SEAL
You will need: work board, white and brown self-drying modelling clay, rolling pin, modelling tool, ruler, needle, PVA glue, water, mixing bowl, paintbrush, soft cord.

1 Roll out a small piece of white self drying modelling clay until it is about 1cm thick. Using a modelling tool, cut a small circle 3cm in diameter.

2 With the modelling tool carve the pattern shown above into the white clay. Leave to dry. This piece is the mould for the seal.

3 Roll a piece of the brown clay into a circle 2cm thick, and 3·5cm in diameter. Gently press the mould into the clay to leave an imprint.

Pillars were used to support the upper floors within the palace. They were made from wood, and painted in bright colours.

LIVING IN LUXURY

The queen had her own set of apartments in the magnificent palace at Knossos. A large fresco decorates the wall in this room. It shows lively dolphins and fish swimming underwater. Most Minoan frescoes show scenes from palace life and the natural world. The paintings are a vital source of information for modern historians.

ROYAL SYMBOL

The double-headed axe was an important symbol in Minoan religion. This one was made from gold in about 1800BC.

PALACE COMPLEX

The ruins of the great palace complex at Knossos have been excavated and partially reconstructed. Many of the Cretan palaces seem to have expanded with the random addition of rooms and corridors. Knossos was the largest of these palaces.

A DANGEROUS DANCE

Bull-leaping was a popular form of entertainment in Crete. Both men and women took part in the sport. The young man would somersault over a charging bull's horns and then leap off its back. This sport may have been part of a religious rite.

4 Cut around the imprint leaving an edge 1cm wide. Make 2 small holes on each side of the circle with the needle. Leave to dry. This piece is the seal.

5 Prepare the varnish by mixing 2 parts of glue to 1 part of water. Brush the seal with varnish. Make sure that the holes aren't filled in with it.

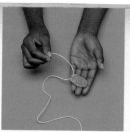

6 Leave the varnish to dry. Cut a length of cord and thread it through either one or both holes. Wear it on your wrist or around your neck.

Seals were used as an identity badge, as a sign of ownership, as a lucky charm or as a piece of art.

The Mycenaeans

THE FIRST IMPORTANT CIVILIZATION on mainland Greece developed in the north-eastern part of the Peleponnese between 1600 and 1200BC. A series of small kingdoms and great fortresses were built during this period. The most powerful of these kingdoms was Mycenae. The Mycenaeans did not keep historical records, and therefore our knowledge of them comes largely from archaelogical evidence. We know that they were an advanced culture as they communicated in a written language and developed technology.

The Mycenaeans had the ability to quarry and build. Excavations have revealed high walls made from huge stone slabs. They learnt how to sail ships and developed extensive trade routes to Egypt, the Near East and the Baltic Sea. From these distant shores they imported gold, tin to make bronze, and amber for jewellery. Local resources such as olive trees were exploited for large financial gain.

Oil was extracted from the olives then perfumed and bottled for export.

Around 1200BC the Mycenaean culture suffered an economic recession that led to its downfall. Historians believe that earthquakes, wars and fires may have triggered the recession.

FRUIT OF LABOUR
This gold pomegranate pendant was found in a tomb on the island of Cyprus. The surface is decorated with fine grains of gold using a process known as the granulation technique. It took a skilled artist to make such a detailed piece of jewellery.

BOAR HELMET
The Mycenaeans favoured elaborate armour, such as this 13th-century BC helmet plated with boar's tusks. Other materials used to make armour included linen, leather and bronze. A great deal of weaponry has been excavated from the royal shaft graves at Mycenae.

COPYCAT CUTTLEFISH
The Mycenaeans developed many of their ideas from those of the Minoans who lived on the island of Crete. Cuttlefish designs similar to the one shown here are also found on Minoan pottery. Mycenaean pottery was widely traded and has been found as far away as northern Italy and eastern Spain. Small jars for holding perfumed olive oil were among the most popular wares.

DECORATED DAGGER

This inlaid bronze dagger came from the tomb of a wealthy Mycenaean who was buried between 1550 and 1500BC. The large number of weapons placed in the tombs of high-ranking individuals suggests that the Mycenaeans were a warlike people. Several such daggers have been discovered during excavations. This one is the most well preserved of them. The scene on the blade of the dagger shows leopards hunting in the forest. The illustration was built-up with inlays of different metals, including gold, silver and copper.

This dagger is the only one discovered with its golden hilt still attached.

MASKED MONARCH

Gold death masks like this are unique to Mycenae. They were made by beating a sheet of gold over a wooden mould, which had been carved in the image of the deceased. The mask was then laid over the face of the dead man when he was buried. This one was discovered by the archaeologist Heinrich Schliemann in the 1870s, after his excavation of Troy. In the past, people have incorrectly thought that the mask belonged to the heroic King Agamemnon. In fact, the mask is approximately three centuries older than first thought and dates from around 1500BC. It is now believed to be the death mask of one the earliest kings of Mycenae.

RICHES FROM GRAVES

Heinrich Schliemann's excavations at Mycenae in 1876 led to the uncovering of five royal shaft graves. They contained 16 bodies and rich treasures made of gold, silver, ivory and bronze. The contents of the graves prove that the Mycenaeans were a wealthy civilisation. Important tombs were hollowed out of soft rock or built of stone. Ordinary people were buried in stone-slab coffins or simple pits.

Politics and Government

THE GREEK WORLD WAS MADE UP of about 300 separate city states. Some were no bigger than villages, while others centred around cities such as Sparta or Athens. Each city state was known as a *polis* (from which we take our word politics) and had its own laws and government. In the 4th century BC, the Greek philosopher, Aristotle, wrote that there were three types of government. The first was power held by one person. They could either be a king (who ruled on account of his royal birth), or a tyrant (who ruled by force). The second type was government by the few which meant rule by an aristocracy (governing by right of noble birth) or an oligarchy (a ruling group of rich and powerful men). The third type was a democratic government (rule by the many) which gave every male citizen the right to vote, hold public office or serve on a jury. Democracy was only practised in Athens. Even there women, slaves and foreigners were not counted as full citizens.

SET IN STONE
The laws of the city of Ephesus were carved on stone tablets in both Greek and Latin. The Greeks believed that their laws had to be clearly fixed (set in stone) and seen by everyone if all citizens were expected to obey them.

BEHIND THE SCENES
Women were not allowed to take an active part in politics in ancient Greece. However, some played an important role behind the scenes. One such woman was Aspasia. As a professional entertainer, she met and became mistress to Pericles (one of the most influential Athenian statesmen of the 5th century BC). Pericles confided in his mistress about affairs of state, and he came to rely on her insight and wisdom in his judgement of people and situations.

VOTING TOKENS
You will need: pair of compasses, thin card, pencil, ruler, scissors, rolling pin, cutting board, self-hardening clay, modelling tool, balsa wood stick 5cm long, piece of drinking straw 5cm long, bronze-coloured paint, paintbrush, water pot.

1 Make two templates. Use a pair of compasses to draw two circles, on a piece of thin card. Make each one 4cm in diameter. Cut them out.

2 Use a rolling pin to roll out the clay to 3cm thickness. Use a modelling tool to cut around the card circles into the clay. Press down hard as you do this.

3 Make a hole in the centre of each clay circle. Use the balsa wood to make one hole (innocent token). Use the straw to make the other hole (guilty token).

PEOPLE POWER

Solon the Lawgiver was an Athenian statesman and poet who lived from 640 to 559BC. Around 594BC, when serving as chief magistrate, he gave Athens new laws that enabled more people to take part in politics. His actions prevented a potential civil war between the few nobles in power and the people who suffered under their rule.

VOTE HERE

This terracotta urn was used to collect voting tokens. They were used in Athens when votes needed to be taken in law courts or when the voters' intentions needed to be kept secret. Each voter put a bronze disc in the urn to register his decision. Normally, voting was done by a show of hands, which was difficult to count precisely.

FACE TO FACE

The ruins of this council chamber at Priene in present-day Turkey show how seating was arranged. The tiered, three-sided square enabled each councillor to see and hear clearly all of the speakers involved in a debate. Even in the democracies of ancient Greece, most everyday decisions were taken by committees or councils and not by the assembly of voters.

4 Write a name on the innocent token using the modelling tool. Carefully push the balsa stick through the hole. Leave it to dry.

5 Write another name on the guilty token using the modelling tool. Carefully push the drinking straw through the hole. Leave it to dry.

6 Wait until the clay tokens are dry before painting them. The original tokens were made from bronze, so use a bronze-coloured paint.

Jurors were issued with two tokens to vote with. A hollow centre meant that the juror thought the accused was guilty. A solid centre meant that the juror thought the accused was innocent.

Equality and Inequality

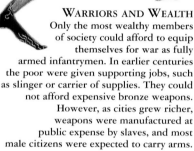

GREEK SOCIETY WAS DIVIDED by a strict social structure, enforced by its governments. Most city states were ruled by a small group of people (oligarchy). Two exceptions to this rule were the powerful cities of Sparta and Athens. Sparta held on to its monarchy, and Athens introduced the first democratic government in history. In Athens, all citizens could vote and hold office. However to be an Athenian citizen, it was necessary to be an adult male, born in Athens. Even so-called democratic Athens was ruled by a minority of its people. The treatment of women, foreign residents (called metics), slaves and children was the same as that of other city states.

Women had no legal rights and rarely took place in public life. Migrants from other parts of Greece were obliged to pay extra taxes and serve in the military, they were called metics. They could not own land or marry an Athenian. The Athenians felt uneasy about the large number of metics living in their city, but their skills helped to make it rich. Slaves made up half the population of Athens. Most had either been born slaves or become slaves as prisoners of war or captives of pirates. Even native Greeks could become slaves by falling into debt, but they were freed once the debt was paid off.

WARRIORS AND WEALTH
Only the most wealthy members of society could afford to equip themselves for war as fully armed infantrymen. In earlier centuries the poor were given supporting jobs, such as slinger or carrier of supplies. They could not afford expensive bronze weapons. However, as cities grew richer, weapons were manufactured at public expense by slaves, and most male citizens were expected to carry arms.

A WOMAN'S PLACE
Greek women spent their lives at home. On this vase, made about 450BC, a woman ties her sandal before going out. As she has attendants, she must be wealthy. Poor women would leave the house to fetch water, work in the fields or shop in the market. Women with slaves, like this one, might leave the home to visit relatives or to pray at a shrine or temple.

LOVED ONES
A young girl and her pet dog are seen on this tombstone from the 4th century BC. The likely expense of such a detailed carving suggests that she was dearly loved. Not all children were cherished. Girl babies, and sick babies of either sex, were often left outside to die. Some were underfed and fell victim to diseases. Greek law required children to support their parents in old age, so childless couples were always keen to adopt and were known to rescue abandoned children.

CRAFTSMAN

Most craftsmen were slaves, ex-slaves, or migrants (metics). They were looked down on by other citizens. This smith might be a slave working in a factory owned by a wealthy man. If a master owned a talented slave, he might set the slave up to run his own business. In return, the master would receive a share of the profits. This smith could also have been a free, self-employed man, with his own workshop and a slave or two working as his assistants.

PATH TO POWER?

Being able to read and write in ancient Greece was not an automatic key to success. The Greek alphabet could be learned quite easily. Even slaves could become highly educated scribes. However, illiterate men were unlikely to hold high positions, except perhaps in Sparta, where written records were rarely kept. Although women were denied the right to a formal education, they were often able to read and write enough to keep a record of household stores.

ENSLAVED BY LANGUAGE

This Roman bottle is made in the shape of an African slave girl's head. The Greeks also owned slaves. The Greek philosopher Aristotle argued that some people were "naturally" meant to be slaves. His opinion was shared by many of his countrymen. He felt that this applied most obviously to people who did not speak Greek. Slaves were treated with varying degrees of kindness and hostility. Some were worked to death by their owners, but others had good jobs as clerks or bailiffs. A few hundred slaves were owned by the city of Athens and served as policemen, coin-inspectors and clerks of the court.

The Golden Age of Athens

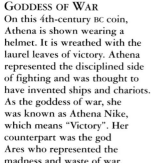

ATHENS WAS THE CHIEF CITY of the fertile region of Attica, in southern Greece. It grew rich from trade, manufacturing and mining silver. The city of Athens reached the height of its wealth and power in the 5th century BC. By this time, it had built up a large empire which encompassed cities on both the mainland and the islands. Its 250,000 citizens enjoyed a vibrant golden age of art and culture. During this period, the Athenians celebrated a victory against Persian invaders by building a series of magnificent temples on the Acropolis in Athens. The Acropolis was a sacred hill that overlooked the city. Its most important temple was the Parthenon, which was dedicated to the city's goddess, Athena. Below, at the heart of the city was the market-place (*agora*). Surrounded by temples and public buildings and crowded with stalls, the agora was the commercial centre of Athens.

Between 431 and 404BC, Athens fought a crippling war against Sparta and the Persians. It lost the war and most of its maritime empire. As a result, Athens gave up its role as commercial and cultural leader in Greece to Sparta.

GODDESS OF WAR
On this 4th-century BC coin, Athena is shown wearing a helmet. It is wreathed with the laurel leaves of victory. Athena represented the disciplined side of fighting and was thought to have invented ships and chariots. As the goddess of war, she was known as Athena Nike, which means "Victory". Her counterpart was the god Ares who represented the madness and waste of war.

CROWNING GLORY
This temple to Hephaestus is a supreme example of the elegant architecture at which the Athenians excelled. It was built between 449 and 444BC at the eastern end of the agora. Hephaestus was the god of fire and armourer of the gods. A bronze statue inside the temple shows Hephaestus at work making armour, wearing a blacksmith's cap and holding a hammer above an anvil. Excavations have revealed that the bronze sculptors worked on one side of the temple, while sculptors in marble worked on the other side.

PANATHENAIC FESTIVAL

Every year, the people of Athens marched or rode in a great procession up to Athena's temple on the Acropolis. Even foreign residents joined in. This frieze from the Parthenon shows young men getting ready to join the procession. At the temple, oxen and other animals were sacrificed, and the meat was given to the people to eat. Every fourth year, there was an extra celebration when a new robe, the peplos, was presented to the goddess Athena. This event was celebrated with days of sporting and musical competitions, with prizes of money or olive oil.

BIRTH OF A GODDESS

According to Greek legend, Zeus swallowed a pregnant lover after a prophecy warned that their child would depose him. Not long after swallowing her, Zeus complained of a painful headache. Hephaestus offered to split open Zeus's head with an axe to ease the pain. When he did, the goddess Athena jumped out. She was fully grown and wearing the armour of a warrior (as seen here in the centre of the painting).

BANISHMENT

Once a year, Athenians were allowed to banish an unpopular member of the community from the city for 10 years. Voters scratched the names on a fragment of pottery called an ostrakon, which is why the procedure was called ostracism. If at least 6,000 votes were cast in favour of exiling a person, they would have to leave the city within 10 days. Ostraka were also used for messages and shopping lists.

GODDESS OF WISDOM

The owl, symbolizing wisdom, was the emblem of Athena. This silver coin was issued in Athens in 479BC, after the Greeks won decisive victories against the Persians. Athenian coins were accepted throughout Greece, Italy and Turkey. This proves just how influential the city of Athens. Coins from other city states were not widely accepted.

The Spartan Order

A T THE HEIGHT OF ITS POWER, Sparta was the only city state to rival the influence of Athens. It controlled most of the area of southern Greece, called the Peleponnese. Sparta was an insular and militaristic state. It became so after losing control of its slave population in a rebellion, which lasted for 17 years. The slaves (helots) were descendants of the people of Messenia whom Sparta overran in the 8th century BC. The helots outnumbered their Spartan overlords by seven to one. Although the Spartans defeated the rebellion, they continued to live in fear of another one. As a result, all male citizens were required by law to serve as full-time warriors. In addition, harsh restrictions were placed on the helots who were forbidden to ride horses or stay out after nightfall. While the citizens were fully occupied with military training, the heavy work and domestic chores were done by the helots.

The Spartans imposed strict living conditions on themselves. Spartan boys and girls were separated from their parents and brought up in barracks. Boys were trained for battle from the age of seven. They were kept cold, barefoot and hungry, and regularly flogged to make them tough. At the age of 20 they joined a group of 15 men who became their comrades. In Sparta, comradeship between men was more important than family life. The girls also took part in physical training so as to be able to bear healthy children. The power of Sparta declined after its defeat by the Theban army in 371 BC.

HEROIC KING
This bust from the 5th century BC may be of King Leonidas. There were two royal families in Sparta. A king was chosen from each family to govern Sparta at the same time. Their powers were limited. Their main responsibility was to lead Spartan forces into battle.

WINE FOR THE WARRIORS
This massive bronze krater (wine vessel) stands 165cm high, weighs 208 km and holds 1,200 litres of liquid. It was made around 530BC by a Spartan craftsman. The neck of the krater is decorated with Spartan warriors and chariots marching to war. The handles are crafted with the heads of female monsters called gorgons. It is thought that the vase was presented as a gift to the king of Lydia who wanted to form an alliance with Sparta. The Spartans were admired for the high quality of their bronze work.

DEATH AND GLORY

This modern monument was erected to commemorate the heroic self-sacrifice of King Leonidas and 300 Spartans. They died in 480BC defending the pass at Thermopylae against a Persian army 250,000 strong. The pass was just 13m wide and the Spartans held their ground for two days while waiting for reinforcements. On the third day, a traitor showed the invading Persians another way through the mountain. Leonidas ordered a retreat, then led the rearguard in a fight to the death.

SEA POWER

The ivory relief pictured here has a Spartan warship carved into it. The pointed ram at the front was used for sinking enemy ships. Sparta was first and foremost a land power. Its navy was no match for that of Athens. A navy was expensive to run because specialized warships could not be used in peace-time. The Athenians financed their navy from their silver mines, but the Spartans were not so wealthy. They sometimes had to borrow money to keep their navy afloat.

BACKBONE OF THE ARMY

Spartan soldiers were easily distinguished on the battlefield because of their long hair and bright red cloaks. This figurine of a Spartan warrior probably dates from the 6th century BC. His crested helmet incorporates a nose guard and cheek guards. He is also wearing greaves (armour to guard his lower legs) and a cuirass (armour to protect his chest).

LAW-GIVER

This Roman mosaic probably shows the figure of Lycurgus, wielding an axe. Little is known of his life, because so few records were kept in Sparta. It is generally believed that Lycurgus lived around 650BC. His main achievement was to re-organize the government of Sparta for effective warfare after its disastrous defeat by the state of Argos.

At Home

the roof was made of pottery tiles

GREEK HOMES WERE BUILT of mud bricks and roofed with pottery tiles. They had small high windows with wooden shutters to keep out thieves, and floors of beaten earth, plaster or mosaic. Most houses started as small structures, and more rooms were added as the owner could afford them. This gave homes a random appearance and meant that streets were rarely straight. In country areas, houses were often surrounded by a stone wall to protect the inhabitants and their domestic animals. Men and women lived in separate rooms and in different areas of the house. The women's quarters were usually found at the rear of the house. Richer households might also have rooms for cooking and bathing in. Most homes contained only a few pieces of plain furniture which might include couches that doubled as beds, chairs and tables. Only wealthier people could afford richly decorated furniture such as couches inlaid with gold and ivory.

the andron was the room in which men entertained

the mosaic floor was made from brightly coloured pebbles

HOME HEATING
In mountainous areas of Greece, the winter can be very cold. This bronze brazier, dating from the 4th century BC, would have been filled with charcoal and used to heat a chilly room.

HEARTH GODDESS
Hestia was the goddess of the hearth and home. A fire was kept burning in her honour all year round. This fire was used for cooking, for heating water and to make charcoal as fuel for the braziers. Traditionally, when the Greeks founded a colony overseas, they took with them fire from their old home to link the new with the old.

DOLPHIN FRESCO
You will need: pencil, sheet of white paper 21cm x 19cm, rolling pin, white self-hardening clay, ruler, cutting board, modelling tool, pin, sandpaper, paintbrush, acrylic paints, water.

1 Draw a dolphin on the piece of white paper. Add some smaller fish and some seaweed. Refer to the final picture as a guide for your drawing.

2 Roll out a piece of clay until it measures 21cm across and 19cm down. The clay should be about 0.5cm thick. Cut off any uneven edges.

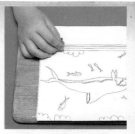

3 While the clay is still damp, place the dolphin picture over it. Following the outline of your picture, prick holes through the paper on to the clay.

wooden shutters were used as windows

HOT WORK

Food was usually cooked over an open fire. Cooking would either take place in an open courtyard, where smoke could escape upwards or in a kitchen where a chimney shaft might be installed.

OPEN HOUSE

At the heart of every Greek house was a courtyard. Many chores were carried out here. Most had an altar where offerings were made to the gods.

Frescoes are paintings applied to damp plaster. This one was inspired by a painting found on a wall of the Minoan palace at Knossos.

clay walls were soft and could easily be burrowed through by enterprising thieves

4 Lift the paper off the clay and leave the base to dry. Once the clay has dried completely, sand it down with fine sandpaper for a smooth finish.

5 Using your pencil, join the dots of each outline together. When this is complete you will have a replica of your original drawing.

6 Paint the base of the fresco with a light blue. Once this is dry, paint in the rest of the picture. Use colours that reflect those of the sea.

7 Finally, paint in the two stripes at the bottom of the picture. These indicate where the fresco would have ended on the wall. Leave to dry.

Country Living

MOST GREEKS LIVED IN the countryside and worked as farmers. The mountainous landscape, poor, stony soil and hot, dry climate restricted what crops they could produce and which animals they could keep. Olive trees and bees flourished in these conditions. Olives provided oil and bees supplied honey (the main sweetener in food) and wax. Grain, such as barley, was difficult to grow, and the land used for its production had to be left fallow every other year to recover its fertility. Country people kept oxen to pull ploughs and drag heavy loads, and they used donkeys to carry goods to market. Rural areas also produced important materials used by city craftworkers. These included timber, flax for linen, horn and bone for glue, and leather.

Country life was hazardous, as droughts, floods, wolves and warfare threatened their livliehoods. Over the centuries, another problem developed. As forests were cut down for timber and fuel, soil erosion increased, leaving even less fertile land. The search for new agricultural land prompted the growth of Greek colonies along the shores of the Mediterranean and the Black Sea.

OLIVE HARVEST
This vase shows men shaking and beating the branches of an olive tree to bring down its fruit. Olives were eaten and also crushed to extract their oil. The oil was used for cooking, cleaning, as a medicine and a fuel for lamps.

FOOD FOR THE POT
Meat was obtained through hunting and the rearing of domesticated animals. Hunting was considered a sport for the rich, but it was a serious business for the poor, who hoped to put extra food on their tables. Simple snares, nets and slings were used to trap lizards and hares and to bring down small birds.

GONE FISHING
Many Greeks lived near water. The sea, rivers and lakes provided fish and shellfish which were their main source of protein. Fish was smoked or salted for future use. Always at the mercy of storms and shipwreck, fishermen prayed to the sea god Poseidon to save them.

PLOUGHING WITH OXEN

This terracotta figure from Thebes shows a farmer ploughing with two oxen. The plough was made of wood, but the part that broke up the earth was tipped with iron. Oxen were stronger and less expensive than horses, making them ideal for heavy work. When oxen died, they yielded hides for leather as well as horn, meat, sinew, which was used as twine, and fat that could be turned into candle tallow.

SNACKS

Drying food was a good way of preserving it in a warm country like Greece. The Greeks ate raisins and dried apricots as a dessert or used them to sweeten other foods. Olives were another popular snack or appetizer.

raisins

olives

apricots

HARVEST GOODDESS

Demeter was the goddess of grain and growth. She looked after plants, children and young people. The first part of her name *deme* is an ancient word for the Earth, the second part, *meter*, means "mother". Farmers believed that their success depended on uncontrollable forces such as the rain, the sun, and diseases which attacked plants and livestock. Special prayers and sacrifices were made to Demeter to ask for her help in preventing such disasters. Festivals were held in honour of the goddess at crucial times during the harvest, before ploughing, when the corn began to sprout, and after it had been harvested.

Food and Drink

MEALS IN ANCIENT GREECE were based around home-baked bread, fish fresh from the sea and such vegetables as onions, beans, lentils, leeks and radishes. Chickens and pigeons were kept for their eggs and meat, and a cow or a few goats or sheep for milk and cheese. Occasionally a pig or goat was slaughtered for the table, or hunting provided boar, deer, hares and even thrushes. The Greeks cooked their meat in olive oil and flavoured it with garlic and wild herbs. They ate fruits such as figs, apples, pears and pomegranates, which could be dried for the winter months. During hard times, people resorted to eating wild berries, hedgehogs and even locusts. Wine was the Greeks' favourite drink. It was usually very thick and had to be strained and then diluted with water for drinking. Sometimes it was mixed with resin, a preservative extracted from pine trees. It could then be kept for three to four years.

WASTE CONVERTER
This terracotta figure shows a butcher killing a pig. Pigs were a cheap source of meat because they could be kept on scrubby pasture and fed on acorns and kitchen scraps. Their skins were tanned to make leather and their hooves melted to make glue.

STORAGE ON A GRAND SCALE
Huge storage jars were used by the Greeks to store food and drink. These come from the palace, at Knossos in Crete. They probably contained olive oil, wine and cereals and were capable of holding hundreds of litres. Handmade from clay, they kept food and drink cool in the hot Mediterranean climate.

PANCAKES WITH HONEY AND SESAME SEEDS
You will need: 100g flour, sieve, mixing bowl, fork, 200ml water, fork, 8 tablespoons clear honey, frying pan, 1 tablespoon sesame seeds, spoon, 1 tablespoon oil, spatula.

1 First make the pancake mix. Sieve the flour into a mixing bowl. Then, using a fork stir the water into the flour. Measure the honey into a small bowl.

2 Spoon the honey into the pancake mixture a bit at a time. Mix it with a fork, making sure that there are no lumps in the pancake mixture.

3 Ask an adult to help you with the next two steps. Heat the frying pan. Sprinkle in the sesame seeds and cook until browned. Set aside.

STAFF OF LIFE

A team of bakers prepare bread for the oven in this terracotta model. In big cities, commercial bakeries produced many different kinds of bread. Ordinary loaves were made of barley or wheat flour, speciality breads were flavoured with mountainside herbs, and delicious pastries came drenched in honey.

PLAY THE GAME

The Greeks drank from large, shallow cups such as this one. This picture shows a man playing a drinking game called cottabus. After much drinking, guests would compete to see who was most in control of their faculties by throwing the wine left in the bottom of their cup at a target. In another game, guests tried to make the loudest noise with their cup without spilling its contents.

GOD OF WINE

This Roman stone panel shows a procession of revellers following the Greek god Dionysus to a drinking party. Dionysus was the god of wine and was worshipped with special enthusiasm in vine-growing regions such as Athens, Boeotia and Naxos.

SERVICE

A carved relief shows servants carrying bowls of food. At formal banquets, the guests lay on their sides to eat as this was thought to aid digestion. The Greeks adopted this custom from the peoples of Asia. They often ate and drank until they passed out on their couches, leaving the servants to clear away without waking them.

4 Heat a teaspoon of the oil in the frying pan. Pour a quarter of the mix into the pan. Cook on both sides for about 4 minutes, until light brown.

5 Serve the pancake on a plate. Sprinkle on a handful of sesame seeds and pour extra honey over it. Cook the rest of the mix the same way.

Pancakes were a popular snack in ancient Greece, especially with theatre- goers. Food stalls were usually set up around theatres to catch the crowds who had come to view the latest play.

Women at Home

RESPECTABLE GREEK WOMEN were rarely seen out in the public domain. Their lives revolved around the household and family. From an early age, girls were trained in domestic skills which would enable them to run a household once married. A girl might be married off by her father at the age of 13 or 14. Her husband was usually much older and would be given a dowry to offset the costs of providing for her. The purpose of marriage was to produce a son to continue the husband's name. A wife assumed a number of responsibilities in her new home. If she was fortunate to have the help of slaves, she would direct them in their daily tasks. If not, she carried out those chores herself. Chores would include cooking meals, cleaning the house and caring for the children. Some women even managed the family finances.

"SO SHE SAID..."
Wealthy women were largely confined to their houses. They often relied on friends or household slaves for news about events in the outside world. Women from poorer families, without slaves, had to leave the house to shop and fetch water. Public fountains were popular meeting places for a gossip.

A CONSTANT TASK
Weaving was considered a respectable occupation for women. This vase painting shows Penelope, wife of the absent hero Odysseus, spinning wool into yarn. Women were expected to produce all the fabric needed to clothe their family. The material they spun was also used for household furnishings such as wall hangings.

KNUCKLEBONES
You will need: self-drying modelling clay, modelling tool, work-board, cream paint, paintbrush.

1 Divide the self-drying modelling clay into 5 equal pieces. Roll each piece into a ball. Press each ball into a figure of eight shape, as above.

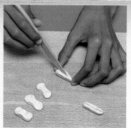

2 With the modelling tool, carve ridges around the middle of each shape. Make small dents in the end of each shape with your finger.

3 When the pieces have dried out, paint them. Use a cream coloured paint. Once the paint has dried, the pieces are ready to play with.

Hoping for Health

Married women from wealthy families rarely left the house. When they did, it was usually to take part in family celebrations or religious ceremonies. The family shown on this carved relief from the 5th century BC are sacrificing a bull to Asclepius, god of health, and Hygieia, his daughter.

Knucklebones were made from the ankle-joints of small animals. These small bones were used in different ways, depending on the type of game. The Greeks also used the knucklebones as dice.

Your Turn

Women were supposed to be fully occupied with household tasks. But many kept slaves, which allowed them some leisure time. These women are playing knucklebones. Another favourite pastime was draughts, played on a board with 36 squares.

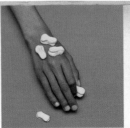

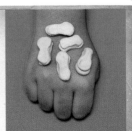

4 To play the game, gather together the five pieces into the palm of one hand. Throw them into the air. Quickly flip your hand over.

5 Try to catch the pieces on the back of your hand. If you're lucky and you catch them all, you win the game. If not, then the game continues.

6 Try to pick up the fallen pieces with the others still on the back of your hand. Throw them with your free hand and try to catch them again.

7 The winner is the first person to have all of the knucklebones on the back of their hand. It may take a few tries for you to get the hang of it.

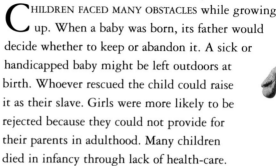

Growing Up

CHILDREN FACED MANY OBSTACLES while growing up. When a baby was born, its father would decide whether to keep or abandon it. A sick or handicapped baby might be left outdoors at birth. Whoever rescued the child could raise it as their slave. Girls were more likely to be rejected because they could not provide for their parents in adulthood. Many children died in infancy through lack of health-care.

Education was considered to be important for boys. Even so, it was usually only sons of rich families who received a complete schooling. They were taught a variety of subjects, including reading, music and gymnastics. Boys from poorer families often learnt their father's trade. Education in domestic skills was essential for most girls. A notable exception was in Sparta, where girls joined boys in hard physical training.

BRINGING UP BABY
This baby is waving a rattle while sitting in a high chair. The chair also served as a potty. It might have wheels on it to help the baby learn how to walk.

BULLY OFF
These two boys are playing a game similar to hockey. On the whole, team sports were ignored in favour of sporting activities where an individual could excel. Wrestling and athletics are two such examples. They were encouraged as training for war.

YOU ARE IT
Two girls play a kind of game in which the loser has to carry the winner. Girls had less free time than boys did. They were supposed to stay close to home and help their mothers with housework, cooking and looking after the younger children.

MAKE A SCROLL
You will need: 2 x 30cm rods of balsa wood, 5cm in diameter, 4 doorknobs, double-sided sticky tape, sheet of paper 30cm x 30cm, 1 x 7cm rod of balsa wood, 2cm in diameter, craft knife, paintbrush, PVA glue, ink powder.

1 Carefully screw a door knob into either end of each 30cm rod of balsa wood, or ask an adult to do it for you. These are the end pieces of the scroll.

2 Cut two pieces of double-sided sticky tape 30cm long. Stick one piece of tape along the top of the paper and another along the bottom.

3 Wrap the top of the paper once around one of the pieces of balsa wood. Repeat this step again for the second piece at the bottom of the paper.

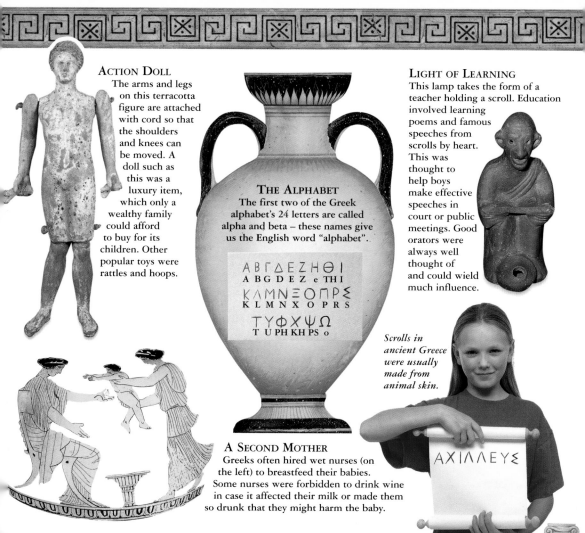

ACTION DOLL

The arms and legs on this terracotta figure are attached with cord so that the shoulders and knees can be moved. A doll such as this was a luxury item, which only a wealthy family could afford to buy for its children. Other popular toys were rattles and hoops.

THE ALPHABET

The first two of the Greek alphabet's 24 letters are called alpha and beta – these names give us the English word "alphabet".

A B Γ Δ E Z H Θ I
A BG D E Z e THI

K Λ M N Ξ O Π P Σ
K L M N X O P R S

T Y Φ X Ψ Ω
T U PH KH PS o

LIGHT OF LEARNING

This lamp takes the form of a teacher holding a scroll. Education involved learning poems and famous speeches from scrolls by heart. This was thought to help boys make effective speeches in court or public meetings. Good orators were always well thought of and could wield much influence.

Scrolls in ancient Greece were usually made from animal skin.

A SECOND MOTHER

Greeks often hired wet nurses (on the left) to breastfeed their babies. Some nurses were forbidden to drink wine in case it affected their milk or made them so drunk that they might harm the baby.

4 Ask an adult to help you with this step. Take the 7cm piece of balsa wood, and use your craft knife to sharpen the end of it into a point.

5 Paint the nib of your pen with glue. This will stop the wood from soaking up the ink. Add water to the ink powder to make ink.

6 Write some letters or a word on your scroll with your pen. We've translated the Greek alphabet above in the fact box. Use this as a guide.

7 We have copied out some letters in ancient Greek. You could also write a word. Ask a friend to translate what you have written, using the alphabet.

Greek Fashion

PHYSICAL BEAUTY AND AN ATTRACTIVE appearance were admired in ancient Greece in both men and women. Clothes were styled simply. Both sexes wore long tunics, draped loosely for comfort in the warm climate, and held in place with decorative pins or brooches. A heavy cloak was added for travelling or in bad weather. The tunics of soldiers and labourers were cut short, so they would not get in the way. Clothes were made of wool and linen, which were spun at home. Fabrics were coloured with dyes made from plants, insects and shellfish. The rich could afford more luxurious garments made from imported cotton or silk. Sandals were usually worn outdoors, though men sometimes wore boots. In such hot weather hats made of straw or wool kept off the sun. A tan was not admired because it signified outdoor work as a labourer or a slave. Men wore their hair short, and women wore it long, coiled up in elaborate styles sometimes decorated with ribbons.

SEE FOR YOURSELF
Glass mirrors were not known to the Greeks. Instead, they used highly polished bronze to see their reflection in. This mirror has a handle in the shaped of a woman. Winged sphinxes sit on her shoulders.

GOLDEN LION
This heavy bracelet dates from around the 4th or 5th century BC. It is made of solid gold and decorated with two lion heads. Gold was valuable because there was little of it to be found in Greece itself. Most of it was imported from Asia Minor or Egypt.

KEEP IT SIMPLE
The figurine above is wearing a peplos. This was a simple, sleeveless dress worn by Greek women. The only adornment was a belt tied underneath the bust. This statue comes from a Greek colony in southern Italy.

CHITON
You will need: tape measure, rectangle of cloth, scissors, pins, chalk, needle, thread, 12 metal buttons (with loops), cord.

1 Ask a friend to measure your width from wrist to wrist, double this figure. Measure your length from shoulder to ankle. Cut your cloth to these figures.

2 Fold the fabric in half widthways. Pin the two sides together. Draw a chalk line along the fabric, 2cm away from the edge of the fabric.

3 Sew along the chalk line. Then turn the material inside out, so the seam is on the inside. Refold the fabric so the seam is at the back.

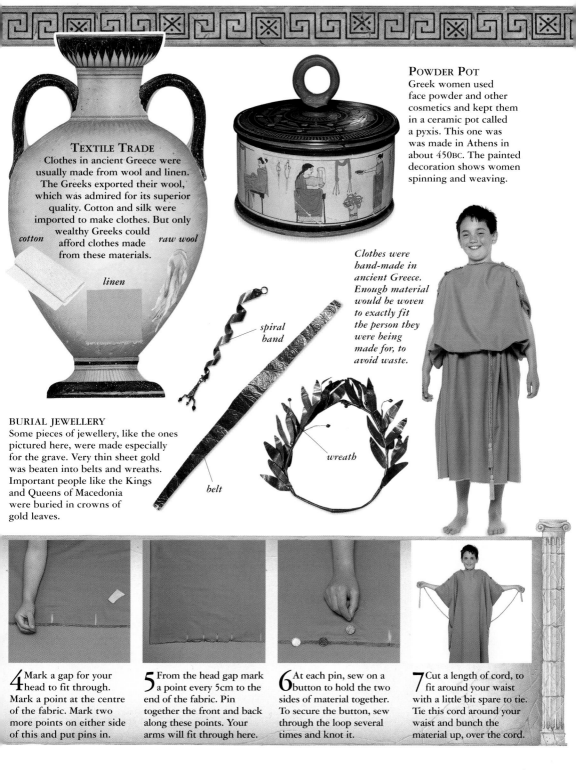

TEXTILE TRADE

Clothes in ancient Greece were usually made from wool and linen. The Greeks exported their wool, which was admired for its superior quality. Cotton and silk were imported to make clothes. But only wealthy Greeks could afford clothes made from these materials.

cotton

raw wool

linen

POWDER POT

Greek women used face powder and other cosmetics and kept them in a ceramic pot called a pyxis. This one was was made in Athens in about 450BC. The painted decoration shows women spinning and weaving.

Clothes were hand-made in ancient Greece. Enough material would be woven to exactly fit the person they were being made for, to avoid waste.

spiral band

BURIAL JEWELLERY

Some pieces of jewellery, like the ones pictured here, were made especially for the grave. Very thin sheet gold was beaten into belts and wreaths. Important people like the Kings and Queens of Macedonia were buried in crowns of gold leaves.

belt

wreath

4 Mark a gap for your head to fit through. Mark a point at the centre of the fabric. Mark two more points on either side of this and put pins in.

5 From the head gap mark a point every 5cm to the end of the fabric. Pin together the front and back along these points. Your arms will fit through here.

6 At each pin, sew on a button to hold the two sides of material together. To secure the button, sew through the loop several times and knot it.

7 Cut a length of cord, to fit around your waist with a little bit spare to tie. Tie this cord around your waist and bunch the material up, over the cord.

Gods and Goddesses

THE ANCIENT GREEKS BELIEVED that their gods looked like human beings and felt human emotions that led them to quarrel and fall in love. People also thought that the gods had magical powers and were immortal (meaning that they could live forever). With these powers, the gods could become invisible or disguise themselves and even turn people into animals. The gods were thought to influence all parts of human life and were kept busy with requests for help, from curing illness to ensuring a victory in war. In order to keep on the right side of the gods, individuals made sacrifices, left offerings and said prayers to them. Communities financed the building of temples, such as the Parthenon, paid for priests to look after them and organised festivals all in honour of the gods.

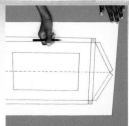

WINGED MESSENGER
Hermes was the god of eloquence and good luck. He was known for his mischievous and adventure-seeking nature. Zeus made him a messenger to the gods, to try and keep him occupied and out of trouble.

WILD GODDESS
Artemis was the goddess of wild places and animals, hunting and the moon. She was a skilful archer, whose arrows caused death and plagues. The power to heal was another of her attributes.

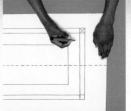

KING OF THE GODS
Zeus ruled over earth and heaven from Mount Olympus, (a real place on the border of Macedonia). He was thought to be a fair god who upheld order and justice. Wrongdoers could be punished with thunderbolts thrown by him.

PARTHENON

You will need: two pieces of white card 62cm by 38.5cm, ruler, black felt-tip pen, shoebox, scissors, blue, red and cream paint, paintbrush, PVA glue, piece of red corrugated card (approximately 39cm x 28.5cm), masking tape, craft knife, 160cm of balsa wood.

1 Draw a horizontal line across the centre of the card. Place the shoebox in the middle. Draw around it. Draw a second box 7cm away from this.

2 Draw a third box 2cm away from the second. Extend the lines of the second box to meet the third, to form four tabs, one in each corner.

3 To make the ends of the roof, draw half a diamond shape along the edge of the second box. Add on two rectangular tabs 1cm deep.

SYMBOLS

Each god and goddess was thought to be responsible for particular aspects of daily life. Each was represented by a symbol. Wheat symbolized Demeter, goddess of living things. Dionysus, god of the vine and wine, was appropriately represented by grapes.

wheat   grapes

GRAPES OF JOY

The god Dionysus was admired for his sense of fun. As god of fertility, the vine and wine, he was popular with both male and female worshippers. However, his followers were too enthusiastic for some city-states which banned celebrations in his name.

LOVE AND PROTECTION

Aphrodite was the goddess of love and beauty. Her vanity was instrumental in causing one of the biggest campaigns in Greek folklore, the Trojan War. Aphrodite promised to win Paris (son of the king of Troy) the love of the most beautiful mortal woman in the world – Helen. In return, Paris was to name Aphrodite as the most beautiful of all the goddesses. However, Helen was already married to the king of Sparta. When she left him to join Paris, the Greeks declared war on Troy. A bloodthirsty war followed in which heroes and gods clashed.

A POWERFUL FAMILY

Hera was the wife of Zeus and goddess of marriage. She was revered by women as the protector of their married lives. Her own marriage was marked by conflicts between herself and her husband. Her jealousy of rivals for her unfaithful husband's affections led her to persecute them. She was also jealous of Heracles, who was Zeus' son by another woman. Hera sent snakes to kill Heracles when he was a baby. Fortunately for Heracles, he had inherited his father's strength and killed the snakes before they harmed him.

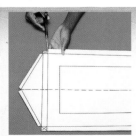

4 Repeat step 3 for the other end of the roof. Cut out both ends of the roof and cut into the four corner tabs. Get your painting equipment ready.

5 Turn the roof piece over. Draw and then paint the above design on to each end piece. Paint a blue, 1cm margin along each side. Leave to dry.

6 Turn the card over. Fold up all the sides of the second box. Fold in each corner tab and glue to its adjoining side. Fold down the rectangular tabs.

7 Cut the piece of red corrugated card in half. Stick them together with tape, along the unridged side. Turn them over and fold along the middle.

Temples and Festivals

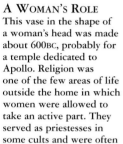

F ESTIVALS TO HONOUR THE GODS were important public occasions in ancient Greece. At the heart of each festival was a temple. At festival time, people flocked to the cities from the countryside. The greatest festivals were occasions of splendour and celebration. They involved processions, music, sports, prayers, animal sacrifices and offerings of food, all of which took place at the temple. The earliest Greek temples were built of wood, and none have survived. Later, temples built from stone echoed the simplicity of tree trunks in their columns and beams. The finest temples were made from marble. They were often decorated with brightly painted friezes, showing mythical stories of gods, goddesses and heroes. No expense was spared because temples were thought to be the gods' earthly homes. Each temple housed a statue of the god to which it was dedicated. The statues were usually elaborate and occasionally made from precious materials such as gold and ivory.

A WOMAN'S ROLE
This vase in the shape of a woman's head was made about 600BC, probably for a temple dedicated to Apollo. Religion was one of the few areas of life outside the home in which women were allowed to take an active part. They served as priestesses in some cults and were often thought to have the gift of seeing into the future.

GRAND ENTRANCE
The monumental gateways to the temple complex on top of the Acropolis were called the Propylaea. The temple beside it honoured Athena who is shown as Nike, goddess of victory.

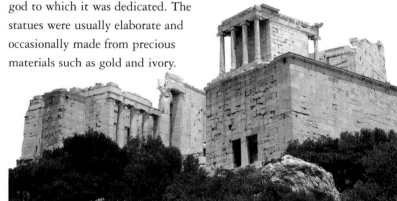

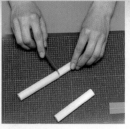

8 Glue the ends of the corrugated card to the folded up edges of the painted card. Leave to dry. This piece forms the roof to your temple.

9 Draw around the shoebox, on to the second piece of card. Draw another box 7cm away. Cut it out, leaving a 1cm border. This is the temple base.

10 Ask an adult to help you with this step. Cut out 32 columns from balsa wood. Each must be 5cm in height. Paint them cream and leave to dry.

11 Mark eight points along each edge of the second box by drawing around a column piece. Draw them an equal distance from each other.

A BIRTHDAY PARADE

A parade of horsemen, chariots and people leading sacrificial animals all formed part of the procession of the annual Panathenaic festival. It was held once a year, in Athens, to celebrate the goddess Athena's birthday. Every fourth year, the occasion involved an even more elaborate ceremony which lasted for six days. During the festivities, the statue of Athena was presented with a new robe.

A TEMPLE FOR THREE GODS

The Erectheum was built on the Acropolis, looking down on Athens 100 metres below. Unusually for a Greek temple, it housed the worship of more than one god: the legendary king Erectheus; Athena, guardian goddess of the city of Athens, and Poseidon, god of the sea. The columns in the shape of women are called caryatids.

BUILDING MATERIALS

Big buildings were often put up near a quarry or navigable water. Limestone was the most commonly used stone, and pine and cypress the commonest woods. Costly marble and cedar were reserved for temples and palaces.

marble   *limestone*

pine

THE LION'S MOUTH

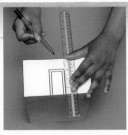

This gaping lion is actually a waterspout from an Athenian temple built in about 570BC. Although rainfall in Greece is low, waterspouts were necessary to allow storm water to drain off buildings with flat roofs. The lion was chosen as a symbol of strength and power.

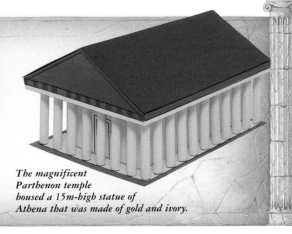

12 Draw a door on to a short end of the shoebox. Glue the roof on to the top of the shoebox. Paint the 1cm border on the temple base, blue.

13 Glue the columns into place, between the roof and the base. Dab glue on to their ends. Position them on the circles marked out in step 11.

The magnificent Parthenon temple housed a 15m-high statue of Athena that was made of gold and ivory.

Religion and Worship

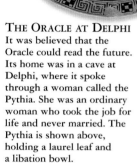

THE WORSHIP OF GODS and goddesses was at the heart of life in ancient Greece. Each god or goddess was in charge of a particular aspect of life, and the Greeks offered prayers and sacrifices according to their needs. The Greek people organized religious festivals, which were celebrated as major public holidays, and gave money to build temples and shrines. Pilgrims seeking favours or forgiveness from the gods made journeys which were often long and hard to sacred places.

The most sacred place of all was the shrine at Delphi in central Greece, which was dedicated to the god Apollo. The Greeks believed Delphi was the centre of the world. Individuals or families could worship privately at a shrine when they felt the need to do so, instead of gathering together with others on a special day. People offered prayers and sacrifices themselves, or they could ask a priest or priestess to approach the god on their behalf. Priests often came from a local noble family. Some inherited their position, others were elected or appointed by a city, others paid for the privilege of being a priest. Priests were highly respected, but their job was only a part-time one.

THE ORACLE AT DELPHI
It was believed that the Oracle could read the future. Its home was in a cave at Delphi, where it spoke through a woman called the Pythia. She was an ordinary woman who took the job for life and never married. The Pythia is shown above, holding a laurel leaf and a libation bowl.

ASK HERE
Questions for the Oracle were submitted in writing to the priests at the Oracle's cave, shown here. Wealthy people made animal sacrifices and paid large sums of money to hear the Oracle's predictions on personal matters such as love or business. Cities sent for advice on matters of public interest and importance. To prepare herself to receive the Oracle's answers, the Pythia first inhaled vapours from the Castalian spring and went into a trance. Her words were then interpreted for the enquirer by the priests.

FAMILY OFFERINGS

On this relief, carved around 200BC, a family is gathered to honour a statue of Zeus. As head of the household, the father leads the ritual. Standing at the altar, he holds a dish that might contain wine, oil or honey. Major occasions involved the sacrifice of an animal. Lesser ones might require an offering of cakes or fruit, or just a pinch of incense.

ACT OF WORSHIP

This female figure was found at a holy sanctuary and is dated around 2000BC. It is thought to be a woman raising her arms in an act of worship. There were rules on how to address the different gods. To speak to most gods, a worshipper held their arms to the sky. Underworld gods were addressed with the arms turned down. To communicate with marine gods the worshipper faced the sea water.

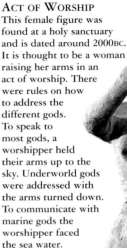

SACRIFICE TO THE GODS

This wooden panel, painted near Corinth around 500BC, shows a worshipper with musicians and priests about to sacrifice a sheep. Usually the meat was cooked and distributed amongst the worshippers, to be eaten. The fat and bones of the animal would be left on the altar for the gods. Animals were also sacrificed as a means of telling the future. Healthy organs meant good fortune, but diseased organs signified bad luck.

SPECIAL STOREHOUSE

This building was one of over a dozen treasuries built at Delphi to hold statues and precious offerings to the gods. The storehouses were ruined by an earthquake, and their contents plundered by treasure-hunters. Some storehouses, including this one, have been rebuilt by archaeologists.

Heroes and Myths

GREEK MYTHOLOGY IS RICH in stories of victorious heroes and heroines, quarrelling gods and goddesses and mysterious and unusual creatures. While keeping people entertained, the stories also tried to answer questions about how the world and humans came into existence. These powerful tales provided inspiration for ancient Greek art and material for their plays. In addition to this, they served as a valuable historical record and encouraged the Greeks to take pride in their vibrant cultural past. Traditionally, mythical stories were passed down through generations by word of mouth. Sometimes travelling bards were paid to recite poems which they had learnt by heart. Eventually, these tales came to be written down. The earliest of these that survive are thought to be the work of the poet Homer. Two poems that we know about are *The Odyssey* and *The Iliad*. Both tell tales of heroes battling against supernatural forces.

MONSTER KILLER
According to Greek lengend the Minotaur was half-bull and half-man. It lived in a maze called the labyrinth on the island of Crete. Many people had entered the maze but never come out. Each year the people of Athens were forced to send human sacrifices to feed the bull. The hero Theseus made it his mission to kill the Minotaur. A princess presented Theseus with a sword and a ball of string to help him. Theseus unwound the string as he walked through the maze. After killing the Minotaur he followed the string back to the entrance of the cave.

SNAKE STRANGLER
The super-strong Heracles was the only human being to become a Greek god. This Roman fresco shows him as a baby strangling serpents sent by the jealous goddess Hera to kill him.

HEAD OF MEDUSA
You will need: board, self-drying modelling clay, rolling pin, ruler, modelling tool, pencil, sandpaper, acrylic paints, one small and one large paintbrush, varnish (1 part water to 1 part PVA glue).

1 With a rolling pin, roll out a slab of clay 20cm by 20cm and 2cm thick. With the modelling tool, cut out a head in the shape shown in the picture.

2 Shape a small piece of clay into a nose. Mould it on to the head with your fingers. Use the modelling tool to smooth the edges into the face.

3 Carve a mouth with lots of teeth and two eyes and etch a gruesome design into the head. Press the end of a pencil into the eyes to make eyeballs.

STONY STARE

Medusa was a winged monster with hair of snakes. She was one of three such female gorgons. Medusa had a face so horrific that any human who looked directly at it was turned to stone. The only way to kill her was to cut off her head. Medusa, whose name means "cunning", outwitted several would-be killers. The hero Perseus finally killed her with help from Athena and Hermes. They lent Perseus a magic cap to make him invisible, a sickle to cut off Medusa's head and a shield in which to see her reflection. Even dead, Medusa remained powerful. Perseus killed his enemy Polydectes by forcing him to look at her face.

FOOLING THE GIANT

King Odysseus was a mythical hero who had many adventures. One escapade found him captured in a cave by a one-eyed giant. To escape, Odysseus stabbed out the giant's eye and rode out of the cave clinging to the underside of a ram.

The word gorgon in Greek suggests the monster's glaring eyes.

FLYING HORSE

The winged horse Pegasus appeared on the coins of Corinth as the city's symbol. Pegasus helped Bellerophon, a Corinthian hero, in his battles. First against the Chimaera which was a monster with a lion's head, a goat's middle and a snake's tail and then against the Amazons, a race of female warriors.

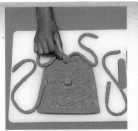

4 Between the palms of your hands, roll out four thin strips of clay to represent the snakes on Medusa's head. Press them into place as shown above.

5 Press a finger down on the end of each roll to make a snake's head. Use the modelling tool and pencil to carve in scales on the snakes' bodies.

6 The head needs to dry completely before you can paint the face. To dry it, let it sit for a few hours on either side. Be careful when you turn it over.

7 When the head is completely dry, sand with fine sandpaper. Paint the face in black, red, white and gold as shown here. Leave to dry and varnish.

Death and the Underworld

PEOPLE IN ANCIENT GREECE would live only about half as long as people in the West do today. It was common for sickly children to die in infancy. Large numbers of men were killed in battle, women often died in childbirth and epidemics could wipe out whole communities.

Most Greeks believed that after death, their souls roamed the Underworld, a cold and gloomy region where the wicked were sent to be punished. In *The Odyssey* the hero Achilles says, "I'd rather be a common labourer on Earth working for a poor man than lord of all the legions of the dead." Very few people, it was thought were good enough to be sent to the Isles of the Blessed. If they were, they could spend eternity amusing themselves with sports and music. People who had led exceptional lives (such as the hero Heracles) were thought destined to become gods and live on Mount Olympus.

When someone died, their body was either buried or cremated. The Greeks believed that only when the body or ashes had been covered with earth, could its spirit leave for the Underworld. Graves contained possessions for use in the afterlife, and women left offerings of food and drink at the graveside to help the spirits.

FRAGRANT FAREWELL
Graves were sometimes marked with lekythoi, white clay flasks holding a perfumed oil that had been used to anoint the body. The lekythoi were usually painted with farewell scenes, funerals or images of the dead.

FOOD FOR THOUGHT
The tradition of leaving food at gravesides began in Mycenaean times. Then people could be buried with their armour, cooking pots and even pets and slaves to accompany them. By 300BC the Greeks were leaving food such as wine and eggs at gravesides as nourishment for the dead.

wine

eggs

A DIVE INTO THE UNKNOWN
The figure on the painting above is shown leaping from life into the ocean of death. The pillars were put up by Heracles to mark the end of the known, living world. This diver was found painted on the walls of a tomb.

TUG OF LOVE

This painting from a vase shows Persephone with
Hades, her husband and ruler of the underworld.
Hades dragged Persephone from earth down to the
Underworld. Her distraught mother, the goddess
Demeter, neglected the crops to search for her. Zeus
intervened and decided that Persephone would spend
six months of every year with her mother and the other
six with Hades. Whenever her daughter returned in
spring, Demeter would look after the crops. However,
Demeter grew sad each time her daughter went back
to the Underworld and wintertime would set in.

LAST JOURNEY

The body of a dead person was taken from their home
to the grave by mourners bearing tributes. To express
their grief, they might cut off their hair, tear at their
cheeks with their nails until blood flowed, and wear
black robes. If there was a funeral feast at the graveside,
the dishes were smashed afterwards and left there.

ROYAL TOMB

Women were less likely to be honoured by tombstone
portraits than men. Philis, seen above, was an exception
to this rule, possibly because she was the daughter of a
powerful Spartan king. Athens enforced a law against
extravagant tombs. No more than 10 men could be
employed for any more than three days to build one.

A Trip to the Theatre

THE FIRST GREEK DRAMAS were performed at temples in honour of the gods. The stories they told were a mixture of history and myth, and featured the adventures of famous Greeks as well as the exploits of gods and legendary heroes. The all-male cast was backed up by a chorus of male singers and dancers, who provided a commentary on the action. Drama became so popular that large open-air theatres were built in major cities and at sacred places such as Delphi and Epidauros. Prizes were awarded to the best dramatists. The three most famous writers of tragedies were Aeschylus, Sophocles and Euripides. They wrote over 300 plays between them, but only a tenth survive. The works of another 150 known writers have all been lost. Greek drama is still performed in theatres today.

SEAT OF HONOUR
Most theatre-goers sat on stone benches. This carved chair might have been reserved for an important official or a sponsor who had paid the expenses of a public performance.

THEATRE
Large theatres like this one at Ephesus on the coast of modern Turkey had excellent acoustics and could hold an audience of over 10,000. The stage, a circle of beaten earth in the centre of the theatre, was called the orchestra, which means 'dancing floor'.

BIRD MASK
You will need: balloon, petroleum jelly, papier-mâché (newspaper soaked in 1 part water to 2 parts PVA glue), black pen, scissors, paint, paintbrush, 2 pieces of ochre card (20cm x 10cm), glue stick, pair of compasses, two pieces of red card (40cm x 40cm), cord.

1 Blow up a balloon to head-size. Cover front and sides in petroleum jelly. Add several layers of papier-mâché. When this is dry, pop the balloon.

2 Ask a friend to mark the position of your eyes and the top of your ears on the mask. Cut out small holes at these points. Paint the mask as shown at the end.

3 Draw and cut out two beak shapes. Repeat for both pieces of ochre card. Mark a point 1cm along the bottom of the beak (the edge marked *a* above).

COMIC TURN
A figurine from the 2nd century BC shows a masked comic actor sitting on an altar. He is hiding in a temple to escape punishment. Comedies were much enjoyed, but considered inferior to tragedies.

SUFFERING COMEDY
In this comic scene the actor in the middle plays the part of a centaur called Cheiron. Centaurs were mythical creatures that were half-man and half-horse. Cheiron was the wisest of them all. But he was also seen as a figure of fun because he was immortal yet suffered from a fatal wound.

PLAYING PARTS
Greek actors wore masks to represent different characters and emotions. The same actor could play different roles in one drama by changing his mask. All the players were male, but some took female roles. Women were not allowed on the stage, and may even have been barred from joining the audience.

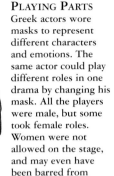

To wear your mask, thread a piece of cord through the holes on each side of the head. Tie them together at the back. This mask is modelled on an original worn by the chorus in Aristophanes' comedy, The Birds.

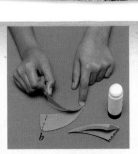

4 Draw a line from the corner of the top edge (*b*) to this point. Fold back the line. Glue the two pieces together along the top edge. Repeat.

5 Put the compass point in the corner of the red card. Draw two arcs, one with a 10cm radius and one with a 20cm radius. Cut out as one piece.

6 Cut feather shapes into the top of the red card. Draw an arc 5cm from the bottom. Cut out 14 tabs, as shown. Repeat both steps for the other piece of card.

7 Glue the two red cards together at the top. Glue the tabs down on to the top of the mask. Glue the beak pieces to the mask. Draw on the eyes.

Music and Dance

MUSIC AND DANCE WERE BOTH AN important part of Greek life. People sang, played and danced at religious ceremonies. Music was enjoyed for pleasure and entertainment at family celebrations, dramatic performances, feasts and drinking parties. Few written records remain of the notes played, but examples of the instruments do. The most popular instruments were the pipes. They were wind instruments similar to the oboe or clarinet. One pipe on its own was called the *aulos*, two played together were known as *auloi*. The stringed lyre and flute were other popular instruments. The stringed lyre produced solemn and dignified music. It was often played by men of noble birth to accompany a poetry recital. The flute was more usually played by slaves or dancing girls.

BREATH CONTROL
The leather strap tied around the auloi-player's cheeks helped to focus the power of his breath. One tube of the auloi supplied the melody, while the other produced an accompanying drone to give more depth to the sound. The aulos had as few as three or as many as 24 fingerholes for making the different notes.

Greek soldiers complained that lack of music was a hardship of war. Spartan soldiers resolved this problem by blowing tunes on pipes as they marched. Music was believed to have magical powers. Greek legend tells of Orpheus soothing savage beasts by playing his lyre. Another myth tells how Amphion (a son of Zeus) made stones move on their own and built a wall around the city of Thebes, by playing his lyre.

BANG! CRASH!
The bronze figurine above is playing the cymbals. They made a sound similar to castanets. The Greeks used the cymbals to accompany dancing. Other percussion instruments included wooden clappers and hand-held drums, like tambourines.

TIMPANON
You will need: scissors, corrugated card, tape measure, plate, white card, pair of compasses, pencil, PVA glue, tape, strips of newspaper, cream paper, red and purple felt-tip pens, ochre card, red and yellow ribbons.

1 Cut out a strip of corrugated card 5cm wide. Wrap it around a dinner plate. Add 6cm on to the length of this card and cut it off.

2 Put the plate upside down on the white card. Draw around it. Draw another circle 3cm inside the first. Cut this out to make a ring.

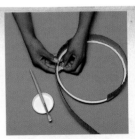

3 Glue the cardboard strip that you made in step 1 to the edge of the cardboard ring you made in step 2. Then tape them together for extra hold.

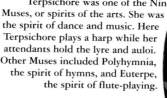

DIVINE MUSIC

Terpsichore was one of the Nine Muses, or spirits of the arts. She was the spirit of dance and music. Here Terpsichore plays a harp while her attendants hold the lyre and auloi. Other Muses included Polyhymnia, the spirit of hymns, and Euterpe, the spirit of flute-playing.

PERCUSSION

The timpanon was a tambourine made of animal skin, stretched over a frame. It was tapped to provide rhythmic accompaniment at dances or recitals. Stringed and wind instruments were thought superior because they made fitting music for solemn or exclusive occasions. Drums, cymbals and clappers were associated with buskers.

To play the timpanon tap on it with your fingers, as the ancient Greeks would have done.

ENTERTAINING

In this plate painting a young man plays the auloi while his female companion dances. Professional musicians were often hired to entertain guests at dinner parties. Sometimes the musicians were household slaves.

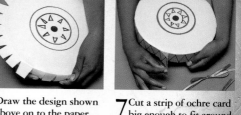

4 Make up some papier mâché solution with 1 part glue to 2 parts water. Soak strips of newspaper in it and cover the card ring with the wet strips.

5 Draw around the plate on to cream paper. Draw another circle 5cm outside this. To make tabs, cut out about 28 small triangles around the edge.

6 Draw the design shown above on to the paper. Place the paper over the top of the card ring. Dab glue on each tab and stick on to the corrugated card.

7 Cut a strip of ochre card big enough to fit around the timpanon. Decorate it as above and glue on. Make 4 bows with the ribbons and glue around the edge.

Arts and Crafts

THE ARTISTS AND CRAFTWORKERS of ancient Greece were admired for the quality of their work. They produced many objects of art including beautiful pottery, fine jewellery and impressive sculptures. Materials they worked with included stone, gold, silver, glass, gemstones and bronze. They also used wood, leather, bone, ivory and horn.

Most goods were made on a small scale in workshops surrounding the agora (market-place). A craftsman might work on his own or with the help of his family and a slave or two. In the larger workshops of such cities as Athens, slaves laboured to produce bulk orders of popular goods. These might include shields, pottery and metalwork which were traded around the Mediterranean Sea for a large profit.

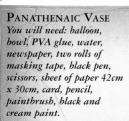

BULK PRODUCTION
Above is a terracotta mould, and on the right, the casting taken from it. Making a mould was a skilled and time-consuming task. Using a mould made it possible to produce items faster and more cheaply than carving each piece individually.

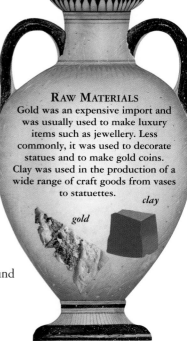

RAW MATERIALS
Gold was an expensive import and was usually used to make luxury items such as jewellery. Less commonly, it was used to decorate statues and to make gold coins. Clay was used in the production of a wide range of craft goods from vases to statuettes.

clay

gold

PANATHENAIC VASE
You will need: balloon, bowl, PVA glue, water, newspaper, two rolls of masking tape, black pen, scissors, sheet of paper 42cm x 30cm, card, pencil, paintbrush, black and cream paint.

1 Blow up the balloon. Cover it with two layers of papier mâché (paper soaked in one part glue, two parts water). Leave on one side to dry.

2 Using a roll of masking tape as a guide, draw and cut out two holes at the top and bottom of the balloon. Throw away the burst balloon.

3 Roll the sheet of paper into a tube. Make sure that it will fit through the middle of the roll of masking tape. Secure the tube with tape or glue.

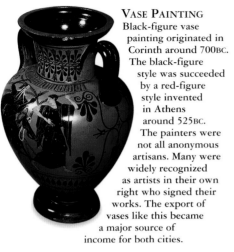

VASE PAINTING

Black-figure vase painting originated in Corinth around 700BC. The black-figure style was succeeded by a red-figure style invented in Athens around 525BC. The painters were not all anonymous artisans. Many were widely recognized as artists in their own right who signed their works. The export of vases like this became a major source of income for both cities.

HOT WORK

In this scene two blacksmiths are forging metal at a brick furnace. Metal goods were expensive to produce. The furnaces themselves were fuelled by charcoal (burnt wood) which was expensive to make because wood was scarce in Greece. In addition, supplies of metal often had to be imported, sometimes from great distances. For example, tin, which was mixed with local copper to make bronze, was brought from southern Spain.

Amphorae like this one were given as prizes at the Panathenaic games. They were decorated with sporting images.

GOLD PECTORAL

This gold pectoral, made on the island of Rhodes in the 7th century BC, was meant to be worn across the breast. Gold was rare in Greece. It was usually imported at great expense from surrounding areas such as Egypt or Asia Minor.

4 Push the tube through the middle of the balloon. Tape into place. Push a roll of masking tape over the bottom of the paper tube and tape.

5 Tape the second roll of masking tape to the top of the tube. Make sure that both rolls are securely attached at either end of the paper tube.

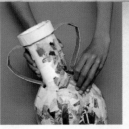

6 Cut two strips of card, 15cm long. Attach them to either side of the vase, as seen above. Cover the entire vase with papier mâché, and leave to dry.

7 Using a pencil, copy the pattern seen on the vase in the picture above on to your vase. Carefully paint in the pattern and leave on one side to dry.

Sports and Fitness

FITNESS WAS VALUED as an essential preparation for war. But the Greeks also enjoyed sport for its own sake, and most cities had a public gymnasium, where men gathered to train and to relax. They preferred individual contests to team games, and often celebrated religious festivals by running races to honour the gods. This is how the Olympic Games first began in 776BC. It was held every four years, and expanded to include long jump, throwing the discus and javelin, boxing, wrestling, chariot races and horse races, as well as poetry and drama competitions. There was also a gruesome fighting sport called *pankration* (total power), a combination of boxing and wrestling in which the only forbidden tactics were eye-gouging and biting. During the Olympics, all wars between cities stopped, so that people could journey safely to the Games. Women were banned from competing or watching the Olympics but they had their own games, also held at Olympia in honour of the goddess Hera.

THE WINNER
A Greek king (on the right) hands a wreath of victory to an Olympic winner. A priest stands by to remind contestants that they are on sacred ground. There were no cash prizes at the Olympics. However, because they brought honour to their cities, winners were sometimes given money on their return home, or even free meals for life.

SPORTING STARS
This vase painting shows a long-jumper holding weights, a discus thrower and two men with javelins. They represent three of the five sports that made up the pentathlon ("penta" is Greek for five). The other two were running and wrestling. The pentathlon began with a foot race, which was followed by javelin throwing, then discus throwing and finished with the long jump. The two contestants who scored highest in these events then wrestled one another to decide the overall winner. Most sportsmen were amateurs. There were also many professionals who trained and competed for a single event.

SPORTING FACILITIES

Much of ancient Olympia, where the first Olympic Games were held, has been uncovered by archaeologists working there since 1829. There were many facilities serving the competitors and spectators. At the centre of the complex were two large temples dedicated to Hera and Zeus. Amongst the buildings surrounding the temples were a hostel, restaurants, a huge gymnasium for training in and a hippodrome for horse and chariot races. Despite its size, Olympia never became a city, because it had no permanent citizens or local government.

DANGEROUS GAME

At the end of a chariot race, an armed man jumped off of the moving vehicle and ran a foot race. This event was eventually dropped from the Games because it often provoked laughter at undignified accidents instead of admiration for the competitors' skill. Chariots frequently overturned with disastrous results. As many as 40 competitors might take part, racing 12 laps of a 1,100 metre circuit. The winner was the owner of the chariot and horses, not the driver.

GOING THE DISTANCE

Long-jumpers carried heavy weights to give them more momentum. The weights also helped them to balance. They jumped on to a bed of crumbled earth (skamma) raked smooth. This helped them to avoid injuries and leave a clear footprint so that the judges could measure the distance they had covered.

STEP THIS WAY

Competitors taking part in the original Olympic Games entered the stadium through this archway. The grassy embankments surrounding the stadium could seat up to 40,000 spectators.

GETTING READY

An athlete binds his hair with a cloth to keep it out of the way. Most athletes competed naked in the Olympic Games. It was felt that sport glorified male strength and beauty. When women competed against each other in the games to honour Hera, they wore short tunics.

Science and Philosophy

THE GREEKS COULD AFFORD to devote time to studying and thinking because their civilization was both wealthy and secure. They learned astrology from the Babylonians, and mathematics from the Egyptians. They used their scientific knowledge to develop many practical inventions, including water clocks, cogwheels, gearing systems, slot machines and steam engines. However these devices were not widely used as there were many slave workers.

Philosophy is a Greek word, meaning love of knowledge. The Greeks developed different branches of philosophy. The three main branches were politics (how best to govern), ethics (how to behave well) and cosmology (how the universe worked).

Greek thinkers recognized the value of recording their observations, and of carrying out experiments. But they did not always see their limitations. Aristotle showed how evaporation could turn salt water into fresh water, and wrongly assumed that wine would turn into water by the same process.

GREAT THINKER
The philosopher Aristotle (384–322BC) is often recognised as the founder of Western science. He pioneered a rational approach to the world, based on observing and recording evidence. For three years, he was the tutor of Alexander the Great.

CLOCK TOWER
The Tower of the Winds in Athens contains a water clock. The original Egyptian invention was a bucket of water with a tiny hole in the bottom. As the water dripped out of it, the water level fell past scored marks on the inside of the bucket, measuring time. The Greeks improved on this design, using the flow of water to work a dial with a moving pointer.

ARCHIMEDES SCREW
You will need: clean, empty plastic bottle, scissors, modelling clay, strong tape, length of clear plastic tube, bowl of water, blue food colouring, empty bowl.

1 Cut off the bottle top. Place the plasticine into the middle of the bottle, about 5cm from the end. Punch in a hole at this point with the scissors.

2 Cut a strip of tape the same length as the bottle. Tape it to the middle of the bottle. This will give the tube extra grip later on.

3 Twist the length of tube around the bottle. Go from one end of the bottle to the other. Tape the tube into place over the first piece of tape.

WATER LIFTER

When the Archimedes screw is turned, it lifts water from one level to another. It is named after its inventor, the scientist Archimedes, who lived about 287–211BC, in Syracuse, Sicily. It is still in use today.

FATHER OF GEOMETRY

Euclid (about 330–260BC) was a mathematician. He lived in the Greek-Egyptian city of Alexandria. He is known as the father of geometry, which comes from the Greek word for "measuring land". Geometry is the study of points, lines, curves, surfaces and their measurements. His geometry textbook was called *Elements*. It was still widely used in the early part of the 20th century AD, over 2,000 years after his death. This picture shows the front page of an edition of the book that was printed in London in 1732.

4 Place a few drops of the blue food colouring into the bowl of water. Stir it in so that the colour mixes evenly throughout the water.

5 Place one end of the bottle into the bowl of blue water. Make sure that the tube at the opposite end is pointing towards the empty bowl.

6 Twist the bottle around in the blue water. As you do so, you will see the water start travelling up the tube and gradually filling the other bowl.

The invention of the Archimedes screw made it possible for farmers to water their fields with irrigation channels. It saved them from walking back and forth to the river with buckets.

Medical Matters

THE GREEKS BELIEVED THAT ultimately only the gods had the power to heal wounds and cure sickness. But they also developed a scientific approach to medicine. Greek doctors could treat injuries and battle wounds by bandaging and bone-setting. They relied on rest, diet and herbal drugs to cure disease. However, they were powerless against large-scale epidemics, such as the plague. Doctors believed that good health was dependent on the balance between four main body fluids – blood, phlegm and yellow and black bile. If this balance was disturbed, they attempted to restore it by applying heated metal cups to the body to draw off harmful fluids. The sweat this produced convinced them it worked. This mistaken practice continued in Europe until the 17th century.

FATHER OF MEDICINE
Hippocrates founded a medical school around 400BC. He taught that observation of symptoms was more important than theory. His students took an oath to use their skills to heal and never to harm.

BODY BALANCE
Bleeding was a common procedure, intended to restore the body's internal balance. This carving shows surgical instruments and cups used for catching blood. Sometimes bleeding may have helped to drain off poisons, but more than often it can only have weakened the patient.

HEALING GOD
The Greeks worshipped Asclepius, as the god of healing. He is shown here with a serpent, representing wisdom. Invalids seeking a cure made a visit to his shrine.

LEG OFFERING
You will need: self-drying modelling clay, rolling pin, board, ruler, modelling tool, paintbrush, cream acrylic paint.

1 Divide the clay into two pieces. With the rolling pin, roll out one piece to 15cm length, 10cm width and 2cm depth. This is the base for the leg.

2 Roll out the second piece of clay. With the modelling tool, carve out a leg and foot shape. It should be big enough to fit on one side of the base.

3 Gently place the leg on the right-hand side of the base. With the tool, draw a shallow outline around the leg into the base. Remove the leg.

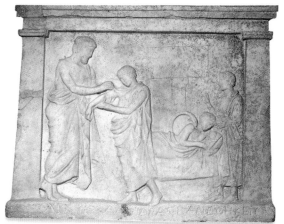

THEORY AND PRACTICE

Patients would explain their dreams to doctors, who then prescribed treatment. In this relief, a healing spirit in the shape of a serpent visits a sleeping patient. In the foreground, the physician bandages the wounded arm.

NATURAL HEALING

The Greeks used a large variety of natural treatments to cure illnesses. Herbal remedies were particularly popular. Lentils, mustard and honey may have been combined in a poultice and applied to a wound.

lentils

mustard

honey

TOOL KIT

The Greeks used bronze surgical instruments, including forceps and probes. Surgery was usually a last resort. Even when it was successful, patients often died from the shock and pain, or from infection afterwards. Operations on limbs were more successful than those on body cavities such as the chest or stomach.

4 With the tool, score the outline with lines. Carve the ancient Greek message seen in the picture above next to the leg.

5 Mould the leg onto the scored area of the base. Use your fingers to press the sides of the leg in place. Carve toes and toenails into the foot.

6 Paint over the entire leg offering with a cream colour, to give it an aged look. Leave to dry overnight. Your leg offering is done.

This model is based on a real one left as a thank-offering to the god Asclepius by someone whose leg was affected by illness. This was a common practice in ancient Greece.

Travel and Trade

THE MOUNTAINOUS LANDSCAPE of ancient Greece was too rocky for carts or chariots, so most people rode donkeys or walked. Sea travel was simpler – the many islands of the eastern Mediterranean made it possible to sail from one port to another without losing sight of land. Merchant ships were sailed because they were too heavy to be rowed. Greek sailors had no compasses. By day they relied on coastal landmarks and at night they navigated by the stars. However, neither method was reliable. A sudden storm could throw a ship off course or cause it to sink.

Merchant ships carried olive oil, wool, wine, silver, fine pottery and slaves. These goods were traded in return for wheat and timber, both of which were scarce in Greece. Other imported products included tin, copper, ivory, gold, silk and cotton.

COINAGE
The gold coin above shows Zeus, ruler of the gods, throwing a thunderbolt. Coins were invented in Lydia (in present-day Turkey) around 635BC, and introduced to Greece soon afterwards. Before that, the Greeks had used bars of silver and rods of iron as money. Greek coins were also made of silver, bronze and electrum, a mixture of gold and silver.

SEA GOD
Poseidon was the god of the sea, horses and earthquakes. Sailors prayed and made sacrifices to him, hoping for protection against storms, fogs and pirates. He is usually pictured holding a trident, the three-pronged spear used by Greek fishermen. At the trading port of Corinth, the Isthmian Games were held every other year in honour of Poseidon.

HARD CURRENCY
The first coins may have been used to pay mercenary soldiers, rather than for trading or collecting taxes. The earliest coins usually bore a religious symbol or the emblem of a city. Only later did they show the head of a ruler. The coin on the right shows the sea god Poseidon with his trident. The coin on the left bears the rose of Rhodes. Many countries that traded with the Greeks copied their idea of using coins for money.

SHIPPING

The ship on the right is a sail-powered merchantman. The criss-cross lines represent a wooden and rope catwalk stretched over the cargo, which was stored in an uncovered hold. Liquids such as wine and olive oil were transported and sold in long narrow pottery jars called amphorae, which could be neatly stacked in the hold. Merchant ships faced many dangers that could cause the loss of their cargo. Pirates and storms were the worst of these.

WEIGHING OUT

Most dry goods were sold loose and had to be weighed out on a balance such as this one. Officials would oversee the proceedings to ensure that they were fair. They stopped merchants and traders from cheating one another. In Athens, these officials were known as metronomoi. It was essential for a merchant to familiarize himself with the various systems of weights and measures used in different countries.

MARKET STALLS

The agora or market-place was to be found in the centre of every Greek town. Market stalls sold a wide range of goods including meat, vegetables, eggs, cheese and fish. Fish was laid out on marble slabs to keep it cool and fresh.

clams

prawns

mussels

RIDING

Mountainous countryside made travelling overland difficult in Greece. The few roads that did exist were in poor condition. For most people, walking was the only way to reach a destination. Horses were usually only used by wealthy people to travel on. Donkeys and mules were used by tradesmen to transport large loads. Longer journeys were made by boat.

Fighting Forces

ALL GREEK MEN were expected to fight in their city's army. In Sparta the army was on duty all year round. In other parts of Greece men gave up fighting in autumn to bring in the harvest and make the wine. The only full-time soldiers in these states were the personal bodyguards of a ruler or mercenaries who fought for anyone who paid them. Armies consisted mainly of hoplites (armoured infantry), cavalry (soldiers on horseback) and a group of foot soldiers armed with stones and bows and arrows. The hoplites were the most important fighting force as they engaged in hand-to-hand combat. The cavalry was less effective in war because riders had no stirrups, which made charging with a lance impossible, as the rider would fall off on contact. They were used for scouting, harassing a beaten enemy and carrying messages.

HARD HELMET

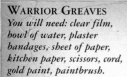

This bronze helmet from Corinth was fashioned to protect the face. It has guards for the cheeks and the bridge of the nose. Iron later replaced bronze as the main metal for weapons.

BOWMEN
The Greek army usually employed Scythian archers to fight for them. Archers were useful for fighting in mountainous countryside where they could position themselves above the enemy. Some Greeks soldiers did fight with bows and arrows. They fought in small units known as *psiloi*. But most of the soldiers in these units could only afford simple missile weapons, such as a javelin or slings from which they shot stones.

WARRIOR GREAVES
You will need: clear film, bowl of water, plaster bandages, sheet of paper, kitchen paper, scissors, cord, gold paint, paintbrush.

1 Ask a friend to help you with steps 1 to 3. Loosely cover both of your lower legs (from your ankle to the top of your knee) in clear film.

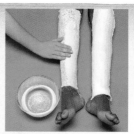

2 Soak each plaster bandage in water. Working from one side of your leg to the other, smooth the bandage over the front of each leg.

3 Carefully remove each greave. Set them on some paper. Dampen some kitchen paper and use it to smooth the greaves down. Leave them to dry.

A RARE SIGHT IN BATTLE

Chariots were not often used in warfare because they could only be used on flat plains. There were usually two people in the chariot, one to drive it, and the other to fight from the back of it.

FIGHTING FORCES

Tin and copper were used to make bronze, the main materials for weapons and armour. Bronze is harder than pure copper and, unlike iron, does not rust. As there was no tin in Greece, it was imported from faraway lands.

copper   *tin*

HOPLITES

This fighting force was made up of middle-class men who could afford the weaponry. A hoplite's armoury consisted of a shield, helmet, spear, sword and greaves. Helmets were made of bronze and were usually crested with horsehair. The body was protected by a bronze cuirass, a one-piece breast- and back-plate, under which the hoplites wore a leather cuirass. Shields were usually round and decorated with a symbol.

4 Trim the edges of the greaves, to make them look neat. Measure four lengths of cord to fit around your leg, below the knee and above the ankle.

5 Turn the greaves on to their front. Lay the cord in place at the point where you want to tie them to your leg. Fix them into place using wet bandages.

6 Leave the plaster bandages to dry, with the cord in place. Now paint each greave with a gold paint. Once they are dry, tie them on.

Greaves were attached to the lower leg to protect it in battle. They were worn by hoplites.

Warfare

WHEN THE GREEKS WENT TO WAR it was usually to engage in raids and sieges of rival city states. Major battles with foreign powers were rare, but the results could be devastating. Army commanders had to choose their ground with care and rely on the discipline and training of their troops to carry through their overall plan. Once the fighting had started, it was almost impossible to control large masses of men or to change their orders. The death or flight of a few key leaders could cause a whole army to break up in chaos.

The core of a Greek army consisted of heavily armed foot soldiers (hoplites) who fought together in solid blocks called phalanxes. As long as they stayed calm, the soldiers were protected by their bristling spears, overlapping shields and sheer weight of numbers. If they panicked and broke up, it was easy for the enemy to pick off individual hoplites, weighed down by 30 kg of armour.

HEROES AT PLAY
Achilles and Ajax were legendary Greek heroes of the Trojan war. This vase shows them playing dice. This game was played by soldiers to while away the time or to decide the share-out of loot. The outcome of the game was sometimes interpreted as a symbol of fate and death.

GREEK TRICK
The Greeks ended the siege of Troy by leaving a wooden horse outside the city and pretending to sail away. The Trojans dragged the horse inside, not realizing that it was filled with Greek soldiers. The soldiers crept out of the horse at night and opened the city gates to let their comrades in. Together they overran the city.

CLOSE COMBAT
The Greek soldiers and heroes of Homer's time fought each other in a series of one-to-one duels. In this engraving, Greek and Trojan warriors are fighting hand to hand. However, as armies began to use more hoplites, methods of fighting changed to accommodate them. This involved men fighting together in a phalanx.

VICTORY AGAINST THE ODDS

At the battle of Issus in 333BC Alexander the Great (left) led the charge against the Persian king Darius (in the chariot). Darius fled in panic, and his much larger army broke up. The Persian army was made up of many different peoples from all over his vast empire. They spoke different languages and did not trust each other, making control harder. In contrast, Alexander had tight control and long experience of fighting with his troops.

SEA FIGHT

In 480BC, the battle of Salamis ended a Persian invasion into Greek territory. The Persians had more and faster ships, but the Greeks defeated them by luring them into narrow waters where these advantages were lost. Then the crowded Persian vessels were rammed to pieces by the much heavier Greek ships.

END OF AN EMPIRE

Greece won another decisive victory against Persia in 331BC. At the battle of Gaugemala the Persian cavalry outnumbered Alexander's almost five to one and the infantry two to one. Discipline, daring and determination overcame the odds and the Persian army lost the battle. Consequently, the Persian empire finally yielded to Alexander.

ANCIENT ROME

Almost 2,000 years ago the powerful Roman Empire ruled the western world. Legions of soldiers marched through country after country, conquering and transforming the primitive lifestyles they came across. But within 400 years, the Empire fell as Rome was destroyed by invaders and the last emperor was deposed.

PHILIP STEELE
Consultant: Jenny Hall, Museum of London

The Story of Rome

T HE CITY OF ROME today is a bustling place, full of traffic and crowds. But if you could travel back in time to around 800BC, you would find only a few small villages on peaceful, wooded hillsides along the banks of the river Tiber. According to legend, Rome was founded here in 753BC. In the centuries that followed, the Romans came to dominate Italy and the Mediterranean. They farmed and traded and fought for new lands. Rome grew to become the centre of a vast empire that stretched across Europe into Africa and Asia. The Empire lasted for centuries and brought a sophisticated way of life to vast numbers of people. Many Roman buildings and artefacts still survive to show us what life was like in the Roman Empire.

ROMAN ITALY
As the city of Rome prospered, the Romans gradually conquered neighbouring tribes. By 250BC they controlled most of Italy. This map shows some of the important towns and cities of that time.

ANCIENT AND MODERN
In Rome today, people live alongside the temples, marketplaces and public buildings of the past. This is the Colosseum, a huge arena called an amphitheatre. It was used for staging games and fights, and first opened to the public in AD80.

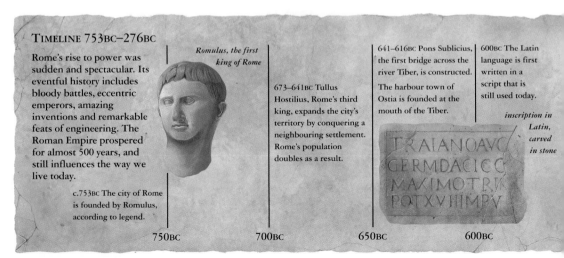

TIMELINE 753BC–276BC

Rome's rise to power was sudden and spectacular. Its eventful history includes bloody battles, eccentric emperors, amazing inventions and remarkable feats of engineering. The Roman Empire prospered for almost 500 years, and still influences the way we live today.

c.753BC The city of Rome is founded by Romulus, according to legend.

Romulus, the first king of Rome

673–641BC Tullus Hostilius, Rome's third king, expands the city's territory by conquering a neighbouring settlement. Rome's population doubles as a result.

641–616BC Pons Sublicius, the first bridge across the river Tiber, is constructed.

The harbour town of Ostia is founded at the mouth of the Tiber.

600BC The Latin language is first written in a script that is still used today.

inscription in Latin, carved in stone

750BC   700BC   650BC   600BC

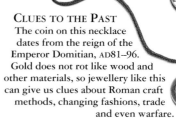

CLUES TO THE PAST
The coin on this necklace dates from the reign of the Emperor Domitian, AD81–96. Gold does not rot like wood and other materials, so jewellery like this can give us clues about Roman craft methods, changing fashions, trade and even warfare.

ARCHAEOLOGISTS AT WORK
These archaeologists are excavating sections of wall plaster from the site of a Roman house in Britain. Many remains of Roman buildings and artefacts, as well as books and documents, have survived from that time. These all help us build up a picture of what life was like in the Roman Empire.

SECRETS BENEATH THE SEA
Divers have discovered Roman shipwrecks deep under the waters of the Mediterranean Sea. Many have their cargo still intact. These jars were being transported over 2,000 years ago. By examining shipwrecks, archaeologists can learn how Roman boats were built, what they carried and where they traded.

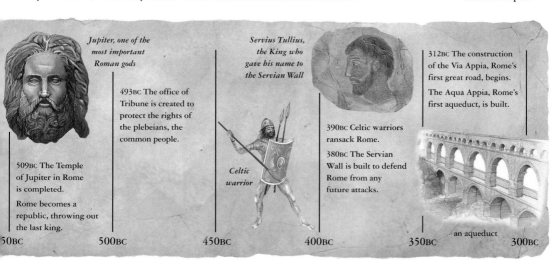

Jupiter, one of the most important Roman gods

493BC The office of Tribune is created to protect the rights of the plebeians, the common people.

509BC The Temple of Jupiter in Rome is completed.

Rome becomes a republic, throwing out the last king.

Servius Tullius, the King who gave his name to the Servian Wall

Celtic warrior

390BC Celtic warriors ransack Rome.

380BC The Servian Wall is built to defend Rome from any future attacks.

312BC The construction of the Via Appia, Rome's first great road, begins.

The Aqua Appia, Rome's first aqueduct, is built.

an aqueduct

| 50BC | 500BC | 450BC | 400BC | 350BC | 300BC |

The Great Empire

BY THE YEAR AD117, the Roman Empire was at its height.
It was possible to travel 4,000km from east to west and still
hear the trumpets of the Roman legions. As a Roman soldier you
might have had to shiver in the snowy winters of northern Britain,
or sweat and toil in the heat of the Egyptian desert.

The peoples of the Empire were very different. There were Greeks,
Egyptians, Syrians, Jews, Africans, Germans and Celts. Many of
them belonged to civilizations that were already ancient when
Rome was still a group of villages. Many revolted against Roman
rule, but uprisings were quickly put down. Gradually, conquered
peoples came to accept being part of the Empire. From AD212
onwards, any free person living under Roman rule had the right to
claim "I am a Roman citizen". Slaves, however, had very few rights.

In AD284, after a series of violent civil wars, this vast empire was
divided into several parts. Despite being reunited by the Emperor
Constantine in AD324, the Empire was doomed. A hundred years
later, the western part was invaded by fierce warriors from the
north, with disastrous consequences. Although the Western Empire
came to an end in AD476, the eastern part continued until 1453. The
Latin language survived, used by the Roman Catholic Church and by
scientists and scholars in Europe. It is still learned today, and is the
basis of languages such as Italian, Spanish, French and Romanian.

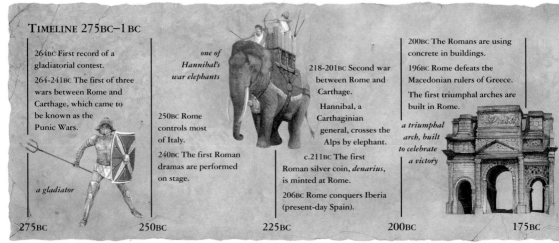

TIMELINE 275BC–1BC

264BC First record of a
gladiatorial contest.

264-241BC The first of three
wars between Rome and
Carthage, which came to
be known as the
Punic Wars.

a gladiator

*one of
Hannibal's
war elephants*

250BC Rome
controls most
of Italy.

240BC The first Roman
dramas are performed
on stage.

218-201BC Second war
between Rome and
Carthage.

Hannibal, a
Carthaginian
general, crosses the
Alps by elephant.

c.211BC The first
Roman silver coin, *denarius*,
is minted at Rome.

206BC Rome conquers Iberia
(present-day Spain).

200BC The Romans are using
concrete in buildings.

196BC Rome defeats the
Macedonian rulers of Greece.

The first triumphal arches are
built in Rome.

*a triumphal
arch, built
to celebrate
a victory*

275BC   250BC   225BC   200BC   175BC

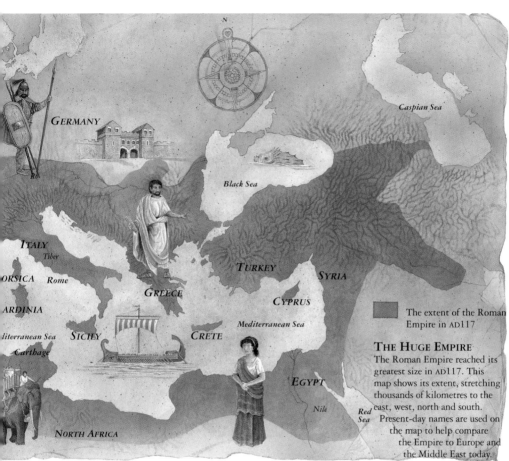

GERMANY

Caspian Sea

Black Sea

ITALY
Tiber

CORSICA Rome

SARDINIA

TURKEY

SYRIA

CYPRUS

GREECE

Mediterranean Sea SICILY CRETE *Mediterranean Sea*

Carthage

EGYPT

Nile

Red
Sea

NORTH AFRICA

The extent of the Roman
Empire in AD117

THE HUGE EMPIRE

The Roman Empire reached its
greatest size in AD117. This
map shows its extent, stretching
thousands of kilometres to the
east, west, north and south.
Present-day names are used on
the map to help compare
the Empire to Europe and
the Middle East today.

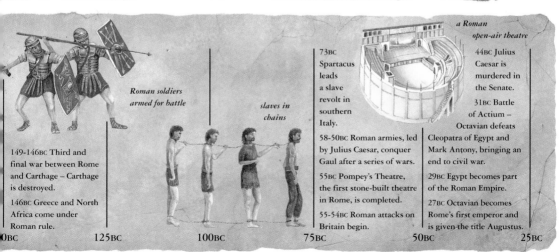

Roman soldiers
armed for battle

slaves in
chains

73BC
Spartacus
leads
a slave
revolt in
southern
Italy.

58-50BC Roman armies, led
by Julius Caesar, conquer
Gaul after a series of wars.

55BC Pompey's Theatre,
the first stone-built theatre
in Rome, is completed.

55-54BC Roman attacks on
Britain begin.

*a Roman
open-air theatre*

44BC Julius
Caesar is
murdered in
the Senate.

31BC Battle
of Actium –
Octavian defeats
Cleopatra of Egypt and
Mark Antony, bringing an
end to civil war.

29BC Egypt becomes part
of the Roman Empire.

27BC Octavian becomes
Rome's first emperor and
is given the title Augustus.

149-146BC Third and
final war between Rome
and Carthage – Carthage
is destroyed.

146BC Greece and North
Africa come under
Roman rule.

150BC   125BC   100BC   75BC   50BC   25BC

The Roman World

THE PEOPLE who made Roman history came from many different backgrounds. The names of the famous survive on monuments and in books. There were consuls and emperors, successful generals and powerful politicians, great writers and historians. However, it was thousands of ordinary people who really kept the Roman Empire going – merchants, soldiers of the legions, tax collectors, servants, farmers, potters, and others like them.

Many of the most famous names of that time were not Romans at all. There was the Carthaginian general, Hannibal, Rome's deadliest enemy. There were also Celtic chieftains and queens, such as Vercingetorix, Caractacus and Boudicca.

ROMULUS AND REMUS

According to legend, Romulus was the founder and first king of Rome. The legend tells how he and his twin brother Remus were abandoned as babies. They were saved by a she-wolf, who looked after them until they were found by a shepherd.

AUGUSTUS (63BC–AD14)

Augustus, born Octavian, was the great-nephew and adopted son of Julius Caesar. After Caesar's death, he took control of the army. He became ruler of the Roman world after defeating Mark Antony at the Battle of Actium in 31BC. In 27BC, he became Rome's first emperor and was given the title Augustus.

CICERO (106–43BC)

Cicero is remembered as Rome's greatest orator, or speaker. Many of his letters and speeches still survive. He was a writer, poet, politican, lawyer and philosopher. He was elected consul of Rome in 63BC, but he had many enemies and was murdered in 43BC.

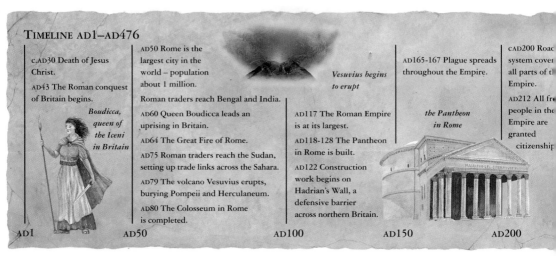

TIMELINE AD1–AD476

c.AD30 Death of Jesus Christ.

AD43 The Roman conquest of Britain begins.

Boudicca, queen of the Iceni in Britain

AD50 Rome is the largest city in the world – population about 1 million.

Roman traders reach Bengal and India.

AD60 Queen Boudicca leads an uprising in Britain.

AD64 The Great Fire of Rome.

AD75 Roman traders reach the Sudan, setting up trade links across the Sahara.

AD79 The volcano Vesuvius erupts, burying Pompeii and Herculaneum.

AD80 The Colosseum in Rome is completed.

Vesuvius begins to erupt

AD117 The Roman Empire is at its largest.

AD118-128 The Pantheon in Rome is built.

AD122 Construction work begins on Hadrian's Wall, a defensive barrier across northern Britain.

AD165-167 Plague spreads throughout the Empire.

the Pantheon in Rome

c.AD200 Road system cover[s] all parts of t[he] Empire.

AD212 All fre[e] people in the Empire are granted citizenship

AD1   AD50   AD100   AD150   AD200

HADRIAN (AD76–138)
Hadrian became emperor in AD117 and spent many years travelling around the Empire. He had many splendid buildings constructed, as well as a defensive barrier across northern Britain, now known as Hadrian's Wall.

NERO (AD37–68) AND AGRIPPINA
Nero became emperor on the death of his adoptive father Claudius, in AD54. A cruel ruler, he was blamed for a great fire that destroyed much of Rome in AD64. Agrippina, his mother, was a powerful influence on him. She was suspected of poisoning two of her three husbands, and was eventually killed on her son's orders.

CLEOPATRA (68–30BC)
An Egyptian queen of Greek descent, Cleopatra had a son by Julius Caesar. She then fell in love with Mark Antony, a close follower of Caesar. They joined forces against Rome, but after a crushing defeat at Actium in 31BC, they both committed suicide. Egypt then became part of the Roman Empire.

JULIUS CAESAR (100–44BC)
Caesar was a talented and popular general and politician. He led Roman armies in an eight-year campaign to conquer Gaul (present-day France) in 50BC. In 49BC, he used his victorious troops to seize power and declare himself dictator for life. Five years later he was stabbed to death in the Senate by fellow politicians.

the cross, a symbol of Christianity

AD270 A new defensive wall is built around Rome by the Emperor Aurelian.

AD284 The Emperor Diocletian brings in new laws and taxes – divisions appear in the Empire.

AD313 Christianity is made legal in the Empire.

AD324 The Emperor Constantine reunites the Empire and founds the city of Constantinople (present-day Istanbul, in Turkey).

AD330 Constantine makes Constantinople his imperial residence and the new capital in the east.

AD395 The Roman Empire is divided again, this time into two parts – Eastern and Western.

AD410 The city of Rome is raided and ransacked by Visigoth armies from Germany.

the Emperor Constantine, depicted on a Roman coin

Vandal warrior

AD455 Vandal armies from Germany ransack Rome.

AD476 Fall of the Western Empire – the Eastern Empire survives until 1453.

D250   AD300   AD350   AD400   AD450

Rulers of Rome

In the early days, the city of Rome was ruled by kings. The first Roman king was said to be Romulus, the founder of the city in 753BC. The last king, a hated tyrant called Tarquinius the Proud, was thrown out in 509BC. The Romans then set up a republic. An assembly of powerful and wealthy citizens, the Senate, chose two consuls to lead them each year. By 493BC, the common people had their own representatives, too – the tribunes. In times of crisis, rulers could take on emergency powers and become dictators. The first Roman emperor, Augustus, was appointed by the Senate in 27BC. The emperors were given great powers and were even worshipped as gods. Some lived simply and ruled well, but others were violent, cruel men. They were surrounded by flatterers, and yet they lived in constant fear of plotters and murderers.

TRIUMPHAL PROCESSION
When a Roman general won a great victory, he was honoured with a military parade called a triumph. Cheering crowds lined the streets as the grand procession passed by. If a general was successful and popular, the way to power was often open to him. Probably the most famous Roman ruler of all, Julius Caesar, came to power after a series of brilliant military conquests.

STATE SACRIFICE
Roman emperors had religious as well as political duties. As *pontifex maximus*, or high priest, an emperor would make sacrifices as offerings to the gods at important festivals.

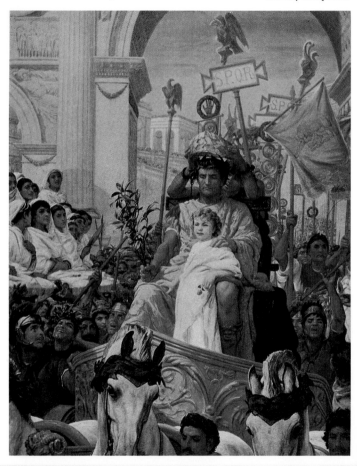

figs

DEADLY FRUIT

Who killed Augustus, the first Roman emperor, in AD14? It was hard to say. It might have been a natural death... but then again, it might have been caused by his wife Livia. She was said to have coated the figs in his garden with a deadly poison. Roman emperors were much feared, but they were surrounded by enemies and could trust no one, least of all their own families.

PRAETORIAN GUARDS

The Praetorian Guards were the emperor's personal bodyguards. They wore special uniforms and were well paid. The guards were the only armed soldiers allowed within the city of Rome and so became very powerful. They also intervened in politics – assassinating the Emperor Caligula and electing his successor, Claudius.

In Rome, wreaths made from leaves of the laurel tree were worn by emperors, victorious soldiers and athletes. The wreath was a badge of honour. The Romans copied the idea from the ancient Greeks.

WREATH OF HONOUR

You will need: tape measure, garden wire, pliers, scissors, clear tape, green ribbon, bay or laurel leaves (real or fake).

1 Measure around your head with the tape measure. Cut some wire the same length, so the wreath will fit you. Bend the wire as shown and tape the ribbon round it.

2 Start to tape the leaves by their stems on to the wire, as shown above. Work your way around to the middle of the wire, fanning out the leaves as you go.

3 Then reverse the direction of the leaves and work your way around the rest of the wire. Fit the finished wreath to your head. Hail, Caesar!

Roman Society

ROMAN SOCIETY was never very fair. At first, a group of rich and powerful noble families, called the patricians, controlled the city and the Senate. Anyone who wanted their voice heard had to persuade a senator to speak on their behalf. Over the centuries the common citizens, known as plebeians, became more powerful until, by 287BC, they shared equally in government. Eventually, in the days of the Empire, even people of humble birth could become emperor, provided they were wealthy or had the support of the army. Emperors always feared riots by the common people of Rome, so they tried to keep the people happy with handouts of free food and lavish entertainments. Roman women had little power outside the family and could not vote. However, many were successful in business or had an important influence on political events. Slaves had very few rights, though Roman society depended on slave labour. Prisoners of war were bought and sold as slaves and many were treated cruelly, making slave revolts common.

A ROMAN CONSUL
This is a statue of a Roman consul, or leader of the Senate, in the days of the republic. At first, only the noble, and often wealthy, ruling class could be senators. However, under the emperors, the power and influence of the Senate slowly grew less and less.

LIFE AS A SLAVE
The everyday running of the Empire depended on slavery. This mosaic shows a young slave boy carrying fruit. In about AD100, a wealthy family might have had as many as 500 slaves. Some families treated their slaves well, and slaves who gave good service might earn their freedom. However, many more led miserable lives, toiling in the mines or labouring in the fields.

SLAVE TAG
This bronze disc was probably worn around the neck of a slave, like a dog-tag. The Latin words on it say: "Hold me, in case I run away, and return me to my master Viventius on the estate of Callistus". Slaves had few rights and could be branded on the forehead or leg as the property of their owners.

COLLECTING TAXES

This stone carving probably shows people paying their annual taxes. Officials counted the population of the Empire and registered them for paying tax. Money from taxes paid for the army and the government. However, many of the tax collectors took bribes, and even emperors seized public money to add to their private fortunes.

ARISTOCRATS

This Italian painting of the 1700s imagines how a noble Roman lady might dress after bathing. Wealthy people had personal slaves to help them bathe, dress and look after their hair. Household slaves were sometimes almost part of the family, and their children might be brought up and educated with their owner's children.

Country Life

THE FIRST ROMANS mostly lived by farming. Even when Rome had become a big city, Roman poets still liked to sing the praises of the countryside. In reality, country life was quite hard. Oxen were used for ploughing. Grain crops were harvested with a sickle, and flour was often ground by hand. Water had to be fetched by hand from the farm's well or a nearby spring.

Many farms were very small. They were often run by retired soldiers, who would raise chickens and geese and perhaps a cow or pig. They would also keep bees and grow olives and a few vegetables.

Other farms in Italy and across the Empire were large estates set up to provide incomes for their wealthy landowners. These estates might have their own olive presses, reaping machines and stores for drying grain. An estate was often laid out around a large, luxurious house or villa. Other villas were grand country houses owned by rich and powerful Romans.

A COUNTRY ESTATE
Life on a country estate was always busy, as this mosaic of a Roman villa in Tunisia, North Africa, shows. North African country estates supplied Rome with vast amounts of grain, fruit and vegetables. The good soil, combined with hot summers and rain in winter, made farming easy.

HADRIAN'S VILLA
One of the grandest country houses of all was built for the Emperor Hadrian between AD124 and 133. Parts of the villa still stand today, as this view of one of its lakeside walks shows. The luxurious villa itself stood on a hilltop, with Rome just visible in the distance. Built on land that belonged to Hadrian's family, the villa had pavilions and pools, terraces, banqueting halls, theatres and libraries. All around the villa were parklands filled with trees, such as laurels, planes and pines, exotic shrubs and formal flowerbeds. Hadrian designed the villa as a holiday palace where he could escape from the cares of government, but he died just four years after it was completed.

HUNTING WILD BOAR

Hunting scenes often decorated the walls of country villas. The hunt was a favourite pastime for young noblemen or army officers visiting the countryside. A wild boar, like the one shown in this mosaic, was one of the most dangerous animals of all when it charged.

FOOD FOR ROME

Rome needed huge amounts of food for all its people. Vegetables, such as leeks, celery, cabbage, beans and peas, were grown at market gardens around the city. Grain crops included wheat, barley, oats and rye. Grapes were made into wine and, as there was no sugar, honey was used to sweeten foods.

grapes

wheat

honey

GROVES OF OLIVE TREES

Olives were, and still are, an important crop in the lands around the Mediterranean. They were grown on small farms as well as on large estates. The oil was pressed and stored in large pottery jars. It was used for cooking or burnt in oil lamps.

PLOUGHING THE LAND

This ploughman from Roman Britain is using a heavy wooden plough drawn by oxen. Large areas of Europe were still covered in thick forest in the days of the Roman Empire. Gradually farmers cleared land to plough, and farmland and orchards spread across the countryside.

Town and City

MANY OF THE TOWNS in Italy and the lands surrounding the Mediterranean Sea were already old and well-established when the Romans invaded. Under Roman rule these towns prospered and grew. In other parts of Europe, where people had never lived in a big town, the Roman invaders built impressive new cities.

Roman towns had straight, paved roads planned on a grid pattern. Some were broad streets with pavements. Others were alleys just wide enough for a donkey. Most streets were busy with noisy crowds, street merchants, carts and rowdy bars. The streets divided the buildings into blocks called *insulae*, which means islands. The homes of wealthy families were spacious and comfortable. Poorer Romans often lived in apartment blocks that were badly built, crowded and in constant danger of burning down.

Fresh water was brought into towns through a system of channels called an aqueduct. The water was piped to fountains, public baths and to the homes of the wealthy.

THE STREETS OF POMPEII
On August 24, AD79, the volcano Vesuvius erupted violently, burying the Roman town of Pompeii in ash and lava. Work began in 1748 to excavate the ancient town, and its streets, shops and houses have slowly been revealed. In this excavated street, the deep ruts in the road made by cart wheels are clearly visible. Streets were often filled with mud and filth, so stepping-stones were laid for pedestrians to cross.

AN AQUEDUCT BRIDGE

You will need: ruler, pencil, scissors, thick and thin card, PVA glue, paintbrush, masking tape, modelling clay, plaster paste, acrylic paints, water pot.

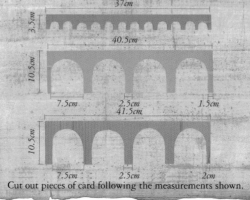

37cm
3.5cm
40.5cm
10.5cm
7.5cm 2.5cm 1.5cm
41.5cm
10.5cm
7.5cm 2.5cm 2cm

Cut out pieces of card following the measurements shown.

1 Draw and cut out the shapes of the arches from the thick card. You need to cut out a pair for each level of the aqueduct – top, middle and bottom.

AQUEDUCTS

Water was carried into Roman towns and cities through a system of channels and pipes called aqueducts. Most of these were underground. Sometimes they were supported on high arches, such as this one, which still stands today in France. The water came from fresh springs, streams and lakes.

HERCULANEUM

The volcanic eruption that buried Pompeii caused a mud flow that buried a nearby coastal town, Herculaneum. Here, too, archaeologists have discovered houses, public baths, shops and workshops side by side on the city's streets. This view shows how crowded parts of the town were, with narrow paved streets separating the buildings.

CITY PLAN

This aerial view of Pompeii clearly shows how Roman streets were laid out on a grid pattern.

Forum baths

Stabian baths

amphitheatre

sports ground

N

large theatre

market

Capitol

Forum

| 0 | 200 | 400m |
| 0 | 200 | 400yds |

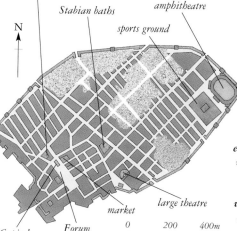

Aqueducts were built at a slight slope to ensure a steady flow of water. Arched bridges carried them across river valleys. The water flowed along a channel at the top of the bridge.

2 Cut strips of thin card in three widths – 4cm, 2.5cm and 2cm. These are for the insides of the arches. Use glue and tape to fix the 4cm strips to the bottom level.

3 Glue on the other side of the bottom level. Fix it securely with tape. Cut a top section from thick card and fix this on. Make the two other levels in the same way.

4 Roll the modelling clay into buttresses and wrap with thick card. Attach these to the three central arches of the bottom level. These will support the aqueduct bridge.

5 Glue the levels together. Cover the model with plaster paste and mark on a brick pattern. Leave to dry. Paint the arches grey. Paint a blue channel of 'water' on top.

House and Garden

ONLY WEALTHY ROMANS could afford to live in a private house. A typical town house was designed to look inwards, with the rooms arranged round a central courtyard and a walled garden. Outside walls had few windows and these were small and shuttered. The front door opened on to a short passage leading into an airy courtyard called an *atrium*. Front rooms on either side of the passage were usually used as bedrooms. Sometimes they were used as workshops or shops, having shutters that opened out to the street.

The centre of the atrium was open to the sky. Below this opening was a pool, set into the floor, to collect rainwater. Around the atrium were more bedrooms and the kitchen. If you were a guest or had important business you would be shown into the *tablinium*. The dining room, or *triclinium*, was often the grandest room of all. The very rich sometimes also had a summer dining room, which looked on to the garden.

Houses were made of locally available building materials. These might include stone, mud bricks, cement and timber. Roofs were made of clay tiles.

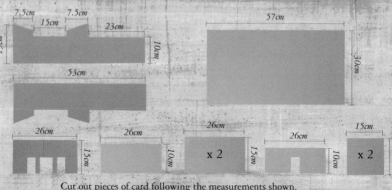

garden

bedroom

tablinium
(living room
and office)

LOCKS AND KEYS
This was the key to the door of a Roman house. Pushed in through a keyhole, the prongs at the end of the key fitted into holes in the bolt in the lock. The key could then be used to slide the bolt along and unlock the door.

INSIDE A ROMAN HOME
The outside of a wealthy Roman's town house was usually quite plain, but inside it was highly decorated with elaborate wall paintings and intricate mosaics. The rooms were sparsely furnished, with couches or beds, small side tables, benches and folding stools. There were few windows, but high ceilings and wide doors made the most of the light from the open atrium and the garden.

MAKE A ROMAN HOME
You will need: pencil, ruler, thick card, scissors, PVA glue, paintbrushes, masking tape, corrugated cardboard, thin card, water pot, acrylic paints.

7,5cm 7.5cm 15cm 23cm 10cm 15cm 53cm 57cm 30cm

26cm 15cm 26cm 10cm 26cm 15cm x 2 26cm 10cm 15cm x 2

Cut out pieces of card following the measurements shown.

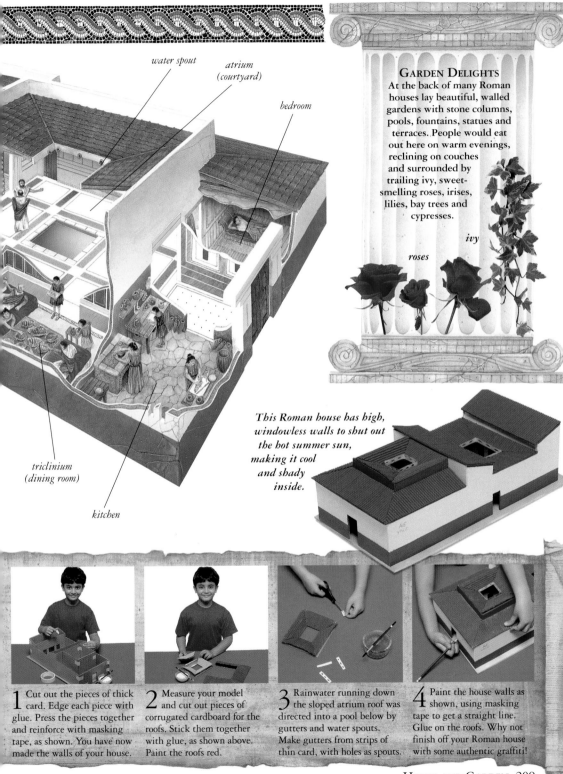

water spout

atrium
(courtyard)

bedroom

triclinium
(dining room)

kitchen

GARDEN DELIGHTS

At the back of many Roman houses lay beautiful, walled gardens with stone columns, pools, fountains, statues and terraces. People would eat out here on warm evenings, reclining on couches and surrounded by trailing ivy, sweet-smelling roses, irises, lilies, bay trees and cypresses.

ivy

roses

This Roman house has high, windowless walls to shut out the hot summer sun, making it cool and shady inside.

1 Cut out the pieces of thick card. Edge each piece with glue. Press the pieces together and reinforce with masking tape, as shown. You have now made the walls of your house.

2 Measure your model and cut out pieces of corrugated cardboard for the roofs. Stick them together with glue, as shown above. Paint the roofs red.

3 Rainwater running down the sloped atrium roof was directed into a pool below by gutters and water spouts. Make gutters from strips of thin card, with holes as spouts.

4 Paint the house walls as shown, using masking tape to get a straight line. Glue on the roofs. Why not finish off your Roman house with some authentic graffiti!

Home Comforts

ROMAN HOUSES were less cluttered with furniture than our own. People kept their clothes in cupboards and wooden chests rather than in wardrobes or drawers. Wooden or metal stools were used more than chairs. Couches were the most important piece of furniture, used for resting, eating and receiving visitors. Roman furniture was often simple, but rich people could afford fine, hand-crafted tables or benches made from wood, marble or bronze. Dining tables were very low, because wealthy Romans ate their evening meal lying on couches. Beds were often made of wood, with slats or ropes to support the mattress and pillows, which were stuffed with wool or straw.

Lighting in both rich and poor homes came from many small, flickering oil lamps made from clay or bronze. Heating came from charcoal burned in open braziers. The most luxurious houses were warmed by underfloor central heating, especially in colder parts of the Empire.

INTERIOR DECORATION
The walls, ceilings and floors of Roman houses were covered with paintings, mosaics and moulded plaster reliefs. Elaborate scenes were painted directly on to the walls, while bright patterns in tiles and mosaics decorated the floor.

A HYPOCAUST
Roman underfloor heating is called a hypocaust. These are the remains of the hypocaust at the palace of Fishbourne in England. Only wealthy Romans could afford this early form of central heating, and many only had it in the dining room.

UNDERFLOOR HEATING
A furnace, burning wood or charcoal, heated the air beneath the floor. The hot air circulated around pillars of brick or tile that supported the floor. It also flowed up inside the walls through special channels. This kept the whole room warm. Slaves would keep the furnace stoked up.

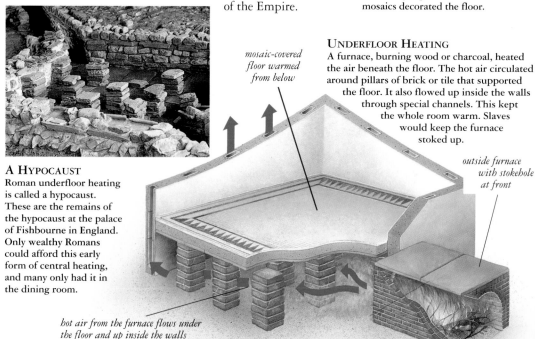

mosaic-covered floor warmed from below

outside furnace with stokehole at front

hot air from the furnace flows under the floor and up inside the walls

HOUSEHOLD SHRINE

The *lararium*, or household shrine, was a small private altar containing images of the family's ancestors. It was usually situated in the *atrium* at the centre of the house. Every day the family would honour their ancestors by burning incense at the shrine.

DINNER IS SERVED

These are guests at a banquet in Roman Germany. Only country folk, foreigners and slaves ate sitting upright at the table. Tables and chairs were usually made of wood and might be carved or painted. There were also woven wicker armchairs. Wealthy Romans ate lying on couches around a central low table.

LAMPLIGHT

Roman homes glowed with the soft light of candles and oil lamps. Lamps were made of pottery or bronze, like this one. They came in many different designs, but they all had a central well containing olive oil. The oil was soaked up by a wick, which provided a steady flame. Sometimes lamps would be grouped together or hung from a tall lampstand.

A LUXURY TO LIE ON

This beautifully decorated bed is made from wood inlaid with ivory and semi-precious stones. It dates back to about 50BC, and was discovered in the remains of a villa in Italy. The villa had been buried under ash from a volcanic eruption. Beds, or couches for sleeping on, were much higher than ours are today and needed steps or a stool to get on to.

In the Kitchen

WHEN A LARGE MEAL was being prepared, slaves would have to carry water and fresh kindling for the fire into the kitchen. As the fires were lit, the room would become quite smoky because there was no chimney. Soon the coals would be glowing red hot and pots would be boiling on trivets and griddles on the raised brick stove. Food was boiled, fried, grilled and stewed. Larger kitchens might include stone ovens for baking bread or spits for roasting meat. A few even had piped hot water.

The kitchens of wealthy Romans were well equipped with all kinds of bronze pots, pans, strainers and ladles. Pottery storage jars held wine, olive oil and sauces. Herbs, vegetables and joints of meat hung from hooks in the roof. There were no tins, and no fridges or freezers to keep food fresh. Food had to be preserved in oil or by drying, smoking, salting or pickling.

mortar

VALUABLE GLASS
This glass bottle or jug was made about 1,900 years ago. Precious liquids or expensive perfumes were sold in bottles like this throughout the Empire. When a bottle was empty, it was far too valuable to throw away, so it was often reused to store food such as honey in the kitchen.

PESTLE AND MORTAR
The Romans liked spicy food. Roman cooks used a pestle and mortar to grind up foods, such as nuts, herbs and spices, into a paste. Both pieces were usually made of a very tough pottery or stone. The rough inside of the mortar was made of coarse grit to help grind the food.

pestle

A ROMAN KITCHEN

You will need: pencil, ruler, cardboard, scissors, paintbrush, PVA glue, masking tape, water pot, acrylic paints, red felt tip pen, plaster paste, balsa wood, sandpaper, self-drying clay, work board, modelling tool.

1 Cut out the walls and floor of the kitchen from cardboard, as shown. Glue the edges and press them together. Reinforce the walls with pieces of masking tape.

2 Paint the floor grey. When dry, use the ruler and pencil to draw on stone flags. Paint the walls yellow, edged with blue. When dry, use the felt tip to draw stripes.

3 Cut out pieces of card to make a stove about 2cm long, 5cm wide and 4cm high. Glue the pieces together and reinforce with masking tape, as shown above.

READY FOR THE COOK

Herbs brought fresh from the garden included coriander, oregano, rue, mint, thyme and parsley. Food was spiced with pepper, caraway, aniseed, mustard seeds and saffron. On the table there might be eggs, grapes, figs and nuts. Much of our knowledge of Roman cooking comes from recipes collected by a Roman gourmet called Apicius nearly 2,000 years ago.

saffron

thyme

mint

quails' eggs

BAKING PAN

This bronze tray was probably used as a mould for baking honey cakes, buns or pastries. The long handle makes it easier to remove from a hot oven. It may also have been used to cook eggs.

STRAINER

This bronze strainer was used by Roman cooks to strain sauces. It was made using the same design as a saucepan, but its bowl has been pierced with an intricate pattern. The hole in the handle was used to hang it from a hook on the wall.

SAUCEPAN

Like many Roman kitchen utensils, this saucepan is made from bronze. Bronze contains copper, which can give food a very strange flavour – the inside of the saucepan has been coated with silver to prevent this from happening.

Foods in a Roman kitchen were stored in baskets, bowls or sacks. Wine, oil and sauces were stored in pottery jars called amphorae.

4 Coat the stove with plaster paste. Leave to dry. Then use sandpaper to rub it smooth. Make a grate from two strips of card and four bits of balsa wood, glued together.

5 Use the acrylic paints to colour the stove and the grate, as shown above. Use small pieces of balsa wood to make a pile of wood fuel to store underneath the stove.

6 Make a table and shelves from balsa wood, as shown. Glue them together, and bind with masking tape. Leave them to dry before painting the pieces brown.

7 Use the clay to model pots, pans, bowls, storage jars, perhaps even a frying pan or an egg poacher. Leave the utensils to dry before painting them a suitable colour.

Food and Drink

For poor Romans, a meal was often little more than a hurried bowl of porridge or a crust of bread washed down with sour wine. Many town-dwellers lived in homes without kitchens. They ate takeaway meals bought from the many food stalls and bars in town. Even for wealthier people, breakfast might be just a quick snack of bread, honey and olives. Lunch, too, was a light meal, perhaps of eggs or cold meats and fruit. The main meal of the day was *cena*, or dinner. This evening meal might start with shellfish or a salad, followed by a main course of roast meat, such as pork, veal, chicken or goose, with vegetables. It finished with a sweet course of fruit or honey cakes.

More lavish banquets might include fattened dormice, songbirds, flamingoes' tongues or a custard made from calves' brains and rose hips! Food was heavily spiced and was often served with a fish sauce called *garum*. Wine was usually mixed with water and sometimes flavoured with honey or spices. Guests could take home any tasty morsels that were left over.

SERVING SLAVES
This mosaic shows a slave called Paregorius helping to prepare his master's table for a banquet. On his head he is carrying a tray with plates of food. During a banquet, dishes were brought in a few at a time and set down on a small table. All the food was cooked and served by slaves.

HONEYED DATES
You will need: chopping board, dates, small knife, walnuts, pecan nuts, almonds, hazelnuts, pestle and mortar, salt, 175ml honey, frying pan, wooden spoon, a few fresh mint leaves.

1 On the chopping board, slit open the dates with the knife. Remove the stone inside. Be sure not to cut the dates completely in half and be careful with the knife.

2 Put aside the hazelnuts. Chop up the rest of the nuts. Use a pestle and mortar to grind them into smaller pieces. Stuff a small amount into the middle of each date.

3 Pour some salt on to the chopping board and lightly roll each date in it. Make sure the dates are coated all over, but do not use too much salt.

CUPS
Pottery cups like this one were used for drinking wine. Many drinking cups had handles and were often highly decorated. Metal cups could make wine taste unpleasant, so coloured glass cups and pottery cups were more popular.

THE FAMILY SILVER
These silver spoons were used by a wealthy family in Roman Britain. Food was usually eaten with the fingers, but spoons were used for sauces. At banquets, Romans liked to bring out their best silver tableware as a sign of status.

AT A BANQUET
This wall painting shows a typical Roman banquet. Guests usually sat three to a couch. After the meal they were entertained with poetry readings and music, or jokes and jugglers. Dress and table manners were very important at a banquet. Arguments and bad language were not allowed, but it was fine to spit, belch or even eat until you were sick!

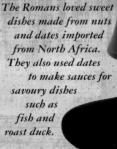

The Romans loved sweet dishes made from nuts and dates imported from North Africa. They also used dates to make sauces for savoury dishes such as fish and roast duck.

4 On a low heat, melt the honey in the frying pan. Lightly fry the dates for five minutes, turning them with a wooden spoon. Take care while using the stove.

5 Arrange the stuffed dates in a shallow dish. Sprinkle over the whole hazelnuts, some chopped nuts and a few leaves of fresh mint. Now they are ready to serve to your friends.

Getting Dressed

MOST ROMAN CLOTHES were made of wool that had been spun and woven by hand at home or in a workshop. Flax was grown in Egypt to make linen, while cotton from India and silk from China were rare and expensive imports. The most common style of clothing was a simple tunic, which was practical for people who led active lives, such as workers, slaves and children. Important men also wore a white robe called a toga. This was a 6m length of cloth with a curved edge, wrapped around the body and draped over the shoulder. It was heavy and uncomfortable to wear, but looked very impressive. Women wore a long dress called a *stola*, over an under-tunic. Often they also wore a *palla* – a large shawl that could be arranged in various ways. Girls wore white until they were married, after which they often wore dresses dyed in bright colours.

DRESSING FOR DIONYSUS
Wall paintings in the homes of wealthy Romans hold many clues about the way people dressed in the Roman world. This scene was found in the Villa of the Mysteries, in Pompeii. It shows young women being prepared as ceremonial brides for Dionysus, the god of wine.

ROMAN FOOTWEAR
This sandal (*left*) and child's shoe (*far left*) were found in York, in Britain. Most Romans wore open leather sandals. There were many different designs, and some had nailed soles to make them harder wearing. Shoes and boots were worn in the colder parts of the Empire.

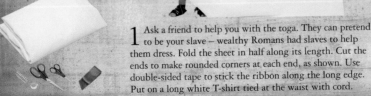

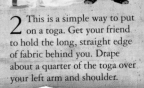

WEAR A TOGA
You will need: old white sheet, tape measure, scissors for cutting cloth and scissors for sticky tape, double-sided sticky tape, purple ribbon, long T-shirt, cord.

1 Ask a friend to help you with the toga. They can pretend to be your slave – wealthy Romans had slaves to help them dress. Fold the sheet in half along its length. Cut the ends to make rounded corners at each end, as shown. Use double-sided tape to stick the ribbon along the long edge. Put on a long white T-shirt tied at the waist with cord.

2 This is a simple way to put on a toga. Get your friend to hold the long, straight edge of fabric behind you. Drape about a quarter of the toga over your left arm and shoulder.

WORKERS' CLOTHES

Not all Romans wore flowing robes. This man is probably a farm worker from Roman Germany. He wears strips of cloth around his legs and a hooded leather cloak to protect him from the cold, wet weather. Hooded cloaks like this were exported from Gaul (present-day France) and Britain.

DRESSED TO IMPRESS

This stone carving shows the family of the Emperor Augustus, dressed for an important state occasion. The women are all shown wearing a *stola*, with a *palla* draped round their shoulders or head. The men and boys are shown in togas. A toga could be worn by all free Roman citizens, but only the wealthy upper classes wore it. This was because it took time – and a helping hand – to put on a toga. Once you had it on, it was also quite awkward to move in!

3 Bring the rest of the toga round to the front, passing it under your right arm. Hook the toga up by tucking a few folds of material securely into the cord around your waist.

4 Now your friend can help you fold the rest of the toga neatly over your left arm, as shown above. If you prefer, you could drape it all over your left shoulder.

Boys from wealthy families wore togas edged with a thin purple stripe until they reached the age of 16. They then wore plain togas. A toga with a broad purple stripe was worn by Roman senators. Purple dye was expensive, so the colour was only worn by high-ranking citizens.

Fashion and Beauty

A ROMAN LADY would spend most of the morning surrounded by her female slaves. Some would bring her a mirror made of bronze or silver and jars of perfumed oils or ointments. Another slave would comb out her hair – and could expect a spiteful jab with a hairpin if she pulled at a tangle.

Most rich women wanted to look pale – after all, only women who had to work outdoors became sunburnt. So chalk, or even a poisonous powder made from white lead, was rubbed into the face. Face packs were made of bread and milk. One remedy for spots and pimples included bird droppings! Lipsticks and blusher were made of red ochre or the sediment from red wine. Eyeshadow was made of ash and saffron. Women's hair was curled, plaited or pinned up, according to the latest fashion.

PORTRAIT OF A LADY
This is a portrait of a lady who lived in the Roman province of Egypt. Her earrings and necklace are made of emeralds, garnets and pearls set in gold. They are a sign of her wealth as they would have been very expensive. Her hair has been curled, and lamp-black or soot may have been used to darken her eyelashes and eyebrows.

CARVED COMB
This comb is carved from ivory and is inscribed in Latin with the words "Modestina farewell". Combs of silver and ivory were used to decorate the intricate hairstyles favoured by many Roman women. The poor used wooden or bone combs, though more out of need than fashion.

SCENT BOTTLES
These lovely perfume bottles belonged to a Roman lady. The round one is made of hand-blown, gold-banded glass. The other is carved from onyx, a precious stone with layers of different colours.

A GOLDEN HEADDRESS
You will need: tape measure, plain card, pencil, scissors, PVA glue, paintbrush, string, plastic beads, gold foil wrappers, sticky tape or paper clip.

1 Measure around your head with the tape measure. Draw the shape of the tiara to the same length on card. Also draw outlines for various sizes of leaf shape, as shown.

2 Carefully cut out the tiara outline from the card. Also cut out the leaf shapes. Then cut out the centre of each one so that they look a bit like arches.

3 Use the PVA glue and a paintbrush to paste the shapes securely on to the front of the tiara. These will be part of an elegant pattern for your tiara.

The Kingdom on the Nile

EGYPT IS A COUNTRY at the crossroads of Africa, Europe and Asia. If you could step back in time 5,000 years, you would discover an amazing civilization – the kingdom of the ancient Egyptians.

HORUS' EYE
This symbol can be seen on many Egyptian artefacts. It is the eye of the god Horus.

Most of Egypt is made up of baking hot, sandy deserts. These are crossed by the river Nile as it snakes its way north to the Mediterranean Sea. Every year, floods cover the banks of the Nile with mud. Plants grow well in this rich soil, and 8,000 years ago farmers were planting crops here. Wealth from farming led to trade and to the building of towns. By 3100BC a great kingdom had grown up in Egypt, ruled by royal families.

Ancient Egypt existed for over 3,000 years, longer even than the Roman Empire. Pyramids, temples and artefacts survive from this period to show us what life was like in the land of the pharaohs.

AMAZING DISCOVERIES
In 1922, the English archaeologist Howard Carter made an amazing discovery. He found the tomb of the young pharaoh Tutankhamun. No single find in Egypt has ever provided as much evidence as the discovery of this well-preserved tomb.

LIFE BY THE NILE
Tomb paintings show us how people lived in ancient Egypt. Here people water and harvest their crops, using water from the river Nile.

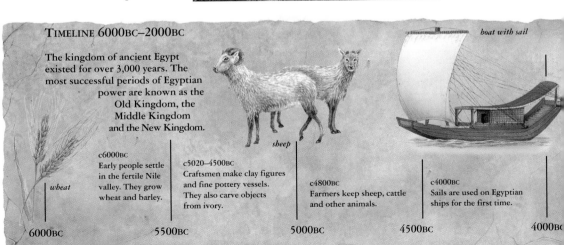

TIMELINE 6000BC–2000BC

The kingdom of ancient Egypt existed for over 3,000 years. The most successful periods of Egyptian power are known as the Old Kingdom, the Middle Kingdom and the New Kingdom.

sheep

boat with sail

wheat

c6000BC
Early people settle in the fertile Nile valley. They grow wheat and barley.

c5020–4500BC
Craftsmen make clay figures and fine pottery vessels. They also carve objects from ivory.

c4800BC
Farmers keep sheep, cattle and other animals.

c4000BC
Sails are used on Egyptian ships for the first time.

6000BC   5500BC   5000BC   4500BC   4000BC

ANCIENT EGYPT

The Egyptian civilization that developed along the fertile banks of the River Nile 5,000 years ago was one of the most wealthy and creative in history. There were mighty tombs and pyramids, built at huge cost, to house priceless treasures and elaborately preserved mummies. The glorious civilization of ancient Egypt lasted over 3,000 years.

PHILIP STEELE
Consultant: Felicity Cobbing

ABORIGINAL AUSTRALIANS

In Australia today, 200 years after the arrival of Europeans, some Aboriginal people are trying to maintain a traditional way of life. Thousands of years ago, their ancestors must have been well aware of how to grow plants such as yams, but they chose to continue as hunter-gatherers. In tune with their environment, they had a wide range of game and food plants available to them, making farming an unnecessary and more difficult way of life.

MARVELS IN STONE

Gigantic stone heads up to 12m high were carved out of volcanic rock and erected on Easter Island between AD1100 and AD1600. Easter Island is one of the remotest islands in the Pacific.

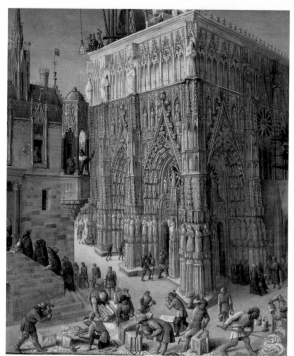

STONEMASONS

This is part of an illustration dating from the AD1400s, showing medieval stonemasons at work. Large workforces and metal tools gradually helped stone to take on a new role as a building material. Stone could be cut, shaped and transported on a much larger scale. Many impressive stone buildings were erected all over the world, some of which have stood for thousands of years.

CROWNING GLORY

This lady's elaborately curled hair is almost certainly a wig. Hairpieces and wigs were always popular with wealthy Roman women– a bride would wear at least six pads of artificial hair at her wedding. Locks of black hair were usually imported from Asia, while blond or red hair came from northern Europe.

MEN'S CHANGING HAIRSTYLES

Roman men were just as concerned with their appearance as women. They usually wore their hair short, either combed forward or curled. They were mostly clean shaven, but beards became fashionable during the reign of the Emperor Hadrian, AD117–138.

A FINE DISPLAY

This picture shows a ceremonial dance at the Temple of the Sun in Rome. Both the men and women are wearing golden headdresses decorated with precious jewels and gold filigree. Lavish displays like this were reserved for grand public occasions to show off the wealth and power of the Empire.

RINGS ON THEIR FINGERS

Both men and women wore jewellery, especially rings. Rich people would wear rings like these, usually made of gold or silver. Emeralds, pearls and amber were also used in rings. The less wealthy would wear rings of bronze.

4 Cut lengths of string and glue them around the inside edges of the shapes. Glue plastic beads at the top of each arch, so that they look like precious stones.

5 Collect gold foil from sweet wrappers and glue it on to the tiara. Use the end of the paintbrush to carefully poke the foil into all the corners around the beads.

The finished tiara can be held together at the back by tape or a clip. Roman ladies liked to wear tiaras made of gold, with jewels in their hair.

Lessons and Learning

MOST CHILDREN in the Roman Empire never went to school. They learned a trade from their parents or found out about sums by trading on a market stall. Boys might be trained to fight with swords or to ride horses, in preparation for joining the army. Girls would be taught how to run the home, in preparation for marriage.

Wealthy families did provide an education for their sons and sometimes for their daughters, too. They were usually taught at home by a private tutor, but there were also small schools. Tutors and schoolmasters would teach children arithmetic, and how to read and write in both Latin and Greek. Clever pupils might also learn public speaking skills, poetry and history. Girls often had music lessons at home, on a harp-like instrument called a lyre.

INKPOTS AND PENS

Pen and ink were used to write on scrolls made from papyrus (a kind of reed) or thin sheets of wood. Ink was often made from soot or lamp-black, mixed with water. It was kept in inkpots such as these. Inkpots were made from glass, pottery or metal. Pens were made from bone, reeds or bronze.

WRITING IN WAX

This painting shows a couple from Pompeii. The man holds a parchment scroll. His wife is probably going through their household accounts. She holds a wax-covered writing tablet and a stylus to scratch words into the wax. A stylus had a pointed end for writing and a flat end for rubbing out.

A WRITING TABLET

You will need: sheets and sticks of balsa wood, craft knife, ruler, PVA glue, paintbrush, brown acrylic paint, water pot, modelling clay, work board, rolling pin, modelling tool, skewer, purple thread, pencil (to be used as a stylus), gold paint.

1 Use the craft knife to cut the balsa sheet into two rectangles 10cm x 22cm. The sticks of balsa should be cut into four lengths 22cm long and four lengths 10cm long.

2 Glue the sticks around the edges of each sheet as shown. These form a shallow hollow into which you can press the 'wax'. Paint the two frames a rich brown colour.

3 Roll out the modelling clay on a board and place a balsa frame on top. Use the modelling tool to cut around the outside of the frame. Repeat this step.

TEACHER AND PUPILS

This stone sculpture from Roman Germany shows a teacher seated between two of his pupils. They are reading their lessons from papyrus scrolls. Children had to learn poetry and other writings by heart. Any bad behaviour or mistakes were punished with a beating.

WRITING IT DOWN

Various materials were used for writing. Melted beeswax was poured into wooden trays to make writing tablets. Letters were scratched into the wax, which could be used again and again. Powdered soot was mixed with water and other ingredients to make ink for writing on papyrus, parchment or wood.

soot

melted beeswax

Roman numerals on papyrus

LETTERS IN STONE

Temples, monuments and public buildings were covered in Latin inscriptions, such as this one. Each letter was beautifully chiselled by a stonemason. These words are carved in marble. The inscription marked the 14th birthday of Lucius Caesar, the grandson of the Emperor Augustus.

4 Cut off about 1cm all around the edge of each modelling clay rectangle. This helps to make sure that the modelling clay will fit inside the balsa wood frame.

5 Carefully press the clay into each side – this represents the wax. Use the skewer to poke two holes through the inside edge of each frame, as shown.

6 Join the two frames together by threading purple thread through each pair of holes and tying it securely together. You have now made your tablet.

Paint the pencil gold to make it look as if it is made of metal. Use it like a stylus to scratch words on your tablet. Why not try writing in Latin? You could write **CIVIS ROMANVS SVM,** *which means "I am a Roman citizen".*

LESSONS AND LEARNING 221

In the Forum

EVERY LARGE ROMAN TOWN had a forum – a market square with public buildings around it. This was where people gathered to do business and exchange friendly gossip. In the morning, while the lady of the house had her hair done and her children struggled with their lessons, her husband would walk over to the forum.

In the forum's central square, crowds thronged around market stalls. Sometimes a public row might break out as inspectors of weights and measures accused some trader of cheating his customers. Around the square were shops, imposing monuments, marble statues and temples to the gods. The walls of buildings were often scrawled with graffiti made up of political messages, personal insults or declarations of love. On one side of the forum was the basilica, a large building used as the town hall, a law court and public meeting place. Some of the crowds may have been members of the *curia* or town council, or one of the trade guilds who had their halls there.

DOWNTOWN POMPEII
The ruins at Pompeii include these remains of a row of columns. They were part of a two-storey colonnade that once took up three sides of the forum. Rows of shops and market stalls were set up behind the colonnade at ground level.

TEMPLES AND PROSPERITY
The forum of every town had splendid temples to the many gods and goddesses of ancient Rome. There were also temples for famous Romans. The grand columns of this temple still remain in the forum at Rome. Today, a Christian church stands behind it. The temple was built in honour of Antoninus Pius, one of Rome's wisest emperors, and his wife Faustina.

MAKING MONEY
Money changers and bankers gathered to make deals and discuss business in the forum. Here, too, tax collectors raised money for the town council – taxes were charged on all goods that passed through the town.

FAST FOOD
As people hurried to work or chatted with friends, they might pick up a snack from a food stall or a street vendor. Pastries filled with spicy meats made popular snacks. On market day, the forum would also be busy with traders and farmers setting up stalls in the central square.

THE BASILICA
This is the Basilica of Maxentius in Rome. A basilica was a huge building used as a cross between a town hall and law courts. It usually had a very high roof, supported by rows of columns. The columns divided the building into a central area with two side aisles. People came here to work, do business or simply chat with friends.

Shopping – Roman Style

I N MOST LARGE TOWNS, shops spread out from the forum and along the main streets. Shops were usually small, family-run businesses. At the start of the working day, shutters or blinds would be taken from the shop front and goods put on display. Noise would soon fill the air as bakers, butchers, fishmongers, fruit and vegetable sellers all began crying out that their produce was the best and cheapest. Joints of meat might be hung from a pole, while ready-cooked food, grains or oils would be sold from pots set into a stone counter. Other shops sold pottery lamps or bronze lanterns, kitchen pots and pans or knives, while some traders repaired shoes or laundered cloth. Hammering and banging coming from the workshops at the back added to the clamour of a busy main street.

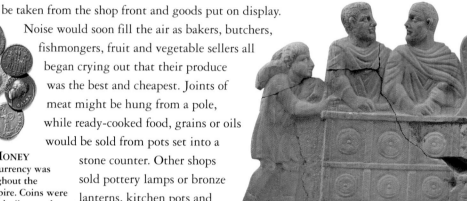

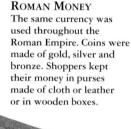

ROMAN MONEY
The same currency was used throughout the Roman Empire. Coins were made of gold, silver and bronze. Shoppers kept their money in purses made of cloth or leather or in wooden boxes.

GOING TO MARKET
This is a view of Trajan's Market, which was a five-storey group of shops set into a hillside in Rome. Most Roman towns had covered halls or central markets like this, where shops were rented out to traders.

A ROMAN DELICATESSEN

About 1,700 years ago this was the place to buy good food in Ostia, the seaport nearest to Rome. Bars, inns and cafés were fitted with stone counters that were often decorated with coloured marble. At lunchtime, bars like this would be busy with customers enjoying a meal.

A BUTCHER'S SHOP

A Roman butcher uses a cleaver to prepare chops while a customer waits for her order. Butchers' shops have changed very little over the ages – pork, lamb and beef were sold, and sausages were popular, too. On the right hangs a steelyard, a metal bar with a pan like a scale, for weighing the meat.

DISHING IT UP

These are the remains of a shop that sold food. Set into the marble counter are big pottery containers, called *dolia*. These were used for displaying and serving up food, such as beans and lentils. They were also used for keeping jars of wine cool on hot summer days. The containers could be covered with wooden or stone lids to keep out the flies.

Trades and Crafts

THERE WERE POTTERY WORKSHOPS throughout the Roman Empire. Clay pots were made by turning and shaping wet clay on a wheel and baking it in a kiln. Some of the best clay came from the district of Arretium, in Italy. Large pottery centres in Gaul (present-day France) produced a very popular red pottery called Samian ware. In Roman Germany, pottery drinking cups were coloured black and decorated in white with mottoes such as "Drink Up!" or "Bring Me Wine!" – in Latin, of course!

The Romans learned from the Syrians how to blow glass into shapes on the end of a long tube. This was a new and simple technique, although ways of making glass had been known for centuries. As a result, glass became widely used in Roman times.

The skills of the blacksmith were called for everyday, all over the Empire. Smiths hammered away on their anvils, shaping iron tools, weapons and pots. Some metalworkers were fine artists, working in gold, silver and bronze.

THE BLACKSMITHS' GOD
The Romans believed in many different gods. This is a statue of Vulcan, the god of smiths, or metal-workers. He is holding a hammer, used to shape hot metal on an anvil.

COPPERSMITHS
A typical busy day at a coppersmiths' workshop. A customer and his son look on as one of the smiths hammers out sheets of hot copper on an anvil. Another smith is bent over his work, decorating a copper bowl. The goods they are selling are displayed on the wall and hung from the ceiling.

SAMIAN POTTERY

This decorated bowl was found at Felixstowe, in Britain. Glossy red Samian ware was made in Gaul (present-day France), in workshops almost as big as factories. This popular pottery was transported all over the Empire, by land and by sea.

ROMAN SHOP

This stone carving shows a Roman shop with cloth and cushions for sale. Customers are seated while the shopkeeper shows them his wares. The Romans were skilled sculptors and much of our knowledge about the Empire comes from detailed carvings in stone such as this one.

ROMAN GLASSMAKING

Quality glass was made into bowls, jugs, flasks and bottles. Some were very simple in design, while others were highly decorated. Bands of coloured glass and even gold were used in some pieces. The finest glassware was used by wealthy Romans, and was always brought out when they entertained guests.

NATURAL DYES

Roman textile workers used a variety of natural dyes on cloth, including onion skins (a golden yellow dye), pine cones (a reddish-yellow dye) and tree bark (a reddish-brown dye). Other natural sources included berries, leaves, minerals, shellfish, nettles and saffron from crocuses.

bark

fir cones

onion

Pictures and Statues

THE ROMANS loved to decorate their homes and public places with paintings and statues. Mosaics were pictures made using *tesserae* – cubes of stone, pottery or glass – which were pressed into soft cement. Mosaic pictures might show hunting scenes, the harvest or Roman gods. Geometric patterns were popular and often used as borders.

Wall paintings, or murals, often showed garden scenes, birds and animals or heroes and goddesses. They were painted on to wooden panels or directly on to the wall. Roman artists loved to trick the eye by painting false columns, archways and shelves.

The Romans were skilled sculptors, using stone, marble and bronze. They imitated the ancient Greeks in putting up marble statues in public places and gardens. These might be of gods and goddesses or emperors and generals.

A COUNTRY SCENE
This man and wild boar are part of a mosaic made in Roman North Africa. Making a mosaic was quite tricky – rather like doing a jigsaw puzzle. Even so, skilled artists could create lifelike scenes from cubes of coloured glass, pottery and stone.

SCULPTURE
Statues of metal or stone were often placed in gardens. This bronze figure is in the remains of a house in Pompeii. It is of a faun, a god of the countryside.

FLOOR MOSAICS
Birds, animals, plants and country scenes were popular subjects for mosaics. These parrots are part of a much larger, and quite elaborate, floor mosaic from a Roman house.

MAKE A MOSAIC

You will need: rough paper, pencil, ruler, scissors, large sheet of card, self-drying clay, rolling pin, wooden board, modelling knife, acrylic paints, paintbrush, water pot, clear varnish and brush (optional), plaster paste, spreader, muslin rag.

1 Sketch out your mosaic design on rough paper. A simple design like this one is good to start with. Cut the card so it measures 25cm x 10cm. Copy the design on to it.

2 Roll out the clay on the board. Use the ruler to measure out small squares on the clay. Cut them out with the modelling knife. Leave to dry. These will be your tesserae.

3 Paint the pieces in batches of different colours, as shown above. When the paint is dry, you can coat them with clear varnish for extra strength and shine. Leave to dry.

MOSAIC MATERIALS

Mosaics were often made inside frames, in workshops, and then transported to where they were to be used. Sometimes, the tesserae were brought to the site and fitted on the spot by the workers. The floor of an average room in a Roman town house might need over 100,000 pieces.

tesserae

pot shards

MUSICIANS AND DANCERS

This dramatic painting is on the walls of an excavated villa in Pompeii. It is one in a series of paintings that show the secret rites, or mysteries, honouring the god Dionysus.

REAL OR FAKE?

Roman artists liked to make painted objects appear real enough to touch. This bowl of fruit on a shelf is typical of this style of painting. It was found on the wall of a villa that belonged to a wealthy Roman landowner.

The Romans liked to have mosaics in their homes. Wealthy people often had elaborate mosaics in their courtyards and dining rooms, as these were rooms that visitors would see.

4 Spread the plaster paste on to the card, a small part at a time. While it is still wet, press in your tesserae following the design, as shown. Use your sketch as an extra guide.

5 When the mosaic is dry, use the muslin rag to polish up the surface. Any other soft, dry cloth would also be suitable. Now your mosaic is ready for display.

Doctors and Medicine

Some Romans lived to a ripe old age, but most died before they reached the age of 50. Archaeologists have found out a lot about health and disease in Roman times by examining skeletons that have survived. They can tell, for example, how old a person was when they died and their general state of health during their life. Ancient writings also provide information about Roman medical knowledge.

Roman doctors knew very little science. They healed the sick through a mixture of common sense, trust in the gods and magic. Most cures and treatments had come to Rome from the doctors of ancient Greece. The Greeks and Romans also shared the same god of healing, Aesculapius. There were doctors in most parts of the Empire, as well as midwives, dentists and eye specialists. Surgeons operated on wounds received in battle, on broken bones and even skulls. The only pain killers were made from poppy juice – an operation must have been a terrible ordeal.

A CHEMIST'S SHOP
This pharmacy, or chemist's shop, is run by a woman. This was quite unusual for Roman times, as women were rarely given positions of responsibility. Roman pharmacists collected herbs and often mixed them for doctors.

GODDESS OF HEALTH
Greeks and Romans honoured the daughter of the god Aesculapius as a goddess of health. She was called Hygieia. The word hygienic, which comes from her name, is still used today to mean free of germs.

MEDICINE BOX
Boxes like this one would have been used by Roman doctors to store various drugs. Many of the treatments used by doctors were herbal, and not always pleasant to take!

MEDICAL INSTRUMENTS
The Romans used a variety of surgical and other instruments. These are made in bronze and include a scalpel, forceps and a spatula for mixing and applying various ointments.

TAKING THE CURE

These are the ruins of a medical clinic in Asia Minor (present-day Turkey). It was built around AD150, in honour of Aesculapius, the god of healing. Clinics like this one were known as therapy buildings. People would come to them seeking cures for all kinds of ailments.

BATHING THE BABY

This stone carving from Rome shows a newborn baby being bathed. The Romans were well aware of the importance of regular bathing in clean water. However, childbirth itself was dangerous for both mother and baby. Despite the dangers, the Romans liked to have large families, and many women died giving birth.

HERBAL MEDICINE

Doctors and travelling healers sold all kinds of potions and ointments. Many were made from herbs such as rosemary, sage and fennel. Other natural remedies included garlic, mustard and cabbage. Many of the remedies would have done little good, but some of them did have the power to heal.

garlic

sage

rosemary

Keeping Clean

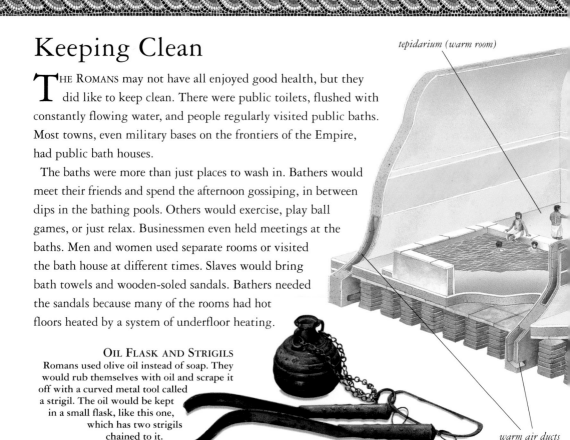

tepidarium (warm room)

T HE ROMANS may not have all enjoyed good health, but they did like to keep clean. There were public toilets, flushed with constantly flowing water, and people regularly visited public baths. Most towns, even military bases on the frontiers of the Empire, had public bath houses.

The baths were more than just places to wash in. Bathers would meet their friends and spend the afternoon gossiping, in between dips in the bathing pools. Others would exercise, play ball games, or just relax. Businessmen even held meetings at the baths. Men and women used separate rooms or visited the bath house at different times. Slaves would bring bath towels and wooden-soled sandals. Bathers needed the sandals because many of the rooms had hot floors heated by a system of underfloor heating.

warm air ducts in walls

OIL FLASK AND STRIGILS
Romans used olive oil instead of soap. They would rub themselves with oil and scrape it off with a curved metal tool called a strigil. The oil would be kept in a small flask, like this one, which has two strigils chained to it.

BATHING AT BATH
This is a view of the Roman baths in the town of Bath, in Britain. The Romans built the baths there because of the natural hot spring, which bubbled up from the rocks at temperatures of up to 50°C. Rich in health-giving minerals, it attracted visitors from far and wide. This large lead-lined pool was used for swimming. In Roman times, it was covered by a roof.

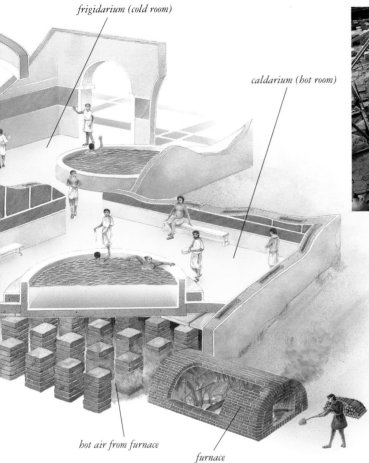

frigidarium (cold room)

caldarium (hot room)

hot air from furnace

furnace

BATH HOUSE DIG
An archaeological dig in Britain has uncovered these remains of the foundations of a bath house. You can see the bottoms of the pillars that once supported the floor. Hot air from a furnace would have flowed around these pillars, heating the floor and the rooms above it.

THE BATHS
The public baths included exercise areas, changing rooms, a sauna and various pools. The rooms and water were heated by hot air from one or more underground furnaces. The *frigidarium*, or cold room, usually had an unheated pool for bathers to take an icy plunge and was often partly open-air. It led on to a warmer area, the *tepidarium*. In the warmth, bathers would rub themselves with oil, then scrape off any dirt or grime. When they were clean, they were ready to take a dip in the pool. The steamy *caldarium*, or hot room, was nearest to a furnace. Here, bathers could soak or sweat to their hearts' content.

PUBLIC TOILETS
The remains of public toilets like these have been found in many parts of the Empire. People used sponges on sticks to clean themselves. They could rinse the sponges in a channel of flowing water in front of them. Another channel of water, under the stone seats, carried away the waste.

Sport and Combat

MOST ROMANS preferred watching sport rather than taking part themselves. There were some, however, who enjoyed athletics and keeping fit. They took their exercise at the public baths and at the sports ground or *palaestra*. Men would compete at wrestling, long jump and swimming. Women would work out with weights.

Boxing matches and chariot races were always well attended. The races took place on a long, oval racetrack, called a circus. The crowds would watch with such excitement that violent riots often followed. Charioteers and their teams became big stars. Roman crowds also enjoyed watching displays of cruelty. Bloody battles between gladiators and fights among wild animals took place in a special oval arena, called an amphitheatre. Roman entertainments became more spectacular and bloodthirsty as time passed. They would even flood the arenas of amphitheatres for mock sea battles.

A COLOSSEUM
This is the colosseum in the Roman city of El Djem, in Tunisia. A colosseum was a kind of amphitheatre. Arenas such as this were built all over the Empire. The largest and most famous is the Colosseum in Rome.

DEATH OR MERCY?
Gladiators usually fought to the death, but a wounded gladiator could appeal for mercy. The excited crowd would look for the emperor's signal. A thumbs-up meant his life was spared. A thumbs-down meant he must die.

COME ON YOU REDS!

Charioteers belonged to teams and wore their team's colours when they raced. Some also wore protective leather helmets, like the one in this mosaic. In Rome, there were four teams – the Reds, Blues, Whites and Greens. Each team had faithful fans and charioteers were every bit as popular as football stars today.

A DAY AT THE RACES

This terracotta carving records an exciting moment at the races. Chariot racing was a passion for most Romans. Chariots were usually pulled by four horses, though just two or as many as six could be used. Accidents and foul play were common as the chariots thundered round the track.

THE CHAMP

Boxing was a deadly sport. Fighters, like this boxer, wore studded thongs instead of padded boxing gloves. Severe injuries, and even brain damage, were probably quite common.

THE GREEK IDEAL

The Romans admired all things Greek, including their love of athletics. This painted Greek vase dates from about 333BC and shows long-distance runners. However, Roman crowds were not interested in athletic contests in the Greek style, such as the Olympic Games.

Music and Drama

MUSIC AND SONGS were an important part of Roman life. Music was played at banquets, at weddings and funerals, at the theatre, in the home, at fights between gladiators and other public events. The Romans played a variety of musical instruments, including double flutes, pan pipes, lyres, cymbals, rattles and tambourines. These had already been well known in either Egypt or Greece. The Romans also had trumpets and horns, and water-powered organs.

Going to the theatre was a popular Roman pastime. The whole idea of drama came from Greece, so Greek comedies and tragedies were often performed. Roman writers produced plays in a similar style, as well as comic sketches and dances. The stage used the stone front of a building as a backdrop. Rising banks of stone or wooden seats curved around it in a half circle.

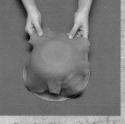

MUSIC LESSONS
Girls from wealthy families often had music lessons at home. This wall painting shows a girl being taught to play the cithara, a type of lyre. The Romans adopted this harp-like instrument from the Greeks.

THE ENTERTAINERS
This mosaic from Pompeii shows a group of actors in a scene from a Greek play. Actors were always men, playing the parts of women whenever necessary. The role of actors in a play was shown by the colours of their costume and their masks. The piper in this mosaic is wearing the white mask of a female character.

MAKE A MASK

You will need: self-drying clay, wooden board, rolling pin, large bowl, modelling knife, acrylic paints, paintbrush, water pot, scissors, cord, pencil, green paper or card, gardening wire, some coloured beads.

1 Put the clay on the board. Roll it out into a sheet that is bigger than the bowl you are using. Drape it over the bowl and shape it, as shown above.

2 Trim off the edges and cut out eye holes and a mouth. Roll out the clay you trimmed off and cut out a mouth and nose piece, as shown above. Make a small ball of clay, too.

3 Mould the nose on to the mask. Press the small ball of clay into the chin and put the mouth piece over it, as shown. Make a hole on each side of the mask, for the cord.

MUSICIANS
Some of the musicians in this procession are playing the *cornu*, a large curved horn. It was played at religious festivals and funerals, at public games, and by the Roman army.

ACTORS' MASKS
Roman actors wore masks and wigs to show the type of character they were playing. This detail of a mosaic from Rome shows the kind of elaborate masks they wore.

DRAMA IN THE OPEN AIR
Roman theatres were usually open to the sky. These are the ruins of the larger of the two theatres in Pompeii. It could seat up to 50,000 people. It had no roof, but could be covered by an awning to protect the audience from the hot summer sun.

4 When the clay is dry, paint the mask in bright colours. You can paint it like this one, shown above, or you could make up your own design. Leave the paint to dry.

5 Cut two lengths of cord. Thread them through the holes in the side of the mask, as shown. Secure with a knot. Tie the cord around your head when you wear the mask.

6 Draw, cut out and paint some leaf shapes. Thread them on to a length of wire, as shown. Thread beads between some of the leaves. Wind the wire round the top of the mask.

Actors' masks had large mouths for them to speak through. The actual masks were probably made of shaped and stiffened linen.

Fun and Games

ROMAN CHILDREN played games such as hide-and-seek, marbles and hopscotch, which are still popular today. Young children played with dolls and little figures of people and animals. These were made of wood, clay or bronze. A child from a wealthy family might be given a child-size chariot, to be pulled along by a goat.

Roman men and women loved playing board games. There were simple games, similar to noughts-and-crosses, and more complicated games, rather like chess or draughts. In some games, players had to race toward the finish. A dice was thrown to decide how many squares they could move at a time. They played with counters made of bone, glass or clay.

The Romans were great gamblers. They would place bets on a chariot race or a cock-fight or on throwing dice. Gambling became such a problem that games of chance were officially banned – except during the winter festival of Saturnalia, when most rules were relaxed. However, the rattle of dice could still be heard in most taverns and public baths.

PLAYING KNUCKLEBONES
Two women play the popular game of knucklebones, or *astragali*. The idea was to throw the knucklebones in the air and catch as many of them as possible on the back of your hand. The number you caught was your score.

KNUCKLEBONES
Most Romans used the ankle bones of sheep to play knucklebones. These had six sides and were also used as dice – each side had a different value. Wealthy Romans might use knucklebones made of glass, bronze or onyx, like these.

MARBLES
Roman children played with these marbles many centuries ago. Two are glass and one is made of pottery. Marbles were either rolled together or on to marked gaming boards. They were also thrown into pottery vases. Nuts, such as hazelnuts and walnuts, were often used like marbles.

MAKE A ROMAN GAME

You will need: self-drying clay, rolling pin, chopping board, modelling knife, ruler, glass tiles for making mosaics, two beads (in the same colours as your tiles).

1 Roll out the clay and trim it to about 25cm square. Use the ruler and knife to mark out a grid, 8 squares across and down, leaving a border around the edge.

2 Decorate the border using the clay you trimmed off, as shown above. Leave to dry. Each player chooses a colour and has 16 tiles and a bead – this is the *dux* or leader.

3 Players take turns to put their tiles on any squares, two at a time. The dux is put on last. Players now take turns to move a tile one square forward, backward or sideways.

Just Rolling Along

Children from poor families had few toys and had to work from a young age. However, even poor children found time to play, and made do with whatever was at hand. This boy is rolling wheels in front of him as he runs.

Your Throw!

This mosaic from Roman North Africa shows three men playing dice games in a tavern. The Romans loved to gamble and would bet on anything, including the roll of the dice. Large amounts could be won or lost on the score when the dice stopped rolling!

Counters

These gaming counters are made of bone and ivory. As well as using quite plain, round ones, the Romans liked to use counters carved in intricate shapes. Here you can see a ram's head, a hare and a lobster. The large round counter has two women carved on it.

Dice

Dice games were played by the poor and the rich. These dice have survived over the centuries. The largest is made of greenstone, the next is made of rock crystal, and the smallest is agate. The silver dice in the form of squatting figures were probably used by wealthy Romans.

During the game, you must move a tile or dux if it is possible to do so – even if it means being captured. The winner is the first player to capture all of the other player's tiles and dux.

4 If you sandwich your opponent's tile between two of yours, it is captured and removed. You then get an extra go. The dux is captured in the same way as any tile.

5 The dux can also jump over a tile to an empty square, as shown. If your opponent's tile is then trapped between your dux and one of your tiles, it is captured.

Religions and Festivals

THE ROMANS believed in many different gods and goddesses. Some of them were the same as the gods of ancient Greece, but with different names. Jupiter, the sky god, was the most powerful of all. Venus was the goddess of love, Mars was the god of war, Ceres the god of the harvest, Saturn the god of farmers, and Mercury of merchants. Household gods protected the home.

Splendid temples were built in honour of the gods. The Pantheon, in Rome, is the largest and most famous. Special festivals for the gods were held during the year, with processions, music, offerings and animal sacrifices. The festivals were often public holidays. The mid-winter festival of Saturnalia, in honour of Saturn, lasted up to seven days.

As the Empire grew, many Romans adopted the religions of other peoples, such as the Egyptians and the Persians.

JUPITER
Jupiter was the chief god of the Romans. He was the all-powerful god of the sky. The Romans believed he showed his anger by hurling a thunderbolt to the ground.

DIANA THE HUNTRESS
Diana was the goddess of hunting and the Moon. In this detail from a floor mosaic, she is shown poised with a bow and arrow, ready for the hunt. Roman gods were often the same as the Greek ones, but were given different names. Diana's Greek name was Artemis.

THE PANTHEON
The Pantheon in Rome was a temple to all the gods. It was built between AD118 and 128. Its mosaic floor, interior columns and high dome still remain exactly as they were built.

A TEMPLE TO THE GODS

You will need: thick stiff card, thin card, old newspaper, scissors, balloon, PVA glue, ruler, pencils, masking tape, drinking straws, acrylic paints, paintbrush, water pot, Plasticine.

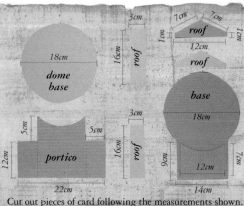

3cm · 7cm · 7cm

roof
1cm · 12cm · 1cm

roof

18cm

dome
base

16cm

roof

base

18cm

5cm · 5cm

3cm

12cm

portico

16cm

roof

9cm · 12cm · 7cm

22cm · 14cm

Cut out pieces of card following the measurements shown.

1 Blow up the balloon. Cover it in strips of newspaper pasted on with glue. Keep pasting until you have a thick layer. Leave to dry. Then burst the balloon and cut out a dome.

PRIESTS OF ISIS

The Egyptian mother-goddess Isis had many followers throughout the Roman Empire. This painting shows priests and worshippers of Isis taking part in a water purification ceremony. The ceremony would have been performed every afternoon.

BLESS THIS HOUSE

This is a bronze statue of a *lar* or household god. Originally gods of the countryside, the *lares* were believed to look after the family and the home. Every Roman home had a shrine to the *lares*. The family, including the children, would make daily offerings to the gods.

MITHRAS THE BULL-SLAYER

Mithras was the Persian god of light. He is shown here, in a marble relief from a temple, slaying a bull. This bull's blood was believed to have brought life to the Earth. The cult of Mithras spread through the whole Empire, and was particularly popular with Roman soldiers. However, only men were allowed to worship Mithras.

The Pantheon was built of brick and then clad in stone and marble. Its huge dome, with a diameter of over 43m, was the largest ever constructed until the 1900s.

2 Put the dome on its card base and draw its outline. Cut out the centre of the base to make a halo shape. Make a hole in the top of the dome, Bind the pieces together, as shown.

3 Glue together the base pieces. Cut a piece of thin card long enough to go round the base circle. This will be the circular wall. Use masking tape to hold the portico in shape.

4 Cut some straws into eight pieces, each 6cm long. These will be the columns for the entrance colonnade. Glue together the roof for the entrance. Secure with tape.

5 Glue together the larger pieces, as shown. Position each straw column with a small piece of Plasticine at its base. Glue on the entrance roof. Paint your model.

Family Occasions

THE FAMILY was very important to Romans. The father was the all-powerful head of the family, which included everyone in the household – wife, children, slaves, and even close relatives. In the early days of Rome, a father had the power of life and death over his children! However, Roman fathers were rarely harsh and children were much loved by both parents.

Childhood was fairly short. Parents would arrange for a girl to be betrothed at the age of 12, and a boy at 14. Marriages took place a few years later. Brides usually wore a white dress and a yellow cloak, with an orange veil and a wreath of sweetly-scented flowers. A sacrifice would be made to the gods, and everyone would wish the couple well. That evening, a procession with flaming torches and flute music would lead the newly-weds to their home.

Funerals were also marked with music and processions. By Roman law, burials and cremations had to take place outside the city walls.

HAPPY FAMILIES
This Roman tombstone from Germany shows a family gathered together for a meal. From the Latin inscription on it, we know that it was put up by a soldier of the legions, in memory of his dead wife. He lovingly describes her as the "sweetest and purest" of women.

D·M·C·IVL·MATERNVS
VET·EX·LEG·I·M·VIVS·SIBI
T·MARIE·MARCELLINAE
COIIVGI·DVLCISSIME
CASTISSIME·OBITAE·F

MOTHER AND BABY
A mother tenderly places her baby in the cradle. When children were born, they were laid at the feet of their father. If he accepted the child into the family, he would pick it up. In wealthy families, a birth was a great joy, but for poorer families it just meant another mouth to feed. Romans named a girl on the 8th day after the birth, and a boy on the 9th day. The child was given a *bulla*, a charm to ward off evil spirits.

TOGETHERNESS
When a couple were engaged, they would exchange gifts as a symbol of their devotion to each other. A ring like this one might have been given by a man to his future bride. The clasped hands symbolize marriage. Gold pendants with similar patterns were also popular.

MOURNING THE DEAD

A wealthy Roman has died and his family have gone into mourning. Laments are played on flutes as they prepare his body for the funeral procession. The Romans believed that the dead went to Hades, the Underworld, which lay beyond the river of the dead. A coin was placed in the corpse's mouth, to pay the ferryman. Food and drink for the journey was buried with the body.

TILL DEATH US DO PART

A Roman marriage ceremony was rather like a present-day Christian wedding. The couple would exchange vows and clasp hands to symbolize their union. Here, the groom is holding the marriage contract, which would have been drawn up before the ceremony. Not everyone found happiness, however, and divorce was quite common.

WEDDING FLOWERS

Roman brides wore a veil on their wedding day. This was often crowned with a wreath of flowers. In the early days of the Empire, verbena and sweet marjoram were a popular combination. Later fashions included orange blossom and myrtle, whose fragrant flowers were sacred to Venus, the goddess of love.

orange blossom

verbena

Soldiers of the Legion

THE ARMY OF THE EARLY EMPIRE was divided into 28 groups called legions. Each of these numbered about 5,500 soldiers. The legion included mounted troops and foot-soldiers. They were organized into cohorts, of about 500 men, and centuries, of about 80 men – even though centuries means 'hundreds'. Each legion was led into battle by soldiers carrying standards. These were decorated poles that represented the honour and bravery of the legion.

The first Roman soldiers were called up from the wealthier families in times of war. These conscripts had to supply their own weapons. In later years, the Roman army became paid professionals, with legionaries recruited from all citizens. During the period of the Empire, many foreign troops also fought for Rome as auxiliary soldiers.

Army life was tough and discipline was severe. After a long march carrying heavy kits, tents, tools and weapons, the weary soldiers would have to dig camp defences. A sentry who deserted his post would be beaten to death.

AT WAR
Trajan's Column in Rome is decorated with scenes from the Dacian wars. These were fought in the region of present-day Romania. Scenes like these can tell us much about Roman soldiers, the weapons they used, their enemies and their allies.

A LEGIONARY
This bronze statue of a legionary is about 1,800 years old. He is wearing a crested parade helmet and the overlapping bronze armour of the period. Legionaries underwent strict training and were brutally disciplined. They were tough soldiers and quite a force to be reckoned with.

ON HORSEBACK
Roman foot-soldiers were backed up by mounted troops, or cavalry. They were divided into groups, of 500 to 1,000, called *alae*. The cavalry were amongst the highest paid of Roman soldiers.

RAISING THE STANDARD

The Emperor Constantine addresses his troops, probably congratulating them on a victory. They are carrying standards, emblems of each legion. Standards were decorated with gold eagles, hands, wreaths and banners called *vexilla*. They were symbols of the honour and bravery of the legion and had to be protected at all costs.

A ROMAN FORT

The Roman army built forts of wood or stone all over the Empire. This fort is in southern Britain. It was built to defend the coast against attacks by Saxon raiders from northern Europe. Today, its surrounding area is called Porchester. The name comes from a combination of the word port and *caster*, the Latin word for fort.

HADRIAN'S WALL

This is part of Hadrian's Wall, which marks the most northerly border of the Roman Empire. It stretches for 120km across northern England, almost from coast to coast. It was built as a defensive barrier between AD122 and 128, at the command of the Emperor Hadrian.

Weapons and Armour

ROMAN SOLDIERS were well equipped. A legionary was armed with a dagger, called a *pugio*, and a short iron sword, called a *gladius*, which was used for stabbing and slashing. He carried a javelin, or *pilum*, made of iron and wood. In the early days, a foot-soldier's armour was a mail shirt, worn over a short, thick tunic. Officers wore a cuirass, a bronze casing that protected the chest and back. By about AD35, the mail shirt was being replaced by plate armour made of iron. The metal sections were joined by hooks or by leather straps. Officers wore varying crests to show their rank. Early shields were oval, and later ones were oblong with curved edges. They were made of layers of wood glued together, covered in leather and linen. A metal boss, or cover, over the central handle could be used to hit an enemy who got too close.

ROMAN SOLDIERS
Artists over the ages have been inspired by the battles of the Roman legions. They imagined how fully armed Roman soldiers might have looked. This picture shows a young officer giving orders.

HEAD GEAR
Helmets were designed to protect the sides of the head and the neck. This cavalry helmet is made of bronze and iron. It would have been worn by an auxiliary, a foreign soldier fighting for Rome sometime after AD43. Officers wore crests on their helmets, so that their men could see them during battle.

ROMAN ARMOUR

You will need: tape measure, A1-size sheets of silver card (one or two, depending on how big you are), scissors, pencil, PVA glue, paintbrush, 2m length of cord, compass.

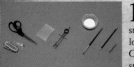

1 Measure yourself around your chest. Cut out three strips of card, 5cm wide and long enough to go round you. Cut out some thinner strips to stick these three together.

2 Lay the wide strips flat and glue them together with the thin strips, as shown above. The Romans would have used leather straps to hold the wide metal pieces together.

3 When the glue is dry, bend the ends together, silver side out. Make a hole in the end of each strip and thread the cord through, as shown above.

TORTOISE TACTICS

Siege tactics were one of the Roman army's great strengths. When approaching an enemy fortress, a group of soldiers could lock their shields together over their heads and crouch under them. Protected by their shields, they could safely advance toward the enemy. This was known as the tortoise, or *testudo*, formation. During a siege, catapults were used to hurl iron bolts and large stones over fortress walls.

DEADLY WEAPONS

These iron spearheads were found on the site of an old Roman fort near Bath, in Britain. The wooden shafts they were on rotted long ago. Roman soldiers carried both light and heavy spears. The lighter ones were used for throwing, and the heavier ones were for thrusting at close range.

SWORDS

Both short and long swords would have been kept in a scabbard. This spectacular scabbard was owned by an officer who served the Emperor Tiberius. It may have been given to him by the emperor himself. It is elaborately decorated in gold and silver.

4 Cut a square of card as wide as your shoulders. Use the compass to draw a 12cm diameter circle in the centre. Cut the square in half and cut away the half circles.

5 Use smaller strips of card to glue the shoulder halves together, leaving a neck hole. Cut out four more strips, two a little shorter than the others. Attach them in the same way.

Put the shoulder piece over your head and tie the chest section round yourself. Now you are a legionary ready to do battle with the enemies of Rome. Metal strip armour was invented during the reign of the Emperor Tiberius, AD14-37. Originally, the various parts were hinged and were joined together either by hooks or by buckles and straps.

Ships and Sailors

THE ROMANS USED SHIPS for trade, transport and warfare. Roman warships were slim, fast vessels called galleys. They were powered by oarsmen who sat below deck. A standard Roman war galley had 270 oarsmen. It also had a large, square sail that was used for more speed when the wind was favourable.

All kinds of goods, from wool and pottery to marble and grain, had to be moved around the Empire. Most goods, especially heavy cargoes of food or building materials, were moved by water. Merchant ships were deeper, heavier and slower than galleys. They had big, flapping sails and longer oars to make steering easier. Barges were used on rivers.

The Romans built lighthouses on treacherous coasts – stone towers topped by big lanterns or blazing beacons. Pirates, uncharted waters and the weather also made sea travel dangerous.

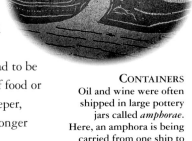

CONTAINERS
Oil and wine were often shipped in large pottery jars called *amphorae*. Here, an amphora is being carried from one ship to another. The amphorae were usually stacked in the ship's hold, with layers of brushwood as padding.

AT THE DOCKS
This wall painting from the port of Ostia shows a merchant ship being loaded. Heavy sacks of grain are being carried on board. You can see the two large steering oars at the stern, or rear, of the ship.

ROLLING ON THE RIVER
Wine and other liquids were sometimes stored in barrels. These were transported by river barges, like the one in this carving. Barrels of wine would be hauled from the vineyards of Germany or southern France to the nearest seaport.

MAKE AN AMPHORA

You will need: large sheet of thin card, ruler, two pencils, scissors, corrugated cardboard – two circles of 10cm and 20cm in diameter, two strips of 40cm x 30cm and another large piece, masking tape, PVA glue, old newspaper, paintbrush, reddish-brown acrylic paint, water pot.

1 Cut two pieces of card – 5cm and 38cm in depth. Tape the short piece to the small circle. Curl the long piece to make the neck. Make two holes in the side and tape it to the large circle.

2 Roll up the strips of corrugated cardboard. Bend them, as shown, fitting one end to the hole in the neck and the other to the cardboard. Fix in place with glue and tape.

3 Cut a piece of card, 40cm square. Roll it into a cylinder shape. Cut four lines, 10cm long, at one end, so it can be tapered into a point, as shown. Bind with tape.

Sailing Off to Battle

This painting imagines the impressive spectacle of a Roman war galley leaving harbour on its way to battle. Galleys were powered by rows of oarsmen, who sat on benches below deck. The helmsman, who controlled the galley's steering, shouted orders down to them. This galley has three banks, or layers, of oars. An underwater battering ram stuck out from the bow, or front, of war galleys. During a sea battle, the mast was lowered and the galley would try to ram the enemy ship. With the ram stuck in its side, Roman soldiers could easily board the enemy ship to finish the fight man to man.

An amphora like this one might have been used to carry wine, oil or fish sauce. Its long, pointed end would be stuck into layers of brushwood for support during transport.

4 To give the amphora a more solid base, roll up a cone of corrugated cardboard and stick it around the tapered end. Push a pencil into the end, as shown. Tape in position.

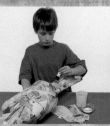

5 Stick the neck on to the main body. Cover the whole piece with strips of newspaper brushed on with glue. Leave to dry. Repeat until you have built up a thick layer.

6 When the paper is dry, paint the amphora. Roman amphorae were made of clay, so use a reddish-brown paint to make yours look like it is clay. Leave to dry.

Builders of the Empire

THE ROMANS were great builders and engineers. As the legions conquered foreign lands, they built new roads to carry their supplies and messengers. The roads were very straight, stretching across hundreds of kilometres. They were built with a slight hump in the middle so that rainwater drained off to the sides. Some were paved with stone and others were covered with gravel or stone chippings. Roman engineers also used their skills to bring water supplies to their cities by building aqueducts.

The Romans constructed great domes, arched bridges and grand public buildings all across the Empire. Local supplies of stone and timber were used. Stone was an important Roman building material, but had to be quarried and transported to sites. The Romans were the first to develop concrete, which was cheaper and stronger than stone.

The rule of the Romans came to an end in western Europe over 1,500 years ago. Yet reminders of their skills and organization are still visible today.

ROMAN ROADS
A typical Roman road, stretching into the distance as far as the eye can see. It runs through the coastal town of Ostia, in Italy. It was the 1800s before anyone in Europe could build roads to match those of ancient Rome.

MUSCLE POWER
This stone carving shows how Romans used big wooden cranes to lift heavy building materials. The crane is powered by a huge treadwheel. Slaves walk round and round in the wheel, making it turn. The turning wheel pulls on the rope, that is tied round the heavy block of stone, raising it off the ground.

MAKE A GROMA

You will need: large, strong piece of cardboard, scissors, ruler, pencil, square of card, PVA glue, masking tape, balsa wood pole, Plasticine, silver foil, string, large sewing needle, acrylic paints, paintbrush, water pot, broom handle.

1 Cut out three pieces of cardboard – two 20cm x 6cm, one 40cm x 6cm. Cut another piece, 15cm x 12cm, for the handle. Then cut them into shape, as shown above.

2 Measure to the centre of the long piece. Use a pencil to make a slot here, between the layers of cardboard. The slot is for the balsa wood pole.

3 Slide the balsa wood pole into the slot and tape the cardboard pieces in a cross. Use the card square to make sure the four arms of the groma are at right angles. Glue in place.

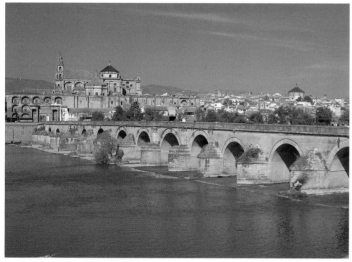

BUILDING MATERIALS

The Romans used a variety of stones for building. Local quarries were the most common source. Limestone and a volcanic rock called tufa were used in Pompeii. Slate was used for roofing in parts of Britain. Fine marble, used for temples and other public buildings, was available in the Carrara region of Italy, as it still is today. However, it was also imported from overseas.

marble

slate

SURVIVING THE CENTURIES

This Roman bridge crosses the River Guadalquivir at Cordoba in Spain. The Romans had no bulldozers or power tools, and yet their buildings and monuments have survived thousands of years.

WALLS OF ROME

The city of Rome's defences were built at many stages in its history. These sturdy walls were raised during the reign of the Emperor Marcus Aurelius, AD121–180. Known as the Aurelian Walls, they are still in good condition today.

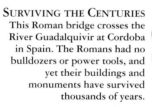

Slot the arms on to the balsa wood pole. Use the plumb lines as a guide to make sure the pole is vertical. The arms can then be used to line up objects in the distance. Romans used a groma to measure right angles and to make sure roads were straight.

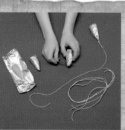

4 Roll the Plasticine into four small cones and cover them with foil. Thread string through the tops, as shown. These are the groma's plumb lines, or vertical guides.

5 Tie the plumb lines to each arm, as shown. They must all hang at the same length – 20cm will do. If the Plasticine is too heavy, use wet newspaper rolled up in the foil.

6 Split the top of the handle piece, and wrap it round the balsa wood pole. Glue it in place, as shown. Do the same on the other end with the broom handle. Paint the groma.

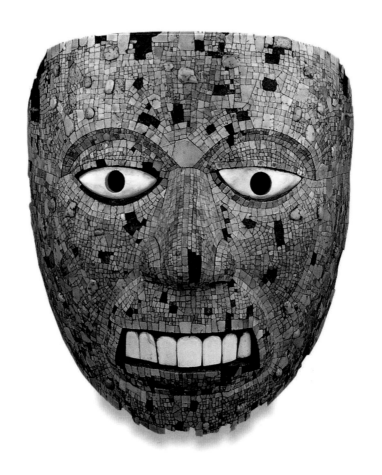

THE
AZTEC & MAYA
WORLDS

The Aztecs, Maya and other peoples of Central America that came before them share a history of fabulous craftsmanship, human sacrifice and marvellous astronomical knowledge. The Aztec and Maya built huge ceremonial temple-pyramids and administrative buildings. Some rulers created empires by conquering neighbouring cities.

FIONA MACDONALD
Consultant: Clara Bezanilla, The Museum of Mankind

Great Civilizations

THE AZTECS LIVED IN MESOAMERICA – the region where North and South America meet. It includes the countries of Mexico, Guatemala, Honduras, El Salvador and Belize. During the past 3,000 years, Mesoamerica has been home to many great civilizations, including the Olmecs, the Maya, the Toltecs and the Aztecs. The Aztecs were the last of these to arrive, coming from the north in around AD1200. In about 1420 they began to conquer a mighty empire. But in 1521 they were themselves conquered by Spanish soldiers, who came to America in search of gold. Over the next hundred years, the rest of Mesoamerica also fell to the Spaniards.

Even so, the descendants of these cultures still live in the area today. Many ancient Mesoamerican words, customs and beliefs survive, as do beautiful hand-painted books, mysterious ruins and amazing treasures.

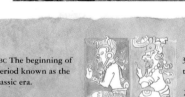

OLMEC POWER
This giant stone head was carved by the Olmecs, the earliest of many great civilizations that flourished in Mesoamerica. Like the Maya and Aztecs, the Olmecs were skilled stone workers and built great cities.

UNCOVERING THE PAST
This temple is in Belize. Remains of such great buildings give archaeologists important clues about the people who built them.

TIMELINE 5000BC–AD800

Many civilizations were powerful in Mesoamerica at different times. The Maya were most successful between AD600–900. The Aztecs were at the height of their power from AD1428–AD1520.

5000BC The Maya settle along the Pacific and Caribbean coasts of Mesoamerica.

2000BC People begin to farm in Guatemala, Belize and south-east Mexico.

Olmec figure

2000BC The beginning of the period known as the Preclassic era.

1200BC Olmec people are powerful in Mesoamerica. They remain an important power until 400BC.

1000BC Maya craftworkers begin to copy Olmec pottery and jade carvings.

900BC Maya farmers design and use irrigation systems.

600BC The Zapotec civilization begins to flourish at Monte Alban.

Maya codex

300BC The Maya population starts to grow rapidly. Cities are built.

292BC The first-known Maya writing is produced.

150BC–AD500 The people living in the city of Teotihuacan grow powerful.

AD250 The beginning of the greatest period of Maya power, known as the Classic Maya era. This lasts until AD900.

mask from Teotihuac

5000BC   2000BC   300BC   AD50

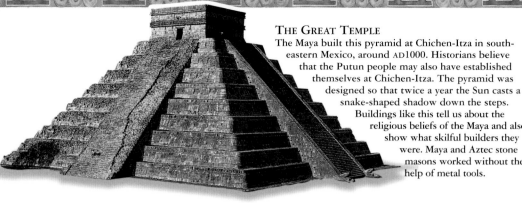

THE GREAT TEMPLE

The Maya built this pyramid at Chichen-Itza in south-eastern Mexico, around AD1000. Historians believe that the Putun people may also have established themselves at Chichen-Itza. The pyramid was designed so that twice a year the Sun casts a snake-shaped shadow down the steps. Buildings like this tell us about the religious beliefs of the Maya and also show what skilful builders they were. Maya and Aztec stone masons worked without the help of metal tools.

THE FACE OF A GOD

This mask represents the god Tezcatlipoca. It is made of pieces of semi-precious stone fixed to a real human skull. Masks like this were worn during religious ceremonies, or displayed in temples as offerings to the gods.

Home of the Mesoamerican civilizations

MESSAGES IN CODE

These are Aztec picture-symbols for days, written in a folding book called a codex. Mesoamerican civilizations kept records of important people, places and events in picture-writing.

MESOAMERICA IN THE WORLD

For centuries, Mesoamerica was home to many different civilizations, but there were links between them, especially in farming, technology and religious beliefs. Until around AD1500, these Mesoamerican civilizations had very little contact with the rest of the world.

AD550 This is the time of the Maya's greatest artistic achievements. Fine temples and palaces in cities such as Kabah, Copan, Palenque, Uxmal and Tikal are built. These great regional city-states are ruled by lords who claim to be descended from the gods. This period of Maya success continues until AD900.

temple at Tikal

AD615 The great Maya leader Lord Pacal rules in the city of Palenque.

AD650 The city of Teotihuacan begins to decline. It is looted and burned by unknown invaders around AD700.

AD684 Lord Pacal's rule in Palenque ends. He is buried in a tomb within the Temple of the Inscriptions.

jade death mask of Lord Pacal

Bonampak mural

AD790 Splendid Maya wall-paintings are created in the royal palace in the city of Bonampak.

AD600   AD700   AD800

Between North and South

MESOAMERICA IS A LAND of contrasts. There are high, jagged mountains, harsh deserts and swampy lakes. In the north, volcanoes rumble. In the south, dense, steamy forests have constant rain for half the year. These features made travelling around difficult, and also restricted contact between the regions.

Mesoamerica was never ruled as a single, united country. For centuries it was divided into separate states, each based on a city that ruled the surrounding countryside. Different groups of people and their cities became rich and strong in turn, before their civilizations weakened and faded away.

Historians divide the Mesoamerican past into three main periods. In Preclassic times (2000BC–AD250), the Olmecs were most powerful. The Classic era (AD250–900) saw the rise of the Maya and the people living in the city of Teotihuacan. During the Postclassic era (AD900–1500), the Toltecs, followed by the Aztecs, controlled the strongest states.

Each civilization had its own language, laws, traditions and skills, but there were also many links between the separate states. They all built big cities and organized long-distance trade. They all practised human sacrifice and worshipped the same family of gods. And, unlike all other ancient American people, they all measured time using their own holy calendar of 260 days.

Sierra Madre Occidental

MEXICO

N

TIMELINE AD800–AD1400

AD800 The Maya palace-city of Palenque begins to decline.

AD856 The Toltecs of northern Mexico begin to create the city-state of Tula.

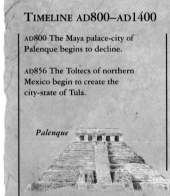

Palenque

AD900 Maya power begins to collapse. Many Maya cities, temples and palaces are deserted and overgrown by the rainforest. This is the beginning of the period known as the Postclassic era. The era lasts until AD1500.

AD950 The city of Tula becomes the centre of fast-growing Toltec power.

AD986 According to legend, the Toltec god-king Quetzalcoatl leaves north Mexico for the Maya lands of Yucatan.

Toltec warrior

AD1000 The Maya city of Chichen-Itza becomes powerful. Historians believe that the Maya may have been helped by Putun warriors from the Gulf coast of Mexico.

AD1000 Toltec merchants do business along long-distance trade routes around the coast. They are helped by Maya craftworkers. Long-distance trade has already been taking place in Mesoamerica for hundreds of years.

AD1011–1063 The Mixtecs are ruled by the leader Eight Deer, in the area of Oaxaca. The Mixtecs are master goldsmiths.

AD800　　　　　　AD900　　　　　　　　　AD1000　　　　　AD11

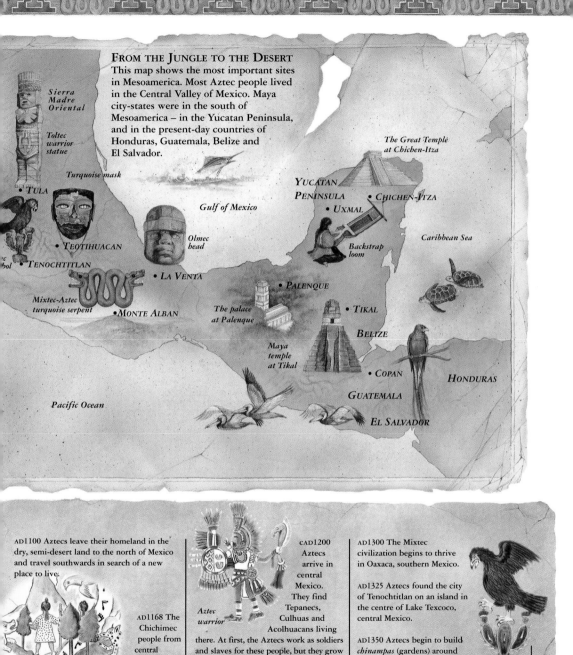

FROM THE JUNGLE TO THE DESERT
This map shows the most important sites
in Mesoamerica. Most Aztec people lived
in the Central Valley of Mexico. Maya
city-states were in the south of
Mesoamerica – in the Yucatan Peninsula,
and in the present-day countries of
Honduras, Guatemala, Belize and
El Salvador.

*Sierra
Madre
Oriental*

*Toltec
warrior
statue*

Turquoise mask

• TULA

• TEOTIHUACAN

• TENOCHTITLAN

*Mixtec-Aztec
turquoise serpent*

•MONTE ALBAN

• LA VENTA

Gulf of Mexico

*Olmec
head*

*The palace
at Palenque*

• PALENQUE

*Maya
temple
at Tikal*

*The Great Temple
at Chichen-Itza*

YUCATAN
PENINSULA   • CHICHEN-ITZA
        • UXMAL

*Backstrap
loom*

Caribbean Sea

• TIKAL

BELIZE

• COPAN

GUATEMALA

HONDURAS

EL SALVADOR

Pacific Ocean

AD1100 Aztecs leave their homeland in the
dry, semi-desert land to the north of Mexico
and travel southwards in search of a new
place to live.

Aztec settlers

AD1168 The
Chichimec
people from
central
Mexico
destroy the city
of Tula and end
Toltec power.

*Aztec
warrior*

cAD1200
Aztecs
arrive in
central
Mexico.
They find
Tepanecs,
Culhuas and
Acolhuacans living
there. At first, the Aztecs work as soldiers
and slaves for these people, but they grow
strong and fight against their masters.

cAD1220 A new Maya city is founded
at Mayapan.

AD1300 The Mixtec
civilization begins to thrive
in Oaxaca, southern Mexico.

AD1325 Aztecs found the city
of Tenochtitlan on an island in
the centre of Lake Texcoco,
central Mexico.

AD1350 Aztecs begin to build
chinampas (gardens) around
Lake Texcoco.

AD1372–1391 The first-known
Aztec ruler, Acamapichtli, reigns.

*eagle on cactus,
the symbol of
Tenochtitlan*

AD1200   AD1300   AD1400

Famous People

FAME IN Maya and Aztec times usually came with power. We know the names of powerful Aztec and Maya rulers, and sometimes of their wives. However, very few ordinary people's names have been discovered.

Rulers' names were written in a codex or carved on a monument to record success in battle or other great achievements. Scribes also compiled family histories, in which rulers often claimed to be descended from gods. This gave them extra religious power. Aztec and Maya rulers made sure their names lived on by building huge palaces, amazing temples and tombs.

Some of the most famous Mesoamerican rulers lived at a time when their civilization was under threat from outsiders. Explorers from Europe have left us detailed accounts and descriptions of the rulers they met.

MAYA RULER
This statue shows a ruler from the Maya city of Kabah, in Mexico. Most Maya statues were designed as symbols of power, rather than as life-like portraits.

ROYAL TOMB
This pyramid-shaped temple was built to house the tomb of Lord Pacal. He ruled the Maya city-state of Palenque from AD615 to 684. Its walls are decorated with scenes from Pacal's life.

TIMELINE AD1400–AD1600

tribute items collected by the Aztecs

AD1400–AD1425 The Aztec city of Tenochtitlan continues to thrive and grow.

AD1415–1426 The Aztec leader Chimalpopoca reigns.

AD1428 Aztecs defeat the Tepanecs and begin to conquer neighbouring lands and collect tribute from them.

AD1428 Aztecs set up the Triple Alliance. This was an agreement with neighbouring city-states Texcoco and Tlacopan that made them the strongest force in Mexico.

AD1440 Moctezuma Ilhuicamina, the greatest Aztec ruler, begins his reign. He reigns until 1468.

AD1441 The Maya city of Mayapan is destroyed by civil war.

AD1468 Aztec ruler Axayacatl reigns.

AD1473 The Aztecs conquer the rich market-city of Tlatelolco in central Mexico.

market traders in the market-city of Tlatelolco

AD1400   AD1425   AD1450   AD14

GOLD-SEEKER

Soldier and explorer Hernan Cortes (1485–1547) came from a poor but noble Spanish family. After Columbus' voyages, many Spanish adventurers travelled to Mesoamerica and the Caribbean hoping to make their fortunes. Cortes sailed to Cuba and then, in 1519, went on to explore Mexico. His example inspired many treasure-seekers. One such man, Pizarro, went on to conquer the Incas of Peru.

BETWEEN TWO WORLDS

Malintzin (*far right above*) was from a Mesoamerican state hostile to the Aztecs. She was of vital help to the Spanish conquerors because she spoke the Aztec language and quickly learned Spanish. The Spanish called her Doña Marina.

THE LAST EMPEROR

Aztec emperor Moctezuma II (*above right*) ruled from 1502 to 1520. He was the last emperor to control the Aztec lands. Moctezuma II was a powerful warrior and a good administrator, but he was tormented by gloomy prophecies and visions of disaster. He was captured when Cortes and his soldiers invaded the capital city of Tenochtitlan in 1519. The following year he was stoned in a riot whilst trying to plead with his own people.

AD1481–1486 Aztec ruler Tizoc reigns.

AD1486 Aztec ruler Ahuitzotl begins his reign.

AD1487 The Aztecs' Great Temple in Tenochtitlan is finished. Twenty thousand captives are sacrificed at a special ceremony to consecrate it (make it holy).

AD1492 The European explorer Christopher Columbus sails across the Atlantic Ocean to America.

Columbus lands

AD1502 Columbus sails along the coast of Mesoamerica and meets Maya people.

a comet appears in the sky

AD1502–1520 Moctezuma II reigns. During his reign, a comet appears in the sky. Aztec astronomers fear that this, and other strange signs, mean the end of the world.

AD1519 Hernan Cortes, a Spanish soldier, arrives in Mexico. A year later, Cortes and his soldiers attack Tenochtitlan. Moctezuma II is killed.

AD1521 The Spanish destroy Tenochtitlan.

AD1525 Spain takes control of Aztec lands.

AD1527 Maya lands are invaded by the Spanish.

AD1535 Mexico becomes a Spanish colony.

AD1600 War and European diseases wipe out 10 million Aztecs, leaving fewer than a million, but the Aztec language and many customs live on. By AD1600, between 75% and 90% of Maya people are also dead, but Maya skills, beliefs and traditions survive.

Spanish soldier

AD1500   AD1525   AD1600

The Order of Things

MESOAMERICAN CITY-STATES were ruled by leaders with three separate tasks. They were army commanders, law-makers and priests. Many rulers claimed to be descended from the gods. Rulers were almost always men. Mesoamerican women – especially among the Maya – had important religious duties but rarely took part in law-making or army life.

Maya rulers were called *ahaw* (lord) or *mahk'ina* (great Sun lord), and each city-state had its own royal family. The Aztec leader was called the *tlatoani* (speaker). Originally, he was elected from army commanders by the Aztec people. Later, he was chosen from the family of the previous ruler. He ruled all Aztec lands, helped by a deputy called *cihuacoatl* (snake woman), by nobles and by army commanders. Priests observed the stars, looking for signs about the future, and held religious ceremonies.

Rulers, priests and nobles made up a tiny part of society. Ordinary citizens were called *macehualtin*. Women looked after their families. Men were farmers, fishermen or craftworkers. There were also thousands of slaves, who were criminals, enemy captives or poor people who had given up their freedom in return for food and shelter.

OFFICIAL HELP
This Maya clay figure shows a scribe at work. Well-trained officials, such as this scribe, helped Mesoamerican rulers by keeping careful records. Scribes also painted ceremonial pottery.

HONOUR TO THE KING
Painted pottery vases like this were buried alongside powerful Maya people. They show scenes from legends and royal palace life. Here, a lord presents tribute to the king.

MAYA NOBLEWOMAN
This terracotta figure of a Maya noblewoman dates from between AD600 and 900. She is richly attired and is protecting her face with a parasol. Women did not usually hold official positions of responsibility in Mesoamerican lands. Instead queens and other noblewomen influenced their husbands by offering tactful suggestions and wise advice. Whether she was rich or poor, a woman's main duty was to provide children for her husband and to support him in all aspects of his work.

THE RULING CLASS

A noble is shown getting ready for a ceremony in this Aztec codex picture. Aztec nobles played an important part in government. They were chosen by rulers to be judges, army commanders and officials. Nobles with government jobs paid no taxes and were given a free house to live in. Noblemen and women were born into ancient noble families, related to the rulers. It was, however, possible for an ordinary man to achieve higher rank if he fought very bravely in battle and captured four enemy soldiers alive.

WAR LEADER

This Maya stone carving shows ruler Shield Jaguar (*below left*) getting ready to lead his army in AD724. He is wearing a padded tunic and holding a knife in his right hand. His wife, Lady Xoc, is handing him his jaguar headdress. Maya rulers also took part in religious ceremonies, where they offered drops of their blood to the gods to ask for their help.

MEN AT WORK

Here, Aztec farmers are harvesting ripe cobs of maize. This painting comes from the Florentine Codex. This 12-volume manuscript was made by a Spanish friar. Codex pictures like this tell us a lot about ordinary peoples' everyday lives. Notice how simply the farmers are dressed compared to the more powerful people on these pages.

The Court, Government and Laws

THE REMAINS OF MANY splendid palaces survive in Mesoamerican lands. In the 1500s European explorers described the vast palace of the Aztec ruler Moctezuma II in Tenochtitlan. It had banqueting rooms big enough to seat 3,000 guests, private apartments, a library, a schoolroom, kitchens, stores, an arsenal for weapons, separate women's quarters, spectacular gardens and a large zoo. Etiquette around the emperor was very strict. Captains of the royal bodyguard had to approach Moctezuma barefoot, with downcast eyes, making low bows and murmuring, "Lord, my lord, my great lord." When they left, they had to walk backwards, keeping their gaze away from his face.

Palaces were not just rulers' homes. They were also official government headquarters where rulers greeted ambassadors from neighbouring city-states and talked with advisors.

Rulers also had the power to make strict laws. Each city-state had its own law-courts, where formidable judges had the power of life and death over people brought before them.

ROYAL RECORD
Maya rulers set up carved stone pillars in their cities to record major events during their reigns. These pillars are called stelae. This one celebrates a Maya ruler in Copan, Honduras.

THE SEAT OF POWER
This carved jade ornament shows a seated Maya king. Although Aztec and Maya leaders had the final responsibility for decisions, they also relied on judges, officials and scribes to help them rule.

MAKE A FEATHER FAN

You will need: pencil, thick card, scissors, thin red card, green paper, double-sided tape, feathers (real or paper), masking tape, paints, paintbrushes, coloured felt, PVA glue and brush, sticky tape, coloured wool, bamboo cane.

1 Draw two rings about 45cm in diameter and 8cm wide on thick card. Cut them out. Make another ring the same size from thin red card, as above.

2 Cut lots of leaf shapes from green paper. Stick them around the edge of one thick card ring using double-sided tape. Add some real or paper feathers.

3 Cut two circles about 12cm in diameter from thin red card. Draw around something the right size, such as a reel of tape. These are for the centre of the fan.

LOCKED UP

Here, a group of Aztec judges discusses how to punish two prisoners. You can see them cowering in a wooden cage. By modern standards, punishments were very severe. If ordinary citizens broke the law, they might be beaten or speared with cactus spines. For a second offence, they might be stoned to death.

THE RULE OF THE GODS

This stone carving shows a human face being swallowed by a magic serpent. Royal and government buildings were often decorated with carvings such as this. They signified the religious power of the ruler of a particular city.

FIT FOR A KING

This picture from an Aztec codex shows visitors to a ruler's palace. It was reported by Spanish explorers that over six hundred nobles came to the Aztec ruler's palace every day to attend council meetings, consult palace officials, ask favours from the ruler and make their views heard. The ruler would sit on a mat on the floor with his council, as was the Aztec tradition.

Aztec nobles and rulers cooled themselves with beautiful feather fans.

4 Paint a flower on one of the two smaller red circles and a butterfly on the other. Cut v-shapes from the felt and glue them to the large red ring.

5 Using sticky tape, fix lengths of coloured wool to the back of one of the red circles, as shown. Place the red circle in the centre of the ring with leaves.

6 Tape the lengths of wool to the outer ring to look like spokes. Coat the ring with PVA glue and place the second card ring on top, putting a cane in between.

7 Use double-sided tape to stick the second red circle face up in the centre. Glue the red ring with felt v-shapes on top of the second thick card ring.

Family Life

FAMILIES WERE very important in Maya and Aztec times. By working together, family members provided themselves with food, jobs, companionship and a home. Each member of a family had special responsibilities. Men produced food or earned money to buy it. Women cared for babies and the home. From the age of about five or six, children were expected to do their share of the family's work by helping their parents. Because family life was so important, marriages were often arranged by a young couple's parents, or by a matchmaker. The role of matchmaker would be played by an old woman who knew both families well. Boys and girls got married when they were between 16 and 20 years old. The young couple usually lived in the boy's parents' home.

Aztec families belonged to local clan-groups, known as *calpulli*. Each *calpulli* chose its own leader, collected its own taxes and built its own temple. It offered help to needy families, but also kept a close eye on how members behaved. If someone broke the law, the whole clan might be punished for that person's actions.

MOTHER AND SON
These Maya clay figures may show a mother and her son. Boys from noble families went to school at about 15. They learned reading, writing, maths, astronomy and religion.

PAINFUL PUNISHMENT
This codex painting shows a father holding his son over a fire of burning chillies as a punishment. Aztec parents used severe punishments in an attempt to make their children honest and obedient members of society.

SPICE
Hot, spicy chilli peppers were an essential part of many Maya and Aztec meals. In fact, the Aztecs said that if a meal lacked chillies, it was a fast, not a feast! Chillies were used in stews and in spicy sauces, and they were used in medicine too. They were crushed and rubbed on aching muscles or mixed with salt to ease toothache.

red chillies

dried chillies, preserved for winter use

green chillies

IXTILTON

This Aztec mask is made of a black volcanic stone called obsidian. It shows the god Ixtilton, helper of Huitzilopochtli, the Aztecs' special tribal god. Aztec legends told how Ixtilton could bring darkness and peaceful sleep to tired children.

HUSBAND AND WIFE

The bride and groom in this codex picture of an Aztec wedding have their clothes tied together. This shows that their lives are now joined. Aztec weddings were celebrated with presents and feasting. Guests carried bunches of flowers, and the bride wore special make-up with her cheeks painted yellow or red. During the ceremony, the bride and groom sat side by side on a mat in front of the fire.

GUARDIAN GODDESS

The goddess Tlazolteotl is shown in this codex picture. She was the goddess of lust and sin. Tlazolteotl was also said to watch over mothers and young children. Childbirth was the most dangerous time in a woman's life, and women who died in childbirth were honoured like brave soldiers.

LEARNING FOR LIFE

A mother teaches her young daughter to cook in this picture from an Aztec codex. The girl is making tortillas, which are flat maize pancakes. You can see her grinding the corn in a *metate* (grinding stone) using a *mano* (stone used with the metate). Aztec mothers and fathers trained their children in all the skills they would need to survive in adult life. Children from the families of expert craftworkers learned their parents' special skills.

In the Home

MESOAMERICAN HOMES were not just safe places to eat and sleep. They were workplaces too. There were no refrigerators or household appliances, so women had to work hard preparing food for the day's meals or for winter storage. Vegetables were cleaned and chopped with stone knives, as there were no metal ones. Beans and chillies were spread out in the Sun to dry, and maize kernels were ground into flour. Homes had to be kept clean as well. Firewood and water had to be fetched and clothes washed. Women and girls spent long hours spinning thread and weaving it into cloth, then sewing it into tunics and cloaks for the family. Some women wove cloth to sell or to give to the government as a tax payment. Homes were also where most sick or elderly people were cared for.

HEART OF THE HOME
Throughout Mesoamerica, the hearth-fire was the heart of the home. This statue shows Xiuhtecuhtli, the Aztec god of fire. The top of his head is hollow, so a fire can be kindled there. The rays on his headdress represent flickering flames.

MAYA POT
The Maya decorated ceremonial pottery with pictures of gods, kings and important people. This pot shows a maize merchant. Pottery used in the home for food and drink would be less ornate.

A BACKSTRAP LOOM
You will need: paintbrush, water-based paint, 2 pieces of thick dowel about 70 cm long, string, scissors, thick card, masking tape, coloured wool.

1 Paint the pieces of dowel brown. Leave them to dry. Tie string to each dowel and wind it around. Leave a length of string loose at each end.

2 Cut a piece of thick card about 70cm x 100cm. This is a temporary base. Lightly fix the stringed dowels to it at the shorter sides with masking tape.

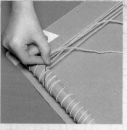

3 Now take your yellow wool. Thread the wool through the string loops and pull through to the other end, as shown. Try to keep the yellow wool taut.

GLOWING COLOURS

Many craftworkers worked at home. This painting by Diego Rivera shows craftworkers from the region of Tarascan dying hanks of yarn before they are woven into cloth. Mesoamerican dyes were made from fruits, flowers, shellfish and the cochineal beetles that lived on cactus plants. Only rich people were allowed to wear clothes made from brightly coloured cloth. Poorer people wore natural colours.

A HELPING HAND

Aztec girls were meant to make themselves useful by helping their mothers around the home. This Aztec codex picture shows a girl sweeping the floor with a bundle of twigs.

WEAVING

Threads spun from plant fibres were woven into cloth on backstrap looms. The finest fabric was made from silky cotton. Rough yucca and cactus fibres made a coarser cloth. Looms like this are still used in Mexico today.

To weave, take the loom off the cardboard. Tie the loose string around your waist. Attach the other end of the loom to a post or tree with the string. Lean back to keep the long warp threads evenly taut.

4 Cut a rectangle of thick card (300mm x 35mm). Now cut a small rectangle of card with one pointed end, as shown. Wind red wool around it.

5 Now take your long card rectangle. This is your shed rod. Carefully slide it through every second thread on your loom, as shown.

6 Turn your shed rod on its side. This will lift the threads up. Tie one end of your red wool to the yellow wool. Feed the card of wool through the lifted threads.

7 Lay the shed rod flat. Use the pointed end of your card to pick up each of the first or alternate threads. Thread the wool on the card through these.

Villages and Towns

MOST PEOPLE in Mesoamerica lived in country villages. They made a living from the land, taking their produce to nearby market towns to sell. Villages and towns all had to obey the strongest city in the region. Usually they also had to pay a tribute (a tax of goods or labour) to it as well. Villages were small, often with fewer than fifty families, but the biggest cities were huge. Historians estimate that over 150,000 people lived in the city of Teotihuacan in AD600. Cities, towns and villages were linked by roads cleared through the forest or by steep paths cut into mountain slopes.

The centre of most Mesoamerican cities was dedicated to religion. The greatest temples stood there, close to a vast open space used for holy ceremonies, dances and processions. Other important buildings, such as royal palaces and ball-courts, stood close by. The homes and workshops of ordinary citizens were built outside the ceremonial area.

HIDDEN IN THE TREES
Today the remains of the great Maya city of Tikal are almost hidden by the rainforest. In Maya times, the trees would have been felled to make room for houses and fields. In around AD800, about 50,000 people lived here.

DESERT FRUITS
Several kinds of cactus thrive in Mexico's dry, semi-desert, regions. The prickly pear had a sweet, juicy fruit, but the maguey cactus was even more useful. Its sap was used as a sweetener and to make an alcoholic drink. Its fibres were made into clothing and baskets. Its spines were used as needles.

BIG CITY
The Maya city of Copan in present-day Honduras covered an enormous area, perhaps 13km long and 3km wide. The religious centre and the nearby Great Plaza are shown here. Both were rebuilt in splendid style on the orders of King Yax Pac around AD750. The temples and royal palace are painted a glowing red – the colour of life and power.

BIRDS OF A FEATHER

These little pictures are from an Aztec codex. They show just some of the many beautiful wild birds that lived in Mesoamerica. The Maya and the Aztecs hunted many of them for their brightly coloured feathers. These feathers could then be used to make fans or shields.

humming bird

quetzal

toucan

parrot

parrot

MOUNTAINS AND MAIZE

On steep, cold mountain slopes, such as those of Popocatapetl, farmers grew hardy crops. *Chia* and *huautli* were both bushy plants with edible seeds. They were well suited to this environment. In sunny, fertile areas, maize was grown.

owl

crocodile

FROM DESERT TO RAINFOREST

The landscape of Mesoamerica is extremely varied. Many different creatures, from crocodiles to deer inhabit it. The Maya and the Aztecs hunted many of these animals for their meat or skins.

deer

butterfly

rabbit

snake

Buildings and Houses

PEOPLE LIVING in Mesoamerica used local materials for building. They had no wheeled transport, so carrying building materials long distances was quite difficult. Stone was the most expensive and longest-lasting building material. It was used for religious buildings, rulers' palaces and tombs. The homes of ordinary people were built more quickly and easily of cheaper materials, such as Sun-dried mud bricks, called adobe, or mud smeared over a framework of wooden poles. For strength, the walls might have stone foundations.

All Mesoamerican homes were very simply furnished. There were no chairs or tables, curtains or carpets – just some jars and baskets for storage and a few reed mats. Everyone, from rulers to slaves, sat and slept on mats on the floor. Most ordinary Aztec homes were L-shaped or built around a courtyard, with a separate bathroom for washing and a small shrine to the gods in the main room.

FAMILY HOME
This present-day Maya family home is built in traditional style, with red-painted mud-and-timber walls. It has one door and no windows. The floor is made of pounded earth. The roof, thatched with dried grass, is steeply sloped so the rain runs off it.

BURIED UNDERGROUND
Archaeologists have discovered these remains of houses at the Maya city of Copan. The roofs, walls and doors have rotted away, but we can still see the stone foundations. The houses are small and tightly packed together.

MAKE A MAYA HOUSE
You will need: thick card, pencil, ruler, scissors, glue, masking tape, terracotta plaster paste (or thin plaster coloured with paint), balsa wood strips, water pot, wide gummed paper tape, brush, short lengths of straw.

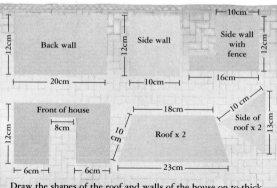

Back wall — 12cm, 20cm

Side wall — 12cm, 10cm

Side wall with fence — 10cm, 12cm, 16cm

Front of house — 12cm, 8cm, 6cm, 6cm

Roof x 2 — 10cm, 18cm, 23cm

Side of roof x 2 — 10cm, 13cm

Draw the shapes of the roof and walls of the house on to thick card, using the measurements shown. (Please note that the templates are not shown to scale.) Cut the pieces out.

1 Cut out a rectangle 25cm x 15cm from thick card for the base. Stick the house walls and base together with glue. Use masking tape for support.

STONEMASONS AT WORK

Mesoamerican masons constructed massive buildings using very simple equipment. Their wedges were made from wood, and their mallets and hammers were shaped from hard volcanic stone. Until around AD900 metal tools were unknown. Fine details were added by polishing stonework with wet sand.

PLASTER

Big stone buildings, such as temples, were often covered with a kind of plaster called stucco. This was then painted with ornate designs. Plaster was made by burning limestone and mixing it with water and coloured earth. By the 1400s, there was so much new building in Tenochtitlan that the surrounding lake became polluted with chemicals from the plaster making.

plaster

limestone

SKILFUL STONEWORK

This carved stone panel from the Maya city of Chichen-Itza is decorated with a pattern of crosses. It was used to provide a fine facing to thick walls made of rubble and rough stone. This wall decorates a palace building.

A Maya house provided a cool shelter from the very hot Mexican Sun, as well as keeping out rain.

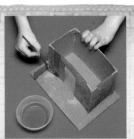

2 Paint the walls and base with plaster paste. This will make them look like Sun-dried mud. You could also decorate the doorway with balsa wood strips.

3 Put the house on one side to dry. Take your roof pieces and stick them together with glue. Use masking tape to support the roof, as shown.

4 Moisten the wide paper tape and use it to cover the joins between the roof pieces. There should be no gaps. Then cover the whole roof with glue.

5 Press lengths of straw into the glue on the roof. Work in layers, starting at the bottom. Overlap the layers. Fix the roof to the house using glue.

City in the Lake

THE AZTECS built their capital city, Tenochtitlan, on an island in the middle of Lake Texcoco in the Central Valley of Mexico. It was founded around AD1325 and soon grew into one of the largest cities in the world. Historians estimate that over 200,000 people lived there by 1500. As the centre of Aztec government, the city saw traders, ambassadors, scribes and porters streaming in with huge loads of tribute from all over Mesoamerica. Thousands of enemy soldiers captured in battle were also brought there to be sacrificed to the gods.

The city was divided into four districts – Flowery Place, Mosquito Fen, Herons' Home and, at the centre, the Sacred Precinct. The four districts of the city were linked to one another, and to the mainland, by countless little canals and causeways of pounded earth. These causeways ran above the surface of the lake. Fresh drinking water from the nearby mountains was carried by a tall stone acqueduct.

EAGLE AND CACTUS

According to legend, the Aztecs chose the site for Tenochtitlan after they received a message from the god Huitzilopochtli. He told them to build their city where they saw an eagle sitting on a cactus, eating a snake. Priests and rulers told legends like this to give reasons for their past actions and make people accept their future plans.

GIVING THANKS

The Aztecs decorated many parts of their city with images of their special god, Huitzilopochtli. Here we can see a brazier decorated with Huitzilopochtli's image, amongst the ruins of the great temple of Tenochtitlan.

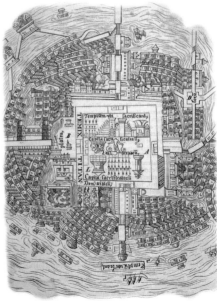

EYE-WITNESS REPORTS

Today Tenochtitlan is buried under modern Mexico City. However, we can gain some idea of what it was like from drawings like this one, made by a European artist in the 1500s. It shows how causeways and canals allowed easy movement around the city.

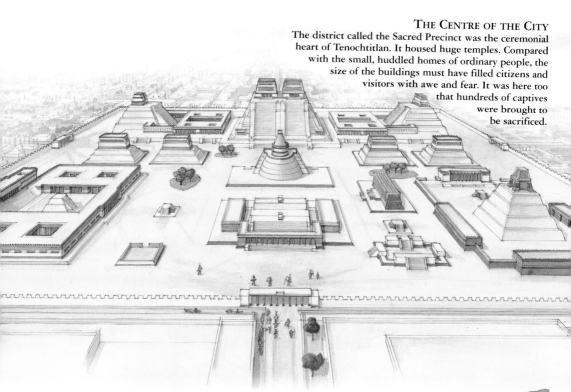

THE CENTRE OF THE CITY

The district called the Sacred Precinct was the ceremonial heart of Tenochtitlan. It housed huge temples. Compared with the small, huddled homes of ordinary people, the size of the buildings must have filled citizens and visitors with awe and fear. It was here too that hundreds of captives were brought to be sacrificed.

STONE WORSHIPPERS

These stone statues of standard bearers were found among the ruins of the Great Temple. This temple stood in the centre of Tenochtitlan. It had two tall pyramids, topped by shrines. These shrines were dedicated to Tlaloc, god of rain, and Huitzilopochtli, the Aztec's own special god of war. The remains of steps leading up to these shrines still remain. When the Spanish conquered the city, they pulled down the Great Temple and built a cathedral near the site.

THE LAKE OF THE MOON

This is the name the Aztecs gave to Lake Texcoco. This fanciful picture shows an 18th-century artist's idea of the Aztec ruler, Tenoch. This ruler founded the city of Tenochtitlan.

Farming

PEOPLE LIVING in different regions of Mesoamerica used various methods to cultivate their land. Farmers in the rainforests grew maize, beans and pumpkins in fields they cleared by slashing and burning. They cut down thick, tangled bushes and vines, leaving the tallest trees standing. Then they burned all the chopped-down bushes and planted seeds in the ashes. But the soil was only fertile for a few years. The fields were left to turn back into forest, and new ones were cleared. Maya farmers also grew crops in raised fields. These were plots of land along the edge of rivers and streams, heaped up with rich, fertile silt dug from the riverbed.

Aztec farmers planted maize wherever they could, on steep rocky hillsides and the flat valley floor. But they grew their biggest crops of fruit, flowers and vegetables in gardens called *chinampas*. These were reclaimed from the marshy shallows along the shores of Lake Texcoco and around the island city of Tenochtitlan.

MAIZE GOD
This stone statue shows Yum Caax (Lord of the Forest Bushes), the Maya god of maize. It was found at Copan. All Mesoamerican people honoured maize goddesses or gods, as the crop was so important.

DIGGING STICKS
Mesoamerican farmers had no tractors, horses or heavy ploughs to help them prepare their fields. Instead, a sharp-bladed wooden digging stick, called an *uictli*, was used for planting seeds and hoeing weeds. Some farmers in Mesoamerica today find digging sticks are more efficient than the kind of spade traditionally used in Europe.

FIELD WORK
This painting by Mexican artist Diego Rivera shows Aztecs using digging sticks to hoe fields of maize. You can see how dry the soil is. If the May rains failed, or frosts came early, a whole year's crop would be lost. Mesoamerican farmers made offerings to the rain god between March and October.

Chinampa soil was made even more fertile by using human manure.

Sticky mud was collected from the lake bottom. Along with compost and manure, this mud was poured on top of the chinampas.

The chinampa was held together by stakes, thick water vegetation and the tangled roots of trees.

FLOATING GARDENS

Chinampas were a sort of floating garden. They were made by sinking layers of twigs and branches under the surface of the lake and weighting them with stones. *Chinampas* were so productive that the government passed laws telling farmers when to sow seeds. This ensured there would be a steady supply of vegetables and flowers for sale in the market.

VEGETARIANS

Many ordinary Mesoamerican people survived on a largely vegetarian diet, based on maize and beans. This would be supplemented by other fresh fruits and vegetables in season. Meat and fish were expensive, luxury foods. Only rulers and nobles could afford to eat them every day.

beans

prickly pear

SLASH AND BURN

Mesoamerican farmers used a technique called slash and burn to clear land for farming. Crops grew very quickly in Mesoamerica's warm climate.

FOREST FRUITS

This Aztec codex painting shows men and women gathering cocoa pods from trees. Cocoa was so valuable that it was sent as tribute to Tenochtitlan.

Hunting and Gathering

MESOAMERICAN FARMERS did not rear many animals to kill for food. Before the Spaniards arrived, there were no cows, sheep, pigs or horses in their lands. Most meat and fish came from wild creatures, which were hunted or trapped. Deer, hares, rabbits and foxes were hunted on the dry mountain slopes. Peccary (wild boar), armadillos and opossums sheltered in the forests. Aztec hunters trapped ducks, geese and pelicans in shallow reed-beds beside the lake. Maya fishermen caught turtles, dolphins and shellfish all around the coast.

Hunters also went in search of many wild creatures that were not used for food. Millions of brightly-coloured birds were killed for their feathers. Poisonous snakes and fierce pumas, jaguars and ocelots (wild cats) were hunted for their beautiful furs and skins.

Mesoamerican people also gathered a great many plants and insects for other uses. Seeds, leaves, bark and flowers were used for medicine and to make paper, mats and baskets. Wild bees supplied honey, and locusts were eaten as snacks.

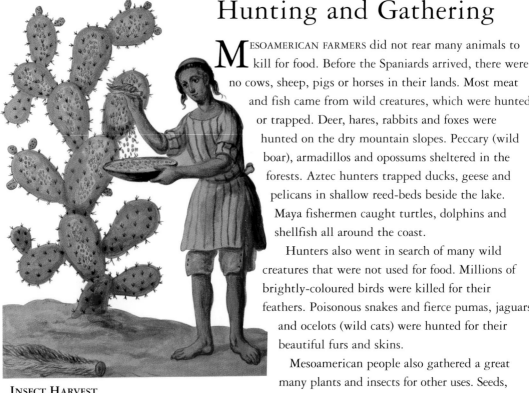

INSECT HARVEST
Mesoamerican people collected many kinds of insects for use in medicines, as dyes and as food. This codex picture shows cochineal beetles being gathered from a cactus. It took about 70,000 beetles to make half a kilo of red dye.

HUNTERS
Mesoamerican men went hunting with bows and arrows, slings, clubs and spears. Hunters' bows were made of wood, and their arrows were tipped with obsidian, a sharp volcanic glass. Their clubs were made from lumps of rock lashed to wooden handles with rope or leather thongs. To make their spears fly further, they used an *atlatl*. This was a grooved piece of wood that acted like an extra-long arm to increase the power behind the throw.

CHOCOLATE TREE

This picture from an Aztec codex shows a cocoa tree and two Aztec gods. Cocoa pods could be gathered from cocoa trees all over Mesoamerica. Once ground, the cocoa beans were mixed with water to make chocolate. Chocolate was a highly prized drink and only nobles could afford to drink it. It was often sweetened with honey and flavoured with vanilla. The Aztecs and Maya did not know how to make bars of solid chocolate, like those we enjoy today.

FAUNA

Wild creatures such as turtles, and rabbits were abundant in Mesoamerica. Rabbits were hunted for their fur. Turtles were a popular catch for many fishermen. Their shells could be used in crafts and their flesh could be eaten.

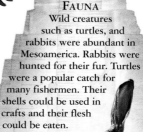

turtle   *blacktail jackrabbit*

FEATHER TRADE

Mesoamerican merchants brought feathers from hunters who lived in the rainforest. The picture above shows different kinds of feathers sorted and ready for sale.

SEA PRODUCE

This Maya beaker is decorated with a picture of a god emerging from a shell. Beautiful seashells were highly prized in Mesoamerica and were often used in jewellery and craftwork. One species of shellfish was caught for its sticky slime. This slime was milked from the shellfish and then used to make a rich purple dye.

fishermen used sticks and paddles to drive fish into nets

flat-bottomed boats could sail across Mexico's shallow, marshy lakes

RIVERS AND LAKES

In this Aztec codex picture, we can see a boy fishing. He is standing in a flat-bottomed boat, hollowed from a single log. This boy is using a bag-shaped net, woven from cactus fibre. Fish were also caught with hooks, lines and harpoons. Long nets, draped across canoes, were used to catch waterfowl.

Food and Drink

MESOAMERICAN PEOPLE usually had two meals a day. They ate their main meal around noon and a smaller snack in the evening. Ordinary people's food was plain and simple but very healthy – if they could get enough of it. When crops failed, there was famine. Everyday meals were based on maize, beans, vegetables and fruit. Peppers, tomatoes, pumpkins and avocado pears were popular vegetables, but the Aztecs also ate boiled cactus leaves (with the spines removed!). Gruel made from wild sage or amaranth seeds was also a favourite. Meat and fish were luxuries. Deer, rabbit, turkey and dog were cooked for feasts, along with frogs, lizards and turtles. The Aztecs also ate fish eggs and green algae from the lake.

USEFUL POTS

Mesoamerican people did not have metal cooking pots, so women cooked and served food in pottery bowls. Special pottery dishes were also used for specific jobs, such as cooking tortillas. The ones above were used for grating chillies and sweet peppers. They have rough ridged bases.

CACTUS WINE

Sweet, sticky sap from the maguey cactus was collected in leather flasks, then left to ferment in open troughs. It quickly turned into a strong alcoholic wine, which the Aztecs called *pulque*. Aztec men and women were not usually allowed to drink much alcohol. On special festivals honouring the dead, *pulque* was served by women wine-makers from huge pottery jars.

MAKE TORTILLAS

You will need: scales, 225g plain or maize flour, 1 tsp salt, bowl, 40g butter, jug, 120ml cold water, spoon, a little plain flour for kneading and flouring, rolling pin, pastry board, butter or oil for frying, frying pan.

1 Carefully weigh out the ingredients. If you cannot find maize flour, use plain flour instead. Aztec cooks had to grind their own flour.

2 Mix the flour and salt together in a bowl. Rub the butter into the mixture with your fingers until it looks like breadcrumbs. Then pour in the water.

3 Use your hands to mix everything together until you have a loose ball of dough. Do not worry if there is still some dry mixture around the bowl.

WARRIOR DISH

This dish was made in the Maya city of Tikal, in present-day Guatemala. It is painted with slip (a liquid clay coloured with minerals) and shows the figure of a warrior. All Mesoamerican pots were shaped by hand – the use of a potter's wheel was not known.

WOVEN TRIBUTE

Cloaks and blankets were sent as tribute to the great city of Tenochtitlan, as well as being sold in markets.

MOULDING GOLD

This painting by Diego Rivera shows Aztec goldsmiths with molten gold. Most jewellery was made by melting gold-dust in a furnace, then pouring it into a mould.

TREASURES

Mesoamerican people treasured many beautiful semi-precious stones, such as turquoise, obsidian and rock-crystal. They paid high prices for corals, pearls and shells from the sea. But they valued jade, a hard, smooth, deep-green stone, most of all, because it symbolized eternal life.

turquoise   *obsidian*

Aztec craftworkers carefully cut semi-precious stones into tiny squares. Turquoise, jade, shell and obsidian were all used for this purpose. The craftworkers used these pieces to create beautiful mosaic masks like this.

4 Cover the mask (except the eyes and mouth) with plaster paste. Press the card pieces into this, using glue to help any awkward ones to stick.

5 Paint the eyes with black and white paint. Cut out teeth from white card and carefully glue in position. Leave the mask in a warm place to dry.

6 Now coat the whole mask with a thin coat of PVA glue. This will seal the surface of the mask.

Merchants and Markets

THE MARKET PLACE was the heart of many Mesoamerican cities and towns. Traders, craftworkers and farmers met there to exchange their produce. Many market traders were women. They sold cloth or cooking pots, made by themselves or their families, and maize, fruit, flowers and vegetables grown by their husbands. In big cities, such as the trading centre of Tlatelolco, government officials also sold exotic goods that had been sent to the Aztec rulers as tribute (taxes) by conquered city-states. After the Aztecs conquered Tlatelolco in 1473, it soon became the greatest market in Mesoamerica. It was reported that almost 50,000 people came there on the busiest days.

Long-distance trade was carried out by merchants called *pochteca*. Gangs of porters carried their goods. The work was often dangerous, but the rewards were great.

MERCHANT GOD
Yacatecuhtli was the Aztec god of merchants and traders. In the codex picture above, he is shown standing in front of a crossroads marked with footprints. Behind him (*right*), is a tired porter with a load of birds on his back.

MAIZE MARKET
Mesoamerican farmers grew many different varieties of maize, with cobs that were pale cream, bright yellow, or even deep blue. Their wives took the maize to market, as selling was women's work. This modern wall-painting shows Aztec women buying and selling maize in the great market at Tlatelolco. At the market, judges sat in raised booths, keeping a lookout for thieves and cheats.

MAKE A MAYA POT

You will need: self-drying clay, board, rolling pin, masking tape, modelling tool, water bowl, small bowl, petroleum jelly, PVA glue, glue brush, yellow and black paint, paintbrush, water pot.

1 Roll out the clay until it is approximately 5mm thick. Cut out a base for the pot with a modelling tool. Use a roll of masking tape as a guide for size.

2 Roll out some long sausages of clay. Coil them around the base of the pot to build up the sides. Join and smooth the clay with water as you go.

3 Model a lip at the top of the pot. Leave it to dry. Cover a small bowl with petroleum jelly. Make a lid by rolling out some clay. Place the clay over the bowl.

JOURNEY'S END

This modern painting shows merchants and porters arriving at the market city of Tlatelolco. Such travellers made long journeys to bring back valuable goods, such as shells, jade and fig-bark paper. Young men joining the merchants' guild were warned about tiredness, pain and ambushes on their travels.

BARTER

Mesoamerican people did not have coins. They bought and sold by bartering, exchanging the goods they wanted to sell for other peoples' goods of equal value. Costly items such as gold-dust, quetzal feathers and cocoa beans were exchanged for goods they wanted to buy.

SKINS

Items such as puma, ocelot and jaguar skins could fetch a high price at market.

colourful feathers   *cocoa beans*

MARKET PRODUCE

In Mexico today, many markets are still held on the same sites as ancient ones. Many of the same types of foodstuffs are on sale there. In this modern photograph, we see tomatoes, avocados and vegetables that were also grown in Aztec times. Today, as in the past, most market traders and shoppers are women.

Mesoamerican potters made their pots by these coil or slab techniques. The potter's wheel was not used at all in Mesoamerica. The pots were sold at the local market.

4 Turn your pot upside down and place it over the rolled-out clay. Trim away the excess clay with a modelling tool by cutting around the top of the pot.

5 Use balls of clay to make a turtle to go on top of the lid. When both the lid and turtle are dry, use PVA glue to stick the turtle on to the centre of the lid.

6 Roll three small balls of clay of exactly the same size for the pot's feet. When they are dry, glue them to the base of the pot. Make sure they are evenly spaced.

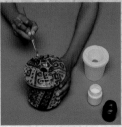

7 Paint the pot with Aztec designs in black and yellow. When you have finished, varnish the pot with a thin coat of PVA glue to make it shiny.

Travel and Transport

MESOAMERICAN PEOPLE knew about wheels but they did not make wheeled transport of any kind. Carriages and carts would not have been suitable for journeys through dense rainforests or along steep, narrow mountain tracks. Many Maya cities were also linked by raised causeways that would have been difficult for wheeled vehicles to travel along.

Most people travelled overland on foot, carrying goods on their backs. Mesoamerican porters carried heavy loads with the help of a *tumpline*. This was a broad band of cloth that went across their foreheads and under the bundles on their backs, leaving their arms free. Rulers and nobles were carried in beds, called litters.

On rivers and lakes, Mesoamericans used simple dug-out boats. At sea, Maya sailors travelled in huge wooden canoes that were able to make voyages of many kilometres in rough seas.

CARRIED HIGH
A Maya nobleman is shown being carried in a litter (portable bed) made from jaguar skins. Spanish travellers reported that the Aztec emperor was carried in the same way. Blankets were also spread in front of the emperor as he walked, to stop his feet touching the ground.

MEN OR MONSTERS?
Until the Spaniards arrived with horses in 1519, there were no animals big and strong enough to ride in the Mesoamerican lands. There were horses in America in prehistoric times, but they died out around 10,000BC. When the Aztecs saw the Spanish riding, they thought they were monsters – half man, half beast.

A WHEELED DOG

You will need: board, self-drying clay, 4 lengths of thin dowel about 5cm long and 2 lengths about 7cm long, water bowl, modelling tool, thick card, scissors, PVA glue, glue brush, paintbrush, modelling tool, paintbrush, paint, masking tape.

1 Roll a large piece of clay into a fat sausage to form the dog's body. Push the 5cm pieces of dowel into the body to make the legs. Leave to dry.

2 Cover the dowel legs with clay, extending the clay 2cm beyond the end of the dowel. Make a hole at the end of each leg with a piece of dowel. Leave to dry.

3 Push the dowel through the holes in the legs to join them horizontally. Make the dog's head and ears from clay. Join them to the body using water.

HARDWORKING PORTERS

This engraving from the 1900s shows Aztec slaves and commoners carrying loads for Spanish conquerors. Being a porter was very hard work. They were expected to cover up to 100 km per day, carrying about 25–30kg on their backs. Like most Mesoamerican people, they travelled these long distances barefoot.

BY BOAT

Aztec soldiers and the citizens of Tenochtitlan used boats with flat bottoms to travel around the city. Boats like this were also used to carry fruits and vegetables to market. Dug-out canoes were popular too. They were made from hollowed out tree trunks.

AZTEC WATERWAYS

The Aztecs paddled their canoes and flat-bottomed boats on Lake Texcoco. Today most of this lake has dried up. The lakeside *chinampas*, where they grew food and flowers, have almost disappeared. This photograph shows modern punts sailing along one of the last remaining Aztec waterways between the few *chinampas* that survive.

Toys like this dog are proof that the wheel was known in Mesoamerica. Wheeled vehicles were not suitable for rugged Mesoamerican land.

4 Cut four circles 3.5cm in diameter from card to make wheels. Pierce a hole in the centre of each. Make the holes big enough for the dowel to fit through

5 Make four wheels from clay, the same size as the card wheels. Glue the clay and card wheels together. Make holes through the clay wheels and leave to dry.

6 Paint the dog's head, body, legs and wheels with Aztec patterns. When the paint is dry, give the dog a thin coat of PVA glue to act as a varnish.

7 Fit the wheels on to the ends of the dowels that pass through the dog's legs. Wrap strips of masking tape around the ends to stop the wheels falling off.

Warriors and Weapons

AZTEC ARMIES were very large. All Aztec men learned how to fight and had to be ready to hurry off to battle when they heard the sound of the great war drum outside the ruler's palace in Tenochtitlan. Ordinary soldiers wore tunics and leg-guards of padded cotton that had been soaked in saltwater. This made it tough – strong enough to protect the wearer from many fierce blows. Aztec army commanders wore splendid uniforms decorated with gold, silver, feathers and fur.

Both the Maya and the Aztecs greatly admired bravery. Aztec armies were led by nobles who had won promotion for brave deeds in battle, or for taking lots of captives. It was a disgrace for an Aztec soldier to try to save his own skin. It was more honourable for him to be killed fighting, or to be sacrificed, than to survive.

Maya soldiers went to war to win captives for sacrifice, but they also fought battles to control trade routes, to obtain tribute and to gain power. They wore a variety of garments, including sleeveless tunics, loincloths, fur costumes and cotton armour.

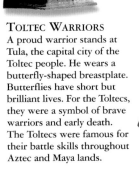

TOLTEC WARRIORS
A proud warrior stands at Tula, the capital city of the Toltec people. He wears a butterfly-shaped breastplate. Butterflies have short but brilliant lives. For the Toltecs, they were a symbol of brave warriors and early death. The Toltecs were famous for their battle skills throughout Aztec and Maya lands.

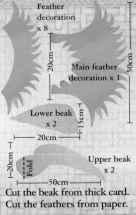

HELD CAPTIVE
An Aztec warrior is shown capturing an enemy in battle in this codex picture. The warrior is dragging his captive along by the hair. Young Aztec men had to grow their hair long at the back and could only cut it when they had taken their first prisoner in battle.

AN EAGLE HELMET

You will need: ruler, thick card, pencil, scissors, masking tape, stapler, self-drying clay, PVA glue, glue brush, gummed paper tape, paints, paintbrush, water pot, ribbon, felt, green paper, Velcro.

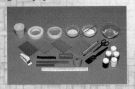

Feather decoration x 8

45cm

20cm

Main feather decoration x 1

50cm

Lower beak x 2

15cm

20cm

Upper beak x 2

20cm

Fold

50cm

Cut the beak from thick card. Cut the feathers from paper.

1 Make your helmet by joining the two parts of the upper beak with masking tape. Join the two parts of the lower beak in the same way, as shown.

2 Fold the two rounded ends of the upper beak towards each other and staple them together. Cover the staples and the join with masking tape.

JAGUAR AND EAGLE KNIGHTS

Ocelotl, the jaguar, is shown in this picture from a codex. Warriors had to prove their bravery in battle and capture lots of prisoners for sacrifice. Those who succeeded were invited to join special fighting brotherhoods of jaguar and eagle knights. They wore costumes made of real feathers and skins.

WARRIOR SPIRIT

This stone carving is from the Maya city of Yaxchilan. In it, Lady Xoc, wife of ruler Shield Jaguar, kneels before a vision serpent. This serpent was made to appear by a special religious ritual. Maya rulers made offerings of their own blood to their ancestor-spirits and to the gods to ask for help in battle.

CLUBS AND SPEARS

Aztec soldiers face Spanish soldiers on horseback. They are armed with war-clubs called *macuahuitl* and protected by wooden shields.

War-clubs, made of wood and razor-sharp flakes of obsidian, could cut an enemy's head off with a single blow. The Spaniards are armed with metal swords and lances.

Fasten your eagle helmet by tying it under the chin. You could make wings from card and attach them to your arms with ribbon. Now you are a brave eagle knight! Eagles were admired by the Aztecs as superb hunters who could move freely to the Sun.

3 Make two eyes from self-drying clay and stick them on to the upper beak with glue. Neaten the edges of the beak and eyes with gummed paper tape.

4 Decorate both parts of the beak with paint. If you wish, add pieces of ribbon, felt or paper, too. Remember that you want to look brave and fierce.

5 Ask an adult to curl the feathers by running a scissor blade along them. Glue the layers of feathers on to the main feather decoration. Trim to fit.

6 Use tape and glue to fix feathers to the inside of the upper beak. Tape ribbon from the upper beak to the lower one to join. Leave some ribbon loose to tie.

Rival City-States

THE MAYA LIVED in many separate city-states, which were always rivals and sometimes at war. Rulers of different states fought to win more land. From around AD200, they also competed with one another to fill their cities with bigger, more beautiful buildings. They competed over political power, control of land and resources, and trade routes.

Between about AD850 and AD900, many Maya cities became poorer, and their power collapsed. The great city centres were abandoned, and Maya scribes and craftworkers no longer carved important dates on temples and tombs. The last date known is AD889. No one knows why this happened. Perhaps it was because of famine, caused by bad weather or farmers over-using the land, or it may have been caused by war. However, Maya civilization did not totally disappear. A few Maya cities, in the far north and south of Mexico, continued to thrive.

Around AD900, the Putun people from the Gulf coast moved into Maya lands. In cities like Chichen-Itza, Putun ideas blended with Maya traditions to create a new culture.

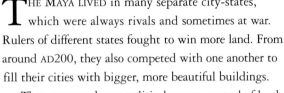

TIKAL
This figure was painted on a pottery vase from the city of Tikal. From about AD600 to 900, Tikal was one of the greatest Maya city-states. It was wealthy, busy and very big. About 75,000 people lived there, and its buildings covered an area of 100 square kilometres. Around AD400, Tikal conquered the nearby Maya state of Uaxactun. Trading and religious links were then developed with the powerful non-Maya city of Teotihuacan.

CHICHEN-ITZA
Pilgrims came from miles around to throw jewellery and fine pottery into the Well of Sacrifice in the city of Chichen-Itza. These items were offerings to the god of rain. Human sacrifices were made here too. Chichen-Itza was founded by the Maya around AD800. Later, Maya craftsmen built a massive new city centre, with temples and ball-courts. Many of these new buildings were based on designs similar to those found in central Mexico. Some historians think this means that the city was conquered by the Putuns.

UXMAL

The city of Uxmal is in the dry Puuc region of Yucatan, Mexico. There are no rivers or streams in the area, so Maya engineers designed and built huge underground tanks, called *chultun*, to store summer rainfall. People living in Uxmal relied on these water tanks for survival.

NAMES AND DATES

This stone slab was once placed above a doorway in the Maya city of Yaxchilan. It is carved with glyphs, or picture-symbols, recording important names and dates. The city of Yaxchilan is famous for the fine quality stone carvings found there, especially on tall pillars and around doors.

COPAN

This stela (tall stone pillar) is from Copan in modern Honduras. The front of the stela is carved with a larger-than-life portrait of 18 Rabbit (Waxaklahun ubah k'awil), the thirteenth ruler of the city. Archaeologists know much about Copan's past from the inscriptions carved in several monuments and buildings.

PALENQUE

Lord Pacal, ruler of the Maya city of Palenque, was buried wearing this mask of green jade. Only the richest city-states could afford to bury their rulers with treasures like this. Palenque was at its strongest between AD600 and 800.

Aztec Conquests

TOTONAC TRIBUTE
Ambassadors from lands conquered by the Aztecs came to Tenochtitlan to deliver the tribute demanded from their rulers. This painting shows splendidly dressed representatives of the Totonac people meeting Aztec tax collectors. The Totonacs lived on the Gulf coast of Mexico, in Veracruz. Here they are shown offering tobacco, fruit and vanilla grown on their lands. They hated and feared the Aztecs.

W AR WAS ESSENTIAL to Aztec life. As newcomers in Mexico, the Aztecs had won their homeland by fighting against the people already living there. From then onwards, they relied on war to bring more land, new cities and extra tribute under their control. Without these riches won through war, the Aztec empire would have collapsed. Big cities such as Tenochtitlan needed steady supplies of tribute to feed their citizens. War was also a source of captives. The Aztecs believed that thousands of prisoners needed to be sacrificed each year.

Each new Aztec ruler had to start his reign with a battle. It was his duty to win fame and glory by conquering new territory and seizing enemy captives. During the 1400s, the Aztec empire grew rapidly, until the Aztecs ruled most of Mexico. This drive to conquer new territory was led by rulers Itzcoatl (1426–1440), Moctezuma Ilhuicamina (1440–1468) and Axayacatl (1468–1481). Conquered cities were often controlled by garrisons of Aztec soldiers and linked to the government in Tenochtitlan by large numbers of officials, such as tax collectors and scribes.

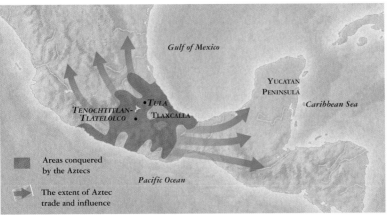

Gulf of Mexico

YUCATAN
PENINSULA

Caribbean Sea

TULA
TENOCHTITLAN-
TLATELOLCO · TLAXCALLA

Areas conquered
by the Aztecs

The extent of Aztec
trade and influence

Pacific Ocean

AZTEC LANDS
This map shows the area ruled by the Aztecs in 1519. Conquered cities were allowed to continue with their traditional way of life, but had to pay tribute to Aztec officials. The Aztecs also put pressure on two weaker city states, Texcoco and Tlacopan, to join with them in a Triple Alliance. One nearby city-state, Tlaxcalla, refused to make an alliance with the Aztecs and stayed fiercely independent.

CANNIBALS

One of the Aztecs' most important reasons for fighting was to capture prisoners for sacrifice. In this codex picture, we can see sacrificed bodies neatly chopped up. In some religious ceremonies, the Aztecs ate the arms and legs of sacrificed prisoners.

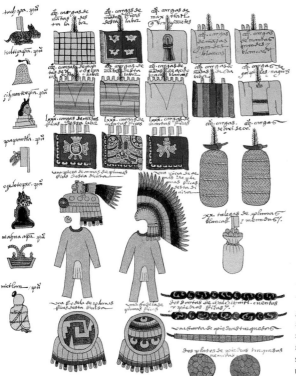

FROM HUMBLE BEGINNINGS

Aztec settlers are shown on their difficult trek through northern Mexico. The Aztecs built up their empire from humble beginnings in a short time. They first arrived in Mexico some time after AD1200. By around 1400, they had become the strongest nation in central Mesoamerica. To maintain their position, they had to be ready for war. The Aztecs invented many legends to justify their success. They claimed to be descended from earlier peoples living in Mexico, and to be specially guided by the gods.

TRIBUTE LIST

The Aztecs received vast quantities of valuable goods as tribute each year. Most of the tribute was sent to their capital city of Tenochtitlan. Aztec scribes there drew up very detailed lists of tribute received, like the one on the left. Among the goods shown are shields decorated with feathers, blankets, turquoise plates, bracelets and dried chilli peppers.

Scholars and Scribes

THE MAYA were the first – and only – Native American people to invent a complete writing system. Maya picture-symbols and sound-symbols were written in books, carved on buildings, painted on pottery and inscribed on precious stones. Maya scribes also developed an advanced number system, including a sign for zero, which Europeans at the time did not have.

Maya writing used glyphs (pictures standing for words) and also picture-signs that stood for sounds. The sound-signs could be joined together, like the letters of our alphabet, to spell out words and to make complete sentences. The Aztecs used picture-writing too, but theirs was much simpler and less flexible.

Maya and Aztec picture-symbols were very difficult to learn. Only specially trained scribes could write them and only priests or rich people could read them. They could spare time for study and afford to pay a good teacher.

MAYA READER
This Maya statue shows a wealthy woman, seated cross-legged with a codex (folding book), on her lap. A Maya or Aztec codex was made of long strips of fig-bark paper, folded like a concertina. The writing was read from top to bottom and left to right.

CITY EMBLEM
This is the emblem-glyph for the Maya city-state of Copan. It is made up of four separate images, which together give a message meaning "the home of the rulers of the royal blood of Copan". At the bottom, you can see a bat, the special picture-sign for the city.

MAKE A CODEX
You will need: thin card, ruler, pencil, scissors, white acrylic paint, eraser, large and small paintbrushes, water pot, paints in red, yellow, blue and black, palette, tracing paper.

1 Draw a rectangle about 100cm x 25cm on to thin card. Cut the rectangle out. Cover it evenly with white acrylic paint. Leave it to dry.

2 Using a pencil and ruler, lightly draw in four fold-lines 20cm apart. This will divide the painted card into five equal sections.

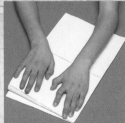

3 Carefully fold along the pencil lines to make a zig-zag book, as shown. Unfold the card and rub out the pencil lines with an eraser.

MAYA CODEX

Maya scribes wrote thousands of codices, but only four survive. All the rest were destroyed by Spanish missionaries. These pages from a Maya codex show the activities of several different gods. The figure at the top painted black with a long nose is Ek Chuah, the god of merchants.

zero	one	four	five	eleven	eighteen

AZTEC ENCYCLOPEDIA

These pictures of Aztec gods come from a book known as the Florentine Codex. This encyclopedia was compiled between 1547 and 1569 by Father Bernardino de Sahagun, a Spanish friar. He was fascinated by Aztec civilization and wanted to record it before it disappeared. This codex is the most complete written record of Aztec life we have.

MAYA NUMBERS

The Maya number system used only three signs – a dot for one, a bar for five, and the shell-symbol for zero. Other numbers were made by using a combination of those signs. When writing down large numbers, Maya scribes put the different symbols on top of one another, rather than side by side as we do today.

4 Trace or copy Aztec or Maya codex drawings from this book. Alternatively, make up your own, based on Mesoamerican examples.

5 Paint your tracings or drawings, using light, bright colours. Using the Maya numbers on this page as a guide, add some numbers to your codex.

If you went to school in Aztec or Maya times, you would find out how to recognize hundreds of different picture-symbols. You would also be taught to link them together in your mind, like a series of clues, to find out what they meant.

Time, Sun and Stars

LIKE ALL OTHER Mesoamericans, the Maya and the Aztecs measured time using a calendar with a year of 260 days. This was used in Mexico as early as 500BC and is probably based on human biology – 260 days is about how long it takes a baby to develop before it is born. The calendar was divided into 13 cycles of 20 days each.

Mesoamerican farmers used a different calendar, based on the movements of the Sun, because sunlight and the seasons made their crops grow. This calendar had 360 days, divided into 18 months of 20 days, plus five extra days that were unlucky. Every 52 years, measured in our time, these two calendars ended on the same day. For five days before the end of the 52 years, people were anxious, because they feared the world might end. A third calendar, of 584 days, also existed for calculating festival days.

SUN STONE
This massive carving was made to display the Aztec view of creation. The Aztecs believed that the world had already been created and destroyed four times and that their Fifth World was also doomed.

STUDYING THE STARS
The Caracol was constructed as an observatory to study the sky. From there, Maya astronomers could observe the planet Venus, which was important in the Mesoamericans' measurement of time.

MAKE A SUN STONE
You will need: pencil, scissors, thick card, self-drying clay, modelling tool, board, rolling pin, masking tape, PVA glue, glue brush, water bowl, pencil, thin card, water-based paints, paintbrush, water pot.

1 Cut a circle about 25cm in diameter from thick card. Roll out the clay and cut out a circle, using the card as a guide. Place the clay circle on the card one.

2 With a modelling tool, mark a small circle in the centre of the clay circle. Use a roll of masking tape as a guide. Do not cut through the clay.

3 Carve the Sun-god's eyes, mouth, teeth and earrings. You can use the real Aztec Sun stone, shown at the top left of this page, as a guide.

alligator

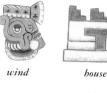
wind

house

lizard

serpent

death's head

deer

rabbit

Water

dog

monkey

grass

reed

jaguar

eagle

vulture

motion

flint knife

rain

flower

NAMES OF DAYS

These pictures from an Aztec codex show the 20 names for days from the farmers' calendar. These symbols were combined with a number from one to 13 to give the date, such as Three Vulture. The days were named after familiar creatures or everyday things, such as the lizard or water. Each day also had its own god. Children were often named after the day on which they were born, a custom that still continues in some parts of Mexico up to the present day.

Your finished Sun stone will not be as big as the original Aztec one. That measures four metres across and is the largest Aztec sculpture discovered so far.

4 Roll out more clay and cut out some Sun's rays, a tongue and eyebrows. Glue them to the clay circle. Smooth the edges with water and leave to dry.

5 Copy the 20 Aztec symbols (*above*) for days on to squares of thin card. The card squares should be no more than 2cm x 2cm. Cut out. Paint brown.

6 Cover the clay circle with a thin coat of dark brown paint. Leave it to dry. Then add a thin coat of white paint to make the circle look like stone.

7 Glue the card symbols evenly around the edge of the clay circle, as shown. Paint the Sun stone with a thin layer of PVA glue to seal and varnish it.

Gods and Goddesses

RELIGION WAS a powerful force throughout Mesoamerica. It affected everything people did, from getting up in the morning to digging in their fields or obeying their ruler's laws. Everyone believed that the gods governed human life. People could not fight their decisions, but the gods could sometimes be persuaded to grant favours if they were offered gifts and sacrifices. The Aztecs and Maya believed in ancient nature gods such as the fire god, the god of maize and the god of rain, and worshipped them with splendid festivals and ceremonies. Mesoamerican people also honoured the spirits of their dead rulers. The Aztecs had their own special tribal god, Huitzilopochtli, Lord of the Sun. He rewarded his followers with victories in war.

Religious ceremonies and sacrifices were led by temple priests. With long, matted hair, red-rimmed eyes and their painted bodies splattered with blood, they were a terrifying sight.

GOD OF SPRING
Xipe Totec was the Aztec god of fertility. He protected the young shoots of maize. Each year, captives were skinned alive as a sacrifice to him. Priests dressed in their skins in religious ceremonies to remind everyone of the skin of young plants.

CHACMOOL FIGURE
This stone statue from the city of Chichen-Itza shows a Chacmool, or reclining figure. It is holding a stone slab on which offerings may have been made.

A STATUE OF A GOD

You will need: pencil, paper, self-drying clay, modelling tool, pastry board, water bowl, petroleum jelly, cotton-wool bud, plaster of Paris, terracotta paint, small paintbrush.

1 Make a drawing of any Aztec god. Model it as a flat figure from self-drying clay. Keep it flat on the bottom. Leave the clay figure to dry.

2 Completely cover the surface of your model with petroleum jelly. Then smooth a layer of clay over the jelly, pressing it down gently into any grooves.

3 Spread more clay on top to make a strong rectangular block, at least 3cm thick. This will become your mould. Leave it to dry thoroughly.

WATER AND RAIN

Tlaloc was the Aztec god of life-giving rain, "the god who makes things grow". Under different names, he was worshipped throughout Mesoamerica. Tlaloc was honoured when he sent water to nourish the crops and feared when he sent deadly floods. In times of drought, the Aztecs sacrificed babies to Tlaloc. They believed the babies' tears would make rain fall.

SUN AND JAGUAR

This Maya carving was part of a wall at Campeche in south-eastern Mexico. It shows the Sun god, whom the Maya called Kinich Ahau. The Maya believed that he disappeared into the underworld every night, at sunset. It was there that he turned into a fierce jaguar god. At the beginning of every new day, they believed that Kinich Ahau then returned to Earth as the life-giving Sun.

EARTH MOTHER

This huge statue of Coatlicue (Great Lady Serpent Skirt) stood in the Sacred Precinct at Tenochtitlan. She was the fearsome Aztec earth-mother goddess. Coatlicue gave birth to the Aztecs' national god Huitzilopochtli, the moon goddess, and the stars.

This model (right) is based on an Aztec statue. It shows a goddess holding two children. Figures of gods were often created from moulds (left).

4 Carefully ease the little model out of the solid block, using the modelling tool. The petroleum jelly should ensure that it comes away cleanly.

5 Clean any loose bits of clay from the mould and smear petroleum jelly inside. Use a cotton-wool bud to make sure the jelly is pushed into every part.

6 Mix up some plaster of Paris and pour it into the mould. Tap the mould gently to remove any air bubbles. Leave the plaster to dry for at least an hour.

7 Gently tip the plaster statue from the mould. Dust it with a brush, then paint it a terracotta colour, so that it looks like an Aztec pottery figure.

Temples and Sacrifices

MESOAMERICAN PEOPLE believed that unless they made offerings of blood and human lives to the gods, the Sun would die and the world would come to an end. Maya rulers pricked themselves with cactus thorns and sting-ray spines, or drew spiked cords through their tongues to draw blood. They pulled out captives' fingernails so the blood flowed or threw them into holy water-holes. Aztecs pricked their ear-lobes each morning and collected two drops of blood to give to the gods. They also went to war to capture prisoners. On special occasions, vast numbers of captives were needed for sacrifice. It was reported that 20,000 victims were sacrificed to celebrate the completion of the Great Temple at Tenochtitlan in 1487. It took four days to kill them all. Mesoamerican temples were tombs as well as places of sacrifice. Rulers and their wives were buried inside. Each ruler aimed to build a great temple as a memorial to his reign.

TEMPLE TOMB
Pyramid Temple 1 at Tikal was built in the AD700s as a memorial to a Maya king. Nine stone platforms were built above the burial chamber, to create a tall pyramid shape reaching up to the sky.

HOLY KNIFE
This sacrificial knife has a blade of a semi-precious stone called chalcedony. It was made by Mixtecs from south Mexico. Mesoamerican priests used finely decorated knives of flint, obsidian and other hard stones to kill captives for sacrifice. These were trimmed to be as sharp as glass.

A PYRAMID TEMPLE
You will need: pencil, ruler, thick card, scissors, PVA glue, glue brush, masking tape, thin strips of balsa wood, thin card, corrugated card, water bowl, paintbrushes, paints.

Cut out pieces for the pyramid and temple-top shrines from thick card, as shown above.

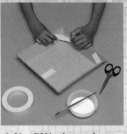

1 Use PVA glue and masking tape to join the thick card pieces to make three flat boxes (A, B and C). Leave the boxes until the glue is completely dry.

2 From the remaining pieces of card, make the two temple-top shrines, as shown. You could add extra details with strips of balsa wood or thin card.

SKULL SHRINE

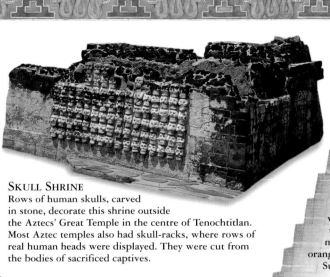

Rows of human skulls, carved in stone, decorate this shrine outside the Aztecs' Great Temple in the centre of Tenochtitlan. Most Aztec temples also had skull-racks, where rows of real human heads were displayed. They were cut from the bodies of sacrificed captives.

RELIGIOUS GIFTS

Mesoamerican people also made offerings of food and flowers as gifts to the gods. Maize was a valuable gift because it was the Mesoamerican people's most important food. Bright orange marigolds were a sign of the Sun, on which every person's life depended.

maize

marigolds

PERFECTION

The ideal victim for human sacrifice was a fit and healthy young man.

HUMAN SACRIFICE

This Aztec codex painting shows captives being sacrificed. At the top, you can see a priest cutting open a captive's chest and removing the heart as an offering to the gods.

This model is based on the Great Temple that stood in the centre of Tenochtitlan.

3 Glue the boxes, one on top of the next. Cut out pieces of card the same size as each side of your boxes. They should be about 1–2cm wide. Stick down, as shown.

4 Cut out two strips of card 2cm x 26cm. Glue them to a third piece of card 14cm x 26cm. Glue corrugated card 9.5cm x 26cm in position, as shown.

5 Stick the staircase to the front of the temple, as shown. Use a ruler to check that the staircase is an equal distance from either side of the temple.

6 Paint the whole temple a cream colour to look like natural stone. Add details, such as carvings or wall paintings, using brightly coloured paint.

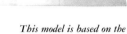

Time for Celebration

FESTIVALS, WITH MUSIC AND DANCING, were a very important part of Mesoamerican life. All big Aztec and Maya cities had a huge open space in the centre, where crowds gathered to sing and dance to honour the gods on festival days. Every twenty days, there were celebrations to mark the start of a new month. There were also festivals, with prayers and sacrifices, to mark important seasons of the farming year. In July and August, the Aztecs celebrated flowering trees and plants. In September, there were harvest festivals, and in October, festivals where hunters gave thanks for plentiful prey. For the Aztec rulers and their guests, feasts and entertainment were a regular event.

All of these special occasions involved music and song. Favourite instruments included rattles, whistles, ocarinas, flutes, bells and shells blown like trumpets. Aztec musicians also played a two-tone wooden drum, called a *teponaztli*, to provide a lively beat for dancing. Stringed instruments were unknown until after the Spanish conquest.

FESTIVAL BEAT
This Maya priest is shown in a wall-painting in the royal palace at the city of Bonampak. He is taking part in a procession to the temple, celebrating the birth of a royal child.

AN AZTEC ORCHESTRA
Musicians played conch shells, rattles and drums while crowds of worshippers sang and danced in the main square of Tenochtitlan.

AN AZTEC RATTLE

You will need: self-drying clay, modelling tool, pastry board, cling film, water bowl, dried melon seeds, bamboo cane, white and terracotta paint, paintbrush, water pot, feather, PVA glue, glue brush.

1 Make a solid model gourd from self-drying clay. You could copy the shape shown above. When it is dry, wrap the gourd completely in clingfilm.

2 Cover the wrapped model gourd with an outer layer of self-drying clay about 1cm thick. Smooth the clay with water to give an even surface.

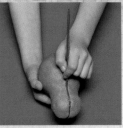

3 Leave the outer layer of clay to get hard but not completely solid. Cut it in half with the thin end of the modelling tool and remove the model gourd.

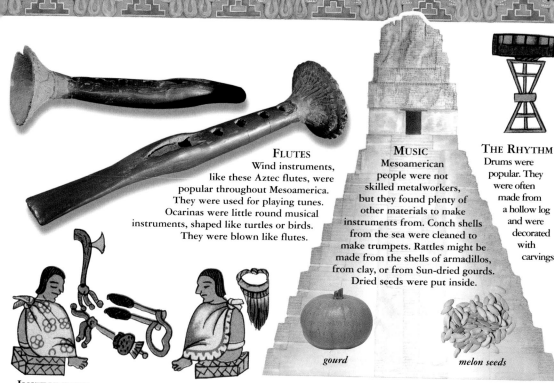

FLUTES

Wind instruments, like these Aztec flutes, were popular throughout Mesoamerica. They were used for playing tunes. Ocarinas were little round musical instruments, shaped like turtles or birds. They were blown like flutes.

MUSIC

Mesoamerican people were not skilled metalworkers, but they found plenty of other materials to make instruments from. Conch shells from the sea were cleaned to make trumpets. Rattles might be made from the shells of armadillos, from clay, or from Sun-dried gourds. Dried seeds were put inside.

gourd

melon seeds

THE RHYTHM

Drums were popular. They were often made from a hollow log and were decorated with carvings.

INSTRUMENTS

This picture from a codex shows two Aztec musicians with some of the instruments they played: a conch shell trumpet, dried-gourd rattles, and flutes made from clay. Some of the instruments are decorated with tassels and bows.

JUMPING FOR JOY

These pictures from an Aztec codex show a rattle-player, a drummer and a juggler. Acrobats, jugglers and contortionists performed at many joyful festivals, such as harvest-time celebrations.

4 Cover the edge of one half of the hollow gourd with wet clay. Put dry seeds or beans inside and a cane through the middle. Press the halves together.

5 When it is dry, decorate the rattle with painted patterns and push a feather into the top of the bamboo cane. Coat the rattle with PVA glue for a shiny finish.

Gourd-shaped rattles were very popular instruments in Mesoamerica. The seeds inside the dried gourds would provide the rattle sound. Codex pictures often show people carrying rattles in processions. The rattles were often decorated with feathers.

Sports and Games

MESOAMERICAN PEOPLE enjoyed sports and games after work and on festival days. Two favourite games were *tlachtli* or *ulama*, the famous Mesoamerican ball-game, and *patolli*, a board-game. The ball-game was played in front of huge crowds, while *patolli* was a quieter game. Mesoamerican games were not just for fun. Both the ball-game and *patolli* had religious meanings. In the first, the court symbolized the world, and the rubber ball stood for the Sun as it made its daily journey across the sky. Players were meant to keep the ball moving in order to give energy to the Sun. Losing teams were sometimes sacrificed as offerings to the Sun god. In *patolli*, the movement of counters on the board represented the passing years.

PATOLLI
A group of Aztecs are shown here playing the game of *patolli*. It was played by moving dried beans or clay counters along a cross-shaped board with 52 squares. It could be very exciting. Players often bet on the result.

THE ACROBAT
This Olmec statue shows a very supple acrobat. Mesoamericans admired youth, fitness and beauty. Sports were fun, but they could also be good training for the demands of war. Being fit was considered attractive.

FLYING MEN
Volador was a ceremony performed on religious festival days. Four men, dressed as birds and attached to ropes, jumped off a high pole. As they spun round, falling towards the ground, they circled the pole 13 times each. That made 52 circuits – the length of the Mesoamerican holy calendar cycle.

PLAY PATOLLI

You will need: thick card, pencil, ruler, black marker pen, paints, small paintbrush, water pot, coloured papers, scissors, PVA glue and glue brush, dried broad or butter beans, self-drying clay.

1 Measure a square of thick card about 50cm x 50cm. Using a marker pen and a ruler, draw three lines from corner to corner to make a cross-shape.

2 Draw seven pairs of spaces along each arm. The third space in from the end should be a double space. Paint triangles in it.

3 Draw eight jaguar heads and eight marigolds on differently coloured paper. Cut them out. Paint the face of the Sun god into the centre.

TARGET RING

This stone ring comes from Chichen-Itza. Ball-game players used only their hips and knees to hit a solid rubber ball through rings like this fixed high on the ball-court walls.

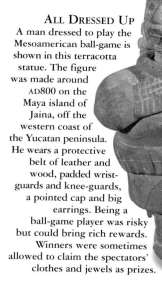

ALL DRESSED UP

A man dressed to play the Mesoamerican ball-game is shown in this terracotta statue. The figure was made around AD800 on the Maya island of Jaina, off the western coast of the Yucatan peninsula. He wears a protective belt of leather and wood, padded wrist-guards and knee-guards, a pointed cap and big earrings. Being a ball-game player was risky but could bring rich rewards. Winners were sometimes allowed to claim the spectators' clothes and jewels as prizes.

PLAY BALL

The ruins of a huge ball-court can still be seen in the Maya city of Uxmal. The biggest courts were up to 60m long and were built next to temples, in the centre of cities. People crowded inside the court to watch. Play was fast, furious and dangerous. Many players were injured as they clashed with opponents.

4 Stick the jaguars and marigolds randomly on the board. Paint a blue circle at the end of one arm, and a crown at the opposite end. Repeat in green on the other arms.

5 Paint five dried beans black with a white dot on one side. The beans will be thrown as dice. Make two counters from clay. Paint one green and one blue.

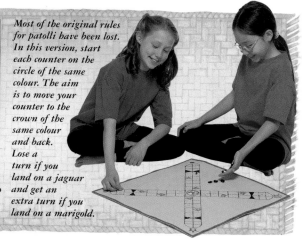

Most of the original rules for patolli have been lost. In this version, start each counter on the circle of the same colour. The aim is to move your counter to the crown of the same colour and back. Lose a turn if you land on a jaguar and get an extra turn if you land on a marigold.

Myths, Legends and Omens

THE AZTECS lived in constant fear that their world might come to an end. Ancient legends told that this had happened four times before. Each time, the world had been born again. Yet Aztec priests and astrologers did not believe that this would happen next time. If the world ended again, it would be forever. The souls of all Aztec people would be banished to a dark, gloomy underworld. The Wind of Knives would cut the flesh from their bones, and living skeletons would feast and dance with the Lord of the Dead. Then the Aztecs would vanish forever when they reached Mictlan (hell). The Maya told similar stories about the underworld – which they called Xibalba (the Place of Fright) in a great epic poem, the Popol Vuh. This poem featured two brothers, called the Hero Twins.

Aztec legends also told that the end of the world would be heralded by strange signs. In AD1519 these gloomy prophecies seemed to be coming true. Ruler Moctezuma II had weird, worrying dreams. Astronomers also observed eclipses of the Sun and a moving comet with a fiery tail.

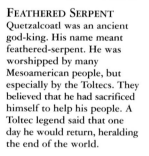

FEATHERED SERPENT
Quetzalcoatl was an ancient god-king. His name meant feathered-serpent. He was worshipped by many Mesoamerican people, but especially by the Toltecs. They believed that he had sacrificed himself to help his people. A Toltec legend said that one day he would return, heralding the end of the world.

HEROS AND LEGENDS
This ball court is in Copan, Guatemala. The ball-game featured in many Maya legends about the Hero Twins. They were skilled ball-game players and also expert hunters with deadly blow guns.

CREATURES OF LEGEND

This Maya bowl is decorated with a picture of a spider-monkey. Many different kinds of monkeys lived in the rainforests of Mesoamerica. Monkey-gods played an important part in Maya myths and legends. Because monkeys were quick and clever, the Maya believed that monkey-gods protected clever people, like scribes.

THE NEW FIRE CEREMONY

Every 52 years, the Aztecs believed that the world might come to an end. To stop this happening, they held a special ceremony. People put out their fires and stayed indoors. At sunset, priests climbed to the top of a hill and waited for the planet Venus to appear in the sky. At the moment it appeared, a captive was sacrificed to the gods. His heart was ripped out and a fire lit in his chest. The priests then sent messengers all over the Aztec lands, carrying torches to relight the fires. People then believed the world was safe for another 52 years.

HEAVENLY MESSENGER

Ruler Moctezuma is shown here observing the brilliant comet that appeared in the Mexican sky in 1519. Priests and Aztec people carefully studied the stars for messages from the gods. They remembered the old Toltec legend that said one day, the god Quetzalcoatl would return and bring the world to an end.

AZTEC HERITAGE

Many Aztec and Maya traditions still survive today. Millions of people speak Nahuatl (the Aztecs' language) or Maya languages. Aztec and Maya beliefs have mingled with Christian traditions to create new religious festivals. The most famous of these festivals is the Day of the Dead. Families bring presents of flowers and sweets shaped like skulls to their ancestors' graves.

The Coming of the Spanish

I N 1493 explorer Christopher Columbus arrived back in Spain from his pioneering voyage across the Atlantic Ocean. He told tales of an extraordinary "new world" full of gold. Excited by Columbus' stories, a group of Spanish soldiers sailed to Mexico in 1519, hoping to make their fortunes. They were led by a nobleman called Hernan Cortes. Together with the Aztecs' enemies, he led a march on Tenochtitlan. For the next two years, the Aztecs fought to stop Cortes and his soldiers taking over their land. At first, they had some success, driving the Spaniards out of Tenochtitlan in May 1520. Then, in 1521, Cortes attacked the city again, set fire to its buildings and killed around three-quarters of the population. In 1535, Mexico became a colony, ruled by officials sent from Spain.

A similar thing happened in Maya lands, but more slowly. The Spanish first landed there in 1523. They did not conquer the last independent city-state, Tayasal, until 1697.

AGAINST THE AZTECS
This picture comes from *The History of the Indies*. It was written by Diego Duran, a Spanish friar who felt sympathy for the Aztecs. Spanish soldiers and their allies from Tlaxcalla are seen fighting against the Aztecs. Although the Aztecs fought bravely, they had no chance of defeating Spanish soldiers mounted on horseback and armed with guns.

A SAD NIGHT
On 6 May 1520, Spanish soldiers massacred Aztecs gathered for a religious festival in Tenochtitlan. The citizens were outraged and attacked the Spaniards, many of whom died. During this night, the emperor Moctezuma II was stoned to death, probably by Aztecs who believed he had betrayed them. Cortes called this the *Noche Triste* (sad night).

THE END OF AZTEC POWER
This Aztec picture shows the surrender of Cuauhtemoc, the last Aztec king, to Cortes. After Moctezuma II died in 1520, the Aztecs were led by two of Moctezuma's descendants – Cuitlahuac, who ruled for only one year, and Cuauhtemoc. He was the last king and reigned until 1524.

RUNNING FOR THEIR LIVES
This illustration from a Spanish manuscript shows Aztec people fleeing from Spanish conquerors. You can see heavily-laden porters carrying stocks of food and household goods across a river to safety. On the far bank, mothers and children, with a pet bird and dog, hide behind huge maguey cactus plants.

WORKING LIKE SLAVES
Spanish settlers in Mexico took over all the Aztec and Maya fields and forced the people to work as farm labourers. They treated them cruelly, almost like slaves. This modern picture shows a Spanish overseer giving orders.

AFTER THE CONQUEST
Mexican artist Diego Rivera shows Mesoamerica after the Spanish conquest. Throughout the 1500s and 1600s, settlers from Spain arrived there. They drove out the local nobles and forced ordinary people to work for them. Spanish missionaries tried to replace local beliefs with European customs and Christianity. In Tenochtitlan, the Spaniards pulled down splendid Aztec palaces and temples to build churches and fine homes for themselves. You can see gangs of Aztec men working as labourers in the background of this picture.

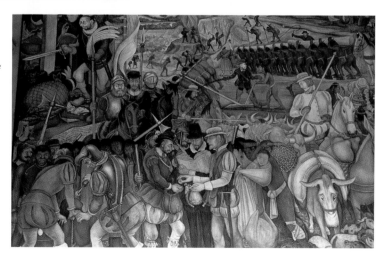

THE INCA WORLD

*The history of South America has seen the rise
and fall of many spectacular civilizations. The
Incas were the last, rising to power about 600
years ago. Hunter-gatherers had first settled the
region 12,000 years ago. Later on, as cities
grew, rulers competed for control of regions, and
so shaped the history of the Americas.*

PHILIP STEELE
Consultant: Dr Penny Dransart

Peoples of the Andes

Snowy peaks and glaciers rim the skyline above high, open plateaus. Cold lakes reflect the blue sky. These are the South American Andes, stretching for about 7,600km from Colombia to southern Chile. To the west, plains and deserts border the Pacific Ocean. To the east, steamy rainforests surround the Amazon River.

Humans settled here in about 11,000BC, or even earlier. Their ancestors crossed into North America from Asia and moved south. As the climate became warmer, tribes settled in the Andes and on the coast. They learned to farm and build villages. From about 1000BC, the seven civilizations of the Parácas, Chavín, Nazca, Moche, Tiwanaku, Wari and Chimú rose and fell. Last of all, from around AD1100 to 1532, came the Inca Empire.

In the High Andes
Alpacas cross a snowfield, high in the Andes. These woolly animals are related to the South American llama, guanaco and vicuña. Their wild ancestors may have been tamed in the Andes as early as 5400BC. Herding and farming were not essential for allowing great civilizations in the Andes, but the Incas developed these activities with great skill.

Workers of Gold
Hollow golden hands from a Chimú tomb may have been used as incense holders. The Chimú people came to power in northern Peru about 400 years before the Incas. Their smiths became very skilled at working gold. These craftsmen were later employed by the Incas.

Digging Up the Past
Archaeologists work near Sipán, in Peru's Lambayeque Valley. Burials of a warrior-priest and of Moche royalty, dating from about AD300, have been found there. The ancient Andean peoples kept no written records, so all we know of them comes from archaeology.

Timeline 11,000BC–AD1

Thousands of years before the Inca Empire was founded, people had settled on the Peruvian coast and in the Andes. The ruins of their cities and temples still stood in Inca times. They were part of the Inca world.

c.11,000BC People settle at Monte Verde, Chile.

c.10,000BC Stone tools are in use in Peru.

c.9000BC The climate becomes warmer, and glaciers retreat.

c.8600BC Beans, bottle gourds and chilli peppers are cultivated.

c.7500BC Guanaco, vicuña and deer become common in the Andes and are hunted for food.

c.5400BC Alpacas, and probably llamas, are herded.

Farming spreads along the coast and in the highlands.

c.4500BC Andean farmers cultivate squash.

stone tools

llama

c.3800BC Maize, manioc and cotton are grown in the Andes.

c.3500BC Llamas are used as pack animals to transport goods.

c.3200–1500BC Mummification is used to preserve the bodies of dead people in the north of Chile.

c.2800BC Pottery is made in Ecuador and in Colombia.

c.2600BC Temples are built on platform mounds on the Peruvian coast.

11,000BC   8600BC   3800BC   2500

VALLEY OF MYSTERY

The Urubamba River winds through steep, forested gorges. In 1911, an American archaeologist called Dr Hiram Bingham came to the area in search of Inca ruins. He discovered a lost city on the slopes of Machu Picchu, high above the river valley.

NAZCA PUZZLES

Mysterious markings on the ground were scraped on the desert on a gigantic scale by the Nazca people. Their civilization grew up on the coast of southern Peru, a thousand years before the Incas. The lines may have marked out routes for religious processions.

ANCIENT PEOPLES

This man is one of the Aymara people who live around Lake Titicaca, on the high border between Peru and Bolivia. Some historians believe they are descended from the builders of a great city called Tiwanaku. Others say that they arrived from the Cañete Valley after Tiwanaku was abandoned in about 1250. Although their way of life has changed over the ages, the Aymara have kept a distinctive identity.

IN SOUTH AMERICA

The great civilizations of South America grew up in the far west of the continent. The area is now occupied by the modern countries of Colombia, Ecuador, Peru, Bolivia, Chile and Argentina.

---

c.2500BC A temple with stepped platforms is built at El Paraíso on the coast of Peru.

Backstrap looms are used.

Potatoes and *quinua* are cultivated.

backstrap loom

There is widespread fishing along the Peruvian coast and the northern coast of Chile.

quinua   Andean farmers use irrigation.

c.2000BC The farming of maize, which first developed on the south-central coast and the north coast, is now widespread along the Peruvian coast and in the highlands.

c.1800BC Pottery-making develops along the coast of Peru.

c.1500BC Metal-working develops in Peru.

c.1000BC Large-scale settlement takes place in the Andes.

c.900BC The Chavín culture develops. The temple complex at Chavín de Huantar is built.

c.700BC The Parácas culture begins to thrive.

c.200BC The Chavín culture comes to an end.

The Nazca culture develops on the coast of southern Peru. Gigantic Nazca lines are marked on the surface of the deserts.

Chavín stone head

2000BC   900BC   AD1

The Great Empire

WHO WERE THE INCAS and where did they come from? If you had asked them, they would have told you proudly that their first great ruler, Manko Qapaq, was sent to Earth by his father Inti, the Sun. Manko Qapaq's queen, Mama Okllo, was believed to be the daughter of the Moon.

The Incas believed that they were superior to all other peoples. In reality, they were just the last link in a long chain of civilizations. They shared many beliefs with these peoples, often taking over their technology and crafts. From their mountain homeland, they learned how to live in the same landscapes and make use of them, ruling coast, desert and rainforest. The Incas started out as just one of many small tribes living in the Peruvian Andes in the 1100s. In the 1300s, led by their ruler Mayta Qapaq, they began to conquer neighbouring lands. During the 1400s, Inca armies and officials created a huge Empire. Although the Incas themselves only numbered about 40,000, they ruled a total population of about 12 million. Of the 20 languages that were spoken in the Inca Empire, the most important was Quechua, which is still widely spoken in the Andes mountains today.

This vast Empire seemed as if it would last for ever. In 1532, something happened to change that. Spanish soldiers landed in Peru, greedy for gold and land.

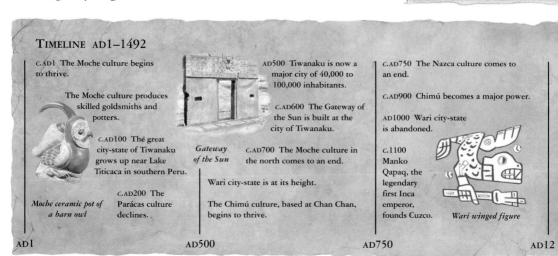

TIMELINE AD1–1492

c.AD1 The Moche culture begins to thrive.

The Moche culture produces skilled goldsmiths and potters.

c.AD100 The great city-state of Tiwanaku grows up near Lake Titicaca in southern Peru.

Moche ceramic pot of a barn owl

c.AD200 The Parácas culture declines.

AD500 Tiwanaku is now a major city of 40,000 to 100,000 inhabitants.

c.AD600 The Gateway of the Sun is built at the city of Tiwanaku.

Gateway of the Sun

c.AD700 The Moche culture in the north comes to an end.

Wari city-state is at its height.

The Chimú culture, based at Chan Chan, begins to thrive.

c.AD750 The Nazca culture comes to an end.

c.AD900 Chimú becomes a major power.

AD1000 Wari city-state is abandoned.

c.1100 Manko Qapaq, the legendary first Inca emperor, founds Cuzco.

Wari winged figure

AD1

AD500

AD750

AD12

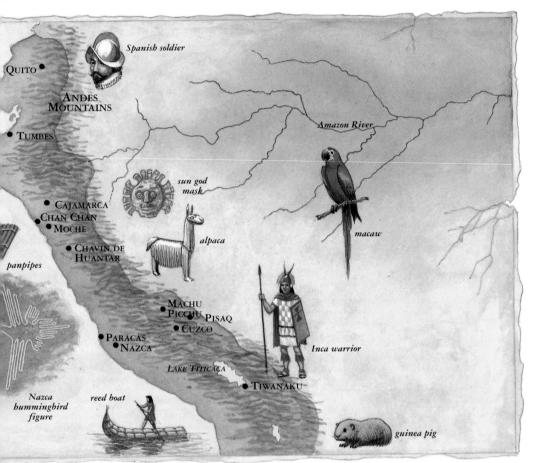

Quito

Spanish soldier

ANDES
MOUNTAINS

Amazon River

TUMBES

sun god
mask

CAJAMARCA
CHAN CHAN
MOCHE

CHAVIN DE
HUANTAR

alpaca

macaw

panpipes

MACHU
PICCHU
PISAQ
CUZCO

PARACAS
NAZCA

Inca warrior

LAKE TITICACA

Nazca
hummingbird
figure

reed boat

TIWANAKU

guinea pig

c.1250 The once-great city of Tiwanaku is abandoned, perhaps because of changes in the climate.

c.1300 Sinchi Roka is the first emperor to use the title *Sapa Inca*.

1370 Chimor, the Empire of the Chimú people, expands.

c.1410 The Incas make new alliances under the emperor Wiraqocha.

1437 Wiraqocha's son Yupanki conquers the mountain State of Chanca.

Chimú gold funeral mask

1438 Wiraqocha backs another son, Urqon, as the next emperor.

Yupanki proclaims himself emperor of a rival Inca State and renames himself Pachakuti.

Urqon is killed, and his father Wiraqocha dies.

The Inca State is reunited under Pachakuti.

c.1440 The powerful emperor, Minchançaman, rules Chimú.

c.1445 Pachakuti's brother, Qapaq Yupanki, explores the coastline to the south.

c.1450 Incas build Machu Picchu high in the Andes.

1450 The Inca Empire grows by conquest. Cuzco is rebuilt.

1470 Incas conquer Chimor.

1471 Topa Inka Yupanki becomes emperor. A great age of road building begins.

Chimú ritual knife

AD1438   AD1445   AD1492

Makers of History

BECAUSE INCA HISTORY was not written down at the time, much of it has to be pieced together from chronicles and diaries recorded in the years after the Spanish conquest in the 1500s. Many accounts describe the everyday lives of ordinary people in the days of the Inca Empire. The names of the people who dug the fields and built the roads are mostly forgotten. Only the names of the Inca royal family and the nobles are known.

The first eight emperors recalled in Inca folklore probably did exist. However over the centuries their life stories, passed on from parent to child over generations, became mixed up with myths and legends. The last 100 years of Inca rule, beginning when Pachakuti Inka Yupanki came to the throne in 1438, were fresh in people's memories when the Spanish invaded. As a result, we know a good deal about the greatest days of the Inca Empire.

MAMA OKLLO

This painting from the 1700s imagines the Inca empress, Mama Okllo, carrying a Moon mask. She reigned in the 1100s. In some Inca myths, she and her brother Manko Qapaq were said to be the children of the Sun and the Moon. Mama Okllo married her brother, who became the first ruler of the Incas. They had a son called Sinchi Roka.

ON THE ROAD TO RUIN

An Inca emperor and empress are carried around their Empire. The Inca rulers had almost unlimited power, but were destroyed by bitter rivalry within the royal family. When the Spanish invaders arrived in 1532, Tawantinsuyu was divided between supporters of Waskar and his brother Ataw Wallpa.

TIMELINE AD1492–1781

1492 The Incas conquer northern Chile.

1493 Wayna Qapaq becomes emperor.

1498 Wayna Qapaq conquers part of Colombia and the Inca Empire reaches its greatest extent.

c.1523 A ship-wrecked Spaniard called Alejo García enters Inca territory from the east with raiding Chiriquana warriors. He dies during his return journey.

quipu used for government records

1525 Wayna Qapaq dies without an agreed successor. His son Waskar is chosen and crowned as the twelfth *Sapa Inca* in Cuzco. Waskar's brother, Ataw Wallpa, claims the imperial throne.

War breaks out in the Inca Empire as the brothers battle for power.

Inca warrior

1526–7 A Spanish naval expedition sights Inca rafts off the Pacific coast.

1529 The Spanish king approves a plan by Francisco Pizarro to conquer Peru.

1532 Waskar is defeated by his brother Ataw Wallpa.

The Spanish, under Francisco Pizarro, enter the inland city of Cajamarca and kill 7,000 Incas.

1533 Ataw Wallpa and his sister, Asarpay, are killed by the Spanish.

Inca rope bridge

AD1492   AD1525   AD1529   AD15

LLOQE YUPANKI

The son of Sinchi Roka, Lloqe Yupanki was chosen to be ruler of the lands around Cuzco in place of his older brother. He was a wise ruler, and his reign in the 1200s was peaceful. His son Mayta Qapaq was more warlike. He expanded his Empire by conquering neighbouring peoples.

PACHAKUTI INKA YUPANKI (REIGNED 1438–71)

Inka Yupanki was still a prince when he proved himself in war by conquering the Chanca people. However, his father Wiraqocha chose another son, Inka Urqon, as the next emperor. Yupanki claimed the throne, calling himself Pachakuti, which means "the world turned upside down". Urqon was killed, and his father died soon after.

ATAW WALLPA (REIGNED 1532–3)

Known as Atahuallpa or Atabaliba to the Spanish, Ataw Wallpa was the son of the great emperor Wayna Qapaq, who died unexpectedly in 1525. When his brother Waskar was crowned in Cuzco, Ataw Wallpa stayed with the army in the north, and a bitter war followed. By 1532, Waskar had been imprisoned, and Ataw Wallpa was ruler. But before the Empire could recover from the war, the Spanish invaded. Ataw Wallpa was captured and executed the following summer.

FRANCISCO PIZARRO (c.1478–1541)

In 1532, this Spanish soldier sailed to the Inca city of Tumbes with just 180 men and 37 horses. They marched inland to Cajamarca. Pizarro used treachery to capture and kill the Inca emperor, Ataw Wallpa. This army went on to loot Inca gold and bring Peru under Spanish rule. Resistance from the local people was fierce – but not as fierce as the rivalry and greed of the Spanish. Pizarro was murdered by one of his fellow countrymen fewer than ten years later.

1535 The Incas rebel against Spain.

1536 Incas lay siege to the city of Cuzco. The city is burnt to the ground by the Incas.

The Inca Empire collapses.

1537 A last Inca State is formed by Cura Okllo and Manko Inka, based at Vilcabamba.

1538 The Spanish invaders fight among themselves at Las Salinas, near Cuzco.

Inca messenger with conch shell

1539 Cura Okllo, the successor to Asarpay and the sister-wife of Manko Inka, is executed by the Spanish.

1541 Pizarro is assassinated.

1545 Manko Inka is assassinated.

1572 Inca resistance under Tupac Amaru I is finally defeated, and he is executed. He is the last Inca ruler.

Vilcabamba and Machu Picchu are abandoned.

1742 Resistance to the Spanish grows. Calls for restoration of the Inca Empire.

1780 Major uprising of indigenous peoples under José Gabriel Condorcanqui He adopts the name of his ancestor and declares himself Tupac Amaru II. He aims to restore the Inca Empire.

1781 Tupac Amaru II is captured and horribly tortured to death.

Spanish conquistador

AD1539

AD1742

AD1781

Lords of the Sun

MANY OF THE EARLY TRIBES that lived in the Andes and on the Pacific coast were small groups of hunters and farmers. As cities and kingdoms grew in size, they began to need strong leadership. By about AD900, the State of Chimor was headed by powerful kings.

The Inca emperor was called *Sapa Inca* (Only Leader). As a descendant of the Sun, he was regarded as a god. He had complete power over his subjects, but he always had to be on his guard. There were many rivals for the throne among his royal relations. Each emperor had a new palace built for himself in the royal city of Cuzco. Emperors were treated with the utmost respect at all times and were often veiled or screened from ordinary people.

The empress, or *Quya* (Star), was the emperor's sister or mother. She was also thought to be divine and led the worship of the Moon goddess. The next

emperor was supposed to be chosen from among her sons. An emperor had many secondary wives. Waskar was said to have fathered eighty children in just eight years.

RELIGIOUS LEADERS
Sacrifices of llamas were made to the gods each month, at special festivals and before battle. The *Sapa Inca* controlled all religious activities. In the 1400s, the emperor Wiraqocha Inka declared that worship of the god Wiraqocha, the Creator (after whom he was named), was more important than worship of Inti, the Sun god. This made some people angry.

A CHOSEN WOMAN
Young girls, the *akllakuna*, were educated for four years in religious matters, weaving and housekeeping. Some became the emperor's secondary wives or married noblemen. Others became priestesses or *mamakuna* (virgins of the Sun). Figurines like these wore specially made clothes, but these have perished or been lost over the years.

A FEATHER FAN
You will need: pencil, card, ruler, scissors, paints in bright colours, paintbrush, water pot, masking tape, wadding, PVA glue, hessian or sackcloth, needle, thread, string or twine.

1 Draw a feather shape 18cm long on to card and cut it out. The narrow part should be half of this length. Draw around the shape on card nine times.

2 Carefully paint the feathers with bright colours. Use red, orange and yellow to look like rainforest birds. Allow the paint to dry completely.

3 Cut out each feather and snip along the sides of the widest part to give a feathery effect. When the paint is dry, paint the other side as well.

COMMANDER IN CHIEF

The emperor sits on his throne. He wears a tasselled woollen headdress or *llautu*, decorated with gold and feathers, and large gold earplugs. He carries a sceptre. Around him, army chiefs await their orders. Emperors played an active part in military campaigns and relied on the army to keep them in power.

COOL SPRINGS

At Tambo Machay, to the south of Cuzco, fresh, cold water is channelled from sacred springs. Here, the great Pachakuti Inka Yupanki would bathe after a hard day's hunting.

THE LIVING DEAD

The dead body of an emperor, preserved as a mummy, is paraded through the streets. When each emperor died, his palace became his tomb. Once a year, the body was carried around Cuzco amid great celebrations. The picture is by Guamán Poma de Ayala, who was of Inca descent. In the 1600s, he made many pictures of Inca life.

Feathers from birds of the tropical forests to the east of the Andes were used to make fans for the emperor.

4 Hold the narrow ends of the feathers and spread out the tops to form a fan shape. Use masking tape to secure the ends firmly in position.

5 Cut a rectangular piece of wadding 9cm high and long enough to wrap the base of the feathers several times. Use glue on one side to keep it in place.

6 Cut a strip of hessian or sackcloth about 5cm wide. Starting at the base of the feathers, wrap the fabric around the stems. Hold it in place with a few stitches.

7 Wind string or twine firmly around the hessian to form the fan's handle. Tuck in the ends and use glue at each end to make sure they are secure.

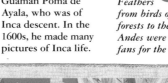

The Inca State

FAMILY CONNECTIONS PLAYED an important part in royal power struggles and in everyday social organization in the Inca world. The nobles were grouped into family-based corporations called *panakas*. Members of each *panaka* shared rights to an area of land, its water, pasture and herds. Linked to each *panaka* was a land-holding *ayllu* (or clan) – a group of common people who were also related to each other.

The Incas managed to control an empire that contained many different peoples. Loyal Incas were sent to live in remote areas, while troublemakers from the regions were resettled nearer Cuzco, where they could be carefully watched. Conquered chiefs were called *kurakas*. They and their children were educated in Inca ways and allowed to keep some of their local powers.

The Inca system of law was quite severe. State officials and *kurakas* (conquered chiefs) acted as judges. Those who stole from the emperor's stores of grain, textiles and other goods faced a death sentence. Torture, beating, blinding and exile were all common punishments. The age of the criminal and the reason for the crime were sometimes taken into account.

A Clever Calculator

One secret of Inca success was the *quipu*. It was used by government officials for recording all kinds of information, from the number of households in a town to the amount of goods of various kinds in a warehouse. The *quipu* was a series of strings tied to a thick cord. Each string had one or more colours and could be knotted. The colours represented anything from types of grain to groups of people. The knots represented numbers.

One State, Many Peoples

The ancestors of these Bolivian women were subjects of the Incas. The Inca Empire was the largest ever known in all the Americas. It included at least a hundred different peoples. The Incas were clever governors and did not always try to force their own ideas upon other groups. Conquered peoples had to accept the Inca gods, but they were allowed to worship in their own way and keep their own customs.

A ROYAL INSPECTION

Topa Inka Yupanki inspects government stores in the 1470s. In the Inca world, nearly all grain, textiles and other goods were produced for the State and stored in warehouses. Some extra produce might be bartered, or exchanged privately, but there were no big markets or shops.

PUBLIC WORKS

Labourers build fortifications on the borders of the Inca Empire. People paid their taxes to the Inca State in the form of labour called *mit'a*. This might be general work on the land. Men were also conscripted to work on public buildings or serve in the army. The Spanish continued to operate the *mit'a* as a form of tax long after they conquered the Inca Empire.

OLLANTAYTAMBO

This building in Ollantaytambo, in the Urubamba Valley, was once a State storehouse for the farm produce of the region. Ollantaytambo was a large town, which was probably built about 550 years ago. It protected the valley from raids by the warriors who lived in the forests to the east. Buildings dating from the Inca Empire were still being lived in by local people when the American archaeologist Dr Hiram Bingham passed through in 1911.

Nobles and Peasants

INCA SOCIETY was strictly graded. At the top were the *Sapa Inca* and his *Quya*. The High Priest and other important officials were normally recruited from members of the royal family.

If noblemen were loyal to the emperor, they might receive gifts of land. They might be given gold or a beautiful *akllakuna* as a wife. They could expect jobs as regional governors, generals or priests. Lords and ladies wore fine clothes and were carried in splendid chairs, called litters.

Next in rank were the conquered non-Inca rulers and chiefs, the *kurakas*. They were cleverly brought into the Inca political system and given traditional honours. They served as regional judges.

Most people in the Empire were peasants. They were unable to leave their villages without official permission. They had no choice but to stay and toil on the land, sending their produce to the government stores.

CRAFT AND CLASS
A pottery figure from the Peruvian coast shows a porter carrying a water pot on his back. In the Inca Empire, craft workers such as potters and goldsmiths were employed by the State. They formed a small middle class. Unlike peasants they were never made to do *mit'a* (public service).

A MOCHE NOBLEMAN
The man's face on this jar is that of a noble. It was made by a Moche potter on the north coast of Peru between 1,500 and 2,000 years ago. The man's headdress sets him apart as a noble, perhaps a high priest.

A WATER POT
You will need: self-drying clay, cutting board, rolling pin, ruler, water, water pot, acrylic paints, paintbrush.

1 Roll out a piece of clay on the board. Make a circle about 17cm in diameter and 1cm thick. This will form the base of your water pot.

2 Roll some more clay into long sausages, about as fat as your little finger. Dampen the base with water and carefully place a sausage around the edge.

3 Coil more clay sausages on top of each other to build up the pot. Make each coil slightly smaller than the one below. Water will help them stick.

A PEASANT'S LIFE

A woman harvests potatoes near Sicuani, to the south of Cuzco. Then, as now, life was hard for the peasant farmers of the Andes. Both men and women worked in the fields, and even young children and the elderly were expected to help. However, the Inca State did provide some support for the peasants, supplying free grain in times of famine.

PLUGGED IN

This Chimú earplug is made of gold, turquoise and shell. It was worn as a badge of rank. Inca noblemen wore such heavy gold earplugs that the Spanish called them *orejones* (big ears). Noblewomen wore their hair long, covered with a head-cloth.

LAND AND SEASONS

One third of all land and produce belonged to the emperor, one third to the priests and one third to the peasants. It was hardly a fair division. A peasant's life, digging, planting and harvesting, was ruled by the seasons. Each new season was celebrated by religious festivals and ceremonies.

Children were expected to help their parents by fetching water from the wells and mountain springs.

4 When you reach the neck of the pot, start making the coils slightly bigger again to form a lip. Carefully smooth the coils with wet fingertips.

5 Use two more rolls of clay to make handles on opposite sides of the pot. Smooth out the joints carefully to make sure the handles stay in place.

6 Leave the clay to dry completely. Then paint the pot all over with a background colour. Choose an earthy reddish brown to look like Inca pottery.

7 Leave the reddish brown colour to dry. Use a fine paintbrush and black paint to draw Inca designs on the pot like the ones in the picture above.

On Land and Water

PERU TODAY is still criss-crossed by the remains of cobbled roads built by the Incas. Two main paved highways ran north to south, one following the coast and the other following the Andes. The first was about 3,600km long, the second even longer. The two roads were joined by smaller roads linking towns and villages. The roads crossed deserts, mountains and plateaus. Markers measured out distances in *topos*, units of about 7km.

Despite these great engineering works, most people in the Empire were not allowed to travel at all. These fine roads were strictly for use by people on official business. Messages to and from the emperor were carried by trained relay runners called *chasquis*, who were stationed in stone shelters along the way. In one day, a message could travel 240km. Government rest-houses called *tambos* were built on the chief routes.

The Incas were very inventive, but they had no wheeled transport. Baggage and goods were carried by porters or on the backs of llamas. Nobles travelled in richly decorated litters, carried by four or more men.

THE WATER CARRIER
A porter carries a jar on his head. Steep mountain roads must have made such work very tiring. The State road network allowed crops, food, drink, precious metal ores and textiles to be brought to the royal court from far-flung regions of the Empire.

TRAVELLING TO WAR
A litter, carried at shoulder height by four strong men, carries the emperor Wayna Qapaq to war. One purpose of the Inca road network was to make sure that armies could be moved quickly from one end of the Empire to the other. Depots and food stores for army use were built along the highways. Depot managers were kept in a state of readiness by royal officials.

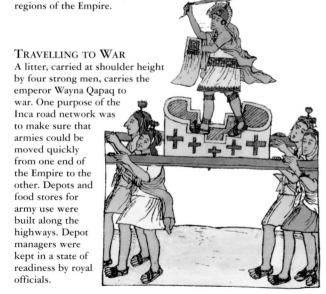

THE ROAD GOES ON
An old Inca road zigzags up steep, terraced slopes near Pisaq. Inca engineers laid down about 16,000km of roads in all. Some highway sections were up to 7m across. Most were just broad enough for a llama – about 1m wide. The steepest sections were stepped.

BOATS OF REEDS

These modern boats were made by the Uru people of Lake Titicaca. The Incas made boats and rafts for travel on lakes, rivers and the ocean. Because there was a shortage of timber in most areas, they made them from a type of reed, called *totora*. These were cut, trimmed and tightly bound in bundles. They were light, buoyant and strong, and could be bent into curved shapes to form the prow and stern of a boat.

HIGHWAY PATROL

The governor of bridges watches as a porter carrying goods on his back crosses a rope bridge across a mountain river. Bridges had to be able to take considerable stress and strain, caused by the tramp of marching armies and by hundreds of heavily burdened llamas. Officials inspected roads and bridges and could order local workers to repair them under the *mit'a* system of conscripted labour.

BRIDGES OF ROPE

Rope bridges are still made from plaited mountain grasses by the Quechua people. This one crosses a gorge of the Apurimac River in Peru. Inca engineers built long rope bridges like this one, as well as stone bridges, causeways over marshy ground and tunnels through rock. Sometimes people crossed rivers in baskets hauled across the water on ropes.

Master Masons

THE ROCKS of the Andes mountains provided high quality granite that was used for impressive public buildings. These included temples, fortresses, palaces, holy shrines and aqueducts (stone channels for carrying water supplies).

The *mit'a* labour system provided the workforce. In the quarries, massive rocks weighing up to 120 tonnes were cracked and shifted with stone hammers and bronze crowbars. They were hauled with ropes on log rollers or sleds. On site, the stones were shaped to fit and rubbed smooth with water and sand. Smaller stone blocks were used for upper walls or lesser buildings.

The expert Inca stonemasons had only basic tools. They used plumblines (weighted cords) to make sure that walls were straight. They used no mortar or cement, but the stones fitted together perfectly. Many remain in place to this day. Most public buildings were on a grand scale, but all were of a simple design.

BUILDING THE TEMPLE
These rectangular stone blocks were part of the holiest site in the Inca Empire, the *Coricancha* (Temple of the Sun). Inca stonework was deliberately designed to withstand the earthquakes that regularly shake the region. The original temple on this site was badly damaged by a tremor in 1650.

BRINGER OF WATER
This beautifully engineered stone water-channel was built across a valley floor by Inca stonemasons. Aqueducts, often covered, were used both for irrigation and for drinking supplies. Irrigation schemes were being built in Peru as early as around 4,500 years ago.

AN INCA GRANARY
You will need: ruler, pencil, beige, dark and cream card, scissors, white pencil, paints, paintbrush, water pot, pair of compasses, masking tape, PVA glue, hay or straw.

1 Use a ruler and pencil to mark eight strips 8.5cm long and 0.25cm wide, and one strip 36cm long and 0.25cm wide on beige card. Cut them out.

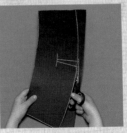

2 On the dark card, draw a curved shape 34cm along the base, 11cm in height and 30cm along the top. Cut it out. Cut out a doorway 6cm high.

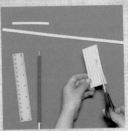

3 Paint another piece of card a stone colour. Leave it to dry. Cut it into "blocks" about 2cm high. Glue them one by one on to the building shape.

HISTORY IN STONE

Stone walls and streets, such as these fine examples still standing in Ollantaytambo, survive to tell a story. Archaeology is much more difficult in the rainforests to the east, where timber structures rot rapidly in the hot, moist air. That is one reason we know more about the way people lived in the Andes than in the Amazon region.

A MASSIVE FORTRESS

Llamas still pass before the mighty walls of Sacsahuaman, at Cuzco. This building was a fortress with towers and terraces. It also served as a royal palace and a sacred shrine. Its multi-sided boulders are precisely fitted. It is said to have been built over many years by 30,000 labourers. It was one of many public buildings raised in the reign of Pachakuti Inka Yupanki.

INCA DESIGN

A building in Machu Picchu shows an example of typical Inca design. Inca stonemasons learned many of their skills from earlier Peruvian civilizations. Openings that are wider at the bottom than the top are seen only in Inca buildings. They are said to be trapezoid.

Storehouses were built of neat stone blocks. They kept precious grain dry and secure.

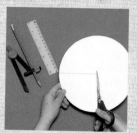

4 Use compasses to draw a circle 18cm across on cream card. Cut it out and cut away one quarter. Tape the straight cut edges together to form a cone.

5 Make a circle by joining the ends of the 36cm strip with masking tape. Then fix the eight 8.5cm strips around the edge and in the middle as shown.

6 Glue short lengths of straw or hay all over the cardboard cone to form the thatched roof of the granary. The thatch should all run in the same direction.

7 Join the edges of the walls with masking tape. Fold in the sides of the doorway. Place the rafters on top. The thatched roof fits over the rafters.

Town Dwellers

REAT CITIES had been built in Peru long before the Incas came to power. In about AD600, the city of Tiwanaku, near Lake Titicaca, may have had a population of nearly 100,000. A hundred years later, the Chimú capital of Chan Chan covered 15 square kilometres of the coastal plain.

The Inca capital, Cuzco, was ringed by mountains and crossed by two rivers that had been turned into canals, the Huatanay and the Tullamayo. Cuzco became dominated by fine public buildings and royal palaces when it was rebuilt in about 1450. At its centre was the great public square, known as *Waqaypata* (Holy Place). At festival time, this square was packed with crowds. Roads passed from here to the four quarters of the Empire. They were lined by the homes of Inca nobles, facing in upon private compounds called *canchas*. The centre of the city was home to about 40,000 people, but the surrounding suburbs and villages housed a further 200,000. Newer Inca towns, such as Pumpo, Huanuco and Tambo Colorado, were planned in much the same way as Cuzco, but adapted to the local landscape.

WATER ON TAP
At Machu Picchu, water was channelled into the town from the mountain springs that bubbled up about 1.5km outside the city walls. The water ran into stone troughs and fountains, and it was used for bathing and drinking.

THE PAST REVEALED
Archaeologists record every detail of what they find with the greatest care. Here at an old Inca town near Cuzco, they are using precision instruments to note the exact position of everything they uncover. Excavations in Inca towns have unearthed pots and jars, fragments of cloth, jewellery, knives and human burials. They are constantly adding to what we know about the Inca civilization.

STEEP STREETS
Machu Picchu was built on a steep slope, using *mit'a* labour. Some of its buildings were set into the rock, while many more were built on raised terraces of stone. Its streets had steps in many places. Incas may have fled to this mountain retreat from Cuzco after the Spanish invaded in 1532. It was abandoned within 40 years and soon covered by creepers and trees.

RUINS OF CHAN CHAN

Chan Chan, capital of Chimor, was built in the north, at the mouth of the Moche River. It was the biggest city of ancient Peru. Far from the granite of the Andes, Chan Chan was constructed with adobe (bricks made from sun-baked mud). The city was laid out in a grid pattern, with 12m-high compound walls marking out the homes of royalty, nobles and craft workers.

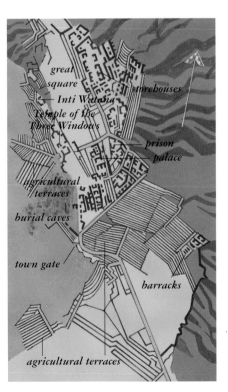

great square
Inti Watana
Temple of the Three Windows
storehouses
prison
palace
agricultural terraces
burial caves
town gate
barracks
agricultural terraces

LIVING IN THE CLOUDS

The small but spectacular Inca town of Machu Picchu clings to a high mountain ridge beneath the peak of Wayna Picchu. In about 1450, it had its own ceremonial square, temples and burial caves. The town also had army barracks, public stores, a prison, housing for craft workers and farmers, and a palace for visiting royalty. The town was defended from attack by a twin wall and a ditch.

A PLAN OF THE TOWN

The long and narrow layout of Machu Picchu was decided by its ridge-top location at 2,743m above sea level. The great square was the religious and political centre of town.

An Inca House

A TYPICAL HOUSE in an Inca town such as Machu Picchu was built from blocks of stone. White granite was the best, being very hard and strong. The roof of each house was pitched at quite a steep angle, so that heavy mountain rains could drain off quickly. Timber roof beams were lashed to stone pegs on the gables, and supported a wooden frame. This was thatched with a tough grass called *ichu*.

Most houses had just one storey, but a few had two or three, joined by rope ladders inside the house or by stone blocks set into the outside wall. Most had a single doorway hung with cloth or hide, and some had an open window on the gable end.

Each building was home to a single family and formed part of a compound. As many as half a dozen houses would be grouped around a shared courtyard. All the buildings belonged to families who were members of the same *ayllu*, or clan.

MUD AND THATCH
Various types of houses were to be seen in different parts of the Inca Empire. Many were built in old-fashioned or in regional styles. These round and rectangular houses in Bolivia are made of mud bricks (adobe). The houses are thatched with *ichu* grass.

upper storey

inside hearth

courtyard

FLOATING HOMES
These houses are built by the Uru people, who fish in Lake Titicaca and hunt in the surrounding marshes. They live on the lake shore and also on floating islands made of matted *totora* reeds. Their houses are made of *totora* and *ichu* grass. Both these materials would have been used in the Titicaca area in Inca times. The reeds are collected from the shallows and piled on to the floor of the lake. New reeds are constantly added.

PICTURES AND POTTERY

Houses with pitched roofs and windows appear as part of the decoration on this pottery from Pacheco, Nazca. To find out about houses in ancient Peru, historians look at surviving towns and ruins, at housing styles still in use today and at old pictures and designs on objects.

SQUARE STONE, ROUND PEG

Squared-off blocks of stone are called ashlars. These white granite ashlars make up a wall in the Inca town of Pisaq. They are topped by a round stone peg. Pegs like these were probably used to support roof beams or other structures, such as ladders from one storey to another.

gable

roofbeam

roof peg

wall niche

BUILDING MATERIALS

The materials used to build an Inca house depended on local supplies. Rock was the favourite material. White granite, dark basalt and limestone were used when possible. Away from the mountains, clay was made into bricks and dried hard in the sun to make adobe. Roof beams were formed from timber poles. Thatch was made of grass or reed.

clay   white granite

thatch   timber

BUILDING TO LAST

The Incas built simple, but solid, dwellings in the mountains. The massive boulders used for temples and fortresses are here replaced by smaller, neatly cut stones. See how the roof beams are lashed to the gables to support the thatch. Stone roofs were very rare, even on the grandest houses. Timber joists provide an upper storey. The courtyard is used just as much as the inside of the house for everyday living.

Inside the Home

L ET'S VISIT THE HOME of an Inca mountain farmer. The outer courtyard is busy, with smoke rising from cooking pots into the fresh mountain air. An elderly woman stacks firewood, while her daughter sorts out bundles of alpaca wool. A young boy brings in a pot of fresh water, splashing the ground as he puts it down.

Pulling aside the cloth at the doorway, you blink in the dark and smoky atmosphere. Cooking has to be done indoors when the weather is poor. The floor of beaten earth is swept clean. There is no furniture at all, but part of the stone wall juts out to form a bench. In one corner there is a clutter of pots and large storage jars. Cloaks and baskets hang from stone pegs on the wall. Niches, inset in the wall, hold a few precious objects and belongings, perhaps a pottery jar or some shell necklaces. Other items include a knife and equipment for weaving or fishing.

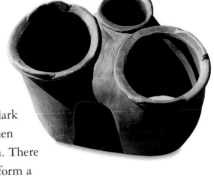

POT STOVES
Cooking stoves of baked clay, very like these, have been used in Peru for hundreds of years. Round cooking pots were placed on top of these little stoves. The fuel was pushed in through a hole in the side. Pot stoves are easily carried and can be used outside. Inside the house, there might be a more permanent hearth, made of clay or stone.

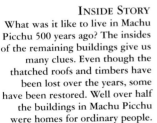

DRINK IT UP!
The shape of this two-handled jar and its simple colouring are typically Inca, but the geometric patterns suggest it may have been the work of a Chimú potter. A jar like this might have been used to carry *chicha* (maize beer) made by the *mamakuna* for one of the great religious festivals. People drank far too much *chicha* on these occasions, and drunkenness was common.

INSIDE STORY
What was it like to live in Machu Picchu 500 years ago? The insides of the remaining buildings give us many clues. Even though the thatched roofs and timbers have been lost over the years, some have been restored. Well over half the buildings in Machu Picchu were homes for ordinary people.

REED MATTING

Totora reed matting, used by the Uru people today, is rolled up in bales by Lake Titicaca. In Inca times, reed mats were used as bedding by most people. They slept fully dressed on the ground. Even the emperor and the nobles slept on the floor, but they had blankets and rugs of the finest cloth to cover themselves. Like the Incas, the Uru people have many household uses for *totora* reed. It is a fuel, its flower is used to make medicines and some parts of it may be eaten.

HOUSEHOLD GOURDS

Decorated gourds are still sold in the highlands of Peru. Gourds are pumpkin-like plants bearing fruits with a hard shell. Gourds were often hollowed out and dried and used by the Incas as simple containers for everyday use around the house. They served as water bottles or pots.

FUEL SUPPLIES

In many parts of the Inca Empire, timber was scarce, and its use was officially limited. Brushwood, sticks and a mountain plant called *llareta* were collected for tinder and fuel. Llama dung was also widely used as a fuel for cooking or for firing pottery. Fires were started with drills. These were sticks rotated at such high speed against another piece of wood that they became very hot indeed and began to smoke.

timber

brushwood

Hunting and Fishing

THE INCAS hunted wild animals for sport as well as for food. Every four years, there was a great public hunt, at which beaters would form a line many kilometres long and comb the countryside for game. The hunters closed in on the animals with dogs. Dangerous animals were hunted, such as bears and pumas (South American cougars or mountain lions), as well as important sources of food such as deer, guanaco (a wild relative of the llama) and partridges. After the hunt, the meat was cut into strips and dried in the sun.

Hunting was a pastime of royalty and nobles, but ordinary people could hunt with permission. Every child learned how to use a sling – ideal for killing small birds. Nets were used to catch wildfowl on lakes and marshes. Spears, clubs, bows and arrows were also used.

BEAK AND TACKLE
The Moche fisherman shown on this jar is using a pelican to catch fish for him with its great pouch of a beak. Fishing crews of the coast used cotton lines, fish hooks of copper or bone, harpoons, or cotton nets with gourd floats.

SPEARS OF THE NAZCA
A painting on a pottery vase shows two hunters attacking vicuña with spears. It dates from the Nazca civilization, which lasted from about 200BC to AD750. The first Peruvians lived by hunting, but the Inca State depended mainly on farming and fishing for its food. Hunting had become a pastime.

BEYOND THE SURF
A fishing boat made of bound *totora* reed is steered towards the surf at Huancacho, to the north of Trujillo on Peru's north coast. This sight would have been much the same in the days of the Inca Empire. The first view Spanish explorers had of the Inca Empire was of fishing boats and rafts at sea.

A REED BOAT
You will need: dry straw or hay, scissors, ruler, strong thread or twine, pencil, darning needle, plastic lid, PVA glue, paintbrush.

1 Take a fistful of straw or hay and gather it together as shown. Trim one end to make a bundle 20cm long. Make another 20cm bundle and two more 18cm long.

2 Tie a length of thread or twine around one end of a bundle. Then wind it along at 3cm intervals. Bind to a point at one end and tie a knot.

3 Gently bend the bound bundle into a banana shape. Tie and bend the remaining three bundles in exactly the same way. Keep the thread tight.

A Day's Fishing

Two Moche fishermen sit on a sea-going raft, drinking beer and arguing, no doubt, about the "fish that got away". Fishing was already a major occupation on the Peruvian coast about 4,500 years ago. Later coastal peoples, such as the Chimú, specialized as fishermen, supplying the inland cities with their catches. In Inca times, freshly caught fish from the coast were hurried by special messenger to the royal palace at Cuzco.

Fishing in Lake and Ocean

The cool currents that sweep up the west coast of Peru provide some of the best fishing in all the Pacific Ocean. Small fish such as sardines and anchovies swarm through these waters. Larger fish and shellfish may also be taken. Inland lakes such as Lake Titicaca are also a rich source of fish.

sardines

anchovies

The Chase

A picture painted on a *kero* (wooden beaker), shows an Inca hunter bringing down a guanaco. His weapon is the *bola*, a heavy cord weighted with three balls. It was hurled at the guanaco's legs in order to entangle it. The *bola* was also used in Argentina in the 1800s by the cowboys called *gauchos*.

The curving sides and pointed prow of a reed boat were designed to cut through the waves.

4 Draw a boat shape on plastic, 14cm long, 6cm at the widest point and 4cm wide at the stern. Cut it out. Prick holes 1cm apart around the edge as shown.

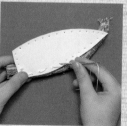

5 Thread the needle and carefully sew one of the shorter bundles to one side of the boat. Repeat on the other side of the boat with the matching bundle.

6 Use PVA glue to fix the longer straw or hay bundles on top of the first ones. Curve the uncut ends upwards slightly to form the prow of the boat.

7 Paint the hull of the boat with glue to make it waterproof. Leave it to dry completely before testing your sea-going craft in a bowl of water!

Living on the Land

THE MOUNTAINS, windy plateaus and deserts of Peru are very difficult to farm. Over thousands of years, humans struggled to tame these harsh landscapes. They brought water to dry areas, dug terraced fields out of steep slopes and improved wild plants such as the potato until they became useful food crops. In Inca times, two-thirds of the farmers' produce was set aside for the emperor and the priests, so there was little personal reward for the people who did the hard work.

Royal officials decided the borders of all the fields and of the pastures for llama and alpaca herds. The soil was broken with hoes and plough-like spades called *takllas*. These simple tools were made of hardened wood. Some were tipped with bronze. The Incas knew how to keep the soil well fertilized, using llama dung in the mountains and guano (seabird droppings) on the coast. In dry areas, the Incas built reservoirs called *qochas* to catch the rain. They were experts at irrigation, carefully controlling water-flow through the fields.

FREEZE-DRIED POTATOES
A woman of the Tinqui people lays out potatoes on the ground, just as farmers would have done in the days of the Incas. Over two hundred potato varieties were grown in the Andes. They were preserved by being left to dry in the hot daytime sun and cold overnight frosts. Dried, pressed potato, called *chuño*, just needed to be soaked to be ready for cooking.

A HIGHLAND CROP
Quinua ripens in the sun. This tough crop can be grown at over 3,800m above sea-level, and can survive both warm days and cold nights. *Quinua* was ideal for the Andes. Its seeds were boiled to make a kind of porridge, and its leaves could be stewed as well.

A SAFE HARVEST
The farmer uses his sling to scare hungry birds from the new maize, while his wife harvests the crop. March was the month when the maize ripened, and April was the month of harvest.

AN ANCIENT PATTERN

Painstaking work over many years created these terraced fields, or *andenes*, near the Inca town of Pisaq. All the soil had to be brought up in baskets from the valley floor far below. Terracing aims to provide a workable depth of level soil, while retaining walls prevent earth being washed away by the rains. The base of each terrace was laid with gravel for good drainage. The Pisaq fields belonged to the emperor and produced maize of the highest quality.

ALL-AMERICAN CROPS

Crops that were once grown in just one part of the world are now grown in other continents as well. Many of the world's most common crops were first grown in the Americas. These include potatoes, tomatoes, maize (sweetcorn), cassava, sweet potatoes and squash.

cassava

sweet potatoes

potatoes

squash

MOTHER EARTH

This gold plate, made by the Chimú people, shows the Earth goddess surrounded by Peruvian crops, each grouped according to its growing season. They include maize, sweet potato and cassava. The Earth goddess was called Pachamama, and she played an especially important part in the religious beliefs of farming villages in the Andes. Most farmers in the Inca Empire spent their lives trying to tame a hostile environment. The fertility of the land was important in religious as well as economic terms.

Food and Feasts

A REGIONAL GOVERNOR might entertain a royal visitor with a banquet of venison (deer meat), roast duck, fresh fish from the lakes or the ocean, and tropical fruits such as bananas and guavas. Honey was used as a sweetener.

Peasants ate squash and other vegetables in a stew, and fish was also eaten where it was available. Families kept guinea pigs for their meat, but most of their food was vegetarian. The bulk of any meal would be made up of starchy foods. These were prepared from grains such as maize or *quinua*, or from root crops such as potatoes, cassava or a highland plant called *oca*. A strong beer called *chicha* was made from maize. The grains were chewed and spat out, then left to ferment in water.

MIXED SPICES
This pottery pestle and mortar may have been used for grinding and mixing herbs. It is about 1,000 years old and was made by the Chimú people. Peruvian dishes were often hot and spicy, using eye-watering quantities of hot chilli peppers. Chilli peppers were one of the first food plants to be cultivated. Peppers of various kinds were grown on the coast and foothills.

MEALS AND MANNERS
Inca nobles ate and drank from wooden plates and painted beakers called *keros*. These continued to be made after the Spanish conquest. Pottery was also used to make beautiful cups and dishes. Most peasants drank and ate from gourds. There were no tables, so food was eaten sitting on the ground. Two main meals were eaten each day, one in the morning and one in the evening.

BEAN STEW
You will need: 250g dried haricot beans, 4 tomatoes, 500g pumpkin, 2 tablespoons paprika, mixed herbs, salt, black pepper, 100g sweetcorn, bowl, large and medium saucepans, knife, chopping board, measuring jug, spoon.

1 Wash the beans in plenty of cold water. Place them in a large bowl and cover them with cold water. Leave them to soak for 3 or 4 hours.

2 Drain the beans and put them in a large saucepan. Cover them with cold water. Bring to the boil. Simmer for 2 hours or until just tender.

3 While the beans are cooking, chop the tomatoes finely on the chopping board. Peel the pumpkin and cut the flesh into 2cm cubes.

A TROPICAL MENU

The mountains were cool because they were high. Down on the lowlands it was much hotter, and tropical crops could be grown wherever there was enough water. These included tomatoes, avocado pears, beans, pumpkin-like squashes, chilli peppers, peanuts and fruits such as guava.

avocado pear

chilli pepper

peanuts

beans

CORN ON THE COB

This maize plant was crafted in Inca silver. The real maize crop would have been almost as precious. Maize could be ground into the flour we call cornmeal, and this was used to make porridge, pancake-like bread and dumplings. The yellow sweetcorn could also be toasted, boiled or puffed up into popcorn.

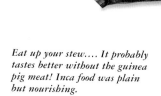

Eat up your stew.... It probably tastes better without the guinea pig meat! Inca food was plain but nourishing.

TO THE LORD OF MAIZE

This maize left in a pottery dish in a Nazca grave is an offering to the Lord of the Maize. Maize played such an important part in the life of Central and South America that it had its own gods, goddesses and festivals.

4 Heat 100ml water in a medium saucepan. Stir in the paprika and bring to the boil. Add the tomatoes and a sprinkling of herbs, salt and pepper.

5 Simmer for 15 minutes until thick and well blended. Drain the beans and return to the large pan with the pumpkin and the tomato mixture. Stir well.

6 Simmer for 15 minutes. Add the sweetcorn and simmer for 5 more minutes until the pumpkin has almost disintegrated and the stew is thick.

7 Taste (but be careful — it's hot!). Add more salt and pepper if necessary. Serve in bowls. Cornbread or tortillas would be an ideal accompaniment.

Textiles and Tunics

IN ALL THE CIVILIZATIONS of the Andes, spinning and weaving were the main household tasks of women of all ranks. Girls learned to weave at an early age, and men wove too. There was a long tradition of embroidery, using bone needles. In Inca times, weaving reached an incredibly high standard. Weaving textiles formed part of the labour tax, like farming or building. Woven cloth was stored in government warehouses and used to pay troops and officials.

Inca men wore a loincloth around the waist, secured by a belt. Over this was a simple knee-length tunic, often made of alpaca wool. On cold nights, they might wear a cloak as well. Women wrapped themselves in a large rectangular cloth of alpaca wool, with a sash around the waist and a shawl. There were many kinds of regional headdresses, caps of looped wool, headbands, hats and feathers. Sandals were made of leather or woven grasses.

PINNED IN STYLE
A long decorative pin called a *tupu* was used by the Incas to fasten dresses and shawls. It might be made from copper, silver or gold. This *tupu* was found at the Sacsahuaman fortress in Cuzco.

INCA FASHION
About 500 years ago, this fine tunic belonged to an Inca nobleman from the south coast of Peru. Its design is simple, but it is beautifully decorated with flower and animal designs. Dress was a status symbol in the Inca Empire. The shape of clothes was much the same for all social classes, but the more important you were, the finer the cloth and the decoration.

AN INCA TUNIC
You will need: blue felt 65cm x 160 cm, red felt 40cm square, PVA glue, brush, tape measure, scissors, ruler, pencil, thread or wool, needle, cream calico fabric, acrylic or fabric paints, paintbrush, water pot.

1 Place the blue felt flat on the table. Position the red felt in the centre of it to form a diamond shape. Glue the red felt carefully in place.

2 For the neck opening, cut a slit 22cm long through the centre of both layers of material as shown, with the long side of the blue felt towards you.

3 Fold the tunic in half along the slit. Halfway along the slit, cut a 12cm slit at right angles to the first. Only cut through one double layer of fabric.

FIBRES AND DYES

Highland animals provided warm woollen fibres. Llamas had the coarsest wool, and vicuñas the softest. Alpaca wool was the one most commonly used. Cotton was grown in the hot lowland regions and was widely worn for its coolness. Plants were used to dye either the yarn or the finished textiles. A scarlet dye called cochineal was obtained from the dried bodies of insects.

alpaca wool *cotton cloth*

dyed cotton yarn

SHIMMERING GOLD

For a religious festival, Inca nobles and priests might wear spectacular costumes. This is part of a tunic made of woven alpaca wool decorated with fine gold work. It comes from Peru's south coast. Clothes like these were produced by craftsmen in special workshops. One Chimú tunic was studded with no fewer than 13,000 pieces of gold!

Many Inca tunics were brightly coloured and decorated with geometric patterns.

BACKSTRAPPERS

This Moche painting shows people weaving with backstrap looms. The upright or warp threads are tensioned between an upright post and a beam attached to the weaver's waist. The cross or weft threads are passed in between. Backstrap looms are still used in Central and South America today.

4 Using the coloured thread or wool, sew together the sides of the tunic with large stitches. Leave enough space for armholes at the top.

5 Draw plenty of 5cm squares in pencil on the cream fabric. Paint them in colourful, geometric Inca designs. Look at the patterns here for ideas.

6 Allow the paint to dry completely. Then carefully cut out the squares and arrange them in any pattern you like on the front of your tunic.

7 When you have a pattern you are happy with, glue the squares in position. Wait until the glue is dry before trying on your unique Inca tunic.

Jewels and Feathers

Festival costumes in the Andes today come in dazzling pinks, reds and blues. In the Inca period it was no different. People loved to wear brightly coloured braids, threads and ribbons. Sequins, beads, feathers and gold were sewn into fabric, while precious stones, red shells, silver and gold were made into beautiful earplugs, necklaces, pendants, nostril-rings and discs. However, it was only the nobles who were allowed to show off by wearing feathers, jewels and precious metals. Some of the most prized ornaments were gifts from the emperor for high-ranking service in the army.

Much of the finest craft work went into making small statues and objects for religious ceremonies, temples and shrines. During the Inca period, craft workers were employed by the State. They produced many beautiful treasures, but some of the best of these were the work of non-Inca peoples, particularly the Chimú. Treasures shipped to Spain after the Conquest astounded the Europeans by their fine craftsmanship.

PLUMES OF THE CHIEF

An impressive headdress like this would have belonged to a high-ranking Inca official or general in northern Chile over 500 years ago. The hat is made from coils of dyed llama wool. It is decorated with bold designs, and topped by a spray of feathers.

A SACRED PUMA

This gold pouch in the shape of a puma, a sacred animal, was made by the Moche people between 1,300 and 1,700 years ago. It may have been used to carry *coca* leaves. These were used as a drug during religious ceremonies. The pattern on the body is made up of two-headed snakes.

A GOLD AND SILVER NECKLACE

You will need: self-drying clay, cutting board, ruler, large blunt needle, gold and silver paint, paintbrush, water pot, card, pencil, scissors, strong thread.

1 Form pieces of clay into beads in the shape of monkey nuts. You will need 10 large beads (about 3.5cm x 2cm) and 10 smaller beads (about 2.5cm x 1.5cm).

2 Use the needle to mark patterns on the beads, so that they look like nut shells. Then carefully make a hole through the middle of each bead. Leave to dry.

3 Paint half the shells of each size gold and half of them silver. You should have 5 small and 5 large gold beads, and 5 small and 5 large silver beads.

PRECIOUS AND PRETTY

The most valued stone in the Andes was blue-green turquoise. It was cut and polished into beads and discs for necklaces, and inlaid in gold statues and masks. Blue lapis lazuli, black jet and other stones also found their way along trading routes. Colombia, on the northern edge of the Inca Empire, mined many precious stones and metals. Seashells were cut and polished into beautiful beads.

emerald   turquoise

lapis lazuli

BIRDS OF A FEATHER

Birds and fish decorate this feather cape. It was made by the Chancay people of the central Peruvian coast between the 1300s and 1500s. It would have been worn for religious ceremonies. Feather work was a skilled craft in both Central and South America. In Inca times, the brilliantly coloured feathers of birds called macaws were sent to the emperor as tribute from the tribes of the Amazon forests.

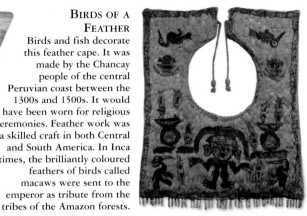

Necklaces made of gold, silver and jewels would only have been worn by Inca royalty, perhaps the Quya *herself.*

TREASURE LOST AND FOUND

A beautifully made gold pendant created in the Moche period before the Incas rose to power. After the Spanish conquest of Peru, countless treasures were looted from temples or palaces by Spanish soldiers. Gold was melted down or shipped back to Europe. A few items escaped by being buried in graves. Some have been discovered by archaeologists.

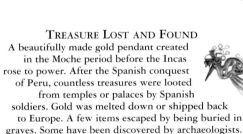

4 Paint some card gold on both sides. On it draw 11 rectangles (3cm x 1cm) with rounded ends. Cut them out and carefully prick a hole in each end.

5 Thread the needle and make a knot 10cm from the end of the thread. Then thread the card strips and large beads alternately, using the gold beads first.

6 Be sure to start and end with card strips. When you have finished, knot the thread tightly next to the last card strip. Cut the thread 10cm from the knot.

7 Repeat steps 5 and 6 using more thread and the small beads, so that the beads are joined as shown. Finally, knot the ends of the two threads together.

Everyday Crafts

MANY BEAUTIFUL OBJECTS produced in the Inca Empire were not made of gold and jewels but of simpler, more down-to-earth materials. Baskets and reed mats were made in early prehistoric times by plaiting and twining various materials. All kinds of small objects, such as bowls, pins, spoons and figures, were carved from bone, stone and wood.

Pottery was being made in Peru by about 2000BC, rather later than in the lands to the north and east. It had a great effect on the way people lived because it affected the production, storage, transportation and cooking of food.

South American potters did not shape their pots on a wheel. They built them up in layers from coils of clay. The coils were smoothed out by hand or with tools, marked or painted, dried in the sun and then baked hard.

Many of the pre-Incan civilizations of the Andes produced beautiful pottery. The Nazca often used bold geometric patterns, while the Moche loved to make jars in the shape of animals and people. Many pots were specially made for religious ceremonies.

POLISHED WOOD
This fine black *kero* (drinking vessel) was made by an Inca craftsman. It is of carved and polished wood. Timber was always scarce in the Inca Empire, but wood was widely used to make plates and cups. Rearing up over the rim of the beaker is a fierce-looking big cat, perhaps a puma or a jaguar.

MODELLED FROM CLAY
A fierce puma bares his teeth. He was made from pottery between AD500 and 800. The hole in his back was used to waft clouds of incense during religious ceremonies in the city of Tiwanaku, near Lake Titicaca.

A TIWANAKU POTTERY JAGUAR
You will need: chicken wire, wire-cutters, ruler, newspaper, scissors, PVA glue, masking tape, flour, water, card, paint, water pot, paintbrush.

1 Cut a rectangle of chicken wire about 14cm long and 20cm wide. Carefully wrap it around to form a sausage shape. Close one end neatly.

2 Squeeze the other end of the sausage to form the jaguar's neck and head. Fold over the wire at the end to make a neat, round shape for his nose.

3 Make rolls of newspaper about 2.5cm long to form the jaguar's legs. Use strips of paper and glue to join them securely to the jaguar's body as shown.

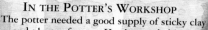

PRETTY POLLY

This pottery jar, like many from Peru, comes with a handle and a spout. It is shaped and painted to look like a parrot and was made, perhaps 1,000 years before the Incas, by the Nazca potters of southern Peru.

WATER OF LIFE

This Inca bottle is carved with a figure inside a tower collecting water. No community could survive very long without a good supply of fresh water. Many pots, bottles and beakers from the South American civilizations are decorated with light-hearted scenes of everyday activities. They give us a vivid idea of how people used to live.

IN THE POTTER'S WORKSHOP

The potter needed a good supply of sticky clay and plenty of water. He also needed large supplies of firewood or dung for fuel. The potter would knead the clay until it was soft and workable. Sometimes he would mix in sand or crushed shells from the coast to help strengthen the clay. Colours for painting the pottery were made from plants and minerals.

shells *sand*

clay

The handle and spout design of your Tiwanaku jaguar is known as a stirrup pot, because the arrangement looks rather like the stirrup of a horse.

4 Mix the flour and water to a paste. Use it to glue a layer of newspaper strips all over the jaguar's body. Allow this layer to dry. You will need 3 layers.

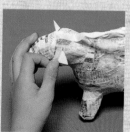

5 Cut ears from card. Fix on with masking tape. Tape on rolls of newspaper to make the handle, spout and tail as in the finished pot above.

6 Leave the model in a warm and airy place to dry. Then paint it all over with reddish brown paint. Allow the paint to dry completely.

7 Use black paint and a fine brush to decorate the jaguar as shown in the picture. When the paint is dry, varnish with PVA glue if you wish.

Metals and Mining

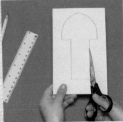

THE WHOLE REGION of the Andes had a very long history of metalworking. A stone bowl that was discovered in the Andahuaylas Valley was nearly 3,500 years old. It contained metalworking equipment and finely beaten gold foil. Braziers found at the town of Machu Picchu, from the end of the Inca period, included traces of molten metal.

The Incas often referred to gold as "sweat of the Sun" and to silver as "tears of the Moon". These metals were sacred not only to the gods but also to their descendants on Earth, the *Sapa Inca* and the *Quya*. At the Temple of the Sun in Cuzco, there was a whole garden made of gold and silver, with golden soil, golden stalks of maize and golden llamas. Imagine how it must have gleamed in the sunshine. Copper, however, was used by ordinary people. It was made into cheap jewellery, weapons and everyday tools. The Incas' love of gold and silver eventually led to their downfall, for it was rumours of their fabulous wealth that lured the Spanish to invade the region.

A SICAN LORD

A ceremonial knife with a crescent-shaped blade is called a *tumi*. Its gold handle is made in the shape of a nobleman or ruler. He wears an elaborate headdress and large discs in his ears. It was made between 1100 and 1300. The knife is in the style of the Sican civilization, which grew up after the decline of the Moche civilization in the AD700s.

A CHIMÚ DOVE

Chimú goldsmiths, the best in the Empire, made this plump dove. When the Incas conquered Chimor in 1470, they forced many thousands of skilled craftsmen from the city of Chan Chan to resettle in the Cuzco area and continue their work.

A TUMI KNIFE

You will need: card, ruler, pencil, scissors, self-drying clay, cutting board, rolling pin, modelling and cutting tools, PVA glue, gold paint, paintbrush, water pot, blue metallic paper.

1 On card, draw a knife shape as shown and cut it out. The rectangular part should be 9cm x 3.5cm. The rounded part is 7cm across and 4.5cm high.

2 Roll out a slab of clay about 1cm thick. Draw a *tumi* shape on it as shown. It should be 12.5cm long and measure 9cm across the widest part at the top.

3 Use the cutting tool to cut around the shape you have drawn. Carefully take away the leftover clay. Make sure the edges are clean and smooth.

MINERAL WEALTH

To this day, the Andes are very rich in minerals. The Incas worked with gold, silver, platinum and copper. They knew how to make alloys, which are mixtures of different metals. Bronze was made by mixing copper and tin. However, unlike their Spanish conquerors, the Incas knew nothing of iron and steel. This put them at a disadvantage when fighting the Europeans.

copper   *silver*

gold

PANNING FOR GOLD

A boy labourer in modern Colombia pans for gold. Some Inca gold was mined, but large amounts also came from panning mountain rivers and streams in the Andes. The river bed was loosened with sticks, and then the water was sifted through shallow trays in search of any flecks of the precious metal that had been washed downstream.

INCA FIGURES

Small ritual figures of women and men from about 6cm high were often made in the Inca period. They were hammered from sheets of silver and gold and were dressed in miniature versions of adult clothing. They have been found on mountain-top shrine sites in the south-central Andes, in carved stone boxes in Lake Titicaca and at important temples.

The Chimú gold and turquoise tumi was used by priests at religious ceremonies. It may have been used to kill sacrifices.

4 Cut a slot into the bottom edge of the clay shape. Lifting it carefully, slide the knife blade into the slot. Use glue to make the joint secure.

5 Use a modelling tool to mark the details of the god on to the clay. Look at the finished knife above to see how to do this. Leave everything to dry.

6 When the clay has hardened, paint the whole knife with gold paint. Leave it to dry completely before painting the other side as well.

7 The original knife was decorated with turquoise. Glue small pieces of blue metallic paper on to the handle as shown in the picture above.

Gods and Spirits

THE FIRST PERUVIANS worshipped nature spirits and creatures such as condors, snakes and jaguars. Later peoples began to believe in gods. Some said the world had been created by the god Wiraqocha, the "old man of the sky". He had made the Sun, Moon and stars, and the other gods. He had carved stone statues and made them live, creating the first humans. Myths tell that he sailed away across the Pacific Ocean.

To the Inca people, the most important god was Inti, the Sun. He was the bringer of warmth and light and the protector of the Inca people. Inti's sister and wife was Mamakilya, the silver Moon goddess. Other gods included Pachamama the Earth goddess, Mamacocha goddess of the sea, Kuychi the Rainbow god and Apu Illapu, god of thunder.

THE GATEWAY GOD
Tiwanaku's 1,400-year-old Gateway of the Sun, in Bolivia, is carved from solid rock and is over 3m high. The figure may represent the Chavín Staff god or Wiraqocha. It may be a Sun god, for his headdress is made up of rays.

END OF THE WORLD?
The Incas believed that Inti, the Sun god, dropped into the ocean each evening, swam underneath the Earth and appeared next morning in the east, above the mountains. An eclipse of the Sun was a terrifying experience, a warning that Inti was abandoning the emperor and his people.

SPIRITS OF THE MAIZE
On this pottery jar, three gods are shown bursting out of bundles of corn cobs. The jar was made by Moche potters between AD300 and AD700. To all the South American peoples, the world of nature was filled with spiritual forces. They believed that the success of the harvest depended on the good will of the gods.

A GOLD SUN GOD MASK
You will need: large piece of card, pencil, ruler, scissors, PVA glue, paintbrush, water pot, gold and black paint.

1 Draw the mask shape on card as shown. It should be 60cm wide and 60cm high overall. The side pieces are 40cm high. The narrowest part is 8cm wide.

2 Draw zigzag patterns all around the edge of the mask as shown in the picture above. These patterns represent the powerful rays of the Sun.

3 Carefully cut out the whole mask shape. Then cut out the rays around the edge, making sure you don't snip all the way through by mistake.

ANCIENT SECRETS

A mysterious figure, carved from a great stone pillar, stands amid the ruined temples of Tiwanaku. It holds a banded *kero* or drinking cup in its left hand and a sceptre in its right. Is this the figure of an ancient god? The monument is 7.3m tall and was excavated in 1932. It dates back over 1,500 years, to the days when Tiwanaku became a great religious centre.

A GOLDEN MASK

Gold face-masks were made by several Peruvian peoples, including the Nazca and the Inca. Some were used during festivals in honour of the Sun. Others were laid on the faces of the dead, just as they were in ancient Egypt. This fine mask was made by Moche goldsmiths in about AD400.

Hail to Inti, the Sun god! Your mask looks as if it is made from shining gold, the magical metal of the Sun.

WORSHIPPING THE SUN

A golden face in a sunburst represents Inti, god of the Sun. This picture from the 1700s imagines how the *Coricancha*, the Temple of the Sun, in Cuzco, must have appeared 200 years earlier. It shows the *Sapa Inca* making an offering of maize beer to Inti in the great hall.

4 Cut out a rectangle of card 15cm x 13cm. Cut a T-shaped piece 14cm across and 11cm high. Also cut out the shapes of eyes, a nose and a mouth.

5 Glue the shapes on to the centre of the mask to form the Sun god's face as shown. Leave the mask flat until the glue is completely dry.

6 Make sure your table top is protected. Cover the whole of the surface of the mask with gold paint. The rays around the edge are fiddly to paint.

7 Finally, use black paint and a fine brush to draw around the face. Add ears and teeth. Decorate the top part with black paint, too.

Temples and Sacrifices

THE INCAS had many *waq'as* (holy places). Some of these shrines were simply streams, rocks or caves that had been visited by pilgrims for thousands of years. Others were wayside idols, or temples built long before the Incas came to power. In Chavín de Huantar, temples were built between 900 and 200BC. They were decorated with carvings of fantastic jaguars and birds of prey. Massive pyramid temples and platforms had been built on the coastal plains. Huaca del Sol, at the Moche capital of Cerro Blanco, was made from over 100 million mud bricks. The Incas themselves built many temples dedicated to the gods Inti, Mama Killa, Wiraqocha and Apu Illapa.

The *Willak Umu* (Inca High Priest) was a member of the royal family. Priests made offerings to the gods and took drugs that gave them dreams and visions. They looked for omens – signs to help them see the future.

HUACA EL DRAGON
Fantastic figures in dried mud decorate Huaca el Dragon, a pyramid burial site to the north-west of Chan Chan. It was a religious site of the Chimú people about 800 years ago, before the Inca Empire.

OFFERINGS TO THE GODS
Llamas are chosen to be sacrificed to the gods. White llamas were offered to the Sun god, Inti, brown ones to the creator god, Wiraqocha, and spotted ones to Apu Illapa, a thunder god. Their entrails were examined for omens. Guinea pigs were also sacrificed. Other offerings to the gods included food, *chicha* beer, maize and cloth. Many offerings were burnt on a fire.

GATEWAY OF THE SUN
The city of Tiwanaku, with its great ceremonial arch, was the centre of many religious activities. It had a raised platform, 15m high, and archaeologists have found the remains of offerings and human sacrifices there. Tiwanaku beliefs seem to have been similar to those of the Wari city-state.

AT PACHACAMAC

Pachacamac, near Lima, was a site of pilgrimage in Inca times. It was named after Pachacamac, a much older creator god. Under Topa Inka, the Incas adopted Pachacamac as their own, worshipping him as a god of fire. They came to Pachacamac to have their fortunes told by an oracle. The site had a pyramid and many shrines. This is the Temple of the Virgins.

HUMAN SACRIFICE

When a new emperor came to the throne, or during times of crisis, Inca priests sacrificed hundreds of people. Victims had to be pure and perfect to please the gods. Boys or girls, *akllakuna*, or sometimes adults were chosen. This girl was one of three sacrificed on a peak in northern Argentina. Her remains were discovered in 1999.

TEMPLES OF THE SUN

The *Coricancha*, or Temple of the Sun, in Cuzco, was the holiest shrine in the Inca Empire. Its remains are seen here topped by a Christian church that was built by the Spanish in 1650. Inca priests believed that power lines called *ceques* radiated out from the *Coricancha*, linking holy sites across the Empire. There were other great Sun temples, too. One was on an island in Lake Titicaca, another was at Vilcashuaman, and a third was near Aconcagua, the highest peak in all the Americas.

Festivals and Rituals

THE INCAS loved to celebrate the natural world and its changing seasons. They marked them with special festivals and religious rituals. Some celebrations were held in villages and fields, others took place at religious sites or in the big cities. It is said that the Incas had as many as 150 festivals each year.

The biggest festival of all was *Inti Raymi*, the Feast of the Sun. It was held in June, to mark midwinter in the southern part of the world. *Qapaq Raymi*, the Splendid Festival, was held in December to mark the southern midsummer. This was when boys were recognized as adult warriors, and young nobles received their earplugs. Crop festivals included the Great Ripening each February, Earth Ripening each March and the Great Cultivation each May. The sowing of new maize was celebrated in August. The Feast of the Moon, held in September, was a special festival for women, while the Day of the Dead, in November, was a time to honour one's ancestors.

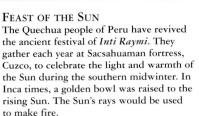

FEAST OF THE SUN
The Quechua people of Peru have revived the ancient festival of *Inti Raymi*. They gather each year at Sacsahuaman fortress, Cuzco, to celebrate the light and warmth of the Sun during the southern midwinter. In Inca times, a golden bowl was raised to the rising Sun. The Sun's rays would be used to make fire.

BRINGER OF RAIN
Drought was feared throughout the Empire, especially in the dry lands of the coast. If rain failed to fall, the life-giving irrigation channels dried up. In desperation, people visited the temples of Apu Illapu, bringer of rain. The priests made offerings and sacrifices, and the pilgrims prayed. The purpose of most Inca ceremonies and festivals was to prevent disaster and to ensure that life carried on.

THE AUGUST FESTIVAL
Quya Raymi (August) was a rainy month. A special festival called *Situa* was held to ward off the sicknesses that were common at that time of year. The people dressed for battle and went out into the streets. They hoped to drive away the evil spirits that made them ill. They carried torches of burning straw and plastered their faces with cornmeal or llama blood.

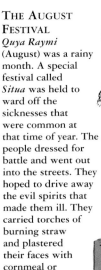

DANCERS AND MASKS

Drums, music and dance were always an important part of *Inti Raymi*, the Sun Festival. The Incas played rattles and whistles, drums and hand-drums, flutes and panpipes to help them celebrate the festival. Musicians played all day long without taking a break, and some of their ancient tunes are still known. Today, masks representing the Spanish invaders are added to the festivities. The modern festival proves that the old way of life has not been forgotten. Modern Peruvians are proud of their Inca past.

THE EMPEROR'S DAY

The modern festival of *Inti Raymi* attracts thousands to Cuzco. In the days of the Incas, too, nobles poured into the Inca capital from every corner of the Empire. Their aim was to honour the emperor as much as the Sun god. They came carrying tributes from the regions and personal gifts, hoping for the Emperor's favour in return.

FIESTA TIME

A drawing from the 1700s shows Peruvian dancers dressed as devils. Many of them are playing musical instruments or carrying long whips. After the conquest, festivals were known by the Spanish term, *fiestas*, and officially celebrated Christian beliefs. However, many of the festivities were still rooted in an Inca past. The dances and costumes often had their origins in Inca traditions.

Flutes, Drums and Dice

A BOY HERDING ALPACAS in the misty fields picks out a tune on a bone whistle. Drums rattle and thump as excited crowds gather in Cuzco for a great festival. The Inca world is full of music.

Music and dance played a very important part in the everyday lives of the Incas. They did not use stringed instruments, but drums and hand-drums, rattles, flutes, whistles and panpipes. Instruments were made from wood, reeds, pottery and bone. At festivals, musicians would play all day without a break. Large bands walked in procession, each panpipe player picking out a different part of the tune. Ancient tunes and rhythms live on in the modern music of the Andes.

The Incas did not have books, but they enjoyed listening to poets and storytellers. They liked tales about the gods, spirits and magic, or princesses and warriors. They enjoyed running races and, like other peoples of the Americas, they loved to gamble. They played games of flicking seeds and rolling dice.

SOUND OF THE PANPIPES
Panpipes made of cane, pottery or bone have been found at many ancient sites in the Inca lands. They are also found in other parts of the world, but their breathy, melodious sound has become very much linked to the Andes. Panpipes are played by blowing across the open end of a sealed tube. They come in many different sizes. In Peru, they are called *antaras* or *zampoñas*.

WHISTLE LIKE A BIRD
A flute is carved to resemble a bird's head and decorated with patterns. It is made from bone and was probably the treasured possession of a Moche musician around AD700.

AN INCA HAND-DRUM

You will need: card, pencil, ruler, scissors, masking tape, cream calico fabric, PVA glue, paintbrush, paints, water pot, wadding, 30cm length of dowel, coloured wool.

1 Use a pencil and ruler to mark two rectangles, measuring 9cm x 85cm, on the card. Cut them out carefully. They will form the sides of the drum.

2 Bend one rectangle round into a circle and use masking tape to join the ends together. It may be easier to ask a friend to help you do this.

3 Lay the cardboard ring on the calico fabric. Draw a circle around it, leaving a gap of about 2cm. Remove the ring and cut out the fabric circle.

Cuzco Drummers

A modern street band in Cuzco plays the haunting music of the Andes, which has become popular around the world. Local peoples such as the Aymara and Quechua took up new instruments after the Spanish conquest, including various kinds of harp and guitar. However, there are still traces of the Inca musical tradition.

Sound of the Conch

A Moche noble is shown on a pot made in about AD500. He is blowing a conch at some royal or religious ceremony. Conches are large seashells, which in many parts of the world are blown as trumpets. The Incas called them *wayllakipa*. Conch trumpets were also carried by royal messengers on the Inca roads. They were blown to warn the next relay station they were on the way. Communication was an important part of running the Inca Empire.

Women played hand-drums like this at festivals in Inca times. Drums were sometimes suspended from wooden frames.

4 Paint glue around the edge of the fabric circle. Turn the fabric over. Carefully stretch it over the cardboard ring. Keep it taut and smooth the edges.

5 Draw a geometric Inca pattern on the remaining strip of card. Use paints to decorate it in bright colours. Lay it flat and leave it to dry.

6 Wrap the painted strip around the drum. Use masking tape to fix one edge to the drum, then use glue to stick down the rest of the patterned strip.

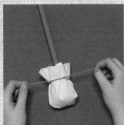

7 Cut out a calico circle 20cm in diameter. Make a beater by wrapping wadding and the calico around one end of the dowel. Tie it with wool.

Medicine and Magic

Like most peoples in the world five hundred years ago, the Incas and their neighbours had some idea of science or medicine. However, curing people was believed to be chiefly a matter of religious rituals and magical spells. No doubt some of these did help people to feel better. Curing sick people was the job either of priests, or of the local healer or medicine man.

As in Europe at that time, Inca healers used fasting and blood-letting (allowing blood to flow from a cut) for many cures. They also tried blood transfusion (putting new blood into someone's body). They succeeded in this far earlier than doctors in other parts of the world, because peoples of the Andes shared the same blood group. The Incas could also set broken bones, amputate limbs, treat wounds and pull teeth. Medicines were made from herbs, roots, leaves and powders.

THE MEDICINE MAN
This Moche healer or priest, from about AD500, seems to be going into a trance and listening to the voices of spirits or gods. He may be trying to cure a sick patient, or he may be praying over the patient's dead body.

MAGIC DOLLS
Model figures like this one, made from cotton and reed, are often found in ancient graves in the Chancay River region. They are often called dolls, but it seems unlikely that they were ever used as toys. They were probably believed to have magical qualities. The Chancay people may have believed that the dolls helped the dead person in another world.

CARRYING COCA
Small bags like these were used for carrying medicines and herbs, especially coca. The leaves of the coca plant were widely used to stimulate the body and to kill pain. Coca is still widely grown in the Andes today. It is used to make the illegal drug cocaine.

MEDICINE BAG
You will need: scissors, cream calico fabric, pencil, ruler, paintbrush, water pot, acrylic or fabric paints, black, yellow, green and red wool, PVA glue, needle and thread, masking tape.

1 Cut two 20cm squares of fabric. Draw a pattern of stripes and diamonds on the fabric and use acrylic or fabric paints to colour them.

2 For the tassels, cut about 10 pieces of wool 8cm long. Fold a piece of wool 15cm long in half. Loop it around each tassel as shown above.

3 Wind a matching piece of wool, 50cm long, around the end of the tassel. When you have finished, knot the wool and tuck the ends inside.

HERBAL REMEDIES

Drugs widely used in ancient Peru included the leaves of tobacco and coca plants. A yellow-flowered plant called calceolaria was used to cure infections. Cinchona bark produced quinine, a medicine we use today to treat malaria. That illness only arrived in South America after the Spanish conquest. However, quinine was used earlier to treat fevers. Suppliers of herbal medicines were known as *hampi kamayuq.*

cinchona tree   *tobacco plant*

SKULL SURGERY

Nazca surgeons were able to carry out an operation called trepanation. This involved drilling a hole in the patient's skull in an attempt to relieve pressure on the brain. The Incas believed this released evil spirits. A small silver plate was sometimes fitted over the hole as a protection.

Doctor on call! An Inca medicine chest took the form of a woven bag, carried on the shoulder.

A BAD OMEN

A comet shoots across the night sky. The Incas believed such sights would bring plague or disease in their wake. Other common causes of illness were believed to include witchcraft, evil spirits and a failure to please the gods. People tried to make themselves better by making offerings to the gods at *waq'as (*local shrines). Healers used charms or spells to keep their patients free from evil spirits.

4 Make nine tassels in all. Place them in groups of three along the bottom of the unpainted side of one of the pieces of fabric. Use glue to fix them in place.

5 Allow the glue to dry. Place the unpainted sides of the fabric pieces together. Sew around the edges as shown. Leave the top edge open.

6 Make a strap by plaiting together strands of wool as shown. Cross each outer strand in turn over the middle strand. Tape will help keep the work steady.

7 Knot the ends of the strap firmly. Attach them to both sides of the top of the bag with glue. Make sure the glue is dry before you pick the bag up.

Inca Knowledge

INCA MATHEMATICIANS used the decimal system, counting in tens. To help with their arithmetic, people placed pebbles or grains of maize in counting frames. These had up to twenty sections. *Quipu* strings were also used to record numbers. Strings were knotted to represent units, tens, hundreds, thousands or even tens of thousands.

The Incas worked out calendars of twelve months by observing the Sun, Moon and stars as they moved across the sky. They knew that these movements marked regular changes in the seasons. They used the calendar to tell them when to plant crops. Inca priests set up stone pillars outside the city of Cuzco to measure the movements of the Sun.

As in Europe at that time, astronomy, which is the study of the stars, was confused with astrology, which is the belief that the stars and planets influence human lives. Incas saw the night sky as being lit up by gods and mythical characters.

FORTUNES FROM THE STARS AND PLANETS
An Inca astrologer observes the position of the Sun. The Incas believed that careful watching of the stars and planets revealed their influence on our lives. For example, the star pattern or constellation that we call the Lyre was known to the Incas as the Llama. It was believed that it influenced llamas and those who herded them.

THE SUN STONE
A stone pillar called *Inti Watana* (Tethering Post of the Sun) stood at the eastern edge of the great square in Machu Picchu. It was like a giant sundial and the shadows it cast confirmed the movements of the Sun across the sky – a matter of great practical and religious importance.

A QUIPU
You will need: scissors, rope and string of various thicknesses, a 90cm length of thick rope, paints, paintbrush, water pot.

1 Cut the rope and string into about 15 lengths measuring from 20cm to 80cm. Paint them in various bright colours. Leave them to dry completely.

2 To make the top part of the *quipu*, take a piece of thick rope, about 90cm long. Tie a knot in each end as shown in the picture above.

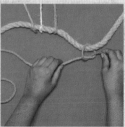

3 Next, take pieces of thinner rope or string of various lengths and colours. Tie them along the thicker rope, so that they all hang on the same side.

THE MILKY WAY

On dark nights, Inca priests looked for the band of stars that we call the Milky Way. They called it *Mayu* (Heavenly River) and used it to make calculations about seasons and weather conditions. In its darker spaces they saw the shadow of the Rain god Apu Illapu. The shape of the Milky Way was believed to mirror that of the Inca Empire.

SUN WATCH

The *Inti Watana* (Tethering Post of the Sun) at Machu Picchu was one of many Sun stones across the Empire. *Sukana* (stone pillars) near Cuzco showed midsummer and midwinter sun positions. The Sun god, Inti, was believed to live in the north and go south each summer.

KEEPERS OF THE QUIPU

Vast amounts of information could be stored on a *quipu*. A large one might have up to 2,000 cords. The *quipu* was rather like an Inca version of the computer, only the memory had to be provided by the operator's brain rather than a silicon chip. Learning the *quipu* code of colours, knots, and major and minor strings took many years. Expert operators were called *quipu-kamayuq*.

You have now designed a simple quipu. Can you imagine designing a system that would record the entire population of a town, their ages, the taxes they have paid and the taxes they owe? The Incas did just that!

4 Tie knots in the thinner ropes or strings. One knot you might like to try begins by making a loop of rope as shown in the picture above.

5 Pass one end of the rope through the loop. Pull the rope taut but don't let go of the loop. Repeat this step until you have a long knot. Pull it tight.

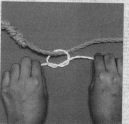

6 Make different sizes of knots on all the ropes or strings. Each knot could represent a family member, school lesson or other important detail.

7 Add some more strings to the knotted strings. Your *quipu* may be seen by lots of people. Only you will know what the ropes, strings and knots mean!

Married Life

WEDDINGS WERE SOME of the happiest occasions in an Inca village. They offered a chance for the whole community to take time off work. The day was celebrated with dancing, music and feasting. The groom would probably be 25 years of age, at which point he was regarded as an adult citizen, and his bride would be rather younger – about 20.

For the first year of the marriage, a couple did not have to pay any tax either in goods or labour. However, most of their lives would be spent working hard. When they were elderly, they would still be expected to help with household chores. Later still, when they became too old or sick to look after themselves, they received free food and clothes from the State warehouse. They would then be cared for by their clan or family group.

Not everyone was expected to get married. The *mamakuna* (virgins of the Sun) lived rather like nuns, in a special convent in Cuzco. They wove fine cloth and carried out religious duties. No men were allowed to enter the *mamakuna*'s building.

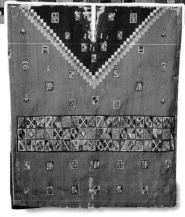

WEDDING CLOTHES
An Inca nobleman would get married in a very fine tunic. This one is from the southern coast of Peru. Commoners had to wear simpler clothes, but couples were presented with free new clothes from the State warehouses when they married.

MARRIAGE PROSPECTS
Two Inca noble women are painted on the side of this *kero* (wooden beaker). Women of all social classes were only allowed to marry with the approval of their parents and of State officials. They were expected to remain married for life and divorce was forbidden. If either the husband or wife was unfaithful, he or she could face trial and might even be put to death.

REAL PEOPLE
This jar from the Moche period is over 1,300 years old. Unlike the portraits on many jars, it seems to show a real person sitting down and thinking about life. It reminds us that ancient empires were made up of individuals who fell in love, raised children and grew old, just as people do today.

A ROYAL MARRIAGE

A prince of the emperor's family marries in Cuzco. The scene is imagined by an artist of the 1800s. An emperor had many secondary wives in addition to his sister-empress. Between them they produced very many princes and princesses. Inca royal familes were divided by jealousy and by complicated relations, which often broke out in open warfare. The emperor ordered his officials to keep tight control over who married whom. His own security on the throne depended on it.

A HOME OF THEIR OWN

When a couple married, they left their parents' houses and moved into their own home, like this one at Machu Picchu. The couple now took official control of the fields they would work. These had been allocated to the husband when he was born. Most couples stayed in the area occupied by their own clan, so their relatives would remain nearby.

HIS AND HERS

The everyday lives of most married couples in the Inca Empire were taken up by hard work. Men and women were expected to do different jobs. Women made the *chicha* beer and did the cooking, weaving and some field work. Men did field work and fulfilled the *mit'a* labour tax in service to the Inca State. They might build irrigation channels or repair roads.

An Inca Childhood

THREE FOR THE POT
A young Inca has been helping out by herding llamas in the mountains. He has taken a net along and caught some wildfowl in the reeds beside the lake. Contemporary pictures like this show that children and teenagers seem to have led a tough, open-air life.

HARD TIMES
Children were often punished severely. Even noble children could expect to be beaten by their teacher on the soles of their feet if they didn't work hard. There were laws to protect children from violence and kidnapping, but in times of famine or war children must have suffered dreadfully.

A NEWBORN INCA BABY was immediately washed in cold water and wrapped in a blanket. It was breast-fed at three set times each day, but cuddling was frowned upon.

Babyhood ended with a naming ceremony at the age of two, during which a lock of hair was cut off. The toddler still spent a lot of time playing – spinning tops were a popular toy. From now on, however, both boys and girls would be expected to start helping out around the house.

Girls came of age at 14. Royal officials decided whether they would become *akllakuna*. Those selected went for training in Cuzco, while the rest remained in their villages. Boys also came of age at 14 and were given a loincloth as a mark of manhood. Boys from noble families were put through special tests of endurance and knowledge. They were then given the weapons and the earplugs that showed their rank in society.

ROCK-A-BYE BABY
At the age of four days, a baby was wrapped up in swaddling clothes and tied into its *quiru* (wooden cradle). This could be placed on the ground and rocked, or tied on the mother's back. After a few months, the baby was taken from the cradle and left in a special pit, which served as a playpen.

LEARNING TO SPIN YARN

Inca girls were taught to spin using a drop spindle and a distaff, a stick round which they wound the prepared fleece or cotton. Using the right hand they twisted the spindle with its whirling weight attached. They guided the fibres from the distaff with the left hand. The fibre was twisted into yarn, which was used for weaving on a backstrap loom. The hunchbacked woman in this drawing is spinning as she walks along the road. She was trained in her youth to be a useful member of Inca society.

HELPING IN THE FIELDS

This Inca boy has a sling and is attacking the flocks of birds that are robbing the maize fields in his village. Both boys and girls were expected to help with the farming and to learn working skills from their parents, such as weaving or terrace-building. Most children in the Inca Empire did not go to school but were educated by their families. They learned what they needed for adult life and no more. The same was true in most parts of the world 500 years ago.

GOING TO SCHOOL

This building at Laris, near Cuzco is a school. Before the Spanish invasion, there was little formal education in Peru. Teenage boys from noble families were taught in Cuzco. Their timetable included Quechua language in Year One, Inca religion and astronomy in Year Two, arithmetic, geometry and *quipu* studies in Year Three, and history in Year Four. *Quipus* were knotted strings used to record information. Pupils also studied music, poetry and the geography of Tawantinsuyu. The only girls to receive formal education were the *akllakuna*, who were taught weaving, cooking and religious studies.

Land of the Dead

ARCHAEOLOGISTS HAVE FOUND many burial sites in the Andes. Bodies are most easily preserved in very dry or very cold conditions, and this region has both. As early as 3200BC, the Andean peoples learned how to embalm or mummify bodies. The insides were often taken out and buried. The rest of the body was dried, and the eyes were replaced with shells. When an Inca emperor died, his mummified body was kept in his former palace. The body was waited on by his descendants and even taken out to enjoy festivals! Respect for ancestors was an important part of Inca religious beliefs.

Inca funerals were sad occasions with slow music. Women cut off their long hair as a sign of grief. When the emperor died, some of his wives and servants were killed. The Incas believed that good people went to *Hanakpacha*, the Empire of the Sun, after death. Bad people had a wretched afterlife, deep in the Earth.

THE LORD OF SIPÁN

In 1988, a Peruvian archaeologist called Dr Walter Alva opened up a royal tomb at Sipán, near Chiclayo in northern Peru. The "Lord of Sipán" had been buried there with his servants, amid treasures made of gold, silver, copper and precious stones. The tomb belonged to the Moche civilization, which flourished between AD1 and 700.

FACING THE NEXT WORLD

Many South American mummies were buried in a sitting position. Their knees were drawn up and bound into position with cord. Over their faces were masks of wood, clay or gold, depending on their status. This mask, perhaps from the pre-Incan Nazca period, was decorated with coloured feathers.

A CHANCAY GRAVE DOLL

You will need: scissors, cream calico fabric, pencil, ruler, paints, paintbrush, water pot, black wool, PVA glue, wadding, 20 red pipecleaners, red wool.

1 Cut two rectangles of fabric 16cm x 11cm for the body. Cut two shield-shaped pieces 7cm wide and 8cm long for the head. Paint one side as shown.

2 Cut 35 strands of black wool, each 18cm long, for the doll's hair. Glue them evenly along the top of the wrong side of the unpainted face shape.

3 Cut a piece of wadding slightly smaller than the face. Glue it on top of the hair and face below. Then glue the painted face on top. Leave to dry.

DEATH WITH HONOUR

This face mask of beaten gold dates back to the 1100s or 1200s, during the Inca Empire. Its eyes are made of emerald, and it is decorated with pendants and a nose ornament. The crest on top, decorated with animal designs, serves as a crown or headdress. This mask was made by a Chimú goldsmith and laid in a royal grave.

TOWERS OF THE DEAD

Various South American peoples left mummies in stone towers called *chullpas*, such as these ones at Nina Marca. Goods were placed in the towers for the dead person to use in the next life. These included food and drink, pins, pots, knives, mirrors and clothes. Discoveries of the goods left in graves have helped archaeologists find out about everyday life long ago.

FACE OF THE MUMMY

This head belonged to a body that was mummified over 1,400 years ago in the Nazca desert. The skin is leathery, and the mouth gapes open in a lifelike manner. Most extraordinary is the skull's high, domed forehead. This shows that the dead person had his head bound with cloth as a small child. An elongated head was a sign of status amongst the Nazca people.

Dolls like these were probably placed in the graves of the Chancay people. They would serve as helpers in the life to come.

4 For each arm, take five pipecleaners and cut them to 11cm. Twist them together to within 1.5cm of one end. Splay this end to make fingers.

5 Make legs in the same way, but this time twist all the way and bend the ends to make feet. Wind wool around the arms and legs to hide the twists.

6 Assemble the doll as in the picture. Use glue to fix the arms and legs and wadding between the body pieces. Glue the front piece of the body in place.

7 Use glue to fix the head to the front of the body, making sure the hair does not become caught. Leave the doll to dry completely before picking it up.

Warriors and Weapons

THE INCA EMPIRE was brought about and held together by military force. Its borders were defended by a string of forts. The cities served as walled refuges when the surrounding countryside was under attack from enemies. There was a standing army of some 10,000 elite troops, but the great bulk of soldiers were conscripts, paying their State dues by serving out their *mit'a*. Badges and headdresses marked the rank of officers. In the 1500s women joined in the resistance to the Spanish conquest, using slings to devastating effect. The Incas were fierce fighters, but they stood no chance against the guns and steel of the Spanish.

TAKE THAT!

This star may have looked pretty, but it was deadly when whirled from the leather strap. It was made of obsidian, a glassy black volcanic rock. Inca warriors also fought with spikes set in wooden clubs, and some troops favoured the *bolas*, corded weights that were also used in hunting. Slings were used for scaring the birds. However, in the hands of an experienced soldier, they could be used to bring down a hail of stones on enemies and crack their heads open.

WAITING FOR THE CHARGE

A Moche warrior goes down on one knee and brings up his shield in defence. He is bracing himself for an enemy charge. All South American armies fought on foot. The horse was not seen in Peru until the Spanish introduced it.

IN THE BARRACKS

Many towns of the Inca Empire were garrisoned by troops. These restored barrack blocks at Machu Picchu may once have housed conscripted soldiers serving out their *mit'a*. They would have been inspected by a high-ranking general from Cuzco. During the Spanish invasion, it is possible that Machu Picchu became a base for desperate resistance fighters.

AN INCA HELMET

You will need: scissors, cream calico fabric, ruler, balloon, PVA glue, paintbrush, paints, water pot, yellow and black felt, black wool.

1 Cut the fabric into strips about 8cm x 2cm as shown in the picture. You will need enough to cover the top half of a blown-up balloon three times.

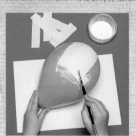

2 Blow up the balloon to the same size as your head. Glue the strips of fabric over the top half. Leave each layer to dry before adding the next.

3 When the last layer is dry, pop the balloon and carefully pull it away. Use scissors to trim round the edge of the helmet. Paint it a reddish orange.

KINGS OF THE CASTLE

The massive fortress of Sacsahuaman at Cuzco was built on a hill. One edge was formed by a cliff and the other defended by massive terraces and zigzag walls. The invading Spanish were excellent castle-builders. They were awestruck by Sacsahuaman's size and defences. The Incas regarded warfare as an extension of religious ritual. Sacsahuaman was certainly used for religious ceremonies. Some historians claim that the Inca capital was laid out in the shape of a giant puma, with Sacsahuaman as its head.

SIEGE WARFARE

An Inca army takes on the enemy at Pukara, near Lake Titicaca. Most South American cities were walled and well defended. Siege warfare was common. The attackers blocked the defenders' ways of escape from the town. After the conquest, in 1536, Inca rebels under Manko Inka trapped Spanish troops in Cuzco and besieged them for over a year.

Inca helmets were round in shape and made of wood or cane. They were decorated with braids and crests.

4 Take the felt. Measure and cut a 3cm yellow square, a yellow circle with a diameter of 3cm, a 9cm yellow square and a 5.5cm black square.

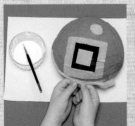

5 Glue the felt shapes on to the helmet as shown above. Glue a 2cm-wide strip of yellow felt along the edge of the helmet to neaten the edge.

6 Take 12 strands of black wool, each 30cm long. Divide them into 3 hanks of 4 strands. Knot the ends together, then plait to the end.

7 Knot the end of the finished braid. Make two more. Glue them inside the back of the helmet. Wait until it is dry before trying it on.

Eclipse of the Sun

THE WORD OF GOD?
When emperor Ataw Wallpa met the Spanish invaders in Cajamarca, he was approached by a Christian priest called Vincente de Valverde. The priest raised a Bible and said that it contained the words of God. Ataw Wallpa grabbed the book and listened to it. No words came out, so he hurled it to the ground. The Spanish were enraged, and the invasion began.

IN NOVEMBER 1532, the emperor Ataw Wallpa met the Spanish invaders, under Francisco Pizarro, in the great square of Cajamarca. The *Sapa Inca* was riding in a litter that was covered in feathers. Surrounding him were troops glinting with gold. The sound of conch trumpets and flutes echoed around the buildings. The Spanish were amazed by the sight, and the Incas looked uneasily at the strangers with their fidgeting horses.

Within just one hour, thousands of Incas had been killed, and their emperor was in the hands of the Spanish. Ataw Wallpa was arrested. He offered to raise a ransom to secure his release. Silver and gold arrived by the tonne, filling up a whole room. The Spanish gained unimagined riches. Even so, in the summer of 1533 they accused Ataw Wallpa of treason, and he was garrotted (executed by strangulation). Resistance to the Spanish continued for another 39 years, but South American civilization had changed for ever that day.

CONQUEST AND SLAVERY
The Spanish conquest was a disaster for all the native peoples of the Americas. Many of them were murdered, enslaved or worked to death in the mines. The Spanish introduced money into Inca life, trading in silver, gold, farm produce and coca. But it was mostly the Spanish settlers who became wealthy, not the native people.

"SANTIAGO!"
Before the 1532 meeting with Ataw Wallpa in the great square of Cajamarca, the Spanish invader Francisco Pizarro had hidden troops behind buildings. When he shouted the pre-arranged signal of *"Santiago!"* (St James), they began to shoot into the crowd. Chaos broke out as the emperor was seized and taken prisoner.

TEARS OF THE MOON

In 1545, the Spanish discovered silver at Potosí in the Bolivian Andes and began to dig mines. The wealth was incredible, but the working conditions were hellish. Local people were forced to work as slaves. Mule trains carried the silver northwards to Colombian ports, making Spain the richest country in the world.

THE TREASURE FLEETS

The Spanish plundered the treasure of the Incas and the minerals of the Andes. Big sailing ships called galleons carried the gold and silver back to Europe from ports in Central and South America. The region was known as the Spanish Main. Rival European ships, many of them pirates from England, France and the Netherlands, began to prey on the Spanish fleets. This led to long years of warfare. Between 1820 and 1824, Spain's South American colonies finally broke away from European rule to become independent countries, but most of the region's native peoples remained poor and powerless.

DESCENDANTS OF THE EMPIRE

Christians of Quechuan and mixed descent take part in a procession through Cuzco. In the Andes, over the past few hundred years, many Inca traditions, festivals and pilgrimages have become mixed up with Christian ones. Indigenous peoples today make up 45 per cent of the total population in Peru, 55 per cent in Bolivia, and 25 per cent in Ecuador.

THE CHINESE EMPIRE

Between the ancient civilizations of Europe and China lay vast distances, and the world's most impenetrable mountains and deserts. The Chinese civilization developed in isolation. It was amazingly inventive, introducing fine ceramics, silk, gunpowder and paper centuries before these skills were mastered in the West.

PHILIP STEELE
Consultant: Jessie Lim

An Ancient Civilization

IMAGINE YOU COULD travel back in time 5,000 years and visit the lands of the Far East. In northern China you would come across smoky settlements of small thatched huts. You might see villagers fishing in rivers, sowing millet or baking pottery. From these small beginnings, China developed into an amazing civilization. Its towns grew into huge cities, with palaces and temples. Many Chinese became great writers, thinkers, artists, builders and inventors. China was first united under the rule of a single emperor in 221BC, and continued to be ruled by emperors until 1912.

China today is a modern country. Its ancient past has to be pieced together by archaeologists and historians. They dig up ancient tombs and settlements, and study textiles, ancient books and pottery. Their job is made easier because historical records were kept. These provide much information about the long history of Chinese civilization.

REST IN PEACE
A demon is trodden into defeat by a guardian spirit. Statues like this were commonly put in tombs to protect the dead against evil spirits.

ALL THE EMPEROR'S MEN
A vast model army marches again. It was dug up by archaeologists in 1974, and is now on display near Xian. The lifesize figures are made of terracotta (baked clay). They were buried in 210BC near the tomb of Qin Shi Huangdi, the first emperor of all China. He believed that they would protect him from evil spirits after he died.

TIMELINE 7000BC–110BC

Prehistoric remains of human ancestors dating back to 600,000BC have been found in China's Shaanxi province. The beginnings of Chinese civilization may be seen in the farming villages of the late Stone Age (8000BC–2500BC). As organized states grew up, the Chinese became skilled at warfare, working metals and making elaborate pottery and fine silk.

*c.*7000BC Bands of hunters and fishers roam freely around the river valleys of China. They use simple stone tools and weapons.

Banpo hut

*c.*3200BC Farming villages such as Banpo produce pottery in kilns. This way of life is called the Yangshao culture.

*c.*2100BC The start of a legendary 500-year period of rule, known as the XIA DYNASTY.

*c.*2000BC Black pottery is made by the people of the so-called Longshan culture.

Shang bronze vessel

*c.*1600BC Beginning of the SHANG DYNASTY. Bronze worked and silk produced. The first picture-writing is used (on bones for telling fortunes).

Zhou spearheads

1122BC Zhou ruler Wu defeats Shang emperor. Wu becomes emperor of the WESTERN ZHOU DYNASTY.

7000BC   2100BC   1600BC

THE HAN EMPIRE (206BC–AD220)

China grew rapidly during the Han dynasty. By AD2 it had expanded to take in North Korea, the southeast coast, the southwest as far as Vietnam and large areas of Central Asia. Northern borders were defended by the Great Wall, which was extended during Han rule.

A HEAVENLY HALL

The Hall of Prayer for Good Harvests (*shown right*) is part of Tiantan, the Temple of Heavenly Peace in Beijing. It was originally built in 1420, but had to be rebuilt in the 1890s after it was destroyed by lightning. Buildings like these tell us about traditional technology and design, as well as about Chinese religious beliefs.

THE JADE PRINCE

In 1968, Chinese archaeologists excavated the tomb of Prince Liu Sheng. His remains were encased in a jade suit when he died in about 100BC. Over 2,400 pieces of this precious stone were joined with gold wire. It was believed that jade would preserve the body.

Zhou soldier

771BC Capital city moves from Anyang to Luoyang. Beginning of EASTERN ZHOU DYNASTY.

*c.*604BC Birth of the legendary Laozi, founder of Daoism.

551BC Teacher and philosopher Kong Fuzi (Confucius) born.

513BC Iron-working develops.

453BC Break-up of central rule. Small states fight each other for 200 years. Work begins on Grand Canal and Great Wall.

221BC China unites as a centralized empire under Zheng (Qin Shi Huangdi). Great Wall is extended.

213BC Qin Shi Huangdi burns all books that are not "practical".

Chinese writing

210BC Death of Qin Shi Huangdi. Terracotta army guards his tomb, near Chang'an (modern Xian).

206BC QIN DYNASTY overthrown. Beginnings of HAN DYNASTY as Xiang Yu and Liu Bang fight for control of the Han kingdom.

202BC The WESTERN HAN DYNASTY formally begins. It is led by the former official Liu Bang, who becomes emperor Gaozu.

200BC Chang'an becomes the capital city of the Chinese empire.

terracotta warrior and horse

112BC Trade with the peoples of Western Asia and Europe begins to flourish along the Silk Road.

80BC   550BC   210BC   140BC   110BC

The Middle Kingdom

CHINA IS A VAST COUNTRY, about the size of Europe. Its fertile plains and river valleys are ringed by many deserts, mountains and oceans. The ancient Chinese named their land Zhongguo, the Middle Kingdom, and believed that it was at the centre of the civilized world. Most Chinese belong to a people called the Han, but the country is also inhabited by 50 or more different peoples, some of whom have played an important part in Chinese history. These groups include the Hui, Zhuang, Dai, Yao, Miao, Tibetans, Manchus and Mongols.

The very first Chinese civilizations grew up around the Huang He (Yellow River), where the fertile soil supported farming villages and then towns and cities. These became the centres of rival kingdoms. Between 1700BC and 256BC Chinese rule spread southwards to the Chang Jiang (Yangzi River), the great river of Central China. All of eastern China was united within a single empire for the first time during Qin rule (221–206BC).

The rulers of the Han dynasty (206BC–AD220) then expanded the empire southwards as far as Vietnam. The Chinese empire was now even larger than the Roman empire, dominating Central and Southeast Asia. The Mongols, from lands to the north of China, ruled the empire from 1279 to 1368. They were succeeded by the Ming dynasty, which was in turn overthown by the Manchu in 1644. In later centuries, China became inward-looking and unable to resist interference from Europe. The empire finally collapsed, with China declaring itself a republic in 1912.

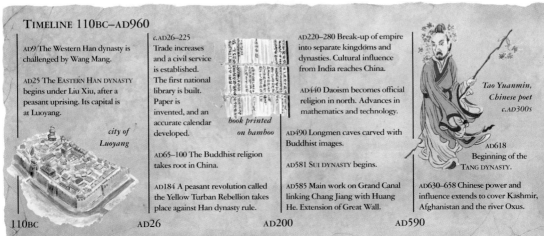

TIMELINE 110BC–AD960

AD9 The Western Han dynasty is challenged by Wang Mang.

AD25 The EASTERN HAN DYNASTY begins under Liu Xiu, after a peasant uprising. Its capital is at Luoyang.

city of Luoyang

c.AD26–225 Trade increases and a civil service is established. The first national library is built. Paper is invented, and an accurate calendar developed.

book printed on bamboo

AD65–100 The Buddhist religion takes root in China.

AD184 A peasant revolution called the Yellow Turban Rebellion takes place against Han dynasty rule.

AD220–280 Break-up of empire into separate kingdoms and dynasties. Cultural influence from India reaches China.

AD440 Daoism becomes official religion in north. Advances in mathematics and technology.

AD490 Longmen caves carved with Buddhist images.

AD581 SUI DYNASTY begins.

AD585 Main work on Grand Canal linking Chang Jiang with Huang He. Extension of Great Wall.

Tao Yuanmin, Chinese poet c.AD300s

AD618 Beginning of the TANG DYNASTY.

AD630–658 Chinese power and influence extends to cover Kashmir, Afghanistan and the river Oxus.

110BC   AD26   AD200   AD590

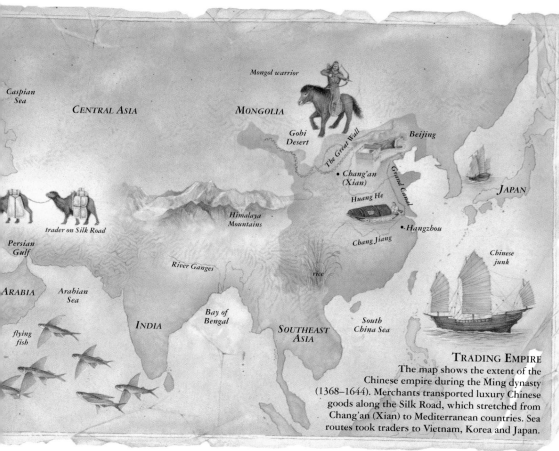

Mongol warrior

Caspian Sea

CENTRAL ASIA

MONGOLIA

Gobi Desert

The Great Wall

Beijing

Chang'an (Xian)

Grand Canal

JAPAN

Huang He

trader on Silk Road

Himalaya Mountains

Hangzhou

Chang Jiang

Persian Gulf

River Ganges

rice

Chinese junk

ARABIA

Arabian Sea

INDIA

Bay of Bengal

SOUTHEAST ASIA

South China Sea

flying fish

TRADING EMPIRE

The map shows the extent of the Chinese empire during the Ming dynasty (1368–1644). Merchants transported luxury Chinese goods along the Silk Road, which stretched from Chang'an (Xian) to Mediterranean countries. Sea routes took traders to Vietnam, Korea and Japan.

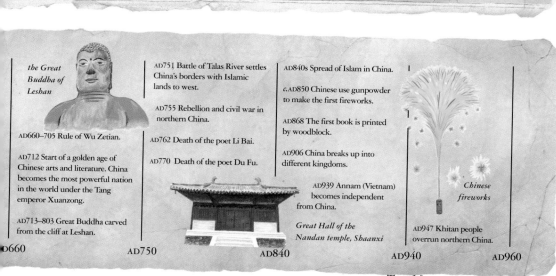

the Great Buddha of Leshan

AD660–705 Rule of Wu Zetian.

AD712 Start of a golden age of Chinese arts and literature. China becomes the most powerful nation in the world under the Tang emperor Xuanzong.

AD713–803 Great Buddha carved from the cliff at Leshan.

AD751 Battle of Talas River settles China's borders with Islamic lands to west.

AD755 Rebellion and civil war in northern China.

AD762 Death of the poet Li Bai.

AD770 Death of the poet Du Fu.

Great Hall of the Nandan temple, Shaanxi

AD840s Spread of Islam in China.

*c.*AD850 Chinese use gunpowder to make the first fireworks.

AD868 The first book is printed by woodblock.

AD906 China breaks up into different kingdoms.

AD939 Annam (Vietnam) becomes independent from China.

AD947 Khitan people overrun northern China.

Chinese fireworks

AD660   AD750   AD840   AD940   AD960

Makers of History

Great empires are made by ordinary people as much as by their rulers. The Chinese empire could not have been built without the millions of peasants who planted crops, built defensive walls and dug canals. The names of these people are largely forgotten, except for those who led uprisings and revolts against their rulers.

The inventors, thinkers, artists, poets and writers of imperial China are better known. They had a great effect on the society they lived in, and left behind ideas, works of art and inventions that still influence people today.

The royal court was made up of thousands of officials, artists, craftsmen and servants. Some had great political power. China's rulers came from many different backgrounds and peoples.

Many emperors were ruthless former warlords who were hungry for power. Others are remembered as scholars or artists. Some women also achieved great political influence, openly or from behind the scenes.

Laozi (born *c*.604BC)
The legendary Laozi is said to have been a scholar who worked as a court librarian. It is thought that he wrote the book known as the *Daodejing*. He believed people should live in harmony with nature, and his ideas later formed the basis of Daoism.

Kong Fuzi (551–479BC)
Kong Fuzi is better known in the West by the Latin version of his name, Confucius. He was a public official who became an influential teacher and thinker. His views on family life, society, and the treatment of others greatly influenced later generations.

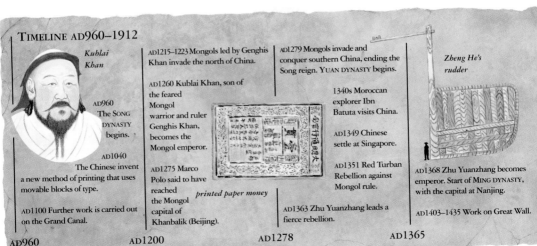

Timeline AD960–1912

Kublai Khan

AD960 The Song Dynasty begins.

AD1040 The Chinese invent a new method of printing that uses movable blocks of type.

AD1100 Further work is carried out on the Grand Canal.

AD1215–1223 Mongols led by Genghis Khan invade the north of China.

AD1260 Kublai Khan, son of the feared Mongol warrior and ruler Genghis Khan, becomes the Mongol emperor.

AD1275 Marco Polo said to have reached the Mongol capital of Khanbalik (Beijing).

printed paper money

AD1279 Mongols invade and conquer southern China, ending the Song reign. Yuan Dynasty begins.

1340s Moroccan explorer Ibn Batuta visits China.

AD1349 Chinese settle at Singapore.

AD1351 Red Turban Rebellion against Mongol rule.

AD1363 Zhu Yuanzhang leads a fierce rebellion.

Zheng He's rudder

AD1368 Zhu Yuanzhang becomes emperor. Start of Ming Dynasty, with the capital at Nanjing.

AD1403–1435 Work on Great Wall.

AD960   AD1200   AD1278   AD1365

HAN GAOZU (256–195BC)

In the Qin dynasty (221–206BC) Liu Bang was a minor public official in charge of a relay station for royal messengers. He watched as the centralized Qin empire fell apart. In 206BC he declared himself ruler of the Han kingdom. In 202BC he defeated his opponent, Xiang Yu, and founded the Han dynasty. As emperor Gaozu, he tried to unite China without using Qin's harsh methods.

QIN SHI HUANGDI (256–210BC)

Scholars plead for their lives before the first emperor. Zheng came to the throne of a state called Qin at the age of nine. He went on to rule all China and was given his full title, meaning First Emperor of Qin. His brutal methods included burying his opponents alive.

EMPRESS WU ZETIAN
(AD624–705)

The emperor Tang Gaozong enraged officials when he replaced his legal wife with Wu, his concubine (secondary wife). After the emperor suffered a stroke in AD660, Wu took control of the country. In AD690 she became the only woman in history to declare herself empress of China.

KUBLAI KHAN (AD1214–1294)

The Venetian explorer Marco Polo visits emperor Kublai Khan at Khanbalik (Beijing). Kublai Khan was a Mongol who conquered northern, and later southern, China.

AD1405–33 Chinese voyages of exploration under Zheng He.

AD1421 Beijing becomes the capital city of the Chinese empire.

Manchu warrior

AD1428 The Chinese are expelled from Annam (Vietnam).

AD1550 Japanese pirates mount raids on China. Mongols invade north again.

AD1644 Li Zicheng leads a rebellion against Ming rule. Manchu invasion. QING DYNASTY founded.

Boxer rebels

AD1673 Rebellions against Qing rule in south.

AD1839–42 First Opium War as Britain forces China to accept opium imports from India.

AD1842 Treaty of Nanjing. Britain gains Hong Kong.

AD1850–64 Taiping rebellion.

AD1858 Treaty of Tianjin. Chinese ports taken over by foreign powers.

AD1862 The Empress Dowager Cixi

becomes regent. 1894–95 War with Japan. Loss of Taiwan.

AD1899–1900 Boxer Rebellion against Qing and foreign governments.

AD1908 Last emperor, Puyi, ascends to throne as a small boy.

AD1912 Declaration of republic by Sun Yatsen. Emperor Puyi abdicates.

Puyi, the last emperor

1405   AD1425   AD1650   AD1880   AD1912

The Sons of Heaven

THE FIRST CHINESE RULERS lived about 4,000 years ago. This
early dynasty (period of rule) was known as the Xia. We know
little about the Xia rulers, because this period of Chinese history
has become mixed up with ancient myths and legends. Excavations
have told us more about the Shang dynasty rulers of over 3,000
years ago, who were waited on by slaves and had fabulous treasures.

During the next period of rule, the Zhou dynasty, an idea grew
up that the Chinese rulers were Sons of Heaven, placed on the
throne by the will of the gods. After China became a powerful,
united empire in 221BC, this idea helped keep the emperors in
power. Rule of the empire was passed down from father to son.
Anyone who seized the throne by force had to show that the
overthrown ruler had offended the gods. Earthquakes and natural
disasters were often taken as signs of the gods' displeasure.

Chinese emperors were among the most powerful rulers in
history. Emperors of China's last dynasty, the Qing (1644–1912),
lived in luxurious palaces that were cut off from the world.
When they travelled through the streets, the
common people had to stay indoors.

WHERE EMPERORS PRAYED
These beautifully decorated pillars
can be seen inside the Hall of Prayer
for Good Harvests at Tiantan in
Beijing. An emperor was a religious
leader as well as a political ruler,
and would arrive here in a great
procession each New Year. The
evening would be spent praying
to the gods for a plentiful harvest
in the coming year.

TO THE HOLY MOUNTAIN
This stele (inscribed stone) is located on the summit of
China's holiest mountain, Taishan, in Shandong
province. To the ancient Chinese, Taishan was the
home of the gods. For over 2,000
years the emperors climbed
the carved steps to
the temple to
offer prayers.

IN THE FORBIDDEN CITY
The vast Imperial Palace in Beijing is best
described as "a city within a city". It was built
between 1407 and 1420 by hundreds of
thousands of labourers under the command of
Emperor Yongle. Behind its high, red walls and
moats were 800 beautiful halls and temples, set
amongst gardens, courtyards and bridges.
No fewer than 24 emperors lived here in
incredible luxury, set apart from their subjects.
The Imperial Palace was also known as the
Forbidden City, as ordinary Chinese people
were not even allowed to approach its gates.

"WE POSSESS ALL THINGS"

This was the message sent from Emperor Qianlong to the British King George III in 1793. Here the emperor is being presented with a gift of fine horses from the Kyrgyz people of Central Asia. By the late 1800s, Chinese rule took in Mongolia, Tibet and Central Asia. All kinds of fabulous gifts were sent to the emperor from every corner of the empire, as everyone wanted to win his favour.

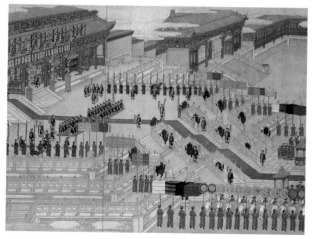

RITUALS AND CEREMONIES

During the Qing dynasty, an emperor's duties included many long ceremonies and official receptions. Here in Beijing's Forbidden City, a long carpet leads to the ruler's throne. Officials in silk robes line the steps and terraces, holding their banners and ceremonial umbrellas high. Courtiers kneel and bow before the emperor. Behaviour at the royal court was set out in the greatest detail. Rules decreed which kind of clothes could be worn and in which colours.

CARRIED BY HAND

The first Chinese emperor, Qin Shi Huangdi, is carried to a monastery high in the mountains in the 200s BC. He rides in a litter (a type of chair) that is carried on his servants' shoulders. Emperors always travelled with a large following of guards and courtiers.

Religions and Beliefs

"THREE TEACHINGS FLOW INTO ONE" is an old saying in China. The three teachings are Daoism, Confucianism and Buddhism. In China they gradually mingled together over the ages.

The first Chinese peoples believed in various gods and goddesses of nature, in spirits and demons. The spirit of nature and the flow of life inspired the writings which are said to be the work of Laozi (born c.604BC). His ideas formed the basis of the Daoist religion.

The teachings of Kong Fuzi (Confucius) come from the same period of history but they stress the importance of social order and respect for ancestors as a source of happiness. At this time another great religious teacher, the Buddha, was preaching in India. Within 500 years Buddhist teachings had reached China, and by the Tang dynasty (AD618–906) Buddhism was the most popular religion. Islam arrived at this time and won followers in the northwest. Christianity also came into China from Persia, but few Chinese were converted to this religion until the 1900s.

THE MERCIFUL GODDESS
Guanyin was the goddess of mercy and the bringer of children. She was a holy figure for all Chinese Buddhists.

DAOISM – A RELIGION OF HARMONY
A young boy is taught the Daoist belief in the harmony of nature. Daoists believe that the natural world is in a state of balance between two forces – yin and yang. Yin is dark, cool and feminine, while yang is light, hot and masculine. The two forces are combined in the black and white symbol on the scroll.

PEACE THROUGH SOCIAL ORDER
Kong Fuzi (Confucius) looks out on to an ordered world. He taught that the well-being of society depends on duty and respect. Children should obey their parents and wives should obey their husbands. The people should obey their rulers, and rulers should respect the gods. All of the emperors followed the teachings of Confucianism.

ISLAM IN CHINA

This is part of the Great Mosque in Xian (ancient Chang'an), built in the Chinese style. The mosque was founded in AD742, but most of the buildings in use today date from the Ming dynasty (1368–1644). Islam first took root in China in about AD700. Moslem traders from Central Asia brought with them the Koran, the holy book of Islam. It teaches that there is only one god, Allah, and that Muhammad is his prophet.

FREEDOM FROM DESIRE

Chinese monks carved huge statues of the Buddha from rock. Some can be seen at the Mogao caves near Dunhuang, where temples were built as early as AD366. The Buddha taught that suffering is caused by our love of material things. Buddhists believe that we are born over and over again until we learn to conquer this desire.

TEMPLE GUARDIANS

Gilded statues of Buddhist saints ward off evil spirits at Puningsi, the Temple of Universal Peace, near Chengde. The temple was built in 1755 in the Tibetan style. It is famed for its Mahayana Hall, a tower roofed in gilded bronze.

Chinese Society

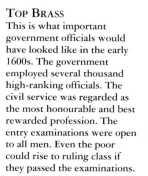

The river valleys and coasts of China have always been among the most crowded places on Earth. Confucius, with his love of social order, had taught that this vast society could be divided into four main groups. At the top were the nobles, the scholars and the landowners. Next came the farmers, including even the poorest peasants. These people were valued because they worked for the good of the whole nation, providing the vast amounts of food necessary to feed an ever-increasing population. In third place were skilled workers and craftsmen. In the lowest place of all were the merchants, because Confucius believed they worked for their own profit rather than for the good of the people as a whole. However, the way in which Chinese society rewarded these groups in practice did not fit the theory at all. Merchants ended up becoming the richest citizens, lending money to the upper classes. In contrast, the highly valued peasants often led a wretched life, losing their homes to floods and earthquakes or starving in years of famine.

Top Brass

This is what important government officials would have looked like in the early 1600s. The government employed several thousand high-ranking officials. The civil service was regarded as the most honourable and best rewarded profession. The entry examinations were open to all men. Even the poor could rise to ruling class if they passed the examinations.

The Ideal Order?

A government official tours the fields, where respectful peasants are happily at work. This painting shows an idealized view of the society proposed by Confucius. The district prospers and flourishes because everybody knows their place in society. The reality was very different – while Chinese officials led comfortable lives, most people were very poor and suffered great hardship. They toiled in the fields for little reward. Officials provided aid for the victims of famine or flood, but they never tackled the injustice of the social order. Peasant uprisings were common through much of Chinese history.

WORKING IN THE CLAYPITS
The manufacture of pottery was one of imperial China's most important industries. There were state-owned factories as well as many smaller private workshops. The industry employed some very highly skilled workers, and also thousands of unskilled labourers whose job was to dig out the precious clay. They had to work very hard for little pay. Sometimes there were serious riots to demand better working conditions.

LIFE BEHIND A DESK
Country magistrates try to remember the works of Confucius during a tough public examination. A pass would provide them with a path to wealth and social success. A failure would mean disgrace. The Chinese civil service was founded in about 900BC. This painting dates from the Qing dynasty (1644–1912). There were exams for all ranks of officials and they were very hard. The classic writings had to be remembered by heart. Not surprisingly, candidates sometimes cheated!

DRAGON-BACKBONE MACHINE
Peasants enlist the aid of machinery to help work the rice fields. The life of a peasant was mostly made up of back-breaking toil. The relentless work was made slightly easier by some clever, labour-saving inventions. The square-pallet chain pump (*shown above*) was invented in about AD100. It was known as the dragon-backbone machine and was used to raise water to the flooded terraces where rice was grown. Men and women worked from dawn to dusk to supply food for the population.

TOKENS OF WEALTH
Merchants may have had low social status, but they had riches beyond the dreams of peasants. They amassed wealth through money-lending and by exporting luxury goods, such as silk, spices and tea. The influence of the merchant class is reflected in the first bronze Chinese coins (c.250BC), which were shaped to look like knives, hoes and spades. Merchants commonly traded or bartered in these tools.

knife

hoe

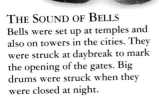

Towns and Cities

Cities grew up in northern China during the Shang dynasty (*c.*1600–1122BC). Zhengzhou was one of the first capitals, built in about 1600BC. Its city wall was seven kilometres long, but the city spilled out far beyond this border. Chinese cities increased in size over the centuries, and by the AD1500s the city of Beijing was the biggest in the world. Some great cities became centres of government, while smaller settlements served as market towns or manufacturing centres.

A typical Chinese city was surrounded by a wide moat and a high wall of packed earth. It was entered through a massive gatehouse set into the wall. The streets were filled with carts, beggars, craft workshops and street markets. Most people lived in small districts called wards that were closed off at night by locked gates. Temples and monasteries were a common sight, but royal palaces and the homes of rich families were hidden by high walls.

The Sound of Bells
Bells were set up at temples and also on towers in the cities. They were struck at daybreak to mark the opening of the gates. Big drums were struck when they were closed at night.

CHINESE SKYSCRAPERS
A pagoda (*shown far left*) soars above the skyline of a town in imperial China. Pagodas were graceful towers up to 15 storeys high, with eaves projecting at each level. Buildings rather like these were first seen in India, where they often marked holy Buddhist sites. The Chinese perfected the design, and many people believed that building pagodas spread good fortune over the surrounding land. Sometimes they were used as libraries, where scholars would study Buddhist scriptures.

MAKE A PAGODA
You will need: thick card, ruler, pencil, scissors, glue and brush, masking tape, corrugated card, 3cm x 1.5cm diameter dowel, embroidery bobbin, half a barbecue stick, paint (pink, terracotta and cream), thick and thin paintbrushes, water pot.

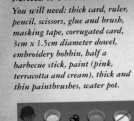

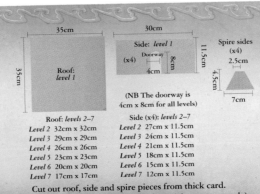

35cm

35cm

Roof: *level 1*

30cm

Side: *level 1*

(x4)   Doorway

4cm   8cm

11.5cm

Spire sides (x4)

2.5cm

4.5cm

7cm

(NB The doorway is 4cm x 8cm for all levels)

Roof: *levels 2–7*
Level 2 32cm x 32cm
Level 3 29cm x 29cm
Level 4 26cm x 26cm
Level 5 23cm x 23cm
Level 6 20cm x 20cm
Level 7 17cm x 17cm

Side (x4): *levels 2–7*
Level 2 27cm x 11.5cm
Level 3 24cm x 11.5cm
Level 4 21cm x 11.5cm
Level 5 18cm x 11.5cm
Level 6 15cm x 11.5cm
Level 7 12cm x 11.5cm

Cut out roof, side and spire pieces from thick card.
Use the measurements shown above (pieces not to scale).

1 Start with level 1. Glue 4 side pieces together. Hold together with masking tape. Then glue pieces of card behind each doorway.

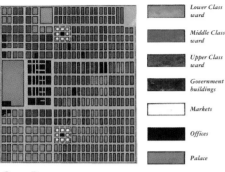

	Lower Class ward
	Middle Class ward
	Upper Class ward
	Government buildings
	Markets
	Offices
	Palace

CITY PLANNING

This grid shows the layout of Chang'an (Xian), the capital city of the empire during the Tang dynasty (AD618–906). The streets were grouped into small areas called wards. The design of many Chinese cities followed a similar pattern.

WESTERN INFLUENCE

The flags of Western nations fly in the great southern port of Guangzhou (Canton) in about 1810. Foreign architectural styles also began to appear in some Chinese cities at this time. In the early 1800s, powerful Western countries competed to take over Chinese trade and force their policies upon the emperor.

LIVING ON THE RIM

Cities around the edge of the empire were unlike those of typical Chinese towns. The mountain city of Lhasa is the capital of Tibet. It stretches out below its towering palace, the Potala. Tibet has had close political links with China since the AD600s. The country did remain independent for most of its history, but was invaded by China in the 1700s and again in 1950.

Pagodas were built in China as early as AD523. Some of the first ones were built by Chinese monks who had seen Buddhist holy temples in India. Extra storeys were sometimes added on over the centuries.

2 Glue level 1 roof on top of level 1 walls. Allow to dry. Centre level 2 sides on roof below. Glue down and hold with tape. Add level 2 roof.

3 Cut four 3cm wide corrugated card strips for each roof. The lengths need to match the roof measurements. Glue to edges of roof and sides.

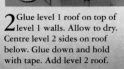

4 Assemble levels 3 to 7. Glue together spire pieces. Wedge dowel piece into the top. Stick barbecue stick on to bobbin. Then glue bobbin on to dowel.

5 Glue spire on to top level. Use a thick brush to paint the base colour. Paint details, such as terracotta for the roof tiles, with a thin brush.

Houses and Gardens

living quarters for owner's immediate family

reception

watch tower

A LL BUILDINGS IN Chinese cities were designed to be in harmony with each other and with nature. The direction they faced, their layout and their proportions were all matters of great spiritual importance. Even the number of steps leading up to the entrance of the house was considered to be significant. House design in imperial China varied over time and between regions. In the hot and rainy south, courtyards tended to be covered for shade and shelter. In the drier climate of the north, courtyards were mostly open to the elements. Poor people in the countryside lived in simple, thatched huts. These were made from timber frames covered in mud plaster. They were often noisy, draughty and overcrowded. In contrast, the spacious homes of the wealthy were large, peaceful and well constructed. Many had beautiful gardens, filled with peonies, bamboo and wisteria. Some of these gardens also contained orchards, ponds and pavilions.

INSIDE A HAN HOUSE

A wealthy family go about their daily lives in a Han dynasty (206BC–AD220) home. The house is built around several courtyards, with a garden at the side and a gatehouse leading out into the streets. A watchtower gives a view of the world outside. The main family building at the rear is two storeys high, but some homes had three or more floors.

main courtyard

MAKE A HOUSE

You will need: thick card, corrugated card, ruler, felt tip pen, scissors, glue and brush, 2.5cm x 0.5cm dowel (x2), masking tape, paint (white, grey, pink), thick and thin paintbrushes, water pot.

Base — 28cm, 24cm

Wall A — 25.5cm, 13.5cm, 9cm, 14.5cm, 3cm, 2cm, 3cm

Wall B (x2) — 17cm, 10.5cm

Stairs — 4cm, 2cm, 5.5cm

Floor (x2) — 6.5cm, 15cm, 7.5cm

Roof Piece A (x4) — 18cm, 7.5cm

Gate — 7cm, 4cm, 0.5cm

Wall C — 25.5cm, 13.5cm, 12.5cm, 11.5cm, 3cm, 1.5cm, 2cm, 3cm

Wall D (x2) — 8.5cm, 11cm, 8.5cm

Roof Piece B (x2) — 18cm, 8.5cm

Wall E (x2) — 8.5cm, 16cm

Wall F (x2) — 9.5cm, 7cm, 9cm

Roof Bracket (x6) — 7.5cm, 4cm, 10.5cm

Bend wall F here

1 Cut out card pieces. Glue walls A, E and F (bend F first) to base. Add floor and stairs. Glue dowel under floor. Glue corrugated card to stairs.

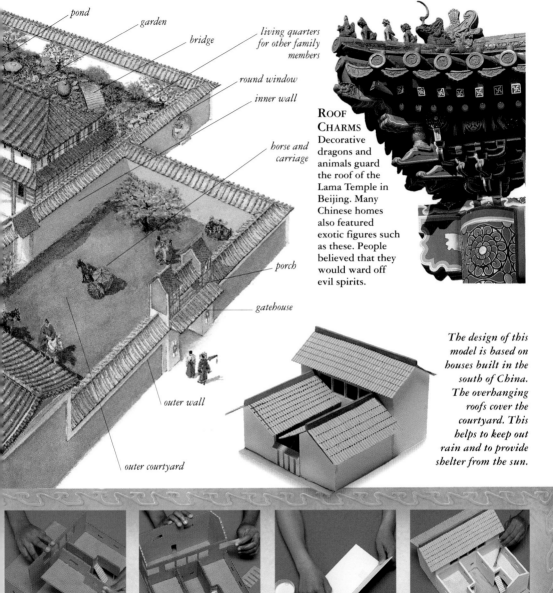

pond

garden

bridge

living quarters for other family members

round window

inner wall

horse and carriage

porch

gatehouse

outer wall

outer courtyard

ROOF CHARMS

Decorative dragons and animals guard the roof of the Lama Temple in Beijing. Many Chinese homes also featured exotic figures such as these. People believed that they would ward off evil spirits.

The design of this model is based on houses built in the south of China. The overhanging roofs cover the courtyard. This helps to keep out rain and to provide shelter from the sun.

2 To assemble second side, repeat method described in step 1. If necessary, hold pieces together with masking tape while the glue dries.

3 Glue B walls to the sides of the base, C wall to the back and D walls to the front. Hold with tape while glue dries. Glue gate between D walls.

4 Assemble A roofs (x2) and B roof (x1). Fix brackets underneath. Glue corrugated card (cut to same size as roof pieces) to top side of roofs.

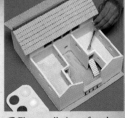

5 Fix a small piece of card over the gate to make a porch. Paint house, as shown. Use a thin brush to create a tile effect on the removable roofs.

Home Comforts

A LARGE HOME in imperial China would include many living rooms for the owner and his wife, their children, the grandparents, and other members of the extended family. There were several kitchens, servants' quarters, and reception rooms where guests would dine. A wealthy scholar's home would even contain its own private library.

Clay stoves provided heat in the cold northern winters. Windows were made of either stiff paper or hemp sacking instead of glass. Walls were tiled, or else decorated with beautiful silk hangings. They could be extended with carved screens. In the early days of the empire, there would be low tables, stools, urns and vases. People slept on low, heated platforms called *kang* in northern China, and the floors of homes would be covered with various mats, rugs and cushions.

Furniture making developed rapidly during the Tang dynasty (AD618–906). Skilled craftsmen began producing beautiful furniture without using nails. Bamboo was widely used in the south. Instead of sitting at floor level, people began to use chairs and high tables. Elaborate furniture was made for the imperial palaces, using rosewood or woods inlaid with ivory or mother-of-pearl. Most people had furniture that was cheaper and simpler in design, but no less beautiful.

BRINGER OF LIGHT
This beautiful lamp is made of gilded bronze, and supported by the figure of a maidservant. It was found in the tomb of Liu Sheng, the Jade Prince. The lamp dates from about 100BC. At that time, homes were lit by oil-lamps or lanterns made of paper, silk or horn.

BEAUTY IN THE HOME
A delicate porcelain plate from the early 1700s shows a young woman standing by a table, leaning on the back of a chair. The neatly arranged books, scrolls and furniture show the importance the Chinese placed on order and harmony in the home. Chairs and tables were put against the walls. There was no clutter or mess, and possessions were always neatly put away.

FURNITURE AND FITTINGS
Richly embroidered hangings and carved tables decorate the office of this Chinese magistrate (*c.* 1600). Wealthy homes and the offices of important people often featured such luxurious decorations and furnishings.

GARDENS OF TRANQUILITY

Chinese gardens offered peace and beauty amidst the hustle and bustle of the city. Bamboo leaves rustled in the wind. Lotus flowers floated gracefully on ponds. Wisteria, with its tumbling blue flowers, wound around the summer houses. There were scented roses, peonies and chrysanthemums. Soft fruits, such as peaches and lychees, were also grown.

lychee

peach

DECORATIVE SCREEN

Standing behind the carved chair is a spectacular folding screen, made in the 1800s. Exotic paintings of landscapes, animals and birds cover its surface, while a glossy lacquer makes it smooth, hard and strong. Many wealthy homes had richly decorated wooden screens, while poorer ones had simpler, carved ones. Screens were used to keep rooms cool in summer and warm in winter.

KEEPING COOL

This wine vessel was made over 3,000 years ago. It was used to store wine for rituals and ceremonies. The vessel was made of bronze, which probably helped to chill the wine. Cooling the wine in this way would improve its flavour.

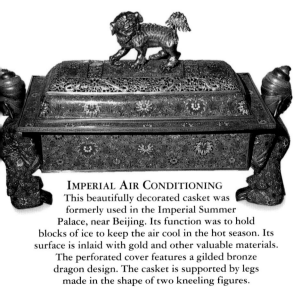

IMPERIAL AIR CONDITIONING

This beautifully decorated casket was formerly used in the Imperial Summer Palace, near Beijing. Its function was to hold blocks of ice to keep the air cool in the hot season. Its surface is inlaid with gold and other valuable materials. The perforated cover features a gilded bronze dragon design. The casket is supported by legs made in the shape of two kneeling figures.

Family Life

KONG FUZI (CONFUCIUS) taught that just as the emperor was head of the state, the oldest man was head of the household and should be obeyed by his family. In reality, his wife ran the home and often controlled the daily lives of the other women in the household.

During the Han dynasty (206BC–AD220) noblewomen were kept apart from the outside world. They could only gaze at the streets from the watchtowers of their homes. It was not until the Song dynasty (AD960–1279) that they gained more freedom. In poor households women worked all day, spending long, tiring hours farming, cooking, sweeping and washing.

For the children of poorer families, education meant learning to do the work their parents did. This involved carrying goods to market, or helping with the threshing or planting. The children of wealthier parents had private tutors at home. Boys hoping to become scholars or civil servants learned to read and write Chinese characters. They also studied maths and the works of Kong Fuzi.

LESSONS FOR THE BOYS
A group of Chinese boys take their school lessons. In imperial China, boys generally received a more academic education than girls. Girls were mainly taught music, handicrafts, painting and social skills. Some girls were taught academic subjects, but they were not allowed to sit the civil service examinations.

FOOT BINDING
This foot looks elegant in its beautiful slipper, but it's a different story when the slipper is removed. Just when life was improving for Chinese women, the cruel new custom of footbinding was introduced. Dancers had bound their feet for some years in the belief that it made them look dainty. In the Song dynasty the custom spread to wealthy and noble families. Little girls of five or so had their feet bound up so tightly that they became terribly deformed.

CHINESE MARRIAGE
A wedding ceremony takes place in the late 1800s. In imperial China, weddings were arranged by the parents of the bride and groom, rather than by the couples themselves. It was expected that the couple would respect their parents' wishes, even if they didn't like each other!

TAKING IT EASY

A noblewoman living during the Qing dynasty relaxes on a garden terrace with her children (c.1840). She is very fortunate as she has little else to do but enjoy the pleasant surroundings of her home. In rich families like hers, servants did most of the hard work, such as cooking, cleaning and washing. Wealthy Chinese families kept many servants, who usually lived in quarters inside their employer's home. Servants accounted for a large number of the workforce in imperial China. During the Ming dynasty (1368–1644), some 9,000 maidservants were employed at the imperial palace in Beijing alone!

RESPECT AND HONOUR

Children in the 1100s bow respectfully to their parents. Confucius taught that people should value and honour their families, including their ancestors. He believed that this helped to create a more orderly and virtuous society.

THE EMPEROR AND HIS MANY WIVES

Sui dynasty emperor Yangdi (AD581–618) rides out with his many womenfolk. Like many emperors, Yangdi was surrounded by women. An emperor married one woman, who would then become his empress, but he would still enjoy the company of concubines (secondary wives).

Farming and Crops

EIGHT THOUSAND YEARS AGO most Chinese people were already living by farming. The best soil lay beside the great rivers in central and eastern China, where floods left behind rich, fertile mud. As today, wheat and millet were grown in the north. This region was mostly farmed by peasants with small plots of land. Rice was cultivated in the warm, wet south, where wealthy city-dwellers owned large estates. Pears and oranges were grown in orchards.

Tea, later to become one of China's most famous exports, was first cultivated about 1,700 years ago. Hemp was also grown for its fibres. During the 500s BC, cotton was introduced. Farmers raised pigs, ducks, chickens and geese, while oxen and water buffalo were used as labouring animals on the farm.

Most peasants used basic tools, such as stone hoes and wooden rakes. Ploughs with iron blades were used from about 600BC. Other inventions to help farmers were developed in the next few hundred years, including the wheelbarrow, a pedal hammer for husking grain and a rotary winnowing fan.

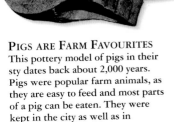

PIGS ARE FARM FAVOURITES
This pottery model of pigs in their sty dates back about 2,000 years. Pigs were popular farm animals, as they are easy to feed and most parts of a pig can be eaten. They were kept in the city as well as in rural country areas.

FEEDING THE MANY
Rice has been grown in the wetter regions of China since ancient times. Wheat and millet are grown in the drier regions. Sprouts of the Indian mung bean add important vitamins to many dishes.

mung beans

millet

rice

wheat

CHINESE TEAS
Delicate leaves of tea are picked from the bushes and gathered in large baskets on this estate in the 1800s. The Chinese cultivated tea in ancient times, but it became much more popular during the Tang dynasty (AD618–906). The leaves were picked, laid out in the sun, rolled by hand and then dried over charcoal fires.

WORKING THE LAND
A farmer uses a pair of strong oxen to help him plough his land. This wall painting found in Jiayuguan dates back to about 100BC. Oxen saved farmers a lot of time and effort. The Chinese first used oxen in farming in about 1122BC.

KEEPING WARM
This model of a Chinese farmer's lambing shed dates from about 100BC, during the Han dynasty. Sheepskins were worn for warmth, but wool never became an important textile for clothes or blankets in China.

HARVESTING RICE – CHINA'S MAIN FOOD
Chinese peasants pull up rice plants for threshing and winnowing in the 1600s. Farming methods were passed on by word of mouth and in handbooks from the earliest times. They advised farmers on everything from fertilizing the soil to controlling pests.

A TIMELESS SCENE
Peasants bend over to plant out rows of rice seedlings in the flooded paddy fields of Yunnan province, in southwest China. This modern photograph is a typical scene of agricultural life in China's warm and wet southwest region. Little has changed in hundreds of years of farming.

Fine Food

CHINESE COOKS TODAY are among the best in the world, with skills gained over thousands of years. Rice was the basis of most meals in ancient China, especially in the south where it was grown. Northerners used wheat flour to make noodles and buns. Food varied greatly between the regions. The north was famous for pancakes, dumplings, lamb and duck dishes. In the west, Sichuan was renowned for its hot chilli peppers. Mushrooms and bamboo shoots were popular along the lower Chang Jiang (Yangzi River).

For many people, meat was a rare treat. It included chicken, pork and many kinds of fish, and was often spiced with garlic and ginger. Dishes featured meat that people from other parts of the world might find strange, such as turtle, dog, monkey and bear. Food was stewed, steamed or fried. The use of chopsticks and bowls dates back to the Shang dynasty (c.1600–1122BC).

THE KITCHEN GOD
In every kitchen hung a paper picture of the kitchen god and his wife. Each year, on the 24th day of the 12th month, sweets were put out as offerings. Then the picture was taken down and burned. A new one was put in its place on New Year's Day.

A TANG BANQUET
These elegant ladies of the Tang court are sitting down to a feast. They are accompanied by music and singing, but there are no men present – women and men usually ate separately. This painting dates from the AD900s, when raised tables came into fashion in China. Guests at banquets would wear their finest clothes. The most honoured guest would sit to the east of the host, who sat facing the south. The greatest honour of all was to be invited to dine with the emperor.

MAKE RED BEAN SOUP

You will need: measuring jug, scales, measuring spoon, 225g aduki beans, 3 tsp ground nuts, 4 tsp short-grain rice, cold water, tangerine, saucepan and lid, wooden spoon, 175g sugar, liquidizer, sieve, bowls.

1 Use the scales to weigh out the aduki beans. Add the ground nuts and the short-grain rice. Measure out 1 litre of cold water in the jug.

2 Wash and drain the beans and rice. Put them in a bowl. Add the cold water. Leave overnight to soak. Do not drain off the water.

3 Wash and dry the tangerine. Then carefully take off the peel in a continuous strip. Leave the peel overnight, until it is hard and dry.

THAT SPECIAL TASTE

Garlic has been used to flavour Chinese dishes and sauces for thousands of years. It may be chopped, crushed, pickled or served whole. Root ginger is another crucial Chinese taste. Fresh chilli peppers are used to make fiery dishes, while sesame provides flavouring in the form of paste, oil and seeds.

sesame

root ginger

SHANG BRONZEWARE FIT FOR A FEAST

This three-legged bronze cooking pot dates from the Shang dynasty (*c*.1600BC–1122BC). Its green appearance is caused by the reaction of the metal to air over the 3,500 years since it was made. During Shang rule, metalworkers made many vessels out of bronze, including cooking pots and wine jars. They were used in all sorts of ceremonies, and at feasts people held in honour of their dead ancestors.

BUTCHERS AT WORK

The stone carving (*shown right*) shows farmers butchering cattle in about AD50. In early China, cooks would cut up meat with square-shaped cleavers. It was then flavoured with wines and spices, and simmered in big pots over open fires until tender.

Most peasant farmers lived on a simple diet. Red bean soup with rice was a typical daily meal. Herbs and spices were often added to make the food taste more interesting.

4 Put the soaked beans and rice (plus the soaking liquid) into a large saucepan. Add the dried tangerine peel and 500ml of cold water.

5 Bring the mixture to the boil. Reduce the heat, cover the saucepan and simmer for 2 hours. Stir occasionally. If the liquid boils off, add more water.

6 Weigh out the sugar. When the beans are just covered by water, add the sugar. Simmer until the sugar has completely dissolved.

7 Remove and discard the tangerine peel. Leave soup to cool, uncovered. Liquidize the mixture. Strain any lumps with a sieve. Pour into bowls.

Markets and Trade

THE EARLIEST CHINESE TRADERS used to barter (exchange) goods, but by 1600BC people were finding it easier to use tokens such as shells for buying and selling. The first metal coins date from about 750BC and were shaped like knives and spades. It was Qin Shi Huangdi, the first emperor, who introduced round coins. These had holes in the middle so that they could be threaded on to a cord for safe-keeping. The world's first paper money appeared in China in about AD900.

There were busy markets in every Chinese town, selling fruit, vegetables, rice, flour, eggs and poultry as well as cloth, medicine, pots and pans. In the Tang dynasty capital Chang'an (Xian), trading was limited to two large areas – the West Market and the East Market. This was so that government officials could control prices and trading standards.

CHINESE TRADING
Goods from China changed hands many times on the Silk Road to Europe. Trade moved in both directions. Porcelain, tea and silk were carried westwards. Silver, gold and precious stones were transported back into China from central and southern Asia.

raw silk

Chinese tea

CASH CROPS
Tea is trampled into chests in this European view of tea production in China. The work looks hard and the conditions cramped. For years China had traded with India and Arabia. In the 1500s it began a continuous trading relationship with Europe. By the early 1800s, China supplied 90 per cent of all the world's tea.

MAKE A PELLET DRUM

You will need: large roll of masking tape, pencil, thin cream card, thick card, scissors, glue and brush, 2.5cm x 30cm thin grey card, thread, ruler, needle, bamboo stick, paint (red, green and black), water pot, paintbrush, 2 coloured beads.

1 Use the outside of the tape roll to draw 2 circles on thin cream card. Use the inside to draw 2 smaller circles on thick card. Cut out, as shown.

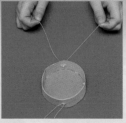

2 Glue grey strip around one of smaller circles. Make 2 small holes each side of strip. Cut two 20cm threads. Pass through holes and knot.

3 Use the scissors to make a hole in the side of the strip for the bamboo stick. Push the stick through, as shown. Tape the stick to the hole.

THE SILK ROAD

The trading route known as the Silk Road developed during the Han dynasty. The road ran for 11,000 kilometres from Chang'an (modern Xian), through Yumen and Kasghar, to Persia and the shores of the Mediterranean Sea. Merchants carried tea, silk and other goods from one trading post to the next.

FROM DISTANT LANDS

A foreign trader rides on his camel during the Tang dynasty. At this time, China's international trade began to grow rapidly. Most trade was still handled by foreign merchants, among them Armenians, Jews and Persians. They traded their wares along the Silk Road, bringing goods to the court at the Tang dynasty capital, Chang'an.

BUYERS AND SELLERS

This picture shows a typical Chinese market in about 1100. It appears on a Song dynasty scroll and is thought to show the market in the capital, Kaifeng, at the time of the New Year festival.

Twist the drum handle to make the little balls rattle. In the hubbub of a street market, a merchant could shake a pellet drum to gain the attention of passers by. He would literally drum up trade!

4 Tape the stick handle down securely at the top of the drum. Take the second small circle and glue it firmly into place. This seals the drum.

5 Draw matching designs of your choice on the 2 thin cream card circles. Cut out a decorative edge. Paint in the designs and leave them to dry.

6 Paint the bamboo stick handle red and leave to dry. When the stick is dry, glue the 2 decorated circles into position on top of the 2 smaller circles.

7 Thread on the 2 beads. Make sure the thread is long enough to allow the beads to hit the centre of the drum. Tie as shown. Cut off any excess.

Medicine and Science

From the empire's earliest days, Chinese scholars published studies on medicine, astronomy and mathematics. The Chinese system of medicine had a similar aim to that of Daoist teachings, in that it attempted to make the body work harmoniously. The effects of all kinds of herbs, plants and animal parts were studied and then used to produce medicines. Acupuncture, which involves piercing the body with fine needles, was practised from about 2700BC. It was believed to release blocked channels of energy and so relieve pain.

The Chinese were also excellent mathematicians, and from 300BC they used a decimal system of counting based on tens. They may have invented the abacus, an early form of calculator, as well. In about 3000BC, Chinese astronomers produced a detailed chart of the heavens carved in stone. Later, they were the first to make observations of sunspots and exploding stars.

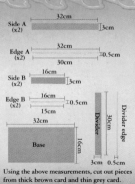

New Ills, Old Remedies
A pharmacist weighs out a traditional medicine. Hundreds of medicines used in China today go back to ancient times. Many are herbal remedies later proved to work by scientists. Doctors are still researching their uses. Other traditional medicines are of less certain value, but are still popular purchases at street stalls.

Pricking Points
Acupuncturists used charts (*shown above*) to show exactly where to position their needles. The vital *qi* (energy) was thought to flow through the body along 12 lines called meridians. The health of the patient was judged by taking their pulse. Chinese acupuncture is practised all over the world today.

Make an Abacus
You will need: thick and thin card, ruler, pencil, scissors, wood glue and brush, masking tape, self-drying clay, cutting board, modelling tool, 30cm x 0.5cm dowel (x11), paintbrush, water pot, brown paint.

Side A (x2) — 32cm — 3cm
Edge A (x2) — 32cm / 30cm — 0.5cm
Side B (x2) — 16cm — 3cm
Edge B (x2) — 16cm / 15cm — 0.5cm
Divider — 30cm / Divider edge
Base — 32cm x 16cm — 3cm / 0.5cm

Using the above measurements, cut out pieces from thick brown card and thin grey card. (pieces not shown to scale).

1 Glue sides A and B to the base. Hold the edges with masking tape until dry. Then glue edges A and B to the tops of the sides, as shown.

2 Roll the clay into a 2cm diameter sausage. Cut it into 77 small, flat beads. Make a hole through the centre of each bead with a dowel.

A Street Doctor Peddles his Wares

This European view of Chinese medicine dates from 1843. It shows snakes and all sorts of unusual potions being sold on the streets. The doctor is telling the crowd of miraculous cures.

Natural Health

Roots, seeds, leaves and flowers have been used in Chinese medicine for over 2,000 years. Today, nine out of ten Chinese medicines are herbal remedies. The Chinese yam is used to treat exhaustion. Ginseng root is used to help treat dizzy spells, while mulberry wood is said to lower blood pressure.

Chinese yam

ginseng root

Burning Cures

A country doctor treats a patient with traditional techniques during the Song dynasty. Chinese doctors relieved pain by heating parts of the body with the burning leaves of a plant called moxa (mugwort). The process is called moxibustion.

The abacus is an ancient counting frame that acts as a simple but very effective calculator. Using an abacus, Chinese mathematicians and merchants could carry out very difficult calculations quickly and easily.

3 Make 11 evenly spaced holes in the divider. Edge one side with thin card. Thread a dowel through each hole. Paint all of the abacus parts. Leave to dry.

4 Thread 7 beads on to each dowel rod – 2 on the upper side of the divider, 5 on the lower. Carefully fit the beads and rods into the main frame.

5 Each upper bead on the abacus equals 5 lower beads in the same column. Each lower bead is worth 10 of the lower beads in the column to its right.

6 Here is a simple sum. To calculate 5+3, first move down one upper bead (worth 5). Then move 3 lower beads in the same column up (each worth 1).

Feats of Engineering

THE ENGINEERING WONDER of ancient China was the Great Wall. It was known as *Wan Li Chang Cheng*, or the Wall of Ten Thousand *Li* (a unit of length). The Great Wall's main length was an incredible 4,000 kilometres. Work began on the wall in the 400s BC and lasted until the AD1500s. Its purpose was to protect China's borders from the fierce tribes who lived to the north. Despite this intention, Mongol invaders managed to breach its defences time after time. However, the Great Wall did serve as a useful communications route. It also extended the Chinese empire's control over a very long distance.

The Grand Canal is another engineering project that amazes us today. It was started in the 400s BC, but was mostly built during the Sui dynasty (AD581–618). Its aim was to link the north of China with the rice-growing regions in the south via the Chang Jiang (Yangzi River). It is still in use and runs northwards from Hangzhou to Beijing, a distance of 1,794 kilometres. Other great engineering feats were made by Chinese mining engineers, who were already digging deep mine shafts with drainage and ventilation systems in about 160BC.

LIFE IN THE SALT MINES
Workers busily excavate and purify salt from an underground mine. Inside a tower *(shown bottom left)* you can see workers using a pulley to raise baskets of mined salt. The picture comes from a relief (raised carving) found inside a Han dynasty tomb in the province of Sichuan.

MINING ENGINEERING
A Qing dynasty official tours an open-cast coalmine in the 1800s. China has rich natural resources and may have been the first country in the world to mine coal to burn as a fuel. Coal was probably discovered in about 200BC in what is now Jiangxi province. Other mines extracted metals and valuable minerals needed for the great empire. In the Han dynasty engineers invented methods of drilling boreholes to extract brine (salty water) from the ground. They also used derricks (rigid frameworks) to support iron drills – over 1,800 years before engineers in other parts of the world.

HARD LABOUR

Peasants use their spades to dig roads instead of fields. Imperial China produced its great building and engineering works without the machines we rely on today. For big projects, workforces could number hundreds of thousands. Dangerous working conditions and a harsh climate killed many labourers.

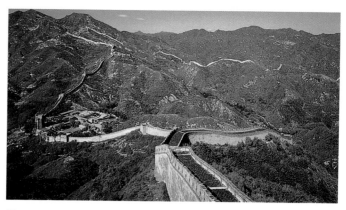

BUILDING THE WALL

The Great Wall snakes over mountain ridges at Badaling, to the northwest of Beijing. The Great Wall and Grand Canal were built by millions of workers. All men aged between 23 and 56 were called up to work on them for one month each year. Only noblemen and civil servants were exempt.

A GRAND OPENING

This painting from the 1700s imagines the Sui emperor Yangdi opening the first stage of the Grand Canal. Most of the work on this massive engineering project was carried out from AD605–609. A road was also built along the route. The transport network built up during the Sui dynasty (AD561–618) enabled food and other supplies to be moved easily from one part of the empire to another.

THE CITY OF SIX THOUSAND BRIDGES

The reports about China supposedly made by Marco Polo in the 1200s described 6,000 bridges in the city of Suzhou. The Baodai Bridge (*shown above*) is one of them. It has 53 arches and was built between AD618 and AD906 to run across the Grand Canal.

Famous Inventions

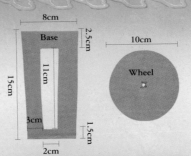

WHEN YOU WALK DOWN a shopping street in any modern city, it is very difficult to avoid seeing some object that was invented in China long ago. Printed words on paper, silk scarves, umbrellas or locks and keys are all Chinese innovations. Over the centuries, Chinese ingenuity and technical skill have changed the world in which we live.

A seismoscope is a very useful instrument in an earthquake-prone country such as China. It was invented in AD132 by a Chinese scientist called Zhang Heng. It could record the direction of even a distant earth tremor. Another key invention was the magnetic compass. In about AD1–100 the Chinese discovered that lodestone (a type of iron ore) could be made to point north. They realized that they could magnetize needles to do the same. By about AD1000, they worked out the difference between true north and magnetic north and began using compasses to keep ships on course.

Gunpowder is a Chinese invention from about AD850. At first it was used to blast rocks apart and to make fireworks. Later, it also began to be used in warfare.

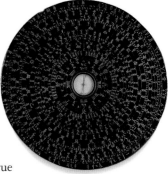

SHADE AND SHELTER
A Qing dynasty woman uses an umbrella as a sunshade to protect her skin. The Chinese invented umbrellas about 1,600 years ago and they soon spread throughout the rest of Asia. Umbrellas became fashionable with both women and men and were regarded as a symbol of high rank.

THE SAILOR'S FRIEND
The magnetic compass was invented in China in about AD1–100. At first it was used as a planning aid to ensure new houses faced in a direction that was in harmony with nature. Later it was used to plot courses on long sea voyages.

MAKE A WHEELBARROW

You will need: thick card, ruler, pencil, scissors, compasses, 0.5cm diameter balsa strips, glue and brush, paintbrush, paint (black and brown), water pot, 3.5cm x 0.5cm dowel, 2cm diameter rubber washers (x4).

Base
8cm
2.5cm
11cm
15cm
3cm
2cm
1.5cm

10cm
Wheel

Using the measurements above, draw the pieces on to thick card. Draw the wheel with the compasses. Cut out pieces with scissors.

1 Cut 7cm, 8cm and 26cm (x2) balsa strips. Glue 7cm strip to short edge of base and 8cm strip to top edge. Glue 26cm strips to side of base.

Su Song's Masterpiece

This fantastic machine is a clock tower that can tell the time, chime the hours and follow the movement of the planets around the Sun. It was designed by an official called Su Song, in the city of Kaifeng in AD1092. The machine uses a mechanism called an escapement, which controls and regulates the timing of the clock. The escapement mechanism was invented in the AD700s by a Chinese inventor called Yi Xing.

Earthquake Warning

The decorative object shown above is the scientist Zhang Heng's seismoscope. When there was an earthquake, a ball was released from one of the dragons and fell into a frog's mouth. This showed the direction of the vibrations. According to records, in AD138 the instrument detected a earth tremor some 500 kilometres away.

One-Wheeled Transport

In about AD100, the Chinese invented the wheelbarrow. They then designed a model with a large central wheel that could bear great weights. This became a form of transport, pushed along by muscle power.

The single wheelbarrow was used by farmers and gardeners. Traders wheeled their goods to market, then used the barrow as a stall. They would sell a variety of goods, such as seeds, grain, plants and dried herbs.

2 Turn the base over. Cut two 2cm x 1cm pieces of thick card. Make a small hole in the middle of each, for the wheel axle. Glue pieces to base.

3 Use compasses and a pencil to draw 1 circle around centre of wheel and 1 close to the rim. Mark on spokes. Paint spaces between spokes black.

4 Paint the barrow and leave to dry. Cut two 7cm balsa strips with tapered ends to make legs. Paint brown. When dry, glue to bottom of barrow.

5 Feed dowel axle between axle supports, via 2 washers, wheel, and 2 more washers. Dab glue on ends of axle, to allow wheel to spin without falling off.

Stone Relics

CHINESE CIVILIZATION BEGAN over 5,000 years ago in the Neolithic period (New Stone Age). Stone was one of the first materials to be worked. It was used to make practical objects, such as hand mills for grinding grain or tools for the farm, as well as for ornaments.

The Chinese valued one type of stone above all others – jade. Many figures and statues were made of the stone. People thought it had magical properties and could preserve the dead. The Han dynasty prince Liu Sheng and his wife, Dou Wan, were buried in suits made of over 2,000 thin jade plates sewn together with gold wire.

On a very different scale, the spread of Buddhism led to the popularity of gigantic stone sculptures. The Great Buddha above the town of Leshan, Sichuan, was carved into the rock in the AD700s. It is 70 metres high and took 90 years to carve from the rockface. Inside, a system of drains helps to prevent the stone from weathering.

BUFFALO IN JADE
Water buffalo were highly prized animals in imperial China. This beautiful carving measures about 43 centimetres in length. It was carved from a single large piece of jade during the 1300s. The precious stone was mined in the northwest of the country, in the region that is now known as Xinjiang.

STONY ELEPHANT
An uncomfortable-looking elephant (*shown above*) is one of many statues of animals that line the seven kilometres of the Spirit Way. This is a ceremonial avenue that leads to the Ming tombs at Shisanling, to the north of Beijing. The elephant statue was carved during the 1400s.

FOLLY IN MARBLE
A Mississippi paddle steamer was the model for this fake boat. It will never sail, as it is made of marble. It was built in the last days of the empire for Empress Dowager Cixi. She used funds meant for the navy to build it at her Summer Palace in Yiheyuan.

THE AFTERLIFE

This stone statue is one of many that guard the tombs at Shisanling, north of Beijing. Yong Li and 12 other Ming emperors were buried here from the 1400s onwards. The statues were made in the form of both humans and animals. They were probably placed there to protect each emperor in his next life.

CARVED FROM ROCK

A great Buddha dominates the spectacular stone carvings of the Yungang cave temples. It is located in what is now Shanxi province, northern China. The huge figure is some 15 metres in height. The elaborate stone carvings at the caves were completed at some point between AD460 and the early AD500s. In total, they take up a kilometre of the rockface.

JADE AXEHEAD

Simple decorative notches are carved on to this Shang dynasty jade axehead. Jade is a tough and difficult stone to cut. Early craftsmen did not have sharp enough tools to cut more detailed or elaborate patterns.

JADE DISCS

Bi are large discs made of jade. The one shown here measures about 27 centimetres in diameter. *Bi* were usually hung from cords of silk and were meant to represent heaven. These patterned discs were worn by priests at ceremonies from about 2500BC until Han times.

Workers of Metal

THE CHINESE MASTERED THE secrets of making alloys (mixtures of two or more metals) during the Shang dynasty (*c*.1600BC–1122BC). They made bronze by melting copper and tin to separate each metal from its ore, a process called smelting. Nine parts of copper were then mixed with one part of tin and heated in a charcoal furnace. When the metals melted they were piped off into clay moulds. Bronze was used to make objects such as ceremonial pots, statues, bells, mirrors, tools and weapons.

By about 600BC the Chinese were smelting iron ore. They then became the first people to make cast iron by adding carbon to the molten metal. Cast iron is a tougher metal than bronze and it was soon being used to make weapons, tools and plough blades. By AD1000 the Chinese were mining and working a vast amount of iron. Coke (a type of coal) had replaced the charcoal used in furnaces, which were fired up by water-driven bellows. Chinese metal workers also produced delicate gold and silver ornaments set with precious stones.

BEWARE OF THE LION
This gilded *fo* (Buddhist) lion guards the halls and chambers of Beijing's imperial palace, the Forbidden City. It is one of a fearsome collection of bronze guardian figures, including statues of dragons and turtles.

SILVER SCISSORS
This pair of scissors is made of silver. They are proof of the foreign influences that entered China in the AD700s, during the boom years of the Tang dynasty. The metal is beaten, rather than cast in the Chinese way. It is decorated in the Persian style of the Silk Road, with engraving and punching.

MAKE A NECKLACE

You will need: tape measure, thick wire, thin wire, masking tape, scissors, tin foil, measuring spoon, glue and brush, fuse wire.

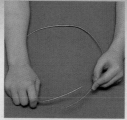

1 Measure around your neck using a tape measure. Ask an adult to cut a piece of thick wire to 1½ times this length. Shape it into a rough circle.

2 Cut two 4cm pieces of thin wire. Coil loosely around sides of thick wire. Tape ends to thick wire. Slide thick wire through coils to adjust fit.

3 Cut out an oval-shaped piece of tin foil. Shape it into a pendant half, using a measuring spoon or teaspoon. Make 9 more halves.

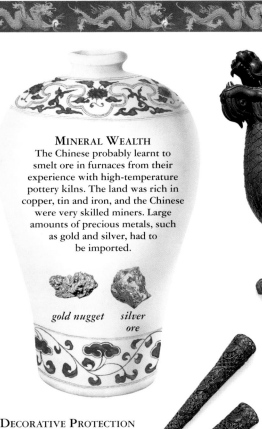

MINERAL WEALTH

The Chinese probably learnt to smelt ore in furnaces from their experience with high-temperature pottery kilns. The land was rich in copper, tin and iron, and the Chinese were very skilled miners. Large amounts of precious metals, such as gold and silver, had to be imported.

gold nugget   silver ore

PEACE BE WITH YOU

The Hall of Supreme Harmony in Beijing's Forbidden City is guarded by this bronze statue of a turtle. Despite its rather fearsome appearance, the turtle was actually a symbol of peace.

DECORATIVE PROTECTION

These nail protectors are made of gold, with inlaid feathers. They were worn by the Empress Dowager Cixi in the 1800s to stop her 15-cm-long little fingernails breaking.

GOLDEN FIREBIRDS

Chinese craftsmen fashioned these beautiful phoenix birds from thin sheets of delicate gold. The mythical Arabian phoenix was said to set fire to its nest and die, only to rise again from the ashes. During the Tang dynasty the phoenix became a symbol of the Chinese empress Wu Zetian, who came to power in AD660. It later came to be a more general symbol for all empresses.

4 Glue the 2 pendant halves together, leaving one end open. Drop some rolled-up balls of foil into the opening. Seal the opening with glue.

5 Make 4 more pendants in the same way. Thread each pendant on to the neckband with pieces of thin fuse wire. Leave a gap between each one.

People of all classes wore decorative jewellery in imperial China. The design of this necklace is based on the metal bell bracelets worn by Chinese children.

Porcelain and Lacquer

Although pottery first developed in Japan and parts of western Asia, Chinese potters were hard at work over 6,000 years ago. In 3200BC, clay was being fired (baked) in kilns at about 900°C.

By 1400BC, potters were making beautiful, white stoneware, baked at much higher temperatures. Shiny glazes were developed to coat the fired clay. Later, the Chinese invented porcelain, the finest, most delicate pottery of all. It was to become one of China's most important exports to other parts of Asia and Europe. In the English language, the word china is used for all fine-quality pottery.

The Chinese were the first to use lacquer. This plastic-like material is a natural substance from the sap of a tree that grows in China. The sap makes a smooth, hard varnish. From about 1300BC onwards, lacquer was used for coating wooden surfaces, such as house timbers, bowls or furniture. It could also be applied to leather and metal. Natural lacquer is grey, but in China pigment was added to make it black or bright red. It was applied in many layers until thick enough to be carved or inlaid with mother-of-pearl.

Enamel Ware
Ming dynasty craft workers made this ornate flask. It is covered with a glassy material called enamel, set inside thin metal wire. This technique, called cloisonné (partitioned), was introduced from Persia.

Floral Bottle
This attractive Ming dynasty bottle is decorated with a coating of bright red lacquer. The lacquer is coloured with a mineral called cinnabar. It would have taken many long hours to apply and dry the many layers of lacquer. The bottle is carved with a design of peonies, which were a very popular flower in China.

China's History Told on the Big Screen
This beautifully detailed, glossy lacquer screen shows a group of Portuguese merchants on a visit to China. It was made in the 1600s. Chinese crafts first became popular in Europe at this time, as European traders began doing business in southern China's ports.

FISH ON A PLATE

Pictures of fish decorate the border of this precious porcelain plate. It was made during the reign of the Qing emperor Yongzheng (1722–1736), a period famous for its elegant designs. It is coloured with enamel. Porcelain is made from a fine white clay called kaolin (china clay) and a mineral called feldspar. They are fired (baked) to a very high temperature.

A JUG OF WINE

An unknown Chinese potter made this beautiful wine jug about 1,000 years ago. It has been fired to such a high temperature that it has become glassy stoneware. It is coated with a grey-green glaze called celadon.

LIFE-LIKE FIGURES

A Ming dynasty entertainer smiles at his audience. All sorts of pottery figures have been found in Ming dynasty tombs. Potters made lively figures of merchants, musicians, court ladies and animals. Some are comic, while others are beautiful.

DEEP BLUE, PURE WHITE

These blue-and-white vases are typical of the late Ming dynasty (1368–1644). In the 1600s large numbers were exported to Europe. Many were produced at the imperial potteries at Jingdezhen, in northern Jiangxi province. These workshops were set up in 1369, as the region had plentiful supplies of the very best clay. Some of the finest pottery ever made was produced there in the 1400s and 1500s.

The Secret of Silk

For years, the Chinese tried to stop outsiders finding out how they made their most popular export – *si*, or silk. The shimmering colours and smooth textures of Chinese silk made it the wonder of the ancient world. Other countries such as India discovered the secret of silk making, but China remained the producer of the world's best silk.

Silk production probably dates back to late Stone Age times (8000BC–2500BC) in China. Legend says that the process was invented by the empress Lei Zu in about 2640BC. Silkworms (the caterpillars of a type of moth) are kept on trays and fed on the leaves of white mulberry trees. The silkworms spin a cocoon (casing) of fine but very strong filaments. The cocoons are plunged into boiling water to separate the filaments, which are then carefully wound on to reels.

A filament of silk can be up to 1,200 metres long. Several filaments are spun together to make up thread, which is then woven into cloth on a loom. The Chinese used silk to make all kinds of beautiful products. They learned to weave flimsy gauzes and rich brocades, and they then wove elaborate coloured patterns into the cloth in a style known as *ke si*, or cut silk.

PREPARING THE THREAD
A young woman winds silk thread on to bobbins in the late 1700s. Up to 30 filaments of silk could be twisted together to make silk thread for weaving. The Chinese made ingenious equipment for spinning silk into thread. They also built looms for weaving thread into large rolls of fabric. By the 1600s, the city of Nanjing alone had an estimated 50,000 looms.

LOAD THOSE BALES!
Workers at a Chinese silk factory of the 1840s carry large bales of woven silk down to the jetty. From there the woven cloth would be shipped to the city. It might be used to make a costume for a lady of the court, or else exported abroad. The Chinese silk industry reached its peak of prosperity in the mid-1800s.

THE DRAGON ON THE EMPEROR'S BACK

A scaly red dragon writhes across a sea of yellow silk. The dragon was embroidered on to a robe for an emperor of the Qing dynasty. The exquisite clothes made for the Chinese imperial court at this time are considered to be great works of art.

WINDING SILK

Silk is being prepared at this workshop of the 1600s. The workers are taking filaments (threads) from the cocoons and winding them on to a reel. Traditionally, the chief areas of silk production in imperial China were in the east coast provinces of Zhejiang and Jiangsu. Silk was also produced in large quantities in Sichuan, in the west.

MAKING SILK

Raising silkworms is called sericulture. It can be a complicated business. The caterpillars have to be kept at a controlled temperature for a month before they begin spinning their silk cocoons.

adult silkmoth and cocoons

silkmoth larva

MAGIC MULBERRIES

These Han dynasty workers are collecting mulberry leaves in big baskets, over 2,000 years ago. These would have been used to feed the silkworms. Silkworms are actually the larva (caterpillars) of a kind of moth. Like most caterpillars, silkworms are fussy feeders and will only eat certain kinds of plant before they spin cocoons.

Dress and Ornament

CHINESE PEASANTS dressed in simple clothes made from basic materials. They mostly wore cotton tunics over loose trousers, with sandals made of rushes or straw. In the south, broad-brimmed, cone-shaped hats helped to protect the wearer from the hot sun and heavy rain. In the north, fur hats, sheepskins and quilted jackets were worn to keep out the cold. Rich people often dressed in elaborate, expensive clothes. Government officials wore special robes that reflected their rank and status. Beautiful silk robes patterned with dragons (*lung pao*) were worn by court ladies, officials, and the emperor himself.

CLOTHES FIT FOR AN EMPEROR
This magnificent imperial robe was made from interwoven, heavy silks in the 1800s. The narrow sleeves, with their horse hoof cuffs, are typical of the Qing dynasty.

MONKEY PENDANT
Wealthy people often wore very expensive, well-crafted jewellery. This beautiful piece from the AD700s is a pendant necklace. It could have been worn by both men and women. The pendant is made from white jade set in a beaded frame of gilded bronze.

Court dress varied greatly over the ages. Foreign invasions brought new fashions and dress codes. Under the Manchus, who ruled as the Qing dynasty from AD1644, men had to wear a long pigtail. Rich people grew their little fingernails so long that special nail guards were worn to prevent them from breaking off.

FASTEN YOUR BELT
Belt hooks and buckles became an essential part of noblemen's clothing from about the 300s BC. They were highly decorated, and made of bronze.

MAKE A FAN

You will need: masking tape, red tissue paper, thick card base, ruler, pencil, compasses, paint (pink, light blue, cream, light green), thin paintbrush, water pot, scissors, 16cm x 1cm balsa strips (x15), barbecue stick, glue and brush, thin card.

1 Tape tissue paper on to base. Make a compass hole 1cm from the edge. From this mark, draw a 16cm radius semicircle and a 7cm radius semicircle.

2 Place one end of the ruler at compass hole. Mark the point with a pencil. Draw evenly spaced lines 1cm apart between the semi-circles.

3 Draw your design on to the tissue paper. Paint in the details. Allow to dry. Remove paper from base. Cut out fan along edges of the semicircles.

OFFICIAL DRESS

A well-dressed civil servant cools down in the summer heat. Chinese government officials wore elegant clothes that showed their social rank. This picture was painted by a European artist in about 1800. The official is wearing his summer outfit, which consists of a long narrow-sleeved tunic, slippers and a brimmed hat. It is a hot day, so he also carries a fan to provide a cool breeze.

LADIES OF THE COURT

These Tang ladies are dressed in the high fashion of the AD700s. Silk was the material worn by the nobles of the day, and court costume included long robes and skirts, various tunics and sashes. The clothes were often beautifully decorated, with colourful patterns and elaborate designs.

ADDED STYLE

Over the ages, all kinds of accessories became part of Chinese costume. These included elaborate hats and headdresses for men and women, sunshades, fans, belts and buckles. Tiny leather shoes lined with silk were worn by noble women.

ladies' shoes

earring

fans

The earliest Chinese fans were made of feathers or of silk stretched over a flat frame. In about AD1000 folding fans were introduced into China, probably from Japan.

back of fan

4 Using scissors, cut each balsa strip 1cm narrower (0.5cm each side) for half of its length. Make a compass hole at the base of each strip.

5 Stack strips. Pass a barbecue stick through holes. It must be long enough to fit through and overlap either side. Make sure strips can move freely.

6 Fold the paper backwards and forwards to form a concertina. Glue each alternate fold of the paper to the narrow ends of the strips, as shown.

7 Paint the top strip of the fan pink. Allow to dry. Cut out small card discs. Glue them over the ends of the barbecue stick to secure the strips.

Chinese Art

IN IMPERIAL CHINA, painting was believed to be the finest of all the arts. It was considered to be a mark of civilization and a suitable pastime for scholars and even emperors. Painting was based upon the same ideas of harmony and simplicity that were important in the Daoist and Buddhist faiths. Paintings appeared on scrolls of silk and paper, walls, screens and fans. Popular subjects for pictures varied over the ages. They included the misty mountains and rivers of southern China, as well as landscapes set off by lone human figures. Artists also painted birds, animals and plants, such as bamboo or lotus. Sometimes just a few brush strokes were used to capture the spirit of the subject. Chinese writing in the form of a poem often played an important part in many pictures. Chinese artists also produced woodcuts, which are prints made from a carved wooden block. Traditionally these were not valued as much as the paintings, but many beautiful woodcuts were produced during the reign of the Ming dynasty (1368–1644).

SYMBOLS OF WISDOM
To the Chinese, the dragon embodied wisdom, strength and goodness. This intricate ivory seal belonged to a Ming emperor and shows a dragon guarding the pearl of wisdom.

WINDOW ON THE PAST
A royal procession makes its way along a mountain range. This detail from a painting on silk is by the great master Li Sixun (AD651–716). Many Tang dynasty paintings show court life and royal processions, but they are far from dull. They provide a colourful glimpse of life in China at that time. This picture shows what people wore and how they travelled.

MAKE PAPER CUT-OUTS
You will need: A4 sized coloured paper, pencil, ruler, scissors.

1 Take a piece of coloured paper and lay it flat on a hard surface. Fold it exactly in half widthways. Make a firm crease along the fold, as shown above.

2 Draw a Chinese-style design on the paper. Make sure all the shapes meet up at the fold. Make a tracing of your design so you can use it again.

3 Keeping card folded, cut out shapes. Make sure you don't cut along the folded edge. Cut away areas you want to discard in between the shapes.

AT FULL GALLOP

Chinese artists greatly admired horses and loved to try to capture their strength and movement in paintings. This lively wall painting was found in a Han dynasty tomb.

PAINTING NATURE

Morning mist hangs over a mountain backdop. This detail from a masterpiece by Qiu Ying (1494–1552) is inspired by the forests and mountain landscapes of his homeland. Artists such as Qiu Ying were successful and well paid.

ART IN PORCELAIN

China's craft workers and designers were also great artists. This blue-and-white porcelain wine jar was made in the 1600s in the form of a mandarin duck and drake. Its hand-painted details would have taken many long hours of work to complete. Blue-and-white porcelain was very popular during the Ming dynasty.

SPRINGTIME ON PAPER

A watercolour painting from the 1800s shows peach blossom just as it comes into flower. It is painted in a very realistic, fresh and simple style. This approach is a common characteristic of much Chinese art.

4 Now open up your design. Be careful not to tear it. To add details to the figures, fold paper again. Mark the details to be cut along the crease.

5 Using a pair of scissors, carefully cut out the detail along the crease. The cut-out detail will be matched perfectly on the other side of the figure.

Carefully open up your finished cut-out. Display the design by sticking it to a window, so that light shines through. In China, paper cut-outs are traditionally used to bring luck and good fortune.

The Written Word

THE CHINESE LANGUAGE is written with symbols called characters, which stand for sounds and words. They have changed and developed over the ages. A dictionary published in 1716 lists over 40,000 of them. Each character was written by hand with a brush, using 11 basic brush strokes. The painting of these beautiful characters is called calligraphy, and was always seen as a form of art.

The Chinese began using woodblocks for printing in about 1600BC. Before that, books had often been handwritten on bamboo strips. Ancient Chinese writers produced all sorts of practical handbooks and encyclopedias. Poetry first developed about 3,000 years ago. It was the Chinese who invented paper, nearly 2,000 years ago. Cloth or bark was shredded, pulped and dried on frames. Movable type was invented in the 1040s. During the 1500s popular folk tales such as *The Water Margin* were published, and in the 1700s the writer Cao Xuequin produced China's greatest novel, *A Dream of Red Mansions*.

MAGICAL MESSAGES
The earliest surviving Chinese script appears on animal bones. They were used for telling fortunes in about 1200BC. The script was made up of small pictures representing objects or ideas. Modern Chinese script is made up of patterns of lines.

ART OF CALLIGRAPHY
This text was handwritten during the Tang dynasty (AD618–906). Traditional Chinese writing reads down from right to left, starting in the top right-hand corner.

MAKE PRINTING BLOCKS
You will need: plain white paper, pencil, paint, soft Chinese brush or thin paintbrush, water pot, tracing paper, board, self-drying clay (15cm x 20cm, 2.5cm thick), modelling tool, wood glue, block printing ink, damp rag.

1 Copy or trace the characters from the reversed image block (see opposite). Start off with a pencil outline, then fill in with paint. Leave to dry.

2 Copy design on to tracing paper. Turn the paper over. Place it on the clay. Scribble on the clean side of the paper to leave a mirror image in the clay.

3 Use a modelling tool to carve out characters. Cut away clay all around characters to make a relief (raised pattern). Smooth clay base with your fingertips.

THE BEST WAY TO WRITE
A calligrapher of the 1840s begins to write, surrounded by his assistants. The brush must be held upright for the writing of Chinese characters. The wrist is never rested on the table. Many years of practice and study are necessary to become a good calligrapher.

THE PRINTED PAGE
The Buddhist scripture called the Diamond Sutra (*shown right*) is probably the oldest surviving printed book in the world. It includes both text and pictures. The book was printed from a woodblock on 11 May AD868 and was intended to be distributed at no cost to the public.

INKS AND COLOURS
Watercolours and inks were based on plant and mineral pigments in reds, browns, blues, greens and yellows. Black ink was made from carbon, obtained from soot. This was mixed with glue to form a solid block. The ink block would be wetted during use. Brushes were made from animal hair fitted into bamboo handles.

Chinese brushes

reversed image   *actual image*

Block rubbings of characters were an early form of printing.

Moon   Ruler

Mouth   Sun

4 When the relief has dried, paint the clay block with wood glue. Leave it to dry thoroughly. When dry, the glue seals and protects the pattern.

5 Now paint the design. Apply a thick layer of printing ink to the raised parts of the clay with a Chinese brush or a soft paintbrush.

6 Lay a thin piece of plain white paper over the inked block. Use a dry brush to press the paper into the ink, so that the paper takes up the design.

7 Lift up the paper to reveal your design. Look after your printing block by cleaning it with a damp rag. You can then use it again and again.

Musicians and Performers

THE EARLIEST CHINESE POETRY was sung rather than spoken. *Shijing* (the Book of Songs) dates back over 3,000 years and includes the words to hymns and folk songs. For most of China's history, musicians were employed in rich households. Orchestras played drums, gongs, pan pipes, racks of bronze bells, fiddles and other stringed instruments. Music was considered an important part of life, and models of musicians were often put in tombs to provide entertainment in the afterlife.

Musicians were frequently accompanied by acrobats, jugglers and magicians. Such acts were as popular in the markets and streets of the town as in the courtyards of nobles. Storytelling and puppet shows were equally well loved. Plays and opera became hugely popular in the AD1200s, with tales of murder, intrigue, heroism and love acted out to music. Most of the female roles would be played by men.

THE COURT DANCER
Arching her right arm upwards, an elegant dancer performs at the royal court. The model's flowing dress belongs to the fashions of the Tang dynasty (AD618–906).

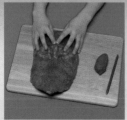

PUTTING ON A PUPPET SHOW
Children put on a show with marionettes (puppets moved by strings) in the 1600s. Drumming was used to provide musical accompaniment, just like in a professional play of the period.

MAKE A MASK

You will need: tape measure, large block of self-drying clay, board, modelling tool, petroleum jelly, newspaper, wood glue and brush, scissors, thick card, masking tape, 2 large white beads, paintbrush, paints (grey, cream, terracotta and yellow), water pot, needle, black wool, string.

1 Measure the width and length of your face with a tape measure. Make a clay mould. Carve out the eyes and attach a clay nose to the mask.

2 Paint front of mask with petroleum jelly. Apply 4–6 layers of papier-mâché. This is made by soaking torn newspaper in water and glue. Leave to dry.

3 Remove mask from the clay mould. Cut a 2.5cm wide strip of card long enough to fit around your face. Bend it into a circle, and tape to the mask.

MUSIC IN THE GARDEN

Musicians in the 1800s play *qins* (lutes) and *sheng* (flutes) in a garden setting. The music tried to reflect nature's harmony. It was intended to make the listener feel peaceful and spiritual.

CHINESE OPERA

These stars of the Chinese opera are performing in the 1700s. Well-known folk tales were acted out to the dramatic sound of crashing cymbals and high-pitched singing. Elaborate make-up and fancy costumes made it clear to the audience whether the actor was playing a hero or a villain, a princess or a demon.

Elaborate masks like these were worn to great effect in Chinese opera. When your mask is finished, you can wear it to scare your friends!

SOUND THE DRUMS!

The cavalcade that followed an important government official or general might have included mounted drummers or trumpeters. These figures of musicians on horseback were found in the tomb of a high-ranking official from the Tang dynasty.

4 Cut 2 pointed ear shapes from card. Fold card at the edge to make flaps. Cut out and glue on small, decorative pieces of card. Glue ears to the mask.

5 Glue on 2 large white beads for the eyes. Cut out more small pieces of card. Glue these on above the eyes. Add another piece of card for the lips.

6 Paint the mask with the grey base colour first. Leave to dry. Then add details using the brighter colours. When dry, varnish with wood glue.

7 Use a needle to thread black wool through for the beard. Tape wool to back of the mask. Thread string through side of mask behind ears to tie it on.

Games and Pastimes

FROM EARLY IN CHINA's history, kings and nobles loved to go hunting for pleasure. Horses and chariots were used to hunt deer and wild boar. Dogs and even cheetahs were trained to chase the prey. Spears, bows and arrows were then used to kill it. Falconry (using birds of prey to hunt animals) was commonplace by about 2000BC.

In the Ming and Qing dynasties ancient spiritual disciplines used by Daoist monks were brought together with the battle training used by warriors. These martial arts (*wu shu*) were intended to train both mind and body. They came to include the body movements known as tai chi (*taijiquan*), sword play (*jianwu*) and the extreme combat known as kung fu (*gongfu*).

Archery was a popular sport in imperial China. The Chinese also loved gambling, and may have invented the first card games over 2,000 years ago.

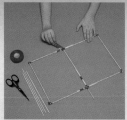

PEACE THROUGH MOVEMENT
A student of tai chi practises his art. The Chinese first developed the system of exercises known as tai chi more than 2,000 years ago. The techniques of tai chi were designed to help relax the human body and concentrate the mind.

CHINESE CHESS
The traditional Chinese game of xiang qi is similar to western chess. One army battles against another, with round discs used as playing pieces. To tell the discs apart, each is marked with a name.

pieces

xiang qi board

MAKE A KITE

You will need: 30cm barbecue sticks (x12), ruler, scissors, glue and brush, plastic insulating tape, A1-size paper, pencil, paint (blue, red, yellow, black and pink), paintbrush, water pot, string, piece of wooden dowel, small metal ring.

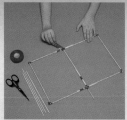

1 Make a 40cm x 30cm rectangle by joining some of the sticks. Overlap the sticks for strength, then glue and tape together. Add a centre rod.

2 Make another rectangle 15cm x 40cm long. Overlay the second rectangle on top of the first one. Tape rectangles together, as shown above.

3 Place frame on to a sheet of white A1-size paper. Draw a 2.5cm border around outside of frame. Add curves around the end of the centre rod.

ALL-IN WRESTLING

This bronze figure of two wrestling muscle men was made in about 300BC. Wrestling was a very popular entertainment and sport in imperial China. It continues to be an attraction at country fairs and festivals.

BAMBOO BETTING

Gamblers place bets in a game of *liu po*. Bamboo sticks were thrown like dice to decide how far the counters on the board should move. Gambling was a widespread pastime during the Han dynasty. People would bet large sums of money on the outcome of card games, horse races and cock fights.

POLO PONIES

These women from the Tang dynasty are playing a fast and furious game of polo. They are probably noblewomen from the Emperor's royal court. The sport of polo was originally played in India and central Asia. It was invented as a training game to improve the riding skills of soldiers in cavalry units.

Chinese children today still play with home-made paper kites. Kites were invented in China in about 400BC.

4 Cut out the kite shape from the paper. Using a pencil, draw the details of your dragon design on the paper. Paint in your design and leave to dry.

5 Cut a triangular piece of paper to hang from the end of your kite as a tail. Fold tail over rod at bottom of kite, as shown. Tape tail into position.

6 Carefully tape and glue your design on to the frame. Fold over border that you allowed for when cutting out the paper. Tape to back of paper, as shown.

7 Wrap 10m of string around dowel. Tie other end to ring. Pass 2 pieces of string through kite from the back. Tie to centre rod. Tie other ends to ring.

Travel by Land

The Chinese empire was linked by a network of roads used only by the army, officials and royal messengers. A special carriageway was reserved for the emperor himself. Ordinary people travelled along dusty or muddy routes and tracks.

China's mountainous landscape and large number of rivers meant that Chinese engineers became expert at bridge-building. Suspension bridges made of rope and bamboo were being used from about AD1 onwards. A bridge suspended from iron chains crossed the Chang Jiang (Yangzi River) as early as AD580. A stone arch bridge built in about AD615 still stands today at Zhouxian in Hebei province. Most people travelled by foot and porters often had to carry great loads on their backs. They also carried wealthy people from place to place on litters (chairs).

China's small native ponies were interbred with larger, stronger horses from central Asia sometime after 100BC. This provided fast, powerful mounts that were suitable for messengers and officials, and they were also capable of pulling chariots and carriages. Mules and camels were widely used along the trade routes of the north, while shaggy yaks carried loads in the high mountains of the Himalayas. Carts were usually hauled along by oxen.

HEADING OUT WEST
Chinese horsemen escort the camels of a caravan (trading expedition). The traders are about to set out along the Silk Road. This trading route ran all the way from Chang'an (Xian) in China right through to Europe and the lands of the Mediterranean.

RIDING ON HORSEBACK
A Chinese nobleman from about 2,000 years ago reins in his elegant horse. Breaking in the horse would have been difficult, as the rider has no stirrups and could easily be unseated. Metal stirrups were in general use in China by AD302. They provided more stability and helped to improve the rider's control of the horse.

CARRIED BY HAND

A lazy landowner of the Qing dynasty travels around his estates. He is carried along in a litter, a platform supported by the shoulders of his tired, long-suffering servants. An umbrella shades the landowner from the heat of the summer sun.

CAMEL POWER

Bactrian (two-humped) camels were originally bred in central Asia. They could endure the extremes of heat and cold of the region, and travel for long distances without water. This toughness made them ideal for transporting goods along the Silk Road.

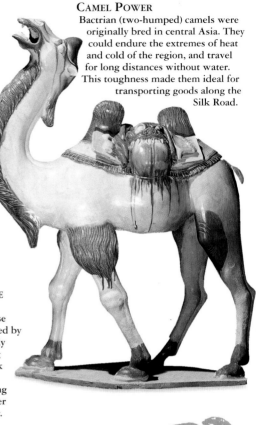

HAN CARRIAGE

During the Han period, three-horse carriages were used by the imperial family only. This carving from a tomb brick is probably of a messenger carrying an important order from the emperor.

TRAVELLING IN STYLE

During the Han dynasty, government officials travelled in stylish horse-drawn carriages. This picture is taken from a decorative brick found in a Han tomb. After larger, stronger breeds of horses were introduced into China from central Asia, the horse became a status symbol for the rich and powerful. Such horses were considered to be celestial (heavenly).

Junks and Sampans

From early in China's history, its rivers, lakes and man-made canals were the country's main highways. Fishermen propelled small wooden boats across the water with a single oar or pole at the stern. These small boats were often roofed with mats, like the sampans (which means "three planks" in Chinese) still seen today. Large wooden sailing ships, which we call junks, sailed the open ocean. They were either keeled or flat-bottomed, with a high stern and square bows. Their sails were made of matting stiffened with strips of bamboo. By the AD800s, Chinese shipbuilders had built the first ships with several masts and proper rudders.

In the 1400s, admirals Zheng He and Wang Jinghong led seven sea expeditions that visited Southeast Asia, India, Arabia and East Africa. The flagship of their 300-strong naval fleet was over five times the size of the largest European ships of the time.

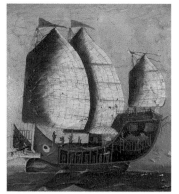

IN FULL SAIL
Junks were a type of sailing vessel used by merchants in the East and South China seas. They were also used by pirates. The China seas could be blue and peaceful, but they were often whipped into a fury by typhoons (tropical storms).

RIVER TRAFFIC
All sorts of small trading boats were sailed or rowed along China's rivers in the 1850s. River travel was often difficult and could be dangerous. Floods were common along the Huang He (Yellow River), which often changed course. The upper parts of China's longest river, the Chang Jiang (Yangzi River), were rocky and had powerful currents.

MAKE A SAMPAN

You will need: ruler, pencil, thick and thin card, scissors, glue and brush, masking tape, 6 wooden barbecue sticks, string, thin yellow paper, paint (black, dark brown), paintbrush, water pot.

Runner A (x2) — 39cm — 1cm

Side B (x2) — 33.5cm — 5cm — 15cm

Base C (x2) — 15cm — 7cm
Base D — 18cm

Floor E — 7cm — 10cm — 4cm
Floor F (x2) — 4cm — 7cm
Edge G (x2) — 1cm — 6.5cm

Cut pieces B, C, D and G from thick card. Cut pieces A, E, and F from thin card.

1 Glue base pieces C and D to side B, as shown. Hold the pieces with masking tape while the glue dries. When dry, remove the masking tape.

2 Glue remaining side B to the boat. Stick runner A pieces to top of the sides. Make sure the ends jut out 2.5cm at the front and back of the boat.

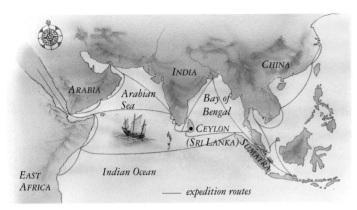

THE VOYAGES OF ZHENG HE

Chinese admirals Zheng He and Wang Jinghong carried out seven fantastic voyages of exploration between 1405 and 1433. This map shows how far and wide they travelled on these expeditions. Their impressive fleets included over 60 ships crewed by about 27,000 seamen, officers and interpreters. The biggest of their vessels was 147 metres long and 60 metres wide.

FISHERMEN'S FEASTS

Seas, lakes and rivers were an important food source in imperial China. Drying fish was often the only way to preserve it in the days before refrigeration. Dried fish made strong-tasting sauces and soups. Popular seafoods included crabs, prawns and squid.

dried fish

dried squid

THE FISHING TRIP

A fisherman poles his boat across the river in the 1500s. The bird shown in the picture is a tamed cormorant, used for catching the fish. The cormorant was normally attached to a line, with a ring around its neck to prevent it from swallowing the fish.

To add the finishing touch to your sampan, make a boatman and oar to propel the vessel through the waterways.

3 Glue floor E to centre of base. Add floor F pieces to the ends of the base, as shown. Stick edge G pieces in between the ends of the runners.

4 Bend 2 barbecue sticks into 10cm high arches. Cut 2 more sticks into five 10cm struts. Glue and tie 2 struts to sides of arches and 1 to the top.

5 Repeat step 4 to make a second roof. To make roof matting, cut thin yellow paper into 1cm x 10cm strips. Fold strips in half and stick to roofs.

6 Paint boat and roofs. Allow to dry. Glue the matting strips to the roofs, as shown. When the glue is dry, place roofs inside the boat.

Soldiers and Weapons

IN CHINA'S EARLY HISTORY, bitter warfare between local rulers devastated the countryside with an appalling cost in human lives. Battle tactics and campaigns were discussed in *The Art of War* by Master Sun, who lived in the 500s BC at around the same time as the thinker Kong Fuzi (Confucius). This was the first book of its kind and its ideas are still studied today. After the empire was united in 221BC, rulers still needed large armies to stay in power and to guard against invasion.

The first Chinese armies fought with horse-drawn chariots and bronze weapons. Later, battles were fought with iron weapons, horsemen and hundreds of thousands of footsoldiers. Armour was made of metal, lacquered leather or padded quilting. Weapons included bows and arrows, powerful crossbows, swords and halberds (long blades on poles). As the empire grew, the Han Chinese came into conflict with the many peoples whose lands now lay in China.

PRECIOUS SPEAR
This spearhead is over 3,200 years old. It was made from the precious stone jade set in bronze and turquoise. The spear was intended for ceremonial use, as it was far too precious to be used in combat.

SOLDIER ON HORSEBACK
A Tang dynasty warrior sits astride his horse, ready for battle. His horse is also ready to fight, covered by a protective jacket. The warrior's feet are supported by stirrups. These were useful in combat, as they allowed a soldier to remain steady in the saddle as he fought.

MAKE CHINESE ARMOUR

You will need: 150cm x 70cm felt fabric, scissors, large sewing needle, string, silver card, ruler, pencil, tape, split pins, silver paint, paintbrush, water pot, thick card, glue and brush.

1 Fold felt fabric in half. Cut a semicircle along fold to make a neck hole. Put garment on. Trim so it just reaches your hips and covers your shoulders.

2 Use scissors to make 2 holes either side of the waist. Pass string through holes. Secure as shown. The string will be used to tie the garment to your waist.

3 Cut 70 squares (5cm x 5cm) out of silver card. Lay a row of overlapping squares face down at the top of the fabric. Tape the rows together.

FIGHTING ON THE GREAT WALL

In 1884–1885, heavily armed French soldiers engaged in battle with the Chinese. The empire was in decline by the 1880s, and its outdated tactics were no match for the superior might of the French forces.

BATTLING HAN

This battered-looking helmet would once have protected a Han soldier's head from crossbow bolts, sword blows and arrows. Young men were conscripted into the Chinese army and had to serve as soldiers for at least two years. During this time they received no payment. However, they were supplied with food, weapons and armour.

FRONTIER GUARD

A battle-hardened soldier keeps guard with his shield and spear. A warrior like this would have kept watch over the precious Silk Road in a distant outpost of the Chinese empire. This model dates from the reign of the Tang emperor Taizong (AD626–649).

To put on your armour, pull the undergarment over your head. Ask a friend to help with the waist ties. Make holes in the shoulder pads and tie on with string.

4 Make enough rows to cover fabric. Trim card to fit at neck. Tape rows together. Take armour off fabric and turn over. Attach split pins at all corners.

5 Place armour over fabric. Push split pins through top and bottom corners of armour. Pass pins through fabric and fasten. Paint split pins silver.

6 Cut shoulder pads out of thick card. Cut out 5cm squares of silver card to cover pads. Glue to card. Push split pins through. Paint pins silver.

Festivals and Customs

THE CHINESE FESTIVAL best known around the world today is the New Year or Spring Festival. Its date varies according to the traditional Chinese calendar, which is based on the phases of the moon. The festival is marked by dancers carrying a long dragon through the streets, accompanied by loud, crackling firecrackers to scare away evil spirits. The festival has been celebrated for over 2,000 years and has always been a time for family feasts and village carnivals. The doorways of buildings are traditionally decorated with hand-written poetry on strips of red paper to bring luck and good fortune for the coming year.

Soon after New Year, sweet dumplings made of rice flour are prepared for the Lantern Festival. Paper lanterns are hung out to mirror the first full moon of the year. This festival began during the Tang dynasty (AD618–906). In the eighth month of the year, the autumn full moon is marked by the eating of special moon cakes. Chinese festivals are linked to agricultural seasons. They include celebrations of sowing and harvest, dances, horse races and the eating of specially prepared foods.

DANCING ANIMALS
Chinese New Year parades are often headed by a lion (*shown above*) or dragon. These are carried by dancers accompanied by crashing cymbals. The first month of the Chinese calendar begins on the first full moon between 21 January and 19 February.

HORSE RACING
The Mongols, who invaded China in the 1200s, brought with them their love of horses and superb riding skills. Today, children as young as three years old take part in horse-racing festivals in northern China and Mongolia. Archery and wrestling competitions are also regularly held.

MAKE A LANTERN

You will need: thick card, pencil, ruler, scissors, compasses, glue and brush, red tissue paper, blue paint, paintbrush, water pot, thin blue and yellow card, wire, tape, bamboo stick, torch, fringing fabric.

25cm

Frame (x4)

18cm

1cm

18cm

2.5cm

Side (x4)

16cm

End (x2)

18cm

Using the measurements above, draw the 10 pieces on to thick card (pieces not drawn to scale). Cut out pieces with scissors.

1 Using compasses, draw an 8cm diameter circle in the middle of one of the end pieces. Cut out the circle with scissors. Glue on the 4 sides, as shown.

2 Glue together the frame pieces. Then glue the end pieces on to the frame. When dry, cover frame with red tissue paper. Glue one side at a time.

DRAGON BOATS

In the fifth month of the Chinese year, races are held in the Dragon Boat festival. This is in memory of a famous statesman called Qu Yuan, who drowned himself in 278BC when his advice to his ruler was ignored. Rice dumplings are eaten at the Dragon Boat festival every year in his memory.

CHINESE LANTERNS

Elaborate paper lanterns brighten up a wedding in the 1800s during the Qing dynasty. Lanterns were also strung up or paraded on poles at other private celebrations and during Chinese festivals.

3 Paint top of lantern blue. Cut borders out of blue card. Glue to top and bottom of frame. Stick a thin strip of yellow card to bottom border.

4 Make 2 small holes opposite each other at top of lantern. Pass the ends of a loop of wire through each hole. Bend and tape ends to secure wire.

5 Make a hook from thick card. Split end opposite hook. Glue and wrap around bamboo stick. Hang lantern by wire loop from hook.

Light up your lantern by placing a small torch inside it. Decorate with a fringe. Now you can join in Chinese celebrations!

ANCIENT JAPAN

*Japan is made up of four main islands –
Kyushu, Shikoku, Honshu and Hokkaido – plus
almost 4,000 smaller islands. Around 1,500
years ago, the rulers of Yamato in central Japan
claimed the right to control all Japan and to be
honoured as emperors. They were later succeeded
by the military rulers known as shoguns.*

FIONA MACDONALD

Consultant: Heidi Potter, Japanese Festival Society

The Land of the Rising Sun

I MAGINE YOU COULD TRAVEL BACK in time 32,000 years. That was when the first settlers reached Japan – a chain of islands between the Asian mainland and the vast Pacific Ocean. On their arrival, the early settlers would have encountered a varied and extreme landscape of rugged cliffs and spectacular volcanoes. Over the centuries, a distinctive Japanese civilization grew up, shaped by this dramatic environment. The Japanese people became experts at surviving in a harsh land. Emperors and shoguns, feuding samurai and peasant workers all played their part in the history of these islands. Many castles, temples, inventions and works of art have survived from the past to tell us what Japanese life was like in ancient times.

ANCIENT POTTERY
This decorated clay pot was made by Jomon craftworkers around 3000BC. The Jomon people were some of the earliest inhabitants of Japan. Jomon craftworkers were probably the first in the world to discover how to bake clay in fires to produce tough, long-lasting pots.

EARLY SETTLERS
The Ainu people live at the northern tip of Japan. They look unlike most other people in Japan, and speak a different language. Historians believe that they are probably descended from early settlers from Siberia.

TIMELINE 30,000BC–AD550

From around 30,000BC onwards the Japanese islands have been inhabited. For long periods during its history, Japan was isolated from the outside world. In 1854 that isolation came to an end.

*c.*30,000BC The first inhabitants of Japan arrive, probably across a bridge of dry land, from the continent of Asia.

*c.*20,000BC Sea-levels rise and the Japanese islands are cut off from the rest of the world.

*c.*10,000BC The JOMON PERIOD begins. The Jomon people are hunter-gatherers who live mainly on the coasts. The world's first pottery is invented in Japan.

early pottery

*c.*3000–2000BC People from the Jomon culture move inland. They begin to grow food crops.

*c.*2000–300BC The Jomon people move back towards the coasts and develop new sea-fishing techniques.

rice fields

*c.*300BC The YAYOI PERIOD begins. Settlers from South-east Asia and Korea arrive in Japan, bringing knowledge of paddy-field rice cultivation, metalwork and cloth-making techniques. Japanese society is transformed from wandering groups of hunters and gatherers. Communities of farmers live together in settled villages.

Yayoi bell

30,000BC   10,000BC   500BC   AD30

DAIMYO AND SAMURAI

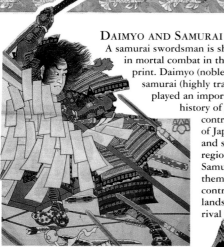

A samurai swordsman is shown locked in mortal combat in this woodblock print. Daimyo (noble warlords) and samurai (highly trained warriors) played an important part in the history of Japan. Daimyo controlled large areas of Japan (domains), and served as regional governors. Samurai helped them to keep control of their lands, and fight rival warlords.

CHINA

RUSSIA

Sea of Okhotsk

HOKKAIDO

NORTH KOREA

JAPAN

Sea of Japan

SOUTH KOREA

HONSHU

N

SHIKOKU

KYUSHU

Pacific Ocean

MAGNIFICENT CASTLES

During the 1500s and 1600s, Japanese craftworkers built many magnificent castles. This one at Matsumoto was completed in 1594–97. Originally, castles were built for defence, but later they became proud status symbols. They were signs of their owners' great power and wealth.

THE ISLANDS OF JAPAN

The four main islands of Japan stretch across several climate zones, from the cold north-east to the semi-tropical south-west. In the past, each island had its own character. For example, northerners were said to be tough and patient, people from the central region were believed to value glory and honour more than money, while men from the south were regarded as the best fighters.

*c.*AD300 KOFUN (Old Tomb) PERIOD begins. A new culture develops. New bronze- and iron-working techniques are invented. Several small kingdoms grow up in different regions of Japan. Rulers of these kingdoms build huge mound-shaped tombs. There are wars between the kingdoms.

花刺蟲飛

Chinese writing

*c.*AD400 The Chinese method of writing arrives in Japan. It is brought by Buddhist scholars and monks who come from China to work for the emperors of Japan.

royal tomb

*c.*AD500 The YAMATO PERIOD begins. Kings from the Yamato region become powerful. They gradually take control of large areas of Japan by making alliances with local chiefs. The Yamato rulers also claim spiritual power, by descent from the Sun goddess, Amaterasu. Calling themselves emperors, they set up a powerful imperial court, appoint officials and award noble titles.

Mount Fuji

AD400

AD500

AD550

Eastern Islands

JAPAN IS MADE UP of four main islands – Kyushu, Shikoku, Honshu and Hokkaido – plus almost 4,000 smaller islands around the coast. According to legend, these islands were formed when tears shed by a goddess dropped into the sea. The first settlers arrived on the Japanese islands about 30,000BC and by 10,000BC, a hunter-gatherer civilization, called Jomon, had developed there. At first, the Jomon people lived by the sea and survived by collecting shellfish and hunting animals. Later, they moved inland, where they cultivated garden plots. After 300BC, settlers arrived from Korea, introducing new skills such as rice-growing and iron-working. People began to live in rice-growing villages around AD300 and, in time, groups of these villages came to be controlled by local lords.

Around AD500, the rulers of Yamato in central Japan became stronger than the rulers of the other regions. They claimed the right to rule all of Japan, and to be honoured as emperors. These emperors built new cities, where they lived with their courtiers. However, by 1185 rule of the country had passed to the shogun (a military ruler). There were bitter civil wars when rival warlords fought to become shogun. In 1600, the wars ended when the mighty Tokugawa Ieyasu became shogun. For over 250 years the shogun came from the Tokugawa family. This family controlled Japan until 1868, when Emperor Meiji regained the emperor's ancient ruling power.

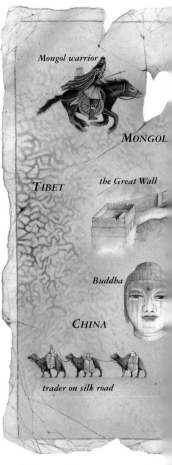

Mongol warrior

MONGOL

TIBET

the Great Wall

Buddha

CHINA

trader on silk road

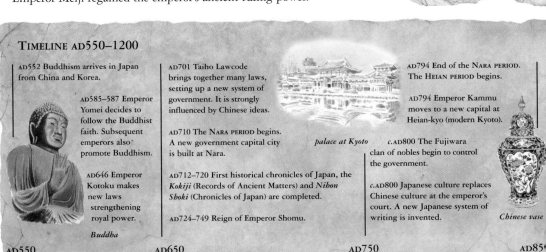

TIMELINE AD550–1200

AD552 Buddhism arrives in Japan from China and Korea.

AD585–587 Emperor Yomei decides to follow the Buddhist faith. Subsequent emperors also promote Buddhism.

AD646 Emperor Kotoku makes new laws strengthening royal power.

Buddha

AD701 Taiho Lawcode brings together many laws, setting up a new system of government. It is strongly influenced by Chinese ideas.

AD710 The NARA PERIOD begins. A new government capital city is built at Nara.

AD712–720 First historical chronicles of Japan, the *Kokiji* (Records of Ancient Matters) and *Nihon Shoki* (Chronicles of Japan) are completed.

AD724–749 Reign of Emperor Shomu.

palace at Kyoto

AD794 End of the NARA PERIOD. The HEIAN PERIOD begins.

AD794 Emperor Kammu moves to a new capital at Heian-kyo (modern Kyoto).

c.AD800 The Fujiwara clan of nobles begin to control the government.

c.AD800 Japanese culture replaces Chinese culture at the emperor's court. A new Japanese system of writing is invented.

Chinese vase

AD550   AD650   AD750   AD85•

POWERFUL NEIGHBOURS

Japan's nearest neighbours are China and Korea, two of the world's most advanced civilizations during the period AD550–1185. From them, Japanese people learned many valuable skills, including writing and woodblock printing. However, because it was surrounded by sea, Japan remained independent and developed a unique civilization of its own.

N
W   E
S

Ainu man

Hokkaido

China

southern gate, Seoul

Yellow Sea

samurai warrior

Sea of Japan

Rynkyn Islands

Korea

Honshu

rice terraces

torrii

Okinawa

East China Sea

Mount Fuji

Dutch trading vessel

Shikoku

Pacific Ocean

Kyushu

Kong Fuzi (Confucius)

to the Rynkyn Islands

AD894 Links with China are broken.

c.AD900 The invention of new scripts for written Japanese leads to the growth of various kinds of literature. These works include collections of poetry, diaries, notebooks and novels. Many of the finest examples are written by rich, well-educated women at the emperor's court.

c.AD965 The birth of Sei Shonagon. Sei Shonagon is a courtier admired for her learning and for her witty and outspoken comments on people, places and events. She writes a famous pillow book (diary).

c.AD1000 *The Tale of Genji,* written by Lady Murasaki Shikibu, is completed. This was the story of love, politics and intrigue within the royal court. *The Tale of Genji* is one of the world's first novels. Lady Murasaki was the daughter of a powerful nobleman. She began to write after the death of her husband.

Lady Murasaki

AD1159 The Heiji civil war breaks out between two powerful clans, the Taira and the Minamoto. The Taira are victorious.

AD1185 Successive emperors lose control of the regions to warlike nobles. The HEIAN PERIOD ends. The Minamoto family, led by Minamoto Yoritomo, defeat the Taira. They gain control of most of Japan and set up a rival government at Kamakura, far from the imperial capital of Kyoto. Yoritomo takes the title of shogun.

Minamoto Yoritomo

AD1000   AD1100   AD1200

The Powerful and Famous

THE HISTORY OF ANCIENT JAPAN records the deeds of famous heroes, powerful emperors and bold warriors. Men and women who had won respect for their achievements in learning, religion and the arts were also held in high regard. In early Japanese society, royal traditions, honour, skill and bravery in battle were considered to be important, as was devotion to serious study. These principles mattered far more than the accumulation of wealth, or the invention of something new. Business people, no matter how successful, were in the lowest social class. However, during the Tokugawa period (1600–1868) many did gain financial power. Hard-working farmers, though in theory respected, led very difficult lives.

PRINCE YAMATO
Many stories were told about the daring adventures of this legendary hero. Prince Yamato probably never existed, but he is important because he symbolizes the power of Japan's first emperors. These emperors came from the Yamato region.

EMPRESS JINGU (ruled *c.*AD200)
According to Japanese legends, Empress (Kogo) Jingu ruled in about AD200, on behalf of her son. Many legends tell of her magic skills, such as her ability to control the waves and tides.

TIMELINE AD1200–1868

*c.*AD1200 Trade increases and a new coinage is developed. Zen Buddhism becomes popular during this period, especially with samurai warriors.

AD1274–1281 Mongols attempt to invade, but are driven back by storms.

samurai warrior

AD1331–1333 Emperor Godaigo tries to win back royal power. He fails, but his bid leads to a rebellion against the shogun.

AD1336 Ashikaga Takauji takes power and installs Emperor Komyo. He moves his court to Kyoto and encourages art and culture. Links with China are re-opened.

AD1338 Ashikaga Takauji takes the title shogun. The MUROMACHI PERIOD begins.

samurai swords

AD1467–1477 The Onin War – a civil war between rival nobles and provincial governors. The shogun's power collapses for a time. This is the first in a series of civil wars lasting until the 1590s. New daimyo (warlords) conquer vast territories in different regions.

AD1540 The first European traders and missionaries arrive in Japan. European traders hope to find spices and rich silks. European missionaries want to spread the Christian faith throughout Japan.

Portuguese sailor

AD1200   AD1300   AD1400   AD1500

TOYOTOMI HIDEYOSHI (1536–1598)

Hideyoshi was a famous war-leader. Along with two other great warlords, Oda Nobunaga and Tokugawa Ieyasu, he helped to unite Japan. The country was unified in 1590, after years of bloody civil war. As a peace measure, Hideyoshi banned everyone except samurai from carrying swords.

LADY MURASAKI SHIKIBU (c.AD978–1014)

The writer Lady Murasaki spent much of her life at the royal court as an attendant to Empress Akiko. Her book, *The Tale of Genji*, tells the story of the life and loves of Genji, a Japanese prince, in a sensitive and poetic style.

THE MEIJI EMPEROR (1852–1912)

The Meiji imperial family are shown in this painting. The emperor began his reign in 1867. The following year the shoguns' long period in office was ended when nobles (daimyo) engineered their downfall. The nobles then installed the emperor as a figurehead ruler.

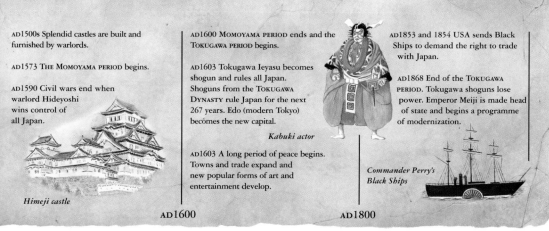

AD1500s Splendid castles are built and furnished by warlords.

AD1573 THE MOMOYAMA PERIOD begins.

AD1590 Civil wars end when warlord Hideyoshi wins control of all Japan.

Himeji castle

AD1600 MOMOYAMA PERIOD ends and the TOKUGAWA PERIOD begins.

AD1603 Tokugawa Ieyasu becomes shogun and rules all Japan. Shoguns from the TOKUGAWA DYNASTY rule Japan for the next 267 years. Edo (modern Tokyo) becomes the new capital.

Kabuki actor

AD1603 A long period of peace begins. Towns and trade expand and new popular forms of art and entertainment develop.

AD1853 and 1854 USA sends Black Ships to demand the right to trade with Japan.

AD1868 End of the TOKUGAWA PERIOD. Tokugawa shoguns lose power. Emperor Meiji is made head of state and begins a programme of modernization.

Commander Perry's Black Ships

AD1600

AD1800

God-like Emperors

HANIWA FIGURE
From around AD300 to AD550, hollow clay figures were placed around the edges of tombs. These figures, shaped like humans or animals, are known as Haniwa.

THE JAPANESE PEOPLE began to live in villages in about 300BC. Over the next 600 years, the richest and most powerful of these villages became the centres of small kingdoms, controlling the surrounding lands. By about AD300, a kingdom based on the Yamato Plain in south-central Japan became bigger and stronger than the rest. It was ruled by chiefs of an *uji* (clan) who claimed to be descended from the Sun goddess. The chiefs of this Sun-clan were not only army commanders – they were priests, governors, law-makers and controllers of their people's treasure and food supply. Over the years, their powers increased. By around AD500, Sun-clan chiefs from Yamato ruled over most of Japan. They claimed power as emperors, and organized lesser chiefs to work for them, giving them noble titles as a reward. Each emperor chose his own successor from within the Sun-clan, and handed over to him the sacred symbols of imperial power – a jewel, a mirror and a sword. Sometimes, if a male successor to the throne was not old enough to rule, an empress would rule as regent in his place.

Descendants of these early emperors still rule Japan today. However, at times they had very little power. Some emperors played an active part in politics, but others spent their time shut away from the outside world. Today, the emperor has only a ceremonial role in the government of Japan.

NARA
This shrine is in the ancient city of Nara. Originally called Heijokyo, Nara was founded by Empress Gemmei (ruled AD707–715) as a new capital for her court. The city was planned and built in Chinese style, with streets arranged in a grid pattern. The Imperial Palace was situated at the northern edge.

FANTASTIC STORIES

Prince Shotoku (AD574–622) was descended from the imperial family and from another powerful clan, the Soga. He never became emperor, but ruled as regent for 30 years on behalf of Empress Suiko. Many fantastic stories were told about him – for example, that he was able to speak as soon as he was born. It was also said that he could see into the future. More accurate reports of his achievements list his introduction of a new calendar, and his reform of government, based on Chinese ideas. He was also a supporter of the new Buddhist faith, introduced from China.

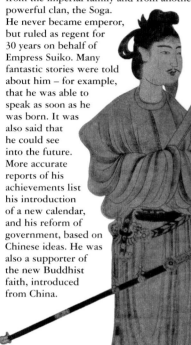

LARGEST WOODEN STRUCTURE

The Hall of the Great Buddha at Nara was founded on the orders of Emperor Shomu in AD745. The whole temple complex is said to be the largest wooden structure in the world. It houses a bronze statue of the Buddha, 16m tall and weighing 500 tonnes, and was also designed to display the emperor's wealth and power. There is a treasury close to the Hall of the Great Buddha, built in AD756. This housed the belongings of Emperor Shomu and his wife, Empress Komyo. The treasury still contains many rare and valuable items.

BURIAL MOUNDS

The Yamato emperors were buried in huge, mound-shaped tombs surrounded by lakes. The largest, built for Emperor Nintoku, is 480m long. From above, the tombs have a keyhole-shaped layout. Inside, they contain many buried treasures.

THE SUN GODDESS

The Sun goddess Amaterasu Omikami is shown emerging from the earth in this print. She was both honoured and feared by Japanese farmers. One of the emperor's tasks was to act as a link between the goddess and his people, asking for her help on their behalf. The goddess's main shrine was at Ise, in central Japan. Some of its buildings were designed to look like grain stores – a reminder of the Sun's power to cause a good or a bad harvest.

Nobles and Courtiers

I**N EARLY JAPAN**, everyone from the proudest chief to the poorest peasant owed loyalty to the emperor. However, many nobles ignored the emperor's orders – especially when they were safely out of reach of his court. There were plots and secret schemes as rival nobles struggled to influence the emperor and to seize power for themselves.

Successive emperors passed laws to try to keep their nobles and courtiers under control. The most important new laws were introduced by Prince Shotoku (AD574–622) and Prince Naka no Oe (AD626–671). Prince Naka considered his laws to be so important that he gave them the name Taika (Great Change). The Taika laws created a strong central government, run by a Grand Council of State, and a well-organized network of officials to oversee the 67 provinces.

BUGAKU
A Bugaku performer makes a slow, stately movement. Bugaku is an ancient form of dance that was popular at the emperor's court over 1,000 years ago. It is still performed there today.

POLITE BEHAVIOUR
A group of ladies watches an archery contest from behind a screen at the edge of a firing range. The behaviour of courtiers was governed by rigid etiquette. Noble ladies had to follow especially strict rules. It was bad-mannered for them to show their faces in public. Whenever men were present, the ladies crouched behind a low curtain or a screen, or hid their faces behind their wide sleeves or their fans. To protect their faces when travelling, they concealed themselves behind curtains or sliding panels fitted to their ox-carts. They also often left one sleeve dangling outside.

THE SHELL GAME
You will need: fresh clams, water bowl, paintbrush, gold paint, white paint, black paint, red paint, green paint, water pot.

1 Ask an adult to boil the clams. Allow them to cool and then remove the insides. Wash the shells and leave them to dry. When dry, paint the shells gold.

2 Carefully pull each pair of shells apart. Now paint an identical design on to each of a pair of clam shells. Start by painting a white, round face.

3 Add features to the face. In the past, popular pictures, such as scenes from the *Tale of Genji*, were painted on to the shell pairs.

THE IMPERIAL COURT

Life at court was both elegant and refined. The buildings were exquisite and set in beautiful gardens. Paintings based on the writings of courtiers show some of the famous places they enjoyed visiting.

NOBLES AT COURT

Two nobles are shown here riding a splendid horse. Noblemen at the imperial court spent much of their time on government business. They also practised their riding and fighting skills, took part in court ceremonies, and read and wrote poetry.

THE FUJIWARA CLAN

Fujiwara Teika (1162–1241) was a poet and a member of the Fujiwara clan. This influential family gained power at court by arranging the marriages of their daughters to young princes and emperors. Between AD724 and 1900, 54 of the 76 emperors of Japan had mothers who were related to the Fujiwara clan.

A LOOK INSIDE

This scroll-painting shows rooms inside the emperor's palace and groups of courtiers strolling in the gardens outside. Indoors, the rooms are divided up by silken blinds and the courtiers sit on mats and cushions.

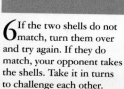

4 Paint several pairs of clam shells with various designs. Make sure that each pair of shells has an identical picture. Leave the painted shells to dry.

5 Turn all your shells face down and mix them up well. Turn over one shell then challenge your opponent to pick the matching shell to yours.

6 If the two shells do not match, turn them over and try again. If they do match, your opponent takes the shells. Take it in turns to challenge each other.

The person with the most shells wins! Noble ladies at the imperial court enjoyed playing the shell game. This is a simplified version of the game they used to play.

Shoguns and Civil Wars

IN 1159, a bloody civil war, known as the Heiji War, broke out in Japan between two powerful clans, the Taira and the Minamoto. The Taira were victorious in the Heiji War, and they controlled the government of the country for 26 years. However, the Minamoto rose again and regrouped to defeat the Taira in 1185.

Yoritomo, leader of the Minamoto clan, became the most powerful man in Japan and set up a new headquarters in the city of Kamakura. The emperor continued to act as head of the government in Kyoto, but he was effectively powerless. For almost the next 700 years, until 1868, military commanders such as Yoritomo were the real rulers of Japan. They were known by the title *sei i tai shogun*, an army term meaning Great General Subduing the Barbarians.

SHOGUN FOR LIFE
Minamoto Yoritomo was the first person to take the title shogun and to hand the title on to his sons. In fact, the title did not stay in the Minamoto family for long because the family line died out in 1219. But new shogun families soon took its place.

FIRE! FIRE!
This scroll-painting illustrates the end of a siege during the Heiji War. The war was fought between two powerful clans, the Taira and the Minamoto. The rival armies set fire to buildings by shooting burning arrows and so drove the inhabitants out into the open where they could be killed.

MAKE A KITE
You will need: A1 card, ruler, pencil, dowelling sticks tapered at each end (5 x 50cm, 2 x 70cm), masking tape, scissors, glue, brush, thread, paintbrush, paints, water pot, paper (52cm x 52cm), string, bamboo stick.

1 Draw a square 50cm x 50cm on card with a line down the centre. Lay the dowelling sticks on the square. Glue the sticks to each other and then tape.

2 When the glue has dried, remove the masking tape. Take the frame off the card. Bind the corners of the frame with the strong thread.

3 Now position your two longer dowelling sticks so that they cross in the middle of the square. Glue and then bind the corners with the strong thread.

DYNASTY FOUNDER

Tokugawa Ieyasu (1542-1616) was a noble from eastern Japan. He was one of three powerful warlords who brought long years of civil war to an end and unified Japan. In 1603 he won the battle of Sekigahara and became shogun. His family, the Tokugawa, ruled Japan for the next 267 years.

RESTING PLACE

This mausoleum (burial chamber) was built at Nikko in north-central Japan. It was created to house the body of the mighty shogun Tokugawa Ieyasu. Three times a year, Ieyasu's descendants travelled to Nikko to pay homage to their great ancestor.

UNDER ATTACK

Life in Nijo Castle, Kyoto, is shown in great detail on this painted screen. The castle belonged to the Tokugawa family of shoguns. Like emperors, great shoguns built themselves fine castles, which they used as centres of government or as fortresses in times of war. Nijo Castle was one of the finest buildings in Japan. It had 'nightingale' floors that creaked loudly when an intruder stepped on them, raising the alarm. The noise was made to sound like a bird call.

Kites were sometimes used for signalling during times of war. The Japanese have also enjoyed playing with kites for over 1,000 years.

4 Paint a colourful kite pattern on to the paper. It is a good idea to tape the edges of the paper down so it does not move around or curl up.

5 Draw light pencil marks 1cm in from the corners of the paper on all four sides. Carefully cut out the corners of the paper, as shown.

6 Glue the paper on to the kite frame. You will need to glue along the wooden frame and fold the paper over the edge of the frame. Leave to dry.

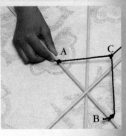

7 Tie a short length of string across the centre of the kite frame (A to B). Knot a long kite string on to it as shown (C). Wind the string on the bamboo.

Samurai

BETWEEN 1185 AND 1600 there were a great many wars as rival nobles (known as 'daimyo') fought to become shogun. Some emperors also tried, unsuccessfully, to restore imperial rule. During this troubled time in Japanese history, emperors, shoguns and daimyo all relied on armies of well-trained samurai (warriors) to fight their battles. The samurai were men from noble families, and they were skilled at fighting battles. Members of each samurai army were bound together by a solemn oath, sworn to their lord. They stayed loyal from a sense of honour – and because their lord gave them rich rewards. The civil wars ended around 1600, when the Tokugawa dynasty of shoguns came to power. From this time onwards, samurai spent less time fighting. Instead, they served their lords as officials and business managers.

RIDING OFF TO WAR
Painted in 1772, this samurai general is in full armour. A samurai's horse had to be fast, agile and strong enough to carry the full weight of the samurai, his armour and his weapons.

TACHI
Swords were a favourite weapon of the samurai. This long sword is called a *tachi*. It was made in the 1500s for ceremonial use by a samurai.

METAL HELMET
Samurai helmets like this were made from curved metal panels, carefully fitted together, and decorated with elaborate patterns. The jutting peak protected the wearer's face and the nape-guard covered the back of the neck. This helmet dates from around 1380.

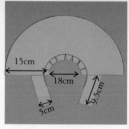

SAMURAI HELMET
You will need: *thick card, pin, string, felt-tip pen, ruler, scissors, tape measure, newspaper, bowl, water, PVA glue, balloon, petroleum jelly, pencil, modelling clay, bradawl, paper, gold card, paints, brush, water pot, glue brush, masking tape, paper fasteners, 2 x 20cm lengths of cord.*

1 Draw a circle 18cm in diameter on card using the pin, string and felt-tip pen. Using the same method, draw two larger circles 20cm and 50cm.

2 Draw a line across the centre of the three circles using the ruler and felt-tip pen. Draw tabs in the middle semi-circle. Add two flaps as shown.

3 Now cut out the neck protector piece completely, as shown above. Make sure that you cut around the tabs and flaps exactly.

15cm
18cm
5cm
5cm

PROTECTIVE CLOTHING

This fine suit of samurai armour dates from the Tokugawa period (1600–1868). Armour gave the samurai life-saving protection in battle. High-ranking warriors wore suits of plate armour, made of iron panels, laced or riveted together and combined with panels of chain mail or rawhide. Lower-ranking soldiers, called *ashigaru*, wore thinner, lightweight armour, made of small metal plates. A full suit of samurai armour could weigh anything up to 18kg.

SURCOAT FINERY

For festivals, ceremonies and parades samurai wore surcoats (long, loose tunics) over their armour. Surcoats were made from fine, glossy silks, dyed in rich colours. This example was made during the Tokugawa period (1600–1868). Surcoats were often decorated with family crests. These were originally used to identify soldiers in battle, but later became badges of high rank.

MAKING BOWS

Japanese craftworkers are busy at work making bows, around 1600. The bow was the Japanese warrior's most ancient weapon. Bows were made of wood and bamboo and fired many different kinds of arrow.

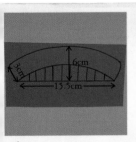

4 Draw the peak template piece on another piece of card. Follow the measurements shown in the picture. Cut out the peak template.

5 To make papier-mâché, tear the newspaper into small strips. Fill the bowl with 1 part PVA glue to 3 parts water. Add the newspaper strips.

6 Blow up the balloon to the size of your head. Cover with petroleum jelly. Build up three papier-mâché layers on the top and sides. Leave to dry between layers.

7 When dry, pop the balloon and trim. Ask a friend to make a mark on either side of your head.

Instructions for the helmet continue on the next page...

The Way of the Warrior

SAMURAI were highly-trained warriors who dedicated their lives to fighting for their lords. However, being a samurai involved more than just fighting. The ideal samurai was supposed to follow a strict code of behaviour, governing all aspects of his life. This code was called *bushido* – the way of the warrior. *Bushido* called for skill, self-discipline, bravery, loyalty, honour, honesty, obedience and, at times, self-sacrifice. It taught that it was nobler to die fighting than to run away and survive.

Many samurai warriors followed the religious teachings of Zen, a branch of the Buddhist faith. Zen was introduced into Japan by two monks, Eisai and Dogen, who went to China to study in the 1100s and 1200s and brought Zen practices back with them. Teachers of Zen encouraged their followers to meditate (to free the mind of all thoughts) in order to achieve enlightenment.

THE TAKEDA FAMILY
The famous daimyo (warlord) Takeda Shingen (1521–1573), fires an arrow using his powerful bow. The influential Takeda family owned estates in Kai province near the city of Edo and kept a large private army of samurai warriors. Takeda Shingen fought a series of wars with his near neighbour, Uesugi Kenshin. However, in 1581, the Takeda were defeated by the army of General Nobunaga.

SWORDSMEN
It took young samurai many years to master the skill of swordsmanship. They were trained by master swordsmen. The best swords, made of strong, springy steel, were even given their own names.

8 Place clay under the pencil marks. Make two holes – one above and one below each pencil mark – with a bradawl. Repeat on the other side.

9 Fold a piece of A4 paper and draw a horn shape on to it following the design shown above. Cut out this shape so that you have an identical pair of horns.

10 Take a piece of A4 size gold card. Place your paper horns on to the gold card and draw around them. Carefully cut the horns out of the card.

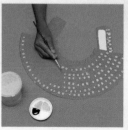

11 Paint the papier-mâché helmet brown. Paint a weave design on the neck protector and a cream block on each flap. Leave to dry.

OFF TO WAR

A samurai warrior (on horseback) and foot-soldiers set off for war. Samurai had to command and inspire confidence in others, so it was especially important for them to behave in a brave and honourable way.

MARTIAL ARTS

Several sports that people enjoy playing today have developed from samurai fighting skills. In aikido, players try to throw their opponent off-balance and topple them to the ground. In kendo, players fight one another with long swords made of split bamboo. They score points by managing to touch their opponent's body, not by cutting or stabbing them!

kendo   *aikido*

SURVIVAL SKILLS

Samurai had to know how to survive in wild countryside. Each man carried emergency rations of dried rice. He also used his fighting skills to hunt wild animals for food.

ZEN

The Buddhist monk Rinzai is shown in this Japanese brush and ink scroll-painting. Rinzai was a famous teacher of Zen ideas. Many pupils, including samurai, travelled to his remote monastery in the mountains to study with him.

Samurai helmets were often decorated with crests made of lacquered wood or metal. These were mounted on the top of the helmet.

12 Bend back the tabs on the peak piece. Position it at the front of the helmet. Stick the tabs to the inside with glue. Hold in place with tape.

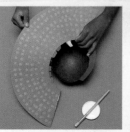

13 Now take the neck protector. Bend back the front flaps and the tabs. Glue the tabs to the helmet, as shown. Leave the helmet to dry.

14 Stick the horns to the front of the helmet. Use paper fasteners to secure, as shown. Decorate the ear flaps with paper fasteners.

15 Thread cord through one of the holes made in step 8. Tie a knot in the end. Thread the other end of the cord through the second hole. Repeat on the other side.

Peasant Farmers

Until the 1900s, most Japanese people lived in the countryside and made a living either by fishing or by farming small plots of land. Japanese farmers grew crops for three different reasons. They grew rice to sell to the samurai or to pay taxes. Barley, millet, wheat and vegetables were used for their own food.

Traditionally, Japanese society was divided into four main classes – samurai, peasant farmers, craftworkers and merchants. Samurai were the most highly respected. Farmers and craftworkers came next because they produced useful goods. Merchants were the lowest rank because they produced nothing themselves.

During the Tokugawa period (1600–1868), society began to change. Towns and cities grew bigger, small industries developed and trade increased. Farmers began to sell their crops to people who had no land of their own. For the first time, some farmers had money to spend on better clothes, houses, and more food.

WRESTLERS
Sumo wrestling has long been a favourite sport in Japan. It developed from religious rituals and from games held at farmers' festivals in the countryside. Sumo wrestlers are usually very fat. They use their massive weight to overbalance their opponents.

RICE FARMING
Planting out tiny rice seedlings in shallow, muddy water was tiring, back-breaking work. Rice farming was introduced to Japan soon after 300BC. Most varieties of rice need to grow in flooded fields, called *tanbo* (paddy-fields). To provide extra food, farmers also reared fish in the *tanbo*.

TERRACING
It was difficult to find enough flat land for growing crops in Japan, so terraces were cut, like steps, into the steep hillsides. Farmland could be shaken by earthquakes or ruined by floods. In years when the harvests failed, there was often famine.

FAVOURITE FOODS
Soya beans and *daikon* (white radishes) were two popular Japanese foods. The Japanese developed storage methods that would allow them to last for months. The radishes were covered in earth and the beans were dried to provide essential winter food supplies. Farmers grew vegetables like these in small garden plots or in terraced fields.

daikon
radish

soya beans

A HARD LIFE
A woman farm-worker carries heavy baskets of grain on a wooden yoke. Although farmers were respected, their lives were often very hard. Until the late 1800s, they had to pay heavy taxes to the emperor or the local lord and were not free to leave their lord's land. They were also forbidden from wearing silk clothes, and drinking tea or *sake* (rice wine).

THRESHING
Japanese farmers are busy threshing wheat in this photograph taken in the late 1800s. Although this picture is relatively recent, the method of threshing has changed little over the centuries. The workers at the far right and the far left are separating the grains of wheat from the stalks by pulling them through wooden sieves. In the background, one worker carries a huge bundle of wheat stalks, while another stands ready with a rake and a winnowing fan. The fan was used to remove the chaff from the grain by tossing the grain in the air so that the wind blew the chaff away.

Treasures from the Sea

JAPAN IS A NATION OF ISLANDS, and few people live very far from the sea. From the earliest times, Japanese people relied on the sea for food. Farms, fishing villages and huts for drying fish and seaweed were all built along Japan's rugged coastline. Heaps of oyster shells and fish bones, thrown away by the Jomon people, have survived from over 10,000 years ago.

Japanese men and women took many different kinds of food from the sea. They found crabs, shrimps and limpets in shallow water by the shore, or set sail in small boats to catch deep-sea varieties such as tuna, mackerel, shark, whale and squid. Japanese people also gathered seaweed (which contains important minerals) and other sea creatures such as jellyfish and sea-slugs. Underwater, they found treasures such as pearls and coral which were both highly prized. Specially trained divers, often women, risked their lives by holding their breath for long periods underwater to harvest these precious items. The sea also provided salt, which was collected in salt-pans (hollows built next to the sea). Salt was used to preserve fish and vegetables and to make pickles of many different kinds.

INSPIRATIONAL
Strange and beautiful sea creatures inspired Japanese painters and print-makers to create many works of art. This painting shows two flat fish and a collection of shellfish. Tuna, sea bream and salmon were all popular fish caught around the coast of Japan. They were usually grilled or preserved by salting or drying.

DANGEROUS SEAS
Japanese sailors and their boat are tossed around by wind and waves in a rough sea. This scene is depicted in a woodblock print by Utagawa Kuniyoshi. The seas around Japan's rocky coasts are often wild and stormy. Being a fisherman was, and still is, a very risky job. Late summer is the most dangerous season to go fishing because monsoon winds from the Pacific Ocean cause very violent typhoon storms. These storms can easily sink a fishing boat.

FISHING METHODS

For many centuries, Japanese fishermen used only baited hooks and lines. This limited the number of fish they could catch on any one trip. But after 1600 they began to use nets for fishing, which allowed them to make bigger catches.

SEAFOOD

Sea products have always been very important in Japan. Oysters were collected for their pearls and also for eating. Oyster stew is still a favourite dish in southern Japan. Mussels were cooked to make many tasty dishes. They flourish in the wild, but in Japan today they are also farmed. Seaweed was used to give flavour to foods. Today it is also used as the wrapping for *maki sushi* (rolls of vinegared rice with fish and vegetable fillings).

oysters

seaweed

mussel

MOTHER-OF-PEARL

Made around 1500, this domed casket is decorated with mother-of-pearl, a beautiful material that forms the coating on the inside of an oyster shell. With great skill and patience, Japanese craftworkers cut out and shaped tiny pieces of mother-of-pearl. These pieces were used to decorate many valuable items.

OYSTER COLLECTING

Gangs of oyster gatherers collect shellfish from the sea bed. Both men and women are shown working together. Oysters have thick, heavy shells, so the workers have to be fit and strong to carry full buckets back to the shore.

GATHERING SHELLFISH

Painted in the 1800s, this picture makes shellfish-gathering look like a pleasant task. In fact, hands and feet soon became numb with cold and the salt water made them red and raw.

Meals and Manners

JAPANESE FOOD has always been simple but healthy. However, for many centuries famine was a constant fear, especially among the poor. The traditional Japanese diet was based on grains – rice, millet, wheat or barley – boiled, steamed or made into noodles. Many foods were flavoured with soy sauce, made from crushed, fermented soya beans. Another nutritious soya product, *tofu* (beancurd), was made from soya beans softened and pulped in water. The pulp was formed into blocks and left to set. *Tofu* has a texture somewhere between custard and cheese, and a mild taste.

What people ate depended on who they were. Only the wealthy could afford rice, meat (usually poultry) or the finest fish. Poor families lived on what they could grow or catch for themselves.

Until the 1900s, people in Japan did not eat red meat or dairy products. But Japanese farmers grew many fruits, including pears, berries and oranges. One small, sweet orange is named after the Satsuma region in the warm southern lands of Japan.

FRESH VEGETABLES
A vegetable seller is shown here taking his produce to market. He carries it in big baskets hanging from a yoke supported on his shoulders. This photograph was taken around 1900, but the tradition of going to market every day to sell vegetables started some time around 1600. At this time many more people began to live in towns. The Japanese have always liked their food to be very fresh.

ONIGIRI - RICE BALLS
You will need: 7 cups Japanese rice, saucepan, wooden spoon, sieve, bowls, 1 tbsp salt, cutting board, 1 tbsp black sesame seeds, $^1/_2$ sheet yaki nori seaweed (optional), knife, cucumber, serving dish.

1 Ask an adult to boil the rice. Sieve to drain, but do not rinse. The rice should remain gluey. Place the rice in one bowl and the salt into another one.

2 Wet the palms of both hands with cold water. Next, put a finger into the bowl of salt and rub a little on to your palms.

3 Place one eighth of the rice on one hand. Use both hands to shape the rice into a triangle. You should use firm but not heavy pressure.

SAKE

This *sake* bottle was made almost 600 years ago, in the Bizen pottery style. *Sake* is a sweet rice wine. It was drunk by wealthy noble families and by ordinary people on very special occasions. Traditionally, it was served warm from pottery flasks or bottles such as this one and poured into tiny cups.

CHOPSTICKS

Japanese people eat using chopsticks. Traditionally, chopsticks were made from bamboo, but today many different materials, including lacquered wood, are used.
In the past, rich nobles used silver chopsticks. This was mainly to display their wealth. However, they also believed the silver would help them detect any poison that had been slipped into their food. They thought that on contact with the poison, the silver would turn black.

ornate chopsticks

ordinary chopsticks

TEA

A servant offers a bowl of tea to a seated samurai. The Japanese believed that no matter how poor or humble people were, it was important to serve food in a gracious way. Good table manners were essential.

TABLEWARE

Food was served and eaten in pottery bowls and on plates. In contrast to the round and flat dishes found in many other countries, Japanese craftworkers often created tableware in elegant shapes, such as this six-sided dish.

4 Make more rice balls in the same way. Place each rice ball in one hand and sprinkle sesame seeds over the rice ball with the other.

5 If available, cut a strip of yaki nori seaweed into four and wrap some of your rice balls in it. To serve your *onigiri*, garnish them with sliced cucumber.

Rice was introduced to Japan in AD100. It has remained the staple food of the islands ever since. Serve your Japanese meal on a pretty dish and eat it with chopsticks.

Houses and Homes

JAPANESE BUILDERS faced many challenges when they designed homes for Japan's harsh environment. They built lightweight, single-storey houses made of straw, paper and wood. These materials would bend and sway in an earthquake. If they did collapse, or were swept away by floods, they would be less likely than a stone building to injure the people inside.

Japanese buildings were designed as a series of box-like rooms. One room was sufficient for the hut of a farming family, but a whole series of rooms could be linked together to form a royal palace. The space within was divided by screens which could be moved around to suit people's needs. Most houses had raised timber floors that were about $^1/_2$m off the ground.

LAMPS

This pottery lantern has a delicate, cut-out design and was probably for use outdoors. Inside, Japanese homes were lit by candles. A candle was placed on a stand which had four paper sides. The paper protected the candle from draughts. One side could be lifted to insert and remove the candle. There were many different styles and designs. House-fires, caused by cooking and candles, were a major hazard. They were a particular problem because so many homes were made of wood.

SILK HOUSE

For many people in Japan, home was also a place of work. Tucked under the thatched roof of this house in Eiyama, central Japan, was an attic where silk producers bred silk-worms.

MAKE A SCREEN

You will need: gold paper (44cm x 48cm), scissors, thick card (22cm x 48cm), craft knife, metal ruler, cutting board, glue stick, ruler, pencil, paints, paintbrush, water pots, fabric tape.

1 Cut two pieces of gold paper (22cm x 48cm). Use a craft knife to cut out a piece of card the same size. Stick the gold paper to both sides of the card.

2 Use a ruler and pencil to carefully mark out six equal panels, on one side of the card. Each panel should measure 22cm x 8cm.

3 Now turn your card over. Paint a traditional picture of Japanese irises, as shown above. When you have finished, leave the paint to dry.

SAKE

This *sake* bottle was made almost 600 years ago, in the Bizen pottery style. *Sake* is a sweet rice wine. It was drunk by wealthy noble families and by ordinary people on very special occasions. Traditionally, it was served warm from pottery flasks or bottles such as this one and poured into tiny cups.

CHOPSTICKS

Japanese people eat using chopsticks. Traditionally, chopsticks were made from bamboo, but today many different materials, including lacquered wood, are used. In the past, rich nobles used silver chopsticks. This was mainly to display their wealth. However, they also believed the silver would help them detect any poison that had been slipped into their food. They thought that on contact with the poison, the silver would turn black.

ornate chopsticks

ordinary chopsticks

TEA

A servant offers a bowl of tea to a seated samurai. The Japanese believed that no matter how poor or humble people were, it was important to serve food in a gracious way. Good table manners were essential.

TABLEWARE

Food was served and eaten in pottery bowls and on plates. In contrast to the round and flat dishes found in many other countries, Japanese craftworkers often created tableware in elegant shapes, such as this six-sided dish.

4 Make more rice balls in the same way. Place each rice ball in one hand and sprinkle sesame seeds over the rice ball with the other.

5 If available, cut a strip of yaki nori seaweed into four and wrap some of your rice balls in it. To serve your *onigiri*, garnish them with sliced cucumber.

Rice was introduced to Japan in AD100. It has remained the staple food of the islands ever since. Serve your Japanese meal on a pretty dish and eat it with chopsticks.

Family Life

FAMILIES IN ANCIENT JAPAN survived by working together in the family business or on the family land. Japanese people believed that the family group was more important than any one individual. Family members were supposed to consider the well-being of the whole family first, before thinking about their own needs and plans. Sometimes, this led to quarrels or disappointments. For example, younger brothers in poor families were often not allowed to marry so that the family land could be handed on, undivided, to the eldest son.

Daughters would leave home to marry if a suitable husband could be found. If not, they also remained single, in their parents' house.

Family responsibility passed down the generations, from father to eldest son. Japanese families respected age and experience because they believed it brought wisdom.

LOOKING AFTER BABY
It was women's work to care for young children. This painting shows an elegant young mother from a rich family dressing her son in a *kimono* (a robe with wide sleeves). The family maid holds the belt for the boy's *kimono*, while a pet cat watches nearby.

WORK
A little boy uses a simple machine to help winnow rice. (Winnowing separates the edible grains of rice from the outer husks.) Boys and girls from farming families were expected to help with work around the house and farmyard, and in the fields.

CARP STREAMER
You will need: pencil, 2 sheets of A1 paper, felt-tip pen, scissors, paints, paintbrush, water pot, glue, wire, masking tape, string, cane.

1 Take the pencil and one piece of paper. Draw a large carp fish shape on to the paper. When you are happy with the shape, go over it in felt-tip pen.

2 Put the second piece of paper over the first. Draw around the fish shape. Next, draw a border around the second fish and add tabs, as shown.

3 Add scales, eyes, fins and other details to both of the fishes, as shown above. Cut them both out, remembering to snip into the tabs. Paint both fishes.

PLAYTIME

These young boys have started two tops spinning close to one another. They are waiting to see what will happen when the tops touch. Japanese children had many different toys with which to play. As well as the spinning top, another great favourite was the kite.

TRADITIONAL MEDICINE

Kuzu and ginger are ingredients that have been used for centuries as treatments in traditional Japanese medicine. Most traditional drugs are made from vegetables. The *kuzu* and ginger are mixed together in different ways depending on the symptoms of the patient. For example, there are 20 different mixtures for treating colds. Ginger is generally used when there is no fever.

kuzu   *ginger*

HONOURING ANCESTORS

A mother, father and child make offerings and say their prayers at a small family altar in their house. The lighted candle and paper lantern help guide the spirits to their home. Families honoured their dead ancestors at special festivals. At the festival of Obon, in summer, they greeted family spirits who had returned to earth.

4 Put the two fish shapes together, with the painted sides out. Turn the tabs in and glue the edges of the fish together, except for the tail and the mouth.

5 Use picture or garden wire to make a ring the size of the mouth. Twist the ends together, as shown Then bend them back. Bind the ends with masking tape.

6 Place the ring in the fish's mouth. Glue the ends of the mouth over the ring. Tie one end of some string on to the mouth ring and the other end to a garden cane.

Families fly carp streamers on Boy's Day (the fifth day of the fifth month) every year. One carp is flown for each son. Carp are symbols of perseverence and strength.

Houses and Homes

JAPANESE BUILDERS faced many challenges when they designed homes for Japan's harsh environment. They built lightweight, single-storey houses made of straw, paper and wood. These materials would bend and sway in an earthquake. If they did collapse, or were swept away by floods, they would be less likely than a stone building to injure the people inside.

Japanese buildings were designed as a series of box-like rooms. One room was sufficient for the hut of a farming family, but a whole series of rooms could be linked together to form a royal palace. The space within was divided by screens which could be moved around to suit people's needs. Most houses had raised timber floors that were about $^1/_2$m off the ground.

LAMPS
This pottery lantern has a delicate, cut-out design and was probably for use outdoors. Inside, Japanese homes were lit by candles. A candle was placed on a stand which had four paper sides. The paper protected the candle from draughts. One side could be lifted to insert and remove the candle. There were many different styles and designs. House-fires, caused by cooking and candles, were a major hazard. They were a particular problem because so many homes were made of wood.

SILK HOUSE
For many people in Japan, home was also a place of work. Tucked under the thatched roof of this house in Eiyama, central Japan, was an attic where silk producers bred silk-worms.

MAKE A SCREEN
You will need: gold paper (44cm x 48cm), scissors, thick card (22cm x 48cm), craft knife, metal ruler, cutting board, glue stick, ruler, pencil, paints, paintbrush, water pots, fabric tape.

1 Cut two pieces of gold paper (22cm x 48cm). Use a craft knife to cut out a piece of card the same size. Stick the gold paper to both sides of the card.

2 Use a ruler and pencil to carefully mark out six equal panels, on one side of the card. Each panel should measure 22cm x 8cm.

3 Now turn your card over. Paint a traditional picture of Japanese irises, as shown above. When you have finished, leave the paint to dry.

SCREENS

Wood and paper screens were used to make both outer and inner walls. These could be pushed back to provide peaceful garden views and welcome cool breezes during Japan's hot summers.

ON THE VERANDA

Japanese buildings often had verandas (open platforms) underneath their wide, overhanging eaves. These could be used for taking fresh air, keeping lookout or enjoying a beautiful view. The people at this inn are relaxing after taking a bath in the natural hot springs.

RICH FURNISHINGS

The interior of a richly furnished building is shown in this print from 1857. Japanese furnishings were often very plain and simple. However, this house has a patterned mat and a carpet on the floor, a tall lampstand, a black and gold side table, and a brightly coloured screen dividing the room. There is also a musical instrument called a *koto* with 13 silk strings.

4 Turn the screen over, so the plain side is facing you. Using scissors or a craft knife, cut out each panel completely along the lines you have drawn.

5 Now use fabric tape to join each of your panels, leaving a small gap between every other panel. The tape will work as hinges for the screen.

Japanese people liked to decorate their homes with pictures of iris flowers. Traditionally, irises reminded them of absent friends.

The City in the Clouds

IT WAS THE CUSTOM for each Japanese ruler to build a new palace when he or she came to power. But in AD710, the Empress Gemmei built a whole new city, at Nara. It became the government centre for all Japan. In AD794, Emperor Kammu decided to build a city that would be bigger and even more beautiful than Nara. He moved his imperial court to a new site, called Heian-kyo. Kammu based the plans for his new capital on the great Chinese city of Chang'an (present-day Xian). The whole city was laid out as a rectangle, with main streets running at right angles to one another. The emperor's palace was in the north of the city, and courtiers lived in elegant *shinden* (single-storey villas) close by. Workers and lower officials lived on the outskirts. Heian-kyo (later called Kyoto) was home to the Japanese emperors for over 1,000 years, until 1868 when Emperor Meiji came to power. Its royal and noble inhabitants became known as the people who lived in the clouds, because they lived shut away from ordinary, everyday life.

IMPERIAL SHRINE
The Heian Shrine was built in 1895. It is a replica of the first Imperial Palace in Kyoto, which was designed for Emperor Kammu in AD794. Like the original palace, it has red-painted beams and spectacular curving roofs in Chinese style. However, the shrine is just over half the size of the original palace. The shrine buildings stand in a garden, which surrounds a beautiful lake.

LIFE IN A *SHINDEN*

In Heian-kyo, nobles and courtiers lived in splendid *shinden* houses like this one. Each *shinden* was designed as a number of separate buildings, linked by covered walkways. It was usually set in a landscaped garden, with artificial hills, ornamental trees, bridges, pavilions and ponds. Sometimes a stream flowed through the garden – and through parts of the house, as well. The various members of the noble family, and their servants, lived in different parts of the *shinden*.

GOLDEN PAVILION

This is a replica of the famous Kinkakuji (Temple of the Golden Pavilion). The original was completed in 1397 and survived until 1950. But, like many of Kyoto's old wooden buildings, it was destroyed by fire. The walls of the pavilion are covered in gold leaf, giving out a golden glow that is reflected in the calm waters of a shallow lake.

SILVER TEMPLE

The Ginkakuji (Temple of the Silver Pavilion) in Kyoto was completed in 1483. Despite its name, it was never painted silver, but left as natural wood.

THRONE ROOM

The Shishinden Enthronement Hall is within the palace compound in Kyoto. The emperor would have sat on the raised platform *(left)* while his courtiers bowed low before him. This palace was the main residence for all emperors from 1331 to 1868.

The Castle Builders

CASTLE OF THE WHITE HERON
The largest surviving Japanese castle is Himeji Castle, in southern Japan. Some people say it is also the most beautiful. It is often called the Castle of the White Heron because of its graceful roofs, curved like a bird's wings. The castle was built by the Akamatsu family in the 1500s. It was taken over by warlord Toyotomi Hideyoshi in 1580.

FOR MANY CENTURIES, powerful nobles lived in the city of Heian-kyo (later called Kyoto). But after about AD1000, some noble families began to build up large *shoen* (private estates in the countryside). These families often went to war against each other. They built castles on their lands to protect themselves, their *shoen* and the soldiers in their private armies.

Unlike all other traditional Japanese buildings (except temples), castles were several storeys high. Most were built on naturally well-defended sites such as rocky cliffs. The earliest had a *tenshu* (tall central tower) surrounded by strong wooden fences or stone walls. Later castles were more elaborate buildings, with ramparts, moats and inner and outer courtyards surrounding the central *tenshu*. The period 1570–1690 is often called the Golden Age of castle design when many magnificent castles were built by daimyo (noble warlord) families. These castles were so strong that they challenged the power of the shogun. In 1615, shogun Tokugawa Ieyasu banned noble families from building more than one castle on their estates.

CASTLE OF WOOD
Himeji Castle is made mostly of wood. The building work required 387 tonnes of timber and 75,000 roof tiles. Outside, strong wooden beams are covered with special fireproof plaster. Inside, there are floors and staircases of polished wood.

CASTLE UNDER SIEGE

The usual way to attack a castle was by siege. Enemy soldiers surrounded it, then waited for the inhabitants to run out of food. Meanwhile, they did all they could to break down the castle's defences by storming the gates and killing the guards.

RUN FOR IT!

This painted screen shows a siege at Osaka Castle in 1615. The inhabitants of the castle are running for their lives, chased by enemy soldiers. The castle moat and walls are visible in the background.

IN THE HEART OF THE CAPITAL

Nijo Castle, Kyoto, was begun by warrior Oda Nobunaga in 1569, and finished by Tokugawa Ieyasu. It was designed to give its owner total control over the emperor's capital city – and all Japan.

BUILDING MATERIALS

Castles were built of wood such as pine and stone. For the lower walls, huge boulders were cut roughly from the quarries or collected from mountainsides. They were fitted together by hand without mortar so that in an earthquake the boulders could move slightly without the whole building collapsing. Castle stonework was usually left rough, but it was occasionally chiselled to a fine, smooth finish. Upper walls were made of wooden planks and spars, covered with plaster made from crushed stone mixed with water.

pine   *limestone*

SURROUNDED BY WATER

Castles were surrounded by wide, deep moats to keep out invaders. A typical moat might be 20m wide and 6m deep. The only way into the castle was across a wooden drawbridge guarded by soldiers at both ends. The castle was also defended by strong stone ramparts, often 5m thick. They sloped into the moat so that any attacker could easily be seen from above.

Towns and Trade

TOWN WOODWORKERS
Netsuke were toggles used to attach small items to a *kimono* belt. Three carpenters are carved on this ivory example. Woodworkers were kept busy in towns, building and repairing houses.

UNTIL MODERN TIMES (after around 1900) most Japanese people lived in the countryside. But after 1600, when Japan was at peace, castle-towns in particular grew rapidly. Towns and cities were great centres of craftwork and trade. As one visitor to Kyoto commented in 1691, "There is hardly a household... where there is not something made or sold." Trade also increased in small towns and villages, linking even the most remote districts into a countrywide network of buying and selling.

Castle-towns were carefully planned. Roads, gates, walls and water supplies were laid out in an orderly design. Areas of the town were set aside for different groups of people to live and work – nobles, daimyo and high-ranking samurai families, ordinary samurai, craftworkers, merchants and traders. Many towns became centres of entertainment with theatres, puppet plays, dancers, musicians and artists. Big cities also had pleasure districts where the inhabitants could escape from the pressures of everyday life.

A TRADITIONAL TOWN
This picture was drawn by a visiting European artist in 1882. It shows a narrow, busy street in a Japanese city. Although it is a relatively recent picture, it shows styles of clothes, shops and houses that had existed for several hundred years. The buildings are made of wood and the shops open directly on to the streets. The cloth hangings above the doorways represent the type of shop, for example, knife shop or fan shop. They are printed or woven with *kanji* characters or special designs. The European artist obviously could not read Japanese because the writing on the shop boards and banners is meaningless squiggles.

SKILLED AT WEAVING SILK

Silk was woven on a loom like the one shown here. This woodblock print dates from about 1770. Towns were great centres of cloth production. Kyoto, in particular, was famous for its silk fabrics patterned with gold and silver flowers.

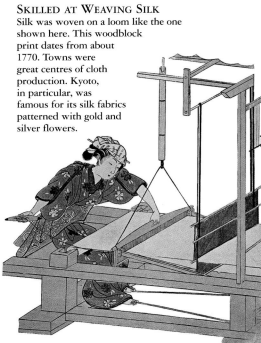

MANY DIFFERENT CRAFTS

These two men are busy making paper lanterns. From the earliest times craftworkers with many different skills worked in Japanese towns. One list of craft guilds, drawn up in Osaka in 1784, included 24 trades. They ranged from makers of porcelain, parasols and face-powder, to basket-weavers, printers, paper-sellers, paint-mixers, cotton-spinners, ivory carvers, and makers of socks.

PLEASURE PURSUIT

Actors, musicians and entertainers, like this well-dressed young woman, lived and worked in the pleasure districts of many towns. The most famous was the Yoshiwara district of Edo. In big cities, they were full of inns and restaurants. Young female entertainers were called *geisha*. Merchants and sometimes samurai would enjoy a meal and a drink while the *geisha* danced and sang for their pleasure.

FIRE HAZARD

Fire was a constant danger in Japanese cities. This was because most buildings were made of wood and packed close together. In an effort to prevent fires from spreading, city rulers gave orders that wooden roof-coverings should be replaced by fireproof clay tiles. They also decreed that tubs of water should be placed in city streets, and watch-towers built to give advance warning of fire.

Palace Fashions

I<small>N ANCIENT</small> J<small>APAN</small>, rich noble men and women at the emperor's court wore very different clothes from ordinary peasant farmers. From around A<small>D</small>600 to 1500, Japanese court fashions were based on traditional Chinese styles. Both men and women wore long, flowing robes made of many layers of fine, glossy silk, held in place by a sash and cords. Men also wore wide trousers underneath. Women kept their hair loose and long, whilst men tied their hair into a topknot and wore a tall black hat. Elegance and refinement were the aims of this style.

After about 1500, wealthy samurai families began to choose new styles. Men and women wore *kimono* – long, loose robes. *Kimono* also became popular among wealthy artists, actors and craftworkers. The shoguns passed laws to try to stop ordinary people from wearing elaborate *kimono*, but they proved impossible to enforce.

PARASOL
Women protected their delicate complexions with sunshades made of oiled paper. The fashion was for pale skin, often heavily powdered, with dark, soft eyebrows.

GOOD TASTE OR GAUDY?
This woman's outfit dates from the 1700s. Though striking, it would probably have been considered too bold to be in the most refined taste. Men and women took great care in choosing garments that blended well together.

MAKE A FAN
You will need: thick card (38cm x 26cm), pencil, ruler, compasses, protractor, felt tip pen (blue), paper (red), scissors, paints, paintbrush, water pot, glue stick.

1 Draw a line down the centre of the piece of card. Place your compasses two-thirds of the way up the line. Draw a circle 23cm in diameter.

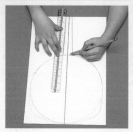

2 Add squared-off edges at the top of the circle, as shown. Now draw your handle (15cm long). The handle should be directly over the vertical line.

3 Place a protractor at the top of the handle and draw a semicircle around it. Now mark lines every 2.5 degrees. Draw pencil lines through these marks.

FEET OFF THE GROUND

To catch insects in a garden by lamplight these women are wearing *geta* (clogs). *Geta* were designed to protect the wearer's feet from mud and rain by raising them about 5–7cm above the ground. They were worn outdoors.

SILK *KIMONO*

This beautiful silk *kimono* was made in about 1600. Women wore a wide silk sash called an *obi* on top of their *kimono*. Men fastened their *kimono* with a narrow sash.

PAPER FAN

Folding fans, made of pleated paper, were a Japanese invention. They were carried by both men and women. This one is painted with gold leaf and chrysanthemum flowers.

It was the custom for Japanese noblewomen to hide their faces in court. They used decorated fans such as this one as a screen. Fans were also used to help people keep cool on hot, humid summer days.

BEAUTIFUL HAIR

Traditional palace fashions for men and women are shown in this scene from the imperial palace. The women have long, flowing hair that reaches to their waists – a sign of great beauty in early Japan.

4 Draw a blue line 1cm to the left of each line you have drawn. Then draw a blue line 2mm to the right of this line. Add a squiggle between sections.

5 Cut out your card fan. Now use this as a template. Draw around the fan top (not handle) on to your red paper. Cut out the red paper.

6 Now cut out the in-between sections on your card fan (those marked with a squiggle). Paint the card fan brown on both sides. Leave to dry.

7 Paint the red paper with white flowers and leave to dry. Paste glue on to one side of the card fan. Stick the undecorated side of the red paper to the fan.

Working Clothes

ORDINARY PEOPLE IN JAPAN could not afford the rich, silk robes worn by emperors, nobles and samurai families. Instead, they wore plain, simple clothes that gave them freedom to move easily as they went about their daily tasks. Men wore baggy jackets and loose trousers, whilst women wore simple, long wrap-over robes.

Ordinary clothes were made from rough, inexpensive fibres, woven at home or purchased in towns. Cotton, hemp and ramie (a plant rather like flax) were all popular. Many other plants were also used to make cloth, including plantain (banana) and the bark of the mulberry tree. From around 1600, clothes were dyed with indigo (a blue dye) and were sometimes woven in complicated *ikat* patterns.

Japan's climate varies from cold and snowy in winter to hot and steamy in summer, so working peoples' clothes had to be adaptable. Usually people added or removed layers of clothing depending on the season. To cope with the rainy summers, they made waterproof clothes from straw. In winter, they wore padded or quilted jackets.

PROTECTIVE APRONS
These women are making salt from sea water. They are wearing aprons made out of leather or heavy canvas cloth to protect their clothes. The woman on the right has tied back her long hair with a scarf.

LOOSE AND COMFY
Farmworkers are shown hard at work planting rice seedlings in a flooded paddy-field. They are wearing loose, comfortable clothes – short jackets, baggy trousers tied at the knee and ankle, and shady hats. For working in water, in rice-fields or by the seashore, ordinary men and women often went barefoot.

MAKE DO AND MEND

Working clothes often got frayed or torn and it was a woman's job to mend them with needle and thread. Women in poor, ordinary families usually made rough, simple clothes for their own families. Sometimes they also bought clothes from travelling pedlars or small shops.

ARMOURERS AT WORK

Loose, flowing *kimono* were originally worn only by high-ranking families. Before long other wealthy and prestigious people, such as these skilled armour makers, copied them. *Kimono* were elegant and comfortable. However, they were certainly not suitable for active outdoor work.

FITTING FOOTWEAR

Out of doors, ordinary people wore clogs or simple sandals. The sandals were woven from straw and held on by twisted straw strings. Before entering a house, people always took off their outdoor footwear so as not to bring mud, grass and dirt inside.

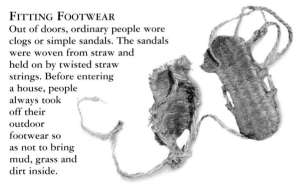

KEEPING THE RAIN OUT

Cone-shaped hats made of woven straw or bamboo protected people's heads from rain. The sloping shape of these hats helped the rainwater to run off before it had time to soak in. Farmworkers also made rain-capes out of straw matting. In this picture you can see one man bent almost double under his rain-cape (*right*). To protect themselves from the rain, rich people used umbrellas made of oiled cloth.

The Decorative Arts

THERE IS A LONG TRADITION among Japanese craftworkers of making everyday things as beautiful as possible. Craftworkers also created exquisite items for the wealthiest and most knowledgeable collectors. They used a wide variety of materials – pottery, metal, lacquer, cloth, paper and bamboo. Pottery ranged from plain, simple earthenware to delicate porcelain, painted with brilliantly coloured glazes. Japanese metalworkers produced alloys (mixtures of metals) that were unknown elsewhere in the ancient world. Cloth was woven from many fibres in elaborate designs. Bamboo and other plants from the grass family were woven into elegant *tatami* mats (floor mats) and containers of all different shapes and sizes. Japanese craftworkers also made beautifully decorated *inro* (little boxes, used like purses) which dangled from men's *kimono* sashes.

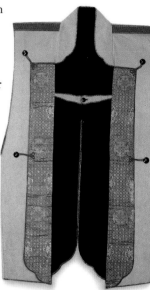

SHINY LACQUER

This samurai helmet was made for ceremonial use. It is covered in lacquer (varnish) and decorated with a diving dolphin. Producing shiny lacquerware was a slow process. An object was covered with many thin layers of lacquer. Each layer was allowed to dry, then polished, before more lacquer was applied. The lacquer could then be carved.

SAMURAI SURCOAT

Even the simplest garments were beautifully crafted. This surcoat (loose, sleeveless tunic) was made for a member of the noble Mori family, probably around 1800. Surcoats were worn by samurai on top of their armour.

MAKE A NETSUKE FOX

You will need: paper, pencil, ruler, self-drying clay, balsa wood, modelling tool, fine sandpaper, acrylic paint, paintbrush, water pot, darning needle, cord, small box (for an inro), scissors, toggle, wide belt.

1 Draw a square 5cm by 5cm on a piece of paper. Roll out a ball of clay to the size of the square. Shape the clay so that it comes to a point at one end.

2 Turn your clay over. Lay a stick of balsa approximately 6cm long, along the back. Stick a thin sausage of clay over the stick. Press to secure.

3 Turn the clay over. Cut out two triangles of clay. Join them to the head using the tool. Make indentations to shape them into a fox's ears.

METALWORK

Craftworkers polish the sharp swords and knives they have made. It took many years of training to become a metalworker. Japanese craftsmen were famous for their fine skills at smelting and handling metals.

BOXES FOR BELTS

Inro were originally designed for storing medicines. The first *inro* were plain and simple, but after about 1700 they were often decorated with exquisite designs. These *inro* have been lacquered (coated with a shiny substance made from the sap of the lacquer tree). Inside, they contain several compartments stacked on top of each other.

MASTERWORK

This beautiful jar is decorated with a design of white flowers, painted over a shiny red and black glaze. It was painted by the master-craftsman Ogata Kenzan, who lived from 1663 to 1743.

Wear your inro *dangling from your belt. In ancient Japan,* inro *were usually worn by men. They were held in place with carved toggles called* netsuke.

4 Use the handle of your modelling tool to make your fox's mouth. Carve eyes, nostrils, teeth and a frown line. Use the top of a pencil to make eye holes.

5 Leave to dry. Gently sand the *netsuke* and remove the balsa wood stick. Paint it with several layers of acrylic paint. Leave in a warm place to dry.

6 Thread cord through the four corners of a small box with a darning needle. Then thread the cord through a toggle and the *netsuke,* as shown.

7 Put a wide belt round your waist. Thread the *netsuke* under the belt. It should rest on the top of it. The *inro* (box) should hang down, as shown.

Wood and Paper

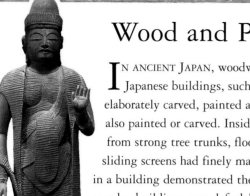

I N ANCIENT JAPAN, woodworking was an art as well as a craft. Most large Japanese buildings, such as temples and palaces, were decorated with elaborately carved, painted and gilded wooden roofs. Doorways and pillars were also painted or carved. Inside, ceiling-beams and supporting pillars were made from strong tree trunks, floors were laid with polished wooden strips, and sliding screens had finely made wooden frames. A display of woodworking skill in a building demonstrated the owner's wealth and power. However, some smaller wooden buildings were left deliberately plain, allowing the quality of the materials and craftsmanship, and the elegance of the design, to speak for themselves.

Paper was another very important Japanese craft. It was used to make many fine objects – from wall-screens to lanterns, sunshades and even clothes. The choice of the best paper for writing a poem or painting a picture was part of an artist's task. Fine paper also showed off a letter-writer's elegance and good taste.

WOODEN STATUES
This statue portrays a Buddhist god. It was carved between AD800 and 900. Many Japanese temples contain carvings and statues made from wood.

SCREENS WITH SCENES
Screens were moveable works of art. This example, made in the 1700s, portrays a scene from Japanese history. It shows Portuguese merchants and missionaries listening to Japanese musicians.

ORIGAMI BOX

You will need: a square of origami paper (15cm x 15cm), clean and even folding surface.

1 Place your paper on a flat surface. Fold it horizontally across the centre. Next fold it vertically across the centre and unfold.

2 Carefully fold each corner to the centre point as shown. Unfold each corner crease before starting to make the next one.

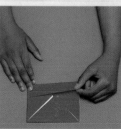

3 Using the creases, fold all the corners back into the centre. Now fold each side 2cm from the edge to make a crease and then unfold.

GRAND PILLARS

This row of red wooden pillars supports a heavy, ornate roof. It is part of the Meiji Shrine in Tokyo. Red (or cinnabar) was the traditional Japanese colour for shrines and royal palaces.

HOLY LIGHTS

Lamps made of pleated paper were often hung outside Shinto shrines. They were painted with the names of people who had donated money to the shrines.

PAPER ART

Paper-making and calligraphy (beautiful writing) were two very important art forms in Japan. This woodcut shows a group of people with everything they need to decorate scrolls and fans– paper, ink, palette, calligraphy brushes and pots of paint.

USEFUL AND BEAUTIFUL

Trees were admired for their beauty as well as their usefulness. These spring trees were portrayed by the famous Japanese woodblock printer, Hiroshige.

Japanese people used boxes of all shapes and sizes to store their possessions. What will you keep in your box?

4 Carefully unfold two opposite side panels. Your origami box should now look like the structure shown in the picture above.

5 Following the crease marks you have already made, turn in the side panels to make walls, as shown in the picture. Turn the origami round 90°.

6 Use your fingers to push the corners of the third side in, as shown. Use the existing crease lines as a guide. Raise the box slightly and fold the wall over.

7 Next, carefully repeat step 6 to construct the final wall. You could try making another origami box to perfect your technique.

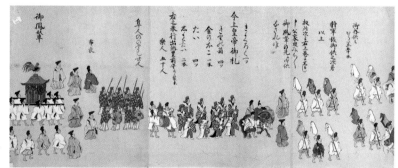

Writing and Drawing

THE JAPANESE LANGUAGE belongs to a family of languages that includes Finnish, Turkish and Korean. It is totally different from its neighbouring language, Chinese. Yet, for many centuries, Chinese characters were used for reading and writing Japanese. This was because people such as monks, courtiers and the emperor – the only people who could read and write – valued Chinese civilization and ideas.

As the Japanese kingdom grew stronger, and Japanese culture developed, it became clear that a new way of writing Japanese was required. Around AD800, two new *kana* (ways of writing) were invented. Both used picture-symbols developed from *kanji* (Chinese characters) that expressed sounds and were written using a brush and ink on scrolls of paper. One type, called *hiragana*, was used for purely Japanese words; the other, called *katakana*, was used for words from elsewhere.

printed kanji → katakana		printed kanji → handwritten kanji → hiragana		

JAPANESE WRITING
Around AD800 two new writing systems, *hiragana* and *katakana,* were invented. For the first time, people could write Japanese exactly as they spoke it. The left-hand side of the chart above shows how a selection of *katakana* symbols developed from the original *kanji*. The right-hand side of the chart shows how *hiragana* symbols evolved, via the handwritten form of *kanji*.

OFFICIAL RECORDS
This illustrated scroll records the visit of Emperor Go-Mizunoo (ruled 1611–1629) to Shogun Tokugawa Iemitsu. The writing tells us that the palanquin (litter) in the picture carries the empress and gives a list of presents for the shogun.

CALLIGRAPHY

You will need: paper, ink, a calligraphy brush. (Please note that you can use an ordinary paint brush and black paint if you cannot find a calligraphy brush or any ink.)

The numbers show the order of the strokes required for this character. Strokes 2, 3 & 4, and 5 & 6, are written in one movement, without lifting the brush.

1 The first stroke is called *soku.* Begin near the top of the paper, going from left to right. Move the brush sharply towards the bottom left, then lift it off the paper.

2 Strokes 2, 3 and 4 are called *roku, do* and *yaku.* Write them together in one movement. Apply pressure as you begin each stroke and then release again.

STORIES ON SCROLLS

Scrolls such as this one were designed to be hand-held, like a book. Words and pictures are side-by-side. Japanese artists often painted buildings with the roofs off, so that readers could see inside.

PAINTING PICTURES

A young boy is shown here mixing ink for his female companion. The ink is made from compressed charcoal that is dissolved in water to give the ink the required consistency. The artist herself has selected a broad brush to begin her painting.

PRINTED PICTURES

Woodblock pictures were created by carving an image in reverse on a block of wood, then using it to print many copies of the same scene. Several different woodblocks might be used to print a single picture, one for each separate colour.

3 For stroke 5 (*saku*) apply an even amount of pressure as you draw your brush left to right. For 6 (*ryo*), apply pressure at the beginning and release it.

4 Stroke 7 is called *taku*. Apply even pressure overall to make this short stroke. Make sure that you also make the stroke quite quickly.

5 Stroke 8 is also called *taku*. Apply an increasing amount of pressure as the brush travels down. Turn the brush back to the right at the last moment, as shown.

This character is called EI (eternal). It uses all eight major Japanese calligraphy strokes.

Poems, Letters and Novels

NEW WAYS OF WRITING the Japanese language were invented around AD800. This led to the growth of forms of literature such as diaries, travel writing and poems. Elegant, refined poetry (called *waka*) was very popular at the emperor's court. From about 1600, *haiku* (short poems with 17 syllables) became the favourite form. *Haiku* were written by people from the samurai class, as well as by courtiers.

Women prose writers were especially important in early Japan. The courtier, Sei Shonagon (born around AD965) won praise for her *Pillow Book* – a kind of diary. Women writers were so famous that at least one man pretended to be a woman. The male poet Ki no Tsurayuki wrote *The Tosa Diary* under a woman's name.

LITERARY LADY
Lady Chiyo was a courtier and poet in the 1700s. Nobles read and wrote a lot of poetry. It was considered a sign of good breeding to quote from literary works. Letters to and from nobles often contained lines from poems.

THE WORLD'S FIRST NOVEL
This scroll shows a scene from the *Tale of Genji*, written in about AD1000 by Lady Murasaki Shikibu. The scroll was painted in the 1700s, but the artist has used a painting style from the period in which the story was written.

MAKE PAPER
You will need: 8 pieces of wood (4 x 33cm and 4 x 28cm), nails, hammer, muslin (35cm x 30cm), staple gun, electrical tape, scissors, torn-up paper, water bowl, masher, washing-up bowl, flower petals, spoon, soft cloths.

1 Ask an adult to make two frames. Staple stretched muslin on to one frame. Cover this frame with electrical tape to make the screen, as shown.

2 Put the frame and screen to one side. Soak paper scraps overnight in water. Mash into a pulp with the potato masher. It should look like porridge.

3 Half-fill the washing-up bowl with the pulp and cold water. You could add a few flower petals for decoration. Mix well with a spoon.

JAPANESE PAPER

Japanese craftworkers made many different kinds of beautiful paper. They used tree bark (especially the bark of the mulberry tree) or other plant fibres, which they blended carefully to create different thicknesses and textures of paper. They sometimes sprinkled the paper mixture with mica or gold leaf to produce rich, sparkling effects.

Japanese paper

mulberry bark

CRANES ON A CARD

This poem-card contains a traditional *waka* (palace-style) poem, in 31 syllables. It is written in silver and black and decorated with cranes.

POET AND TRAVELLER

The poet Matsuo Basho (1644-1694) is portrayed in this print dating from the 1800s. Basho was famous as a writer of short *haiku* poems. He was also a great traveller, and in this picture he is shown (*right*) talking to two farmers he has met on his travels. Here is a typical example of a *haiku* by Basho:

> *The summer grasses –*
> *All that has survived from*
> *Brave warriors' dreams.*

The personality of a Japanese writer was judged by the type of paper they used, as well as by the content of the letter.

4 Place the screen with the frame on top into the washing up bowl. As the frame and screen enter the water, scoop under the pulpy mixture.

5 Pull the screen out of the pulp, keeping it level. Gently move it from side to side over the bowl to allow a layer of pulp to form. Shake the water off.

6 Take the frame off the screen. Carefully lay the screen face down on a cloth. Mop the back of the screen with a cloth to get rid of the excess water.

7 Peel away the screen. Leave the paper to dry for at least 6 hours. When dry, turn over and gently peel away the cloth to reveal your paper.

At the Theatre

GOING TO THE THEATRE and listening to music were popular pastimes in ancient Japan. There were several kinds of Japanese drama. They developed from religious dances at temples and shrines, or from slow, stately dances performed at the emperor's court.

Noh is the oldest form of Japanese drama. It developed in the 1300s from rituals and dances that had been performed for centuries before. Noh plays were serious and dignified. The actors performed on a bare stage, with only a backdrop. They chanted or sang their words, accompanied by drums and a flute. Noh performances were traditionally held in the open air, often at a shrine.

Kabuki plays were first seen around 1600. In 1629, the shoguns banned women performers and so male actors took their places. Kabuki plays became very popular in the new, fast-growing towns.

GRACEFUL PLAYER
This woman entertainer is holding a *shamisen* – a three-stringed instrument, played by plucking the strings. The *shamisen* often formed part of a group, together with a *koto* (zither) and flute.

POPULAR PUPPETS
Bunraku (puppet plays) originated about 400 years ago, when *shamisen* music, dramatic chanting and hand-held puppets were combined. The puppets were so large and complex that it took three men to move them about on stage.

NOH THEATRE MASK

You will need: tape measure, balloon, newspaper, bowl, glue, petroleum jelly, pin, scissors, felt-tip pen, modelling clay, bradawl, paints (red, yellow, black, and white), paintbrush, water pot, cord.

1 Ask a friend to measure around your head above the ears. Blow up a balloon to fit this measurement. This will be the base for the papier-mâché.

2 Rip up strips of newspaper. Soak in a water and glue mixture (1 part glue to 2 parts water). Cover the balloon with a layer of petroleum jelly.

3 Cover the front and sides of your balloon with a layer of papier-mâché. Leave to dry. Repeat 2 or 3 times. When dry, pop the balloon.

TRAGIC THEATRE

An audience watches a scene from an outdoor performance of a Noh play. Noh drama was always about important and serious topics. Favourite subjects were death and the afterlife, and the plays were often very tragic.

LOUD AND FAST

Kabuki plays were a complete contrast to Noh. They were fast-moving, loud, flashy and very dramatic. Audiences admired the skills of the actors as much as the cleverness or thoughtfulness of the plots.

BEHIND THE MASK

This Noh mask represents a warrior's face. Noh drama did not try to be lifelike. The actors all wore masks and moved very slowly using stiff, stylized gestures to express their feelings. Noh plays were all performed by men. Actors playing women's parts wore female clothes and masks.

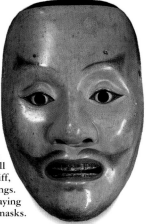

Put on your mask and feel like an actor in an ancient Noh play. Imagine that you are wearing his long, swirling robes, too.

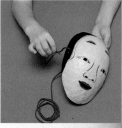

4 Trim the papier-mâché so that it forms a mask shape. Ask a friend to mark where your eyes, nose and mouth are when you hold it to your face.

5 Cut out the face holes with scissors. Put clay beneath the side of the mask at eye level. Use a bradawl to make two holes on each side.

6 Paint the face of a calm young lady from Noh theatre on your mask. Use this picture as your guide. The mask would have been worn by a man.

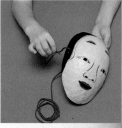

7 Fit the cord through the holes at each side. Tie one end. Once you have adjusted the mask so that it fits, tie the other end.

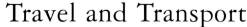

Travel and Transport

JAPAN IS A RUGGED and mountainous
country. Until the 20th century, the
only way to travel through its wild
countryside was along narrow, zig-zag
paths. These mountain paths and fragile
wooden bridges across deep gullies and
rushing streams were often swept away by
landslides or floods.

During the Heian period, wealthy
warriors rode fine horses, while important
officials, wealthy women, children and priests
travelled in lightweight wood and bamboo carts.
These carts were fitted with screens and curtains for
privacy and were pulled by oxen. In places where the route was unsuitable for
ox-carts, wealthy people were carried shoulder-high on palanquins (lightweight
portable boxes or litters). Ordinary people mostly travelled on foot.

During the Tokugawa period (1600–1868) the shoguns encouraged new
road building as a way of increasing trade and control. The longest road was
the Eastern Sea Road, which ran for 480km between Kyoto and the shogun's
capital, Edo. Some people said it was the busiest road in the world.

BEASTS OF BURDEN
A weary mother rests
with her child and ox
during their journey.
You can see that the ox
is loaded up with heavy
bundles. Ordinary
people could not afford
horses, so they used
oxen to carry heavy
loads or to pull carts.

SHOULDER HIGH
Noblewomen on
palanquins (litters) are
shown being taken by
porters across a deep
river. Some of the women
have decided to disembark
so that they can be carried
across the river. Palanquins
were used in Japan right
up to the Tokugawa
period (1600–1868).
When making journeys
to or from the city of
Edo, daimyo and wives
were sometimes
carried the whole route
in palanquins.

HUGGING THE COASTLINE

Ships sail into harbour at Tempozan, Osaka. Cargo between Edo and Osaka was mostly carried by ships that hugged the coastline. The marks on the sails show the company that owned the ships.

STEEP MOUNTAIN PATHS

Travellers on mountain paths hoped to find shelter for the night in villages, temples or monasteries. It could take all day to walk 16km along rough mountain tracks.

CARRYING CARGO

Little cargo-boats, such as these at Edobashi in Edo, carried goods along rivers or around the coast. They were driven through the water by men rowing with oars or pushing against the river bed with a long pole.

IN THE HARBOUR

Sea-going sailing ships, laden with cargo, are shown here at anchor in the harbour of Osaka (an important port in south-central Japan). In front of them you can see smaller river-boats with tall sails. Some families both lived and worked on river-boats.

Remote from the World

JAPAN'S GEOGRAPHICAL POSITION has always kept it separate from the rest of the world, but this has not meant total isolation. The Japanese have established links with their nearest neighbours and, sometimes, with lands far away.

In AD588 the first Buddhist temple was built in Japan. Its construction marked the beginning of an era when Chinese religious beliefs, styles in art, clothes and painting, and beliefs about government and society, began to play an important part in Japan. This Chinese-style era ended between AD800 and 900. By that time, Japanese culture had grown strong and confident.

The next important contact with foreigners came when European traders and missionaries arrived in Japan in the 1540s. At first they were tolerated but, between 1635 and 1640, the shoguns banned Christianity altogether and strictly limited the places where foreigners could trade. Europeans had to live within the Dutch trading factory (trading post) on Dejima Island. Chinese merchants were allowed in only a few streets in Nagasaki. This policy of isolationism continued until 1853, when the USA sent gunboats and demands to trade. Reluctantly, the Japanese agreed and, in 1858, they signed a treaty of friendship with America.

KONG FUZI
The Chinese thinker and teacher Kong Fuzi (often known as Confucius) lived from 551 to 479BC. His ideas about family life, government and society influenced many later generations in both China and Korea. Chinese scribes took Kong Fuzi's ideas to Japan in about AD552.

IN WESTERN STYLE
The young Emperor Meiji took over from the shoguns in 1868. In this picture, leading members of his government meet to discuss foreign policy in 1877. Most of them are wearing Western-style army and navy uniforms.

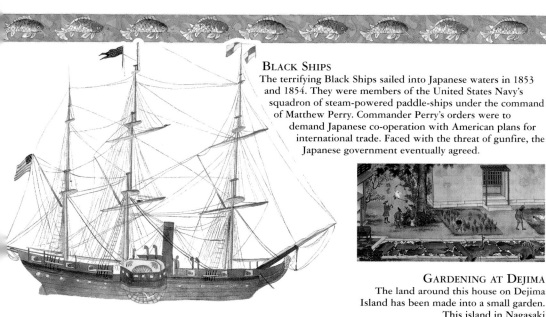

BLACK SHIPS

The terrifying Black Ships sailed into Japanese waters in 1853 and 1854. They were members of the United States Navy's squadron of steam-powered paddle-ships under the command of Matthew Perry. Commander Perry's orders were to demand Japanese co-operation with American plans for international trade. Faced with the threat of gunfire, the Japanese government eventually agreed.

GARDENING AT DEJIMA

The land around this house on Dejima Island has been made into a small garden. This island in Nagasaki harbour was the only area where Europeans were allowed to stay during Japan's period of isolation from the world.

BUSINESS IN DEJIMA

This painting from the 1700s portrays European and Japanese merchants and their servants at the Dutch trading factory at Dejima. The artist has shown the merchants discussing business and taking tea in a Japanese-style house furnished with some European-style contents.

IDEAS FROM ABROAD

An American-style steam train travels across Yokohama harbour. This print is from the Meiji era (1868 onwards), the period when Western-style ideas were introduced by the emperor. In the background you can see Yokohama docks which became a major centre of new industries in the late 1800s.

Gods and Spirits

Almost all of the Japanese people followed a very ancient religious faith called Shinto. Shinto means the way of the gods. It developed from a central idea that all natural things had a spiritual side. These natural spirits – called *kami* in Japanese – were often kindly, but could be powerful or even dangerous. They needed to be respected and worshipped. Shinto also encouraged ancestor-worship – ancestor spirits could guide, help and warn. Special priests, called shamans, made contact with all these spirits by chanting, fasting, or by falling into a trance.

Shinto spirits were honoured at shrines that were often built close to sites of beauty or power, such as waterfalls or volcanoes. Priests guarded the purity of each shrine, and held rituals to make offerings to the spirits. Each Shinto shrine was entered through a *torii* (large gateway) which marked the start of the sacred space. *Torii* always had the same design – they were based on the ancient perches of birds waiting to be sacrificed.

At the Shrine
A priest worships by striking a drum at the Grand Shrine at Izu, one of the oldest Shinto shrines in Japan. A festival is held there every August, with processions, offerings and prayers. An *omikoshi* (portable shrine) is carried through the streets, so that the spirits can bring blessings to everyone.

Offerings to the Spirits
Worshippers at Shinto shrines leave offerings for the *kami* (spirits) that live there. These offerings are neatly-wrapped barrels of *sake* (rice wine). Today, worshippers also leave little wooden plaques with prayers on them.

Votive Dolls
You will need: self-drying clay, 2 balsa wood sticks (12cm long), ruler, paints, paintbrush, water pot, modelling clay, silver foil, red paper, gold paper, scissors, pencil, glue stick, optional basket and dowelling stick.

1 Place a ball of clay on the end of each of the balsa sticks. On one of the sticks, push the clay down so that it is 5mm from the end. This will be the man.

2 Paint hair and features on the man. Stand it up in modelling clay to dry. Repeat with the woman. Cover the 5mm excess stick on the man's head in foil.

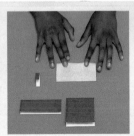

3 Take two pieces of red paper, 6.5cm x 14cm and 6cm x 10cm. Fold them in half. Take two pieces of gold paper, 10.5cm x 10cm and 1cm x 7cm. Fold in half.

HOLY VOLCANO

Fuji-San (Mount Fuji) has been honoured as a holy place since the first people arrived in Japan. Until 1867, women were not allowed to set foot on Fuji's holy ground.

LUCKY GOD

Daikoku is one of seven lucky gods from India, China and Japan that are associated with good fortune. In Japan, he is the special god of farmers, wealth, and of the kitchen. Daikoku is recognized by both Shinto and Buddhist religions.

FLOATING GATE

This *torii* at Miyajima (Island of Shrines), in southern Japan, is built on the seashore. It appears to float on the water as the tide flows in. Miyajima was sacred to the three daughters of the Sun.

In some regions of Japan, dolls like these are put on display in baskets every year at Hinamatsuri (Girls' Day), on 3 March.

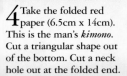

4 Take the folded red paper (6.5cm x 14cm). This is the man's *kimono*. Cut a triangular shape out of the bottom. Cut a neck hole out at the folded end.

5 Dip the blunt end of the pencil in white paint. Stipple a pattern on to the red paper. Add the central dots using the pencil tip dipped in paint.

6 Slip the man's head and body into the red paper *kimono*. Then take the larger piece of gold paper and fold around the stick, as shown. Glue in place.

7 Now stick the gold paper (1cm x 7cm) on to the woman's *kimono*, in the middle. Slip the woman's head and body into the *kimono*. Glue in place.

Monks and Priests

MONK AND PUPIL
A Buddhist sage is pictured with one of his pupils. Thanks to such teachers, Buddhist ideas spread beyond the imperial court to reach ordinary people, and many Buddhist temples and monasteries were built.

AS WELL AS FOLLOWING SHINTO, many Japanese people also practised the Buddhist faith. Prince Siddhartha Gautama, the founder of Buddhism, was born in Nepal around 500BC. He left his home to teach a new religion based on the search for truth and harmony and the ending of all selfish desires. His followers called him the Buddha (the enlightened one). The most devoted Buddhists spent at least part of their life as scholars, priests, monks or nuns.

Buddhist teachings first reached Japan in AD552, brought by monks and scribes from China and Korea. Buddhism encouraged learning and scholarship, and, over the centuries, many different interpretations of the Buddha's teachings developed. Each was taught by dedicated monks or priests and attracted many followers. The Buddhist monk Shinran (1173–1262) urged his followers to place their faith in Amida Buddha (a calm, kindly form of the Buddha). He taught them that Amida Buddha would lead them after death to the Western Paradise. Shinran's rival, Nichiren (1222–1282) claimed that he had been divinely chosen to spread the True Word. This was Nichiren's own interpretation of Buddhism, based on an ancient Buddhist text called the *Lotus Sutra*.

FAMOUS MONK
This woodcut of 1857 shows an episode from a story about the Buddhist monk, Nichiren. He was said to have calmed a storm by the power of his prayers. The influence of Nichiren continued long after his death, and many other stories were told about him.

SCHOLAR MONKS
A group of monks (*left*) study Buddhist scrolls. Monks were among the most important scholars in early Japan. They studied ancient Chinese knowledge and developed new Japanese ideas.

GREAT BUDDHA
This huge bronze statue of Daibutsu (the Great Buddha) is 11.3m high and weighs 93 tonnes. It was made at Kamakura in 1252 – a time when the city was rich and powerful. The statue shows the Buddha in Amida form – inviting worshippers to the Western Paradise.

GOD OF MERCY
Standing over 5m high, this statue of Kannon was made around AD700. Kannon is also known as the god of mercy. Orginally Kannon was a man – in fact, one form of the Buddha himself. However, over the years it became the custom to portray him in female shape.

HOLY FLOWERS
The lotus flower often grows in dirty water and was believed to symbolize the purity of a holy life. It has many associations in literature with Buddhism. Chrysanthemums are often placed on graves or on Buddhist altars in the home. White and yellow flowers are most popular because these colours are associated with death.

white chrysanthemum   *yellow chrysanthemums*

lotus

HOLY WORDS
For many years after Buddhism reached Japan, it was practised mainly by educated, wealthy people. Only they could read the beautiful Buddhist *sutras* (religious texts) like this one, created between AD645 and 794. This sutra was written by hand, but some of the world's first printed documents are Buddhist *sutras* made in Japan.

Temples and Gardens

Land suitable for growing plants was very precious in Japan, so the people made the best use of it – both for growing food and for giving pleasure. All Japanese people who could afford it liked to surround their homes with beautiful gardens where they could take gentle exercise, read or entertain.

Japanese gardens were often small, but they were carefully planned to create a landscape in miniature. Each rock, pool, temple or gateway was positioned where it could best be admired, but also where it formed part of a balanced, harmonious arrangement. Japanese designers chose plants to create a garden that would look good during all the different seasons of the year. Zen gardens – made of stones, sand and gravel – contained no plants at all.

PLANTS TO ADMIRE
Artists created and recorded delicate arrangements of blooms and leaves. This scroll-painting of branches, blossom and flowers dates from the 1500s.

ZEN GARDEN
This is part of a Zen Buddhist garden, made of lumps of rock and carefully-raked gravel. Gardens like this were designed to help people pray and meditate in peaceful surroundings.

HARMONY IN DESIGN
The Eastern Pagoda at the Yakushiji Temple in Nara is one of the oldest temples in Japan. It was founded in AD680 and the pagoda was built in 730. Pagodas are tall towers, housing statues of Buddha or other religious works of art. Often, they form part of a group of buildings standing in a garden.

MAKING AN *IKEBANA* ARRANGEMENT
You will need: vase filled with water, scissors, twig, raffia or string, 2 flowers (with different length stems), a branch of foliage, 2 stems of waxy leaves.

1 Cut the twig so that it can be wedged into the neck of the vase. This will provide a structure to build on and to control the position of the flowers.

2 Remove the twig from the vase. Next, using raffia or string, tie the twig tightly on to the longest flower about halfway down the stem.

3 Place the flower stem in the vase. As you do this, gently slide the twig back into the neck of the vase and wedge it into position as before.

TREES IN MINIATURE

Bonsai is the Japanese art of producing miniature but fully-formed trees. This is achieved by clipping roots and carefully regulating the water supply. Bonsai originated in China, but became popular in Japan around 1500. A tree that might naturally grow to about 6m could end up just 30cm tall after bonsai treatment. Some bonsai trees are grown to achieve a dramatic slanting or twisted shape.

bonsai maple   *bonsai pine*

CHINESE STYLE

The Tenryuji Temple, Kyoto, stands in one of the oldest Buddhist gardens still surviving in Japan. The garden was created before 1300. It is designed in the Chinese style and made of rocks, gravel, water and evergreen plants.

GARDENERS AT WORK

A gardener, his wife and son prepare to plant cedar tree saplings. In the foreground, you can see a wooden bucket for watering plants, and a wooden hoe for digging up weeds. At the back, there are nursery beds where seedlings are carefully tended. Cedar trees were, and still are, popular in Japan. The wood is used in the building of houses and the beautiful trees themselves are used to decorate many gardens.

Ikebana means "living flowers". The three main branches of an arrangement represent heaven, earth and human beings.

4 Add the shorter-stemmed flower to the longer stem. Position it so that it slants forwards. Carefully lean it against the twig and the longer stem.

5 Slip the branch of foliage between the two stems. It should lean out and forward. The foliage should look as though it is a branch growing naturally.

6 Position some waxy leaves at the neck of the vase. *Ikebana* is the arrangement of anything that grows. Foliage is as important as the flowers.

7 Add a longer stem of waxy leaves at the back of the vase. This simple arrangement is typical of those Japanese people have in their homes.

Festivals and Ceremonies

The Japanese people celebrated festivals (*matsuri*) all year round, but especially during the warm months of spring and summer. Many of these festivals had ancient origins and were connected with farming or to the seasons. Others were linked to Shinto beliefs or to imported Buddhist ideas. There were two main kinds of festival. National holidays, such as New Year, were celebrated throughout Japan. Smaller local festivals were often linked to a Buddhist statue or temple, or to an ancient Shinto shrine.

One of the most important ceremonies was the tea ceremony, first held by Buddhist monks between 1300 and 1500. During the ceremony, the host served tea to his or her guests with great delicacy, politeness and precision.

BOWLS FOR TEA
At a tea ceremony, two types of green tea are served in bowls like these. The bowls are often plainly shaped and simply decorated. According to Zen beliefs, beauty can be found in pure, calm, simple things. Toyotomi Hideyoshi fell out with the tea master Sen no Rikyu over this. Hideyoshi liked tea bowls to be ornate rather than plain.

LOCAL FESTIVAL
A crowd of people enjoy a festival day. Local festivals usually included processions of portable Shinto shrines through the streets. These were followed by lots of noisy and cheerful people.

TEA BOWL

You will need: self-drying clay, cutting board, ruler, modelling tool, cut-out bottom of a plastic bottle (about 10cm in diameter), fine sandpaper, paints, paintbrush, water pot, soft cloth, varnish and brush.

1 Roll out a snake of clay 25cm long and 1cm thick. Starting from the centre, curl the clay tightly into a circle with a diameter of 10cm.

2 Now you have made the base of the bowl, start to build up the sides. Roll out more snakes of clay, 25cm long. Join the pieces by pressing them together.

3 Sculpt the ridges of the coil bowl together using your fingers and modelling tool. Use the bottom of a plastic bottle for support (see step 4).

CHERRY BLOSSOM

This woodblock print shows two women dressed in their best *kimonos* strolling along an avenue of flowering cherry trees. The cherry-blossom festival, called Hanami, was a time to meet friends and enjoy an open-air meal in the spring sunshine. Blossoms appeared in late February in the far south, but not until early May in the colder northern lands of Japan.

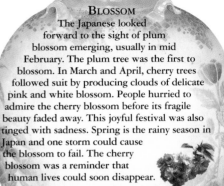

BLOSSOM

The Japanese looked forward to the sight of plum blossom emerging, usually in mid February. The plum tree was the first to blossom. In March and April, cherry trees followed suit by producing clouds of delicate pink and white blossom. People hurried to admire the cherry blossom before its fragile beauty faded away. This joyful festival was also tinged with sadness. Spring is the rainy season in Japan and one storm could cause the blossom to fail. The cherry blossom was a reminder that human lives could soon disappear.

plum blossom

cherry blossom

TEA CEREMONY

Hostess and guests sit politely on *tatami* (straw mats) for a Zen tea ceremony. This ritual often lasted for up to four hours. Many people in Japan still hold tea ceremonies, as a way of getting away from hectic modern life.

Design your bowl in a pure, elegant style, like the Zen potters. If you want to add any decoration, make sure that is very simple, too.

4 Roll out another coil of clay 19cm long and 1cm wide. Make it into a circle 8cm in diameter. Join the ends. This will form a stand for the bowl.

5 Turn the bowl over – still using your drinks bottle for support. Join the circular stand to the bottom of the bowl. Mould it on using your fingers.

6 Leave the bowl to dry. Once dry, remove the plastic bottle and sand the bowl gently. Paint the base colour over it. Leave until it is dry.

7 Apply your second colour using a cloth. Lightly dapple paint over the bowl to make it appear like a glaze. Varnish the bowl inside and out.

PEOPLE AND PLACES

Abu Simbel
The magnificent temple of Ramesses II. It was cut into a solid rock face.

Aeschylus (525–456BC) Founder of Greek tragic drama. Wrote many plays including *Prometheus Bound*.

Akhenaten (ruled 1379–1334BC) Pharaoh of Egypt. He forbade the worship of all gods except the sun god Aten. The change was soon abandoned after his reign.

Alexander the Great (356–323BC) Greek conqueror who led Greece against Persia, captured Egypt and founded an empire that stretched to India.

Antony, Mark (c.83–30BC) Roman general and supporter of Caesar. He ruled Rome jointly with Octavian (Augustus) and Lepidus, but fell out with them when he fell in love with Cleopatra. His force was defeated by Octavian at the battle of Actium, after which he committed suicide.

Archimedes (287–211BC) Greek mathematician famous

for his practical inventions as well as his great contribution to maths and science.

Aristotle (384–322BC) One of the most celebrated Greek philosophers and tutor to Alexander the Great. His enormous body of work influenced both Arab and Christian scholars.

Ataw Wallpa or **Atahualpa** (ruled 1532–33) The last ruler of the Inca Empire and son of Wayna Qapaq. He defeated his half-brother Waskar to gain the throne. He was captured by the Spanish who, despite receiving a huge ransom, executed him.

Athens Ancient capital of Greek learning and art. It was at its most prosperous in the 400sBC when its empire controlled Greece.

Augustus (63BC–AD14) The first Roman emperor from 27BC. Born Octavian, he was Caesar's great-nephew and adopted son. His rule was peaceful and a great period in Roman literature and art.

Beijing The capital of China. It was begun in 1264 by Kublai Khan under the name Khanbalik on the site of the former Chin capital. At its centre is the Imperial Palace known as the Forbidden City built from 1407 to 1420. By the 1500s it was the largest city in the world.

Boudicca or **Boadicea** (died AD61) Queen of the Iceni who led a revolt

against the Romans in Britain, but finally killed herself after her defeat.

Caesar, Julius (100–44BC) Brilliant Roman general and dictator of Rome who was murdered by his enemies in the Senate.

Caligula (AD12–41) Roman emperor from AD374. Caligula was mentally unstable and his reign as emperor was brief and bloody.

Caractacus or **Caradog** (died AD54) King of the Catuvellauni in southern Britain. He was captured by the Romans, but freed by Emperor Claudius.

Carthage Ancient trading city of North Africa destroyed by the Romans in 146BC. It is now a suburb of Tunis.

Çatal Huyuk A large Neolithic settlement in Turkey that dates from about 6500BC.

Chan Chan The largest city of ancient Peru, capital of the Chimú.

Chang'an Capital of the Chinese Empire from 200BC. The Silk Road led from Chang'an to the Mediterranean Sea. Today it is called Xian.

Chavín de Huantar A ceremonial centre high up in the Peruvian Andes. It was the basis for the Chavín culture, which flourished around 1000–200BC.

Chichen-Itza A Maya city

in Mexico that was founded around AD800 and rose to power in about AD1000.

Cicero (106–43BC) Roman statesman and orator whose speeches and writings have had a major influence on Western thought.

Cixi (1835–1908) Dowager empress of China. In 1862 she seized power and prevented reforms.

Claudius (10BC–AD54) Roman Emperor from AD41. Intelligent and scholarly, Britain was conquered during his reign.

Cleopatra VII (68–30BC) Brilliant and ambitious queen of Egypt. Killed herself when she and her lover Mark Antony were defeated by Rome.

Columbus, Christopher (c.1451–1506) Italian explorer who, financed by Spain, "discovered" the Americas when he sailed to the West Indies in 1492.

Constantine (AD274–337) The first Christian Roman emperor and called the Great. He founded a new capital at Constantinople.

Constantinople A city in Turkey, formerly called Byzantium, which today is called Istanbul. It was designed as a new Rome and became the capital of the Eastern Roman Empire.

Copan A vast Mayan city-state in present-day, western Honduras.

Corinth A port in southern Greece. It was the most properous city in Greece by the mid-500sBC.

Cortes, Hernan (1485–1547) Spanish adventurer who captured Mexico for Spain.

Cuzco The Inca capital of Peru from AD1200 and rebuilt in 1438 by Pachacuti. After the Spanish conquest it was replaced by Lima.

Deir el-Medina An Egyptian village built in 1500BC for the craftworkers employed in the Valley of the Kings.

Delphi A site on Mount Parnassus in central Greece. It was the seat of the most respected oracle of ancient times.

Dolni Vestonice A Palaeolithic settlement in the present-day Czech Republic. Some of the oldest fired-clay objects in the world have been found there by archaeologists.

Edo Tokugawa Ieyasu made Edo the capital of

Japan from 1603. Today it is called Tokyo.

Ephesus An ancient city on the west coast of Turkey. Its famous temple to the goddess Artemis was one of the Seven Wonders of the World.

Euclid (c.330–260BC) Greek mathematician famous for his book *Elements of Geometry*.

Euripedes (480–406BC) Greek dramatist who wrote around 80 plays including *Medea*, *Iphigenia* and *Orestes*.

Giza Site of the famous pyramids of Egypt, tombs to the pharaohs Khufu, Khafra and Menkaura. The Great Sphinx guards the pyramid of Khafra.

Hadrian (AD76–138) Roman Emperor from AD117. An able general, he suppressed revolt and encouraged the arts.

Han Gaozu (256–185BC) Born Liu Bang, in 202BC he founded the Han dynasty in China. It lasted until AD220.

Hannibal (247–182BC) Carthaginian general who fought two wars against Rome. He is famous for crossing the Alps with elephants to march on northern Italy.

Harappa An ancient city in northernPakistan built in about 2500BC and an important centre of the Indus civilization.

Hatshepsut (ruled 1498–1483BC) Daughter of Tutmose I, she was the first female ruler in history when she ruled Egypt after the death of her husband and half-brother Tutmose II.

Heian-kyo Built in AD794 by Emperor Kammu, it was home to Japan's emperors for over 1,000 years. Today it is called Kyoto.

Hideyoshi, Toyotomi (1536–1598) A Japanese general, who became shogun in 1585. He tried to invade Korea twice and died in the second attempt.

Hippocrates (c.400BC) Greek physician. He founded medical schools and helped separate medicine from superstition.

Homer (c.700BC) Poet, traditionally believed to be the author of the epic poems the *Iliad* and the *Odyssey*.

Ibn Batuta (1304–1368) Moroccan scholar who wrote of his travels across Africa, India, Russia and China.

Imhotep (c.2700BC) Egyptian architect and chief adviser to Pharaoh Zoser.

Jericho Now in Palestine, one of the oldest continuously inhabited cities in the world, from about 8000BC.

Karnak The religious centre of ancient Thebes in Egypt, the complex of buildings was begun by Ramesses I and took over 2,000 years to complete.

Khafra (ruled 2558–2532BC) Pharaoh of Egypt and son of Khufu. He built the Great Sphinx at Giza.

Khufu (ruled 2589–2558BC) Pharaoh of Egypt. Built the Great Pyramid at Giza, the world's largest stone structure.

Knossos The leading city of the Minoan civilization on Crete.

Kong Fuzi or **Confucius** (551–479BC) The most celebrated Chinese philosopher whose teachings formed the basis of conduct in China from Han times.

Kublai Khan (1216–94) Grandson of Genghis Khan and first Mongol emperor of China from 1279. A great statesman and warrior, he ordered the building of roads and organized charity for the sick and needy.

Laoze (c.600BC) Traditional founder of Daoism in China.

Lascaux A famous cave site in southwest France that contains some of the most beautiful cave paintings, painted in about 15,000BC.

La Venta Centre of the Olmec civilization in western Mexico.

Leonidas (died 480BC) King of Sparta who died defending the pass at Thermopylae against a superior Persian force.

Machu Picchu An Inca town built high up in the Andes Mountains in about 1450.

Mama Oklla (ruled in the 1100s) Famous Inca empress who married her brother Manko Qapaq. Her son was Sinchi Rocha.

Mayapan The most powerful Maya city of Yucatan, Mexico, from about 1200 to 1440.

Meiji (1852–1912) Meaning Enlightened Rule, it was the name chosen by Mutsuhito when he became emperor of Japan in 1867. His reign introduced radical political, social and economic change.

Memphis The capital of Egypt throughout the Old Kingdom between 2686 and 2181BC. Traditionally founded by Pharaoh Narmer who united Upper and Lower Egypt in 3100BC.

Minamoto Yoritomo (1147–99) The first shogun of Japan from 1192. He ruled in the name of emperor at Kamakura.

Moctezuma II (1466–1520) Last Aztec emperor. He was captured by Cortes and stoned to death by his own people.

Monte Alban A great city state in Mexico that flourished around AD300.

Murasaki Shikibu (c.978–1014) A lady of the Japanese court who wrote the famous novel *The Tale of Genji*.

Nanjing Capital of China during the Ming dynasty (1368–1644).

Nara Built by Empress Gemmei in 710, it was Japan's centre of government.

Nefertiti (c.1300sBC) Wife and queen of Akhenaten. She retired from public life before her death.

Nero (AD37–68) Became Roman Emperor on the death of his adoptive father Claudius in AD54. He was a cruel and weak ruler.

Nobunaga, Oda (died 1582) A Japanese warlord who took the capital Kyoto in 1568 and tried to unite Japan. On his death his work was continued by his general Hideyoshi.

Olympia A site in western Greece. It was the seat of the most important shrine to Zeus and every four years a festival of games was held there in his honour.

Pacal (ruled AD615–84) Ruler of the Maya city of Palenque who was buried in a lavish tomb.

Pachakuti (ruled 1438–71) Made himself Inca emperor on the death of his father Wiraqocha. He reunited and increased the empire, reformed government and improved the city of Cuzco.

Palenque A powerful Maya city-state from about AD300 to 800.

Pericles (495–429BC) Athenian statesman who raised Athens to its greatest time of greatest prosperity.

Philip II of Macedonia (382–336BC) Led Macedonia to become the leading kingdom in Greece. Father of Alexander the Great.

Pizarro, Francisco (c.1478–1541) Spanish adventurer who conquered Peru for Spain. He was murdered by his men.

Plato (427–347BC) Athenian philosopher and teacher of Aristotle. He founded the Academy at Athens, and his writings are some of the most influential in history.

Polo, Marco (1256–1323) Venetian traveller who journeyed to China in 1271. He reached the court of Kublai Khan in 1274 and spent 17 years travelling in China.

Pompeii A thriving Roman town near Naples that was completely destroyed by the eruption of Vesuvius in AD79.

Puyi (1906–67) The last emperor of China. He gave up his throne in 1912 at the age of six.

Qin Shi Huangdi (256–210BC) The first emperor of China. He united the warring states into one country in 221BC. He organized the land and people and harshly enforced the laws.

Ramesses II (ruled 1279–1212BC) Pharaoh of Egypt and called the Ramesses the Great. He was the last great military pharaoh, and his rule was one of great prosperity.

Rome A city on the river Tiber that was the heart of the Roman Empire. Traditionally founded by Romulus (after whom the city is named) and Remus in 753BC.

Sappho (c.600BC) Greek woman poet who wrote many love poems.

Sei Shonagon (born c.965) A Japanese courtier admired for her famous pillow book, a type of diary.

Shotoku (AD574–622)
Ruled Japan as regent on
behalf of Empress Suiko.
He reformed government
based on Chinese ideas and
passed laws to keep the
nobility under control.

Sipán Site of a rich Moche
royal tomb in northern Peru.

Socrates (469–399BC)
Athenian philosopher who
attracted many followers,
and greatly influenced
Plato and Xenophon.

Sophocles (496–406BC)
Athenian dramatist who
wrote over 100 plays
including *Oedipus the King*,
Antigone and *Electra*.

Sparta Ancient Greek city
state, the chief rival to the
city of Athens.

Spartacus (died 71BC) A
Roman slave and gladiator
who escaped and led a
successful slave revolt.

Stonehenge A massive
stone circle on Salisbury
Plain, England. It is
prehistoric Europe's most
complex stone monument.

Tenochtitlan The capital
of the Aztecs in Lake
Texcoco, which today is
Mexico City. Traditionally
founded in 1345.

Teotihuacan The earliest
true city in Mesoamerica
(from about 100BC) it
dominated Central Mexico
economically for about
600 years.

Thebes (Egypt) The
capital of Egypt in the
New Kingdom (c. 1550
and 1070BC). Now the site
of modern Luxor.

Thebes (Greece) The most
important city in central
Greece, from 519BC it
was a great rival to the
city of Athens.

Thermopylae A narrow
pass that controlled entry
to Greece from the
northeast. In 480BC it was
the site of a famous Greek
victory against the
invading Persians.

Tikal The largest Maya city
state with a population of
about 50,000. It was at its
height of prosperity from
about AD550 to 900.

Tiwanaku or **Tiahuanaco**
A vast ceremonial site and
city near Lake Titicaca. It
was a centre for art and
culture between about
AD600 and 1000.

Tokugawa Ieyasu
(1542–1616) Japanese
general who, on the death
of Hideyoshi, defeated his
rivals at the battle of
Sekigahara and became
shogun in 1603.

Topa Inca (ruled
1471–93) Son of Pachacuti,
he greatly expanded the
Inca Empire and built
many roads.

Troy An ancient city in
Turkey that flourished
from about 2000BC. In

Greek legend, Troy was
captured by the Greeks
using a wooden horse after
a ten year siege.

Tula Capital of the Toltec
civilization in Mexico. It
was at its height from
about AD950 to 1168.

Tutankhamun (ruled
1334–1325BC) Pharaoh of
Egypt. Little is known
about his reign but he is
famous because only his
tomb in the Valley of the
Kings escaped looting.

Tutmose III (ruled
1479–1425BC) Pharaoh of
Egypt. During the first 15
years of his reign his aunt
Hatshepsut ruled. The
prosperity of his rule was
reflected in magnificent
buildings at Karnak.

Uxmal A powerful Mayan
city state in Yucatan,
Mexico.

Valley of the Kings A
narrow gorge near Thebes
containing the tombs of at
least 60 pharaohs. The
earliest tomb was built for
Tutmose I in about 1550BC.

Vercingetorix (died 46BC)
King of the Averni in Gaul
(France). He led a revolt
against Roman occupation
in 52BC. He was paraded
through Rome by Julius
Caesar before finally
being executed.

Wayna Qapaq (ruled
1493–1525) Successor to
Topa Inca. He extended the
Inca Empire's northern
boundaries and founded
Quito as a second capital.

Wiraqocha or **Viracocha**
(ruled *c.*1390s–1438)
Eighth Inca ruler and the
first empire builder.
Wiraqocha absorbed
neighbouring lands and
set up a strong state.

Wu Zetian (AD624–705)
Second wife to the Tang
emperor Gaozong, she
declared herself empress of
China in 690.

Zheng He (1371–1433)
Commander of the Chinese
fleet. Between 1405 and
1433 he led seven
expeditions into the Indian
Ocean to extend China's
influence abroad.

Zhu Yuanzhang A Chinese
peasant who led revolts
against the Mongols, driving
them out of China. He
founded the Ming dynasty
in 1368.

GLOSSARY

A

abacus A wooden frame with beads on rods used for counting.

acupuncture The treatment of the body with fine needles to relieve pain or cure illness.

AD (Anno Domini, Latin for the year of our Lord.) A system used to calculate dates after the supposed year of Christ's birth.

adobe Sun-dried mud bricks, which are used as a building material.

akllakuna Girls who were selected for special education and training in the Inca Empire.

alabaster A gleaming white stone, which is made of gypsum.

alloy Any metal that is made from a mixture of other metals.

alpaca A South American llama-like animal, valued for its wool.

amaranth A bushy Mexican plant with edible seeds.

ambassador A person who represents the interests of one country in another country.

amphitheatre An oval, open-air arena surrounded by seats. It was used for public entertainment shows, such as gladiator fights in ancient Rome.

amphora A pottery storage jar, often shaped like a tall vase with two handles and a pointed base, used to store wine or olive oil.

amputate Cut off a part of the body.

amulet A lucky charm.

ancestor A member of the same family who died long ago.

anvil A block used by blacksmiths for shaping hot metal.

aqueduct An artificial channel for carrying water over a long distance. Many ran underground or were supported on bridges.

archaeology The scientific study of the historica remains of the past.

arithmetic The calculation of numbers.

arsenal A store of weapons.

artefact An object that has been preserved from the past.

Asia Minor The peninsula where Europe and Asia meet. An area that is today modern Turkey.

assassination The violent killing of a person.

astrology The belief that the stars and planets influence the way we live on Earth.

astronomy The observation and scientific study of the stars, planets and other heavenly bodies.

auxiliaries Soldiers who were recruited from non-Roman citizens.

B

backstrap loom A system of weaving in which the upright (warp) threads are stretched between a post and a belt around the weaver's waist.

ball-court A large open courtyard surrounded by rows of stone seats where the Mesoamerican ball-game was played.

banquet A rich, elaborate feast served with great ceremony.

barracks Buildings used to house soldiers.

barter The exchange of goods for others of equal value. This is how goods may be traded in societies that have no money.

basalt A dark, volcanic rock.

BC (Before Christ) A system used to calculate dates before the supposed year of Christ's birth. Dates are calculated in reverse (e.g. 200BC is longer ago than 1BC).

bellows A machine for pumping air into a fire or furnace.

bolas Three heavy balls tied to cords. It was used by Inca soldiers as a weapon and by hunters and herders to bring down running animals.

brazier A metal container filled with hot coals that is used for heating rooms or for keeping a cooking fire alight.

bronze A metal alloy that is made by mixing tin with copper.

Buddhism The faith based on the religious teachings of the Indian prince Siddhartha Gautama who was given the name Buddha (a name which means the Enlightened One).

C

calligraphy The name given to the art of beautiful hand-writing.

carp A large freshwater fish. Goldfish are small carp.

cartouche An oval ring containing the names and the titles of an Egyptian pharaoh.

cassava A root crop first grown for food in the Americas. Also known as manioc.

catapult A large wooden structure that is used during a siege to fire missiles such as stones at the enemy.

causeway A road or pathway raised above the surrounding land or water.

century A unit of the Roman army, made up of 80 to 100 soldiers. A century also means a period of 100 years.

chacmool A statue from Mesoamerica of a dying warrior or rain god, carrying a dish in his arms. The dish was used to hold blood and hearts from human sacrifices.

chinampa A garden built on fertile, reclaimed land on the shores of Lake Texcoco, Mexico.

chiton A long woollen garment worn by the ancient Greeks.

Christianity The faith that is based on the religious teachings of Jesus Christ.

circus An oval track used for chariot races.

citizen A member of a state, city or community. A Roman or Greek citizen was a freeman with the right to vote in elections.

city state An independent state consisting of a city and its surrounding land. Ancient Greece was made up of about 300 city states, including Athens and Sparta. The Maya also lived in many separate city states.

civilization A society that has made advances in the fields of the arts, science and technology, law or government.

civil servant An official who administers the country for a government.

civil war A war between people of the same country.

clan A group of people related to each other through their ancestors or by marriage.

cloisonné A decorative technique that means partitioned. Glassy enamel is poured inside tiny compartments separated by thin metal wire.

coca A South American plant whose leaves were used by the Incas as a mild drug, as a medicine and for fortune-telling.

cochineal A bright red dye made from the dried bodies of crushed beetles.

codex (plural codices) An ancient text. Maya and Aztec codices were made from strips of bark that were folded in a concertina fashion.

cohort A division of the Roman army, at one time numbering about 500 soldiers.

colony A settlement of people outside their own country, but still bound to it. The ancient Greeks founded many colonies around the shores of the Mediterranean Sea.

comet A ball of rock and ice that orbits the Sun. It forms a long tail as it nears the Sun.

compost Rotting vegetable matter used to make the soil fertile.

compound An enclosed yard surrounding a building or group of buildings.

conch shell The huge, horn-shaped shell of a tropical sea creature. It was blown and used as a musical instrument.

condor A large South American vulture.

Confucianism The Western name for the teachings of the Chinese philosopher Kong Fuzi (Confucius), which call for social order and respect for family and ancestors.

conscript A term of service to the state in which people have to work as soldiers or labourers.

consul One of two leaders of the Roman Republic who were elected each year by the Senate.

contortionist An acrobat who can adopt complicated, twisted positions.

cormorant A coastal and river bird, used in China to catch fish.

cremation The burning of a dead body.

crossbow A mechanical bow that fires small arrows called bolts.

cuirass A one-piece breast and back plate that is worn by soldiers.

cultivate To prepare the land for farming and use it for growing crops.

D

daimyo A Japanese nobleman or warlord.

Daoism A Chinese philosophy based on the contemplation of the natural world. It later became a religion with a belief in magic.

delta Where a river splits into separate waterways as it nears the sea.

democracy A system of government based on rule by the people through elected representatives. Every citizen has the right to vote and hold public office.

derrick The tower-like frame that supports drilling equipment.

dictator A ruler who has total power.

domesticated A tamed wild animal.

dowry A bride's property or money.

dugout canoe A canoe made by hollowing out a tree trunk.

dynasty A series of rulers from the same family.

E

earplug Large discs worn by the Incas in their earlobes as jewellery.

eaves The overhanging edges of a roof.

eclipse When the Moon passes in front of the Sun, obscuring its light.

embalm To preserve a dead body by using mixtures of chemicals, herbs and spices.

empire A state and the conquered lands it rules over.

entrails The bowels, guts and internal organs of an animal.

epidemic When a disease affects many people at the same time.

escapement A type of ratchet used in clockwork timing mechanisms.

estate A large area of land, houses and farms, usually owned by a single person or family.

etiquette The rules governing behaviour in a society.

F

faience A type of opaque glass that is usually blue or green.

famine A time when food is very scarce.

fauna The animals that live in an area.

ferment To brew beer.

filament A very fine strand of fibre.

flax A plant whose fibrous stems are used to make linen cloth. Its blue flowers can be used to make a dye and its seeds are crushed to produce linseed oil.

flint A hard stone used to make tools. It flakes easily to create a very sharp edge.

forage To search for something.

forceps Surgical instruments shaped like pincers or tongs.

fresco A painting applied to damp plaster and used to decorate walls.

frieze A band of sculpture or decoration along a wall.

G

gables The pointed ends of a house, which support the roof.

galley A warship powered by oars.

garrison A force of soldiers posted to guard a fortress or town. A garrison is also

the name given to a fort or similar place.

geisha A Japanese woman who entertained men with songs and dances.

gilded Covered with a thin layer of gold leaf.

glacial A period in the Earth's history when a large area of the world was covered by ice. Glacials are also known as ice ages.

glaze A smooth, shiny coating on pottery.

gladiator A professional fighter, slave or criminal in ancient Rome, who fought to the death for public entertainment.

glyph A picture symbol used in writing.

gorgon A female monster

of Greek myth. One of three snake-haired sisters whose looks turned anyone looking at them to stone. Medusa was one of the gorgons.

gourd A hard-skinned, pumpkin-like plant, which was often hollowed out for use as a container.

graffiti Words or pictures scrawled or scratched in public places, especially on walls.

greave Piece of armour worn to protect the shins.

grid pattern A criss-cross pattern of straight lines at right angles. It was used to divide a town into blocks and straight streets.

groma An instrument used by Roman surveyors to measure right angles and to make sure roads were straight.

gruel A soup of cereal and water, such as porridge.

guanaco A wild relative of

the llama, commonly hunted by the Incas.

guild A society that protected the interests of people working within a trade. A guild ensured members worked to high standards, trained young people and looked after old and sick members.

H

hand-axe A heavy tool that fitted into the palm of the hand.

harem The women's apartments, and the women who lived there, in an Islamic house.

hearth A fireplace.

hemp A fibrous plant often used to make coarse cloth.

henna A red dye for the hair or skin made from plant leaves.

herbalism Using medicines made from herbs to heal the sick.

hieroglyph A picture symbol used in ancient Egypt to represent objects and concepts.

hominid Humans and their most recent ancestors.

hunter-gatherer People who hunt wild animals and gather plant foods as a way of life.

I

ikat A weaving technique in Japan. The threads are dyed in many different colours then woven together to create complicated and

beautiful patterns.

ikebana The Japanese art of flower arranging. The word Ikebana means living flowers.

illiterate A person who is unable to read or write.

imperial Relating to the rule of an emperor or an empress.

incense Sweet-smelling tree gum or bark.

indigenous Belonging by

origin to a certain place, native to.

indigo A dark-blue dye made from a plant.

inro A small, decorated box, which is worn hanging from the sash of a Japanese kimono.

inscribed Letters or pictures that are carved on stone or another hard material.

irrigation Bringing water to dry land so that crops can be grown.

Islam The Muslim faith, which follows the teachings of the 6th-century AD prophet Muhammad.

J

jade Either of two hard, precious minerals called jadeite and nephrite. Jade is white or green in colour.

javelin A long spear for throwing. It is often used as a weapon.

joinery Skilled woodworking needed for making fine furniture.

junk A Chinese sailing ship with square sails.

K

kanji The picture-symbols based on Chinese characters that were used for writing Japanese before about AD800.

kaolin A fine white clay used in porcelain and paper-making.

kernel The edible seed inside its husk.

kiln An oven or furnace.

kimono A loose robe with wide sleeves worn by both men and women in Japan.

kindling Twigs, woodchips or other material used to start a fire.

knucklebones A favourite game of the ancient Greeks. It involved flipping small animal bones from one side of the hand to the other without dropping them.

kuraka One of the local chiefs of lands conquered by the Incas.

L

lacquer A tough, shiny varnish made from tree sap. It is made up of many thin, polished layers that can then be carved. Lacquer was used to coat wood, metal or leather.

legion A section of the Roman army made up only of Roman citizens. Non-Roman citizens could not be legionaries.

libation A drink-offering poured to the gods.

litter A seat or platform in which someone is carried by bearers.

llama A camel-like creature of South America. It was used as a pack animal, shorn for its wool and was sacrificed in religious ceremonies by the Incas.

lodestone A type of magnetic iron ore, also called magnetite.

loincloth A strip of cloth worn around the hips.

loom A frame on which cloth is woven.

loot To plunder a town and steal its goods.

lotus A type of water lily.

lychee A soft Chinese fruit.

lyre A harp-like stringed musical instrument.

M

magistrate A government officer for justice similar to a local judge.

mail Chain armour made of interlocking iron rings.

maize Also called corn or sweetcorn. It was the most important crop in the Americas.

manure Dung or compost spread on soil.

martial arts Physical exercises that are often based upon combat, such as swordplay and kung fu. The Chinese martial arts bring together spiritual and physical disciplines.

merchant Someone who buys and sells goods such as cloth or food for profit.

Mesoamerica An area that is made up of Mexico and northern Central America (Guatemala, Honduras, El Salvador and Belize).

Mesolithic The middle stone age, which began about 12,000 years ago and ended with the spread of farming.

mica A flaky, shiny mineral.

Middle East The countries that sit at the crossroads of three continents – Africa, Europe and the main part of Asia.

Middle Kingdom The period in ancient Egypt between 2050 and 1786BC.

midwife Someone who helps a mother give birth to her child.

millet A type of grain crop.

minerals Natural, solid, non-living substances found in the ground. Rocks are made up of one or more minerals. Metals, such as gold and silver, are minerals.

Minoan The first great Greek civilization and the first in Europe. It flourished on the island of Crete around 2000BC.

mit'a Conscripted labour, owed to the Inca state as a form of tax.

monsoon Winds that blow at certain times of the year in southern Asia bringing heavy rain.

mortar A mixture of cement, sand and water used to join together stones or bricks.

mosaic Small squares or tiny pieces of glass, stone or pottery set in patterns and used to make pictures and to decorate floors and objects.

mother-of-pearl A beautiful, shiny coating found inside seashells. It is also called nacre.

mummy A dead body preserved by drying or extreme cold, or by embalming.

Mycenaean The second great Greek civilization. The Mycenaeans dominated the Greek mainland from around 1600BC.

myrrh A kind of plant resin that is used to make perfume and medicine.

mythology Traditional stories known as myths about the deeds of gods, heroes and fantastic creatures.

N

Near East An area of the world now called the Middle East, but which included Egypt as well.

Neolithic The new stone age which began about 10,000 years ago and lasted until metal working became widespread.

netsuke Small Japanese toggles that are carved from ivory and used to secure items hanging from a belt sash.

New Kingdom The period in ancient Egypt between 1550 and 1070BC.

niche A shallow alcove set into a wall.

O

oasis A place where there is water in a desert area.

obsidian A hard, black, glassy rock that is produced when volcanoes erupt.

ocarina An Aztec wind musical instrument.

ochre Yellow- or red-coloured earth used as pigment in paint.

Old Kingdom The period in ancient Egypt between 2686 and 2181BC.

oligarchy Government by a group of rich and powerful people.

omen A sign of good or bad fortune in the future.

oracle A place where people consulted their gods for advice about the future or fortune-telling.

orator A person who is an eloquent public speaker.

ore A rock that contains metal, such as iron, copper and tin.

origami The Japanese art of folding paper.

overseer A supervisor.

P

pagoda A high, multi-storey tower found in eastern and southern Asia. Pagodas were often used as libraries or places of religious worship. In Japan, they were usually part of a Buddhist temple.

Palaeolithic The old stone age which began about 2 million years ago when the first stone tools were made.

palanquin A covered litter for one person.

Panathenaic festival A yearly procession in Athens. Sacrifices were made to the goddess Athena at the Parthenon.

panpipes A wind musical instrument made of a series of pipes joined together.

papyrus A tall reed that grows in the river Nile. It was used to make a kind of paper.

patrician A member of one of the old, wealthy and powerful families of ancient Rome.

pavilion An ornamental garden building or tent.

peasant An ordinary worker, usually a farm worker, who lives in the country.

pectoral Jewellery or armour worn on the chest.

peninsula A strip of land surrounded by sea on three sides, making it almost like an island.

Persia Modern-day Iran.

phalanx A solid block of hoplites (Greek foot soldiers) in battle.

pharaoh The ruler of ancient Egypt.

philosophy A Greek word that means love of knowledge. Philosophy is the discipline of thinking about the meaning of life.

pictogram A picture symbol used to record information.

pigment Any material used to provide colour for paint or ink.

pilgrim Someone who makes a journey to a sacred place.

pitched roof A roof that slopes.

plate armour Fitted body armour made of linked sheets of solid metal.

plateau An area of high, flat land, usually in a mountainous region.

plaza A large, open space in the centre of a town or city.

plebian A member of the (free) common people of ancient Rome.

porcelain The finest quality pottery.

potter's wheel A circular stone spun round to help shape wet clay into pots.

poultice A soft preparation spread on a strip of cloth and applied to a sore part of the body.

prehistoric The time before written records were made.

preserve To treat food or keep a body so that it does not spoil or go bad and decay.

priest Someone who offered prayers and sacrifices on behalf of worshippers at a temple.

prophecy The foretelling of the future.

prow The front end of a ship.

pyramid A large stone monument with a broad, square base and triangular sides rising to a point, or with steps up to a platform.

Q

quinua A South American plant grown for its edible seeds and leaves.

quipu A series of knotted coloured cords used by the Incas to record information.

Quya The Inca empress, who was the sister-wife or mother of the emperor.

R

radiocarbon dating A very accurate method of dating objects using the breakdown of Carbon 14 present in once-living things.

ram A large pointed beam often attached to the hull of a warship. It was used to ram into the side of an enemy ship, making it easier to board.

ramparts The defensive parapets on the top of castle walls.

regent Someone who rules a country on behalf of another person.

republic A state that is governed by an assembly of its citizens rather than by a monarch or emperor.

ritual An often repeated series of solemn actions or words, usually for a religious purpose.

S

sacrifice The killing of a living thing, or the offering of a possession, in honour of the gods.

saffron The orange stigmas of crocuses, which is used to make a yellow spice and dye.

samurai Members of the Japanese warrior class. Samurai were well-trained and followed a strict code of honourable behaviour.

Sapa Inca One of the titles taken by some Inca emperors. Sapa Inca means the Only Leader.

sarcophagus The outer stone casing of a coffin.

scribe A professional writer, clerk or civil servant.

seismoscope An instrument that reacts to earthquakes and tremors.

Senate The law-making assembly of ancient Rome.

serfs People who are not free to move from the land they farm without the permission of their lord.

shaman A medicine man or woman with powers to heal the sick and contact the spirits.

shinden A large, single-storey house in Japan.

Shinto An ancient Japanese faith, known as the way of the gods and based on honouring holy spirits.

shogun A Japanese army commander. Shoguns ruled Japan in the name of the emperor of Japan from 1185 to 1868.

shrine A place of worship or a container for holy relics such as bones.

sickle A tool with a curved blade used to cut grass or grain crops.

siege A long-lasting attack to capture a fortified place or city by surrounding it and cutting it off.

Silk Road The overland trading route that stretched from China through Asia to Europe.

silt Fine grains of soil found at the bottom of rivers and lakes.

sinew An animal tendon that joins muscle to bone.

slash and burn A method of farming. Bushes and scrub are cut down and burnt and seeds planted in the ash. The soil is fertile for a few years, then new areas are cleared.

slaves People who were not free, but were owned by their masters. Some were worked to death. Others were treated well and given good jobs.

smelt To extract a metal from its ore by heating it in a furnace.

society All classes of people living in a particular community or country.

sphinx A mythical creature that is half lion, half human.

spindle A rod used to twist fibres including wool into yarn while spinning.

squash Any one of various marrow-like vegetables.

stela (plural stelae) A tall stone pillar.

stern The rear or back end of a ship.

sting-ray A fish with a long, poisonous spike in its tail.

stucco A plaster used to cover and decorate important buildings.

suburb An outlying district of a city.

sunspot A dark patch on the Sun's surface.

surcoat A long, loose tunic worn over armour.

survey To map out and measure an area of land. Land is surveyed before the construction of a building or a road or any other structure.

suspension bridge A bridge in which the roadway is suspended (hung) from towers.

swaddling Cloth or cloths that are tightly wrapped around a baby.

T

tax Goods, money or services paid to the government or ruling state.

temple A building used for worship or rituals.

terracotta Baked brown-red clay and sand, which is used to make statues, figurines and pottery.

textile Cloth produced by weaving threads together.

threshing Separating grains of wheat, corn or rice from their stalk.

timpanon A Greek tambourine made with animal skin.

tinder Dry material that quickly catches fire if a spark falls on it.

toga A white woollen robe worn by the upper classes in ancient Rome.

tomb A vault in which dead bodies are placed.

torii The traditional gateway to a Shinto shrine in Japan.

tortillas Flat pancakes made from maize or wheat.

tragedy A play that ends in disaster. It usually concerns a good and noble person with a fatal flaw in his character that causes his downfall in the end.

trapezoid A four-sided shape, of which only two sides are parallel.

treadwheel A wooden wheel that is turned by the feet of people or animals and used to power mills or other machinery.

tribe A group of people that share a common language and way of life.

tribune One of the officials elected to represent the interest of the common people in Rome. It is also a rank in the Roman army.

tribute Goods given by one person, city or country to another as a mark of submission.

trident A three-pronged spear.

trivet A metal stand placed over a flame to support a cooking pot.

tundra A treeless area where the soil is permanently frozen under the surface.

tunic A loose-fitting robe. It was worn as everyday clothing in ancient Greece and Rome where it was usually fastened at the shoulder with a brooch or pin.

tutor A personal teacher.

tyrant An absolute ruler who seizes power.

Tywantinsuyu The name the Incas called their empire, meaning the Four Quarters.

U

underworld A mysterious place to which the spirits of the dead were believed to travel after death and burial.

V

ventilation A way of making fresh air circulate freely in a room.

vicuna A llama-like animal whose wool was used by the Incas to make the finest cloth.

villa A Roman country house, usually part of an agricultural estate.

vizier The treasurer or highest-ranking official in the Egyptian court.

votive An offering.

W

warlord A man who keeps a private army and rules over a large region of land by force.

weathering The wearing away of rocks by rain, wind and ice.

wildfowl Wild ducks, geese and other water birds.

winnowing Separating grains of wheat, rice or corn from the hard outer chaff (husk).

wreath Flowers or leaves wound together into a ring to wear on the head. Wreaths made of olive or laurel leaves were a symbol of honour in ancient Greece and Rome.

Y

yak A long-haired ox that is used as a beast of burden in Tibet.

yin and yang The Daoist belief in two life forces that must be balanced to achieve harmony. Yin is negative, feminine and dark, while yang is positive, masculine and light.

yoke A long piece of wood or bamboo used to carry heavy loads. The yoke was placed across the shoulders and a load was hung from each end to balance it.

yucca A desert plant with long, fleshy leaves.

Z

Zen A branch of the Buddhist faith that was popular among Japanese samurai warriors.

INDEX

ACKNOWLEDGEMENTS

CHILD MODELS

Anness Publishing would like to thank the following children for modelling for this book:

Jake Lewis Courtney Andrews, Mohammed Asfar, Emily Askew, Anthony Bainbridge, Leon R. Banton, Sabirah Bari, Afsana Begum, Sarah Bone, Donna Marie Bradley, Lucilla Braune, Ha Chu, Patrick Clifford, Molly Cooper, Charlene Da Cova, Paula Dent, Daniel Djanan, Frankie Timothy Junior Elliot, Ricky Garrett, Lana Green, Aileen Greiner, Otis Harrington, Sasha Haworth, Rikky Charles Healey, Rachel Herbert, Francesca Hill, Aslom Hussain, Roxanne John, Jodie King, Alex Lindblom-Smith, Sophie Lindblom-Smith, Amarni McKenzie, Imran Miah, Lucy Nightingale, Ifi Obi, Daniel Ofori, Vanessa Ofori, Graham Oppong, Edward Parker, Joshua Adam Laidlaw Parkin, Joshua Parris-Eugene, Rajiv M. Pattani, Mai-Anh Peterson, Emily Preddie, Adrianne S. Punzalan, Susan Quirke, Charlie Ray, Eva Rivera/Razbadavskite, Brendan Scott, Claudia Martins Silva, Levinia de Silva, Clleon Smith, Roxanne Smith, Nicky Stafford, Mark Stefford, Katie Louise Stevens, Samantha Street, Simon Thexton, Shereen Thomas, Saif Uddowlla, Ha Vinh, Reece Warman, Peter Watson, Kirsty Wells, Joseph Williams, Tyrene Williams, Harriet Woollard.

Gratitude also to their parents, and to Hampden Gurney, Johanna Primary and Walnut Tree Walk Schools.

PICTURE CREDITS

(Stone Age, Egypt, Greece, Rome, Aztec, Inca, China, Japan)

b=bottom, t=top, c=centre, l=left, r=right

E. Beintema/AAA Collection: page 452tl; Ronald Sheridan/ AAA Collection: page 453tl, 465tl; A-Z Botanical Collection Ltd: page 243br; Lesley and Roy Adkins Picture Library: pages 195cr, 203t, 221bl, 225b, 228l, 229b, 245tl; AKG London: pages 319cl, 319r, 321tl, 322t, 325c, 351bl, 370b, 434br, 439br, 444tl, 465tl, 479tl, 480br; B and C Alexander: pages 20tl, 22t, 37bl, 48l, 49tl, 49cr, 51t, 55br, 57tl, 70r; The Ancient Art and Architecture Collection Ltd: pages 15tl, 21t, 45tr, 47tl, 52l, 53b, 59cl, 68r, 69tl, 74b, 79tc, 80t, 80b, 81bc, 81tr, 82r, 82/83, 84br, 86, 87bl, 88l, 88r, 89tl, 90t, 91cl, 91br, 92b, 100l, 102r, 103tl, 106r, 107t, 108b, 109bc, 110l, 110r, 111b, 112r, 113r, 114br, 115tl, 115tr, 115b, 116t, 117t, 120/121, 122r, 123tr, 124tr, 126b, 127l, 128l, 129r, 135tr, 138cr, 139br, 141cl, 142cr, 145tl, 148tl, 151br, 151bl, 152tl, 152cl, 154cr, 155br, 157tr, 157cl, 160tr, 162tl, 162cl, 163c, 165cr, 168bl, 169tr, 170cr, 171cl, 172tl, 176tr, 178cl, 179tr, 181br, 184cl, 186bl, 187cl, 188tr, 190tl, 198b, 198l, 199tc, 201tl, 204b, 211tr, 211cl, 211cr, 214/215, 217r, 221bl, 222b, 223tr, 223br, 226, 231tl, 232b, 239tr, 240bl, 242tr, 242bl, 244tr, 247tl, 251bl, 314l, 320l, 321cl, 331t, 361tr, 367tl, 385tr, 426tl, 428cl, 447b, 449tl, 453br, 471tl, 472tl; Andes Press Agency: pages 325t, 330t, 350tr, 45b, 363bl; Heather Angel: pages 35 bc, 4911br; BBC Hulton: page 459c; GDR Barnett Images: pages 270tl; 271bl, 292bl; Bildarchiv Preussischer Kulturbesitz: page 168tl; The Bodleian Library: pages 263cl, 264b, 265br, 267c; The Bridgeman Art Library: pages 14l, 24b, 25tr, 25br, 26l, 34l, 51c, 61br, 68l, 69cr, 71bl, 135cr, 146bl, 150br, 159r, 162tr, 164cl, 164tr, 173r, 203b, 259tl, 295bl, 350cl, 385tl, 386cl, 391tr, 393br, 395bl, 401tl, 401cl, 403bl, 411bl, 415tl, 416cl, 417cl, 417cr, Bridgeman Art Library, London: The Life and Pastimes of the Japanese Court 443tl; Sumo Wrestler Abumatsu Rokunosuki by Kunisada 450tl, Fuji on a Fine Day by Kuniyoshi 453tl, Osen of the Kagiya Serving Tea by Harunobu 455bl, The

Moon by Kunisada 458, Woman by Kikumaru 465bl, Standing Courtesan by Kaigetsudo 466br, Collecting Insects by Harunobu 467tl, Salt Maidens by Harunobu 468tl, Threading a Needle by Chinnen 469tr, Tales of Bunsho by Tosa 475tl, Tale of Genji by Tokugawa 11 476br, Courtesan with Musical Instrument by Kuniyoshi 478tl, Ships Returning to Harbour by Gakutei 481tr, The Stone Bridge by Hiroshige 111 481bl, Retreat in the Mountains by Tomioka 481br, Woodblock by Yoshitaki 482br, Yokohama Seascape 483br, View of Dutch Trading Post 483tr, 483cl, Fuji in Fine Weather by Hokusai 485tl, Nicheren Calming the Storm by Yoshimoro 486bl, Juroku Rakan 486tl, Cherry Blossoms at Asakura by Hiroshige 11 491tl; The following Bridgeman Art Library images are reproduced by kind permission of the Fitzwilliam Museum, Cambridge: Mother Dressing Son by Harunobu 456tl, Celebrated Beauties by Utamaro 466tl, Sudden Shower by Hiroshige 469br, Painting Party by Kunisada 473cr, Fuji from Koshigaya 473cl, Mother and Baby Resting by Kunimaru 480tl; The British Museum: pages 22c, 39tr; 83t, 87tr, 89br, 90b, 98l, 98t, 100r, 105bc, 106bl, 108t, 109tr, 113l, 120l, 124br, 125l, 125br 127r, 142tl, 142bl, 161cl, 165cl, 171tl, 212r, 213tr, 213cr, 213bl, 218c, 218r, 220l, 232c, 238bl, 238br, 239b, 242br, 247b; Jean-Loup Charmet: pages 363t, 363br; Christies Images: pages 443bl, 446bl, 446br, 447tl, 449bl, 453cl, 455br, 459bl, 465br, 467tr, 470br, 471tr, 474br, 483cr, 487cr, 487tl, 490tl, 490br; Peter Clayton: pages 45cr, 59tl, 59tr, 60bl, 61tl, 61cl; 85t, 85b, 89bl, 105bl, 105br, 106br, 114t, 114bl, 123tl, 123bl, 124l, 125tr, 130, 145bl, 149br, 154tl, 160cl, 161tr, 169b, 183tr, 185tl, 185cl, 208l, 215cr, 224tl, 227bc; Bruce Coleman: pages 35t, 38br, 45bl, 50t, 70l, 277c, 329cl, 352br, 359br, 395br, 409tl, 485bl; Colorific pages 71t; Asian Art and Architecture Inc/ Corbis: pages 476tl, 477tl, Corbis-Bettman: page 441tl, Carmen Redondo/ Corbis: page 488br, Hulton-Deutsch/ Corbis: page 451bl, Sakamoto Photo Research Laboratory/ Corbis: pages 458tl, 467bl, 477br, 487br, Seattle Art Museum/ Corbis: page 451bl, Michael S Yamashita/ Corbis: page 462bl; Sylvia Corday: pages 25tl, 32c; Sue Cunningham Photographic: pages 315tr, 326c, 328l, 329tl, 333tl, 333tr, 334t, 341bl, 356t, 360c, 366tr, 366cl, 368tr, 370cr; Dagli Orti: page 309tl; James Davis Worldwide Photographic Travel Library: pages 258br, 268tl, 289bl, 300c, 302tl, 309br, 375tr, 387cl, 406br; C M Dixon: pages 15tr, 18l, 24l, 27tl, 28l, 30r, 33tl, 34r, 36r, 36b, 38t, 39tl, 40b, 43tr, 43c, 44t, 44bl, 44br, 46l, 46r, 47tr, 48r, 50cr, 52r, 54bl, 56l, 58l, 58r, 60t, 60br, 63cr, 64r, 66r, 66b, 67bl, 67br; 78tr, 78b, 79b, 84t, 87tl, 91tr, 101tr, 104, 105t, 109tl, 117b, 118l, 118r, 121, 122l, 131t, 134c, 138c, 139tr, 139cl, 140c, 141tl, 141cr, 143c, 146tr, 146br, 147tr, 147cl, 147br, 149cl, 149bl, 150cl, 153tr, 154bl, 155tl, 156tl, 157cl, 157cr, 158tr, 158c, 159cl, 163tr, 166tl, 169cl, 169cl, 170tl, 171tr, 175tl, 177cl, 182tr, 182cl, 186tr, 186br, 187bl, 188cl, 189tr, 191br, 200l, 202bl, 204r, 205bl, 207tl, 207cr, 210bl, 214bl, 215tr, 215br, 216l, 216r, 217l, 219tl, 219tc, 219tr, 220r, 222/223, 223bl, 224tr, 224b, 225t, 225c, 227tl, 227tr, 228br, 230cl, 230tr, 231bl, 234r, 235tl, 235cl, 235bl, 237t, 237c, 238tr, 239tl, 240tl, 240br, 241cl, 245tr, 245b, 246l, 247tr, 248tr, 248bl, 248br, 250l, 250r, 252r, 260tl, 264tl, 266r, 277bl, 382tl, 384bl, 394tl, 400tr, 413tl, 414tr, 440tl, 464tl, 475bl; Ecoscene: pages 41tr, 54t; Edimedia: pages 454bl, 456br, 468br; E T Archive: pages 19t, 69tr, 259br, 260br, 261bl, 261tr, 263tl, 265bl, 271tr, 272tl, 273br, 274tl, 274bl, 275br, 276tl, 277tr, 278c, 280, 281, 282b, 283, 285tl, 286bl, 289r, 291tl, 291tr, 291bl, 292tl, 297tl, 301l, 301tr, 302c, 303c, 304, 305, 306cr, 306tl, 308t, 310br, 318r, 336t, 336cr, 337bl, 345c, 347tl, 347cl, 349c, 352cl, 364bl, 368tl, 370tl, 378l, 379tl, 379tr, 379bl, 381tr, 381bl,

382bl, 385tr, 385bl, 387tr, 390br, 391br, 392tr, 392bl, 393bl, 394br, 395tr, 396tr, 397tr, 402bl, 410br, 413tr, 417tl, 419cl, 420cr, 424bl, 427cl, 431t, 434tl, 439tl, 441br, 442bl, 450br, 457tl, 472br, 481tr, 482tl; Mary Evans Picture Library: pages 20b, 23tl, 27tr, 37br, 45tl; 94r, 94l, 102l, 138tl, 139tl, 140tl, 143b, 144tr, 164c, 173bl, 175tr, 180tr, 183cl, 184tl, 184cr, 186cl, 189cl, 190bl, 191tr, 191cl, 199bl, 199br, 200r, 210tr, 219bl, 234b, 244br, 246r, 249t, 272br, 289tl, 310tl, 319tl, 319c, 371b, 381br, 382br, 392br, 399tl, 412br, 429tl, 457bl, 464bl; FLPA: pages 21cl, 39br, 61cr, 413tc, 413br; Werner Forman Archive: pages 49bc, 57c, 64l, 211bl, 243t, 254tl, 265tr, 266tl, 278tl, 286tl, 305tl, 314cr, 320r, 324l, 324r, 327c, 337tl, 341tr, 342r, 343cl, 343tr, 344cl, 345cl, 346cr, 348l, 356c, 357c, 358l, 361bl, 362t, 362br, 369cl, 380bl, 383tr, 396cr, 399tr, 399cl, 408tr, 409bl, 409br, 410bl, 414cl, 418c, 420tl, 421cl, 425tr, 429tr, 440bl, 443cl, 445bl, 463cl, 469tl, 470tl, 479bc;

Geoscience Features Picture Library: page 251tr; Fortean Picture Library: pages 55t, 56r, 62c; Garden Picture Library: 487bl, 487bc; Griffith Institute, Ashmolean Museum: pages 74t, 97t, 97b; Sonia Halliday Photographs: pages 150tl, 151tl, 205tl, 228tr; Robert Harding Associates: pages 15cl, 21b, 23b, 25bl, 33cl, 41tl, 41br, 63tl, 63tr, 143r, 190br ; Michael Holford Photographs: pages 84bl, 99bl, 126c, 131b, 149tr, 156tl, 160tl, 161tl, 165tr, 166cr, 173tl, 175cl, 176cl, 177tr, 180bl, 181cr, 187tr, 195tr, 202tr, 202br, 206, 212l, 218l, 219br, 227bl, 230bl, 230br, 235br, 236bl, 241tr, 241bl, 243bl, 244bl, 251tl, 255c, 261br, 262bl, 284tl, 293tr, 300tl, 301r, 311, 339b, 344r, 348cr, 367tr, 374tl, 405tr, 406tr, 407br, 412tl, 428tr, 438br, 446tl, 448br, 452bl, 475bm, 488tl, 491bl; The Hutchison Library: pages 287c, 330bl, 330r, 338t, 357r, 422cl, 430c, 431cl, Hutchison/Jon Burbank: 473tl, 484tl, 487cl, Hutchison/ JG Fuller: 484bc, Hutchison/ Chiran Kyushu: 459cr, 469bl, Hutchison/ Michael Macintyre: 442tl, 461bl, br; The Idemitsu Museum of Arts: pages 459cl, 467cl, 471cl; Images Colour Library: pages 463tr, 487bl; Simon James: pages 233tr, 233br; Japan Archive: pages 435tl, 435bl, 438tl, 439tc, 441tr, 441cr, 443tr, 444br, 445tl, 445tr, 447tr, 448tl, 450bl, 460bl, 461tr, 462tl, 463tl, 463bl, 473tl, 478br, 485tr, 489tr; Chris Kapolka: page 354bl; MacQuitty Collection: pages 375c, 390tr, 391bl, 395tl, 397tl, 402tr, 407b, 411br, 413bl, 415tr, 416tl, 418tr, 423tl, 423tr, 423cl, 424tl, 425cl, 425br, 429cl; Manchester Museum: page 99tl; Museum of London: pages 38bl; Museum of Sweden: page 35c; NHPA: pages 277c, 491cl; Michael Nicholson: pages 141tr, 144c, 145tr, 148bl, 167tl, 167cl, 167bl, 174tr, 174cl, 181tl, 181bl, 181br; Panos: page 326r, 365b; Papilio Photographic: page 400cl; Bob Partridge and the Ancient Egypt Picture Library: pages 89tr, 92t, 119r, 119br; Courtesy of the Petrie Museum of Egyptian Archaeology, University College London: page 111c; Planet Earth Pictures Ltd: page 195b, 275c, 332b; Popperfoto: page 353tr; Radiotimes Hulton Picture Library: page 116b; N.J. Saunders: page 323b; Science Photo Library: pages 345tl, 349tl, 359l, 359cl; South American Photo Library: pages 254br, 255tl, 258tl, 259tl, 262tl, 263tr, 267tl, 268tr, 269tr, 270b, 272bl, 273bl, 274br, 276bl, 279tr, 280bl, 283br, 285bl, 287, 293br, 294tl, 296c, 298c, 303b, 307tl, 307c, 308b, 311; South American Pictures: pages 315cr, 318l, 321tr, 323r, 323c, 325bl, 326bl, 327bl, 327r, 328r, 329r, 331br, 332t, 334l, 334b, 335t, 335bl, 336c, 338bl, 338br, 339t, 340l, 340r, 342l, 346l, 351tl, 351br, 352tr, 353tl, 353bl, 354r, 354br, 355t, 355c, 358bl, 358br, 359tr, 360r, 362bl, 364r, 364br, 365t, 365c, 367cl, 368c, 369r, 371cl, 371tr; Still Pictures: pages 315tl, 322b, 349tr, 350cr, 361bl; Tony Stone Images: pages 194/195, 488bl; Superstock: page 488bl; TRIP: pages 380br, 430tr; Visual Arts Library: pages 229tr, 236/237, 260br, 269r, 269b, 277tl, 279tc, 279tl, 282tl, 283tl, 288cr, 290c, 290tl, 293bl, 295t, 296tl, 297tr, 305tl, 306tr, 306cl, 309tr, 310bl, 378r, 379br, 384tl, 384c, 390bl, 393tl, 398cl, 404tl, 405cl, 410tl, 411tl, 411tr, 414cr, 419tl, 421tl, 421tr, 425tl, 426c; Wilderness Photo Library: page 314r; Zefa: pages 75r, 78tl, 79tl, 79tr, 81tl, 82l, 83b, 92l, 93t, 93b, 96, 96/97, 97c, 99tr, 101b, 103tr, 103cr, 103b, 110/111, 112l, 120r, 128r, 129l, 198r, 205br, 237b, 293tr, 374c, 380tr, 383tl, 383b, 386tl, 388tr, 403tr, 403br, 406bl, 407tl, 407tr, 408tl, 409tr, 417tr

This edition is published by Southwater, an imprint of Anness Publishing Ltd, Hermes House, 88–89 Blackfriars Road, London SE1 8HA; tel. 020 7401 2077; fax 020 7633 9499 www.southwaterbooks.com; www.annesspublishing.com

If you like the images in this book and would like to investigate using them for publishing, promotions or advertising, please visit our website www.practicalpictures.com for more information.

UK agent: The Manning Partnership Ltd; tel. 01225 478444; fax 01225 478440; sales@manning-partnership.co.uk UK distributor: Grantham Book Services Ltd; tel. 01476 541080; fax 01476 541061; orders@gbs.tbs-ltd.co.uk North American agent/distributor: National Book Network; tel. 301 459 3366; fax 301 429 5746; www.nbnbooks.com Australian agent/distributor: Pan Macmillan Australia; tel. 1300 135 113; fax 1300 135 103; customer.service@macmillan.com.au New Zealand agent/distributor: David Bateman Ltd; tel. (09) 415 7664; fax (09) 415 8892

Publisher: Joanna Lorenz
Managing Editor, Children's Books: Gilly Cameron Cooper
Editor: Joy Wotton
The Rise of Civilization: introduction by Dr John Haywood
Senior Editors: Ambreen Husain, Neil Kelly, Nicole Pearson
Project Editors: Joanna Hanks, Charlotte Hurdmann, John Jamieson, Linda Sonntag, Sophie Warne, Joy Wotton
Editors: Nicola Baxter, Leon Gray, Jayne Miller
Designers: Simon Borrough, Matthew Cook, Joyce Mason, Caroline Reeves, Margaret Sadler, Alison Walker
Illustrations: Rob Ashby, Julian Baker, Vanessa Card, Stuart Carter, Stephen Gyapay, Shane Marsh, Clive Spong, Stuart Watkinson at Ideas Into Print
Special Photography: John Freeman
Stylists: Konika Shakar, Thomasina Smith, Melanie Williams
Production Controller: Ben Worley

ETHICAL TRADING POLICY

Because of our ongoing ecological investment programme, you, as our customer, can have the pleasure and reassurance of knowing that a tree is being cultivated on your behalf to naturally replace the materials used to make the book you are holding. For further information about this scheme, go to www.annesspublishing.com/trees

A CIP catalogue record for this book is available from the British Library.

Previously published as *The Encyclopedia of Ancient History*